Bombing Pompeii

Bombing Pompeii

World Heritage and Military Necessity

Nigel Pollard

University of Michigan Press ANN ARBOR

For questions or permissions, please contact um.press.perms@umich.edu

Published in the United States of America by
the University of Michigan Press
Manufactured in the United States of America
Printed on acid-free paper

First published December 2020

A CIP catalog record for this book is available from the British Library.

ISBN 978-0-472-13220-1 (hardcover : alk. paper)

ISBN 978-0-472-12729-0 (ebook)

For Liv and Maria,
who already know much more about Pompeii than teenagers should.

Contents

Acknowledgements

Joanne Berry first suggested to me that I should work on the intersection of archaeology and the Second World War when I was teaching in Italy in 2008–2009, and so thanks are due to her as the original source of inspiration for this book. Long ago I swore I would never undertake research relating to Pompeii, yet here it is.

Swansea University's former Callaghan Centre for the Study of Conflict, Power and Empire funded my 2011 workshop that really got me interested in applying historical lessons to contemporary issues in cultural property protection (CPP), including as it did not just colleagues working on historical material, like Carlotta Coccoli, but also Laurie Rush and Richard Osgood, who have done so much to develop CPP practice in US and UK armed forces. I'm grateful to Nikki Cooper and Jonathan Dunnage for enabling me to put on that workshop.

My colleagues in UK Blue Shield and the UK military Cultural Property Protection Working Group have introduced me to new ways of thinking about CPP and how to apply the historical to the contemporary. In particular, Emma Cunliffe and Paul Fox applied their own unique skill-sets to improve this book with their detailed, generous and insightful comments, Peter Stone's re-establishment of UK Blue Shield opened up many new opportunities, and Tim Purbrick (now commander of the UK military Cultural Property Protection Unit) encouraged my sense that historical lessons do actually have practical value in contemporary contexts. I thank them, and many other colleagues for their contributions.

From the US, Laurie Rush's enthusiasm and insight into practical CPP issues have done much to keep me on track, and Cori Wegener has also been an inspiration. 'Inspiration' is also true of Ilaria Dagnini Brey's book *The Venus Fixers*, and Ilaria herself has been generous in responding to my questions. The staff of the US Air Force Historical Research Agency undertook searches for material on my behalf, and patiently answered my queries. Mike Constandy of Westmoreland Research was efficient in tracking down images and documents in the US National Archives. I also thank Ben Leonard and Susann and Bert Lusnia for their regular help and support.

In Italy, thanks are due to Carlotta Coccoli, to Alessandra Giovenco and Valerie Scott at the British School at Rome, and to Sebastian Hierl and Antonio Palladino at the American Academy at Rome. Simon Pocock generously provided initial copies of photographs previously used in his book, and Ciro Marciano and Filippo Avellino shared their local and professional knowledge of the transport infrastructure in the Pompei area.

In the UK, I am grateful to the staff of the libraries and archives of the Society of Antiquaries, National Archives and Imperial War Museum for their assistance, particularly to Magda Kowalczuk and Danielle Andrean, and also to Bryan Ward-Perkins for responding to my queries about his family history.

Colleagues at Swansea University have provided help and feedback of various kinds, particularly Adi Armoni, Giovanna Donzelli, Jonathan Dunnage, Richard Hall and Chris Stray. The College of Arts and Humanities at Swansea University funded a semester's research leave for me to work on this book in 2017, and a British Academy-Leverhulme Small Research Grant (2018-2020) provided support for my research relating to the Museo Nazionale di Napoli.

Alex Swanston of The Map Archive (https://www.themaparchive.com/) did an excellent job of turning my scribbles into publishable maps.

I also thank all those people who commented on and asked questions at my presentations on this topic at annual meetings of the Archaeological Institute of America, at the German Historical Institute in Rome, and elsewhere in the US, Italy, UK and Australia.

I am very grateful to the anonymous readers for the University of Michigan Press for their feedback, and to Ellen Bauerle, Marcia LaBrenz and Anna Pohlod, also of the University of Michigan Press, for making the process of producing this book a (largely!) smooth and stress-free experience.

Notes on Usage

All dates are given in British/European format (day, month, year) rather than US (month, day, year) except when quoting contemporary documents using the US format.

I use the spelling 'Pompeii' for the ancient site and its wider vicinity, reserving the modern Italian spelling 'Pompei' strictly for the modern town. However, quotations from wartime documents use their original spelling.

Abbreviations

AAI: Allied Armies, Italy
ACC: Allied Control Commission
ACLS: American Council of Learned Societies
ACMF: Allied Central Mediterranean Force
AFHQ: Allied Force Headquarters
AMG: Allied Military Government (from 24 October 1943)
AMGOT: Allied Military Government of Occupied Territories (to 24 October 1943)
AP: Aiming Point
APO: Army Post Office [US]
Art.: Article [in citations of international law]
BG: Bombardment Group [US]
BS: Bombardment Squadron [US]
Br.: British
CAB: Cabinet [British]
CAO: Civil Affairs Officer
CAVU: Ceiling and visibility unlimited
CCAO: Chief Civil Affairs Officer
CMF: Central Mediterranean Force
CP/CPP: Cultural property/cultural property protection
DAF: Desert Air Force [British]
FBG: Fighter-Bomber Group [US]
FBS: Fighter-Bomber Squadron [US]
FO: Foreign Office [UK]
ft.: feet [distance]
HC: House of Commons
HMSO: His Majesty's Stationery Office/Her Majesty's Stationery Office
HQ: Headquarters
Ins.: Insula [Pompeii city block]
IP: Initial Point
IWM: Imperial War Museum [UK]
H.: Heavy

lb./lbs.: pounds [weight—of non-metric bombs]
Lt.: Light
m.: metres [distance]
MAAF: Mediterranean Allied Air Forces
MAC: Mediterranean Air Command
MFAA: Monuments, Fine Arts and Archives
M/T or M.T.: motor transport
MK/Mk: Mark
MPRC: Mediterranean Photographic Reconnaissance Command.
MTO: Mediterranean Theatre of Operations
NAAF: Northwest African Air Forces
NARA: National Archives and Records Administration [US]
NASAF: Northwest African Strategic Air Force
NWAAF: Northwest African Air Forces
OIS: Operations and Intelligence Summary
OPSUM: Operations Summary
ORB: Operations Record Book
OWI: Office of War Information [US]
PBS: Peninsula/Peninsular Base Section [US]
Prov.: Provincia/Province [Italian]
RA: Royal Artillery
RAF: Royal Air Force
RCAF: Royal Canadian Air Force
RR: Railroad [US]
Reg.: Region [Pompeii city quarter]
S/L: Searchlight[s]
Sqn: Squadron [British]
SS: Strada Statale
T: Treasury [UK]
TCI: Touring Club Italiano
TI: Target Identification [bomb]
TNA: The National Archives [UK]
UNESCO: United Nations Educational, Scientific and Cultural Organization
USAAF: US Army Air Force
WO: War Office [UK]

ABBREVIATIONS FOR FREQUENTLY CITED ARCHIVAL DOCUMENTS

AFHRA = [US] Air Force Historical Research Agency
AFHRA documents are cited by their eight-digit IRIS catalogue number.

TNA = The [UK] National Archives, Kew.
Some TNA files contain multiple documents. The page numbers given below denote the place of the document in the currently available (2019) downloadable pdf version of the file when it exists. Page numbers in references denote the page numbers on the original document.

NARA = National Archives and Records Administration (the US National Archives).
All NARA documents cited here were originally accessed on the fold3 website (www.fold3.com). All (except for a few USAAF images, as noted) belong to NARA M1944, the Records of the American Commission for the Protection and Salvage of Artistic and Historic Monuments in War Areas (the Roberts Commission), 1943–46. These documents are cited here by M1944, Record Group, Roll Number, Series, author (where available), title, and date.

INDIVIDUAL DOCUMENTS

AMGOT Plan for Italy = TNA WO 220/333, *AMGOT Plan for Italy*, September 1943.

Bombing Accuracy of Marauder Squadrons = TNA AIR 23/7471, Headquarters Mediterranean Allied Air Forces, *Bombing Accuracy of Marauder Squadrons of D.A.F.* [Desert Air Force] *on Bridge Targets*, C.M.F. [Central Mediterranean Force] Operational Research Section Report No. 27, November 1944.

Collier Report = NARA M1944 RG 239/0062, MFAA Field Reports, *Report of The Allied Commission of Enquiry Appointed to Investigate Damage Alleged to Have Been Caused to Real and Personal Property of Historical and Educational Importance in Italy*, 28 December 1943 to 21 January 1944.

Collier Evidence = NARA M1944 RG 239/0062, MFAA Field Reports, *Report of The Allied Commission of Enquiry Appointed to Investigate Damage Alleged to Have Been Caused to Real and Personal Property of*

Historical and Educational Importance in Italy: Record of Evidence, 28 December 1943 to 21 January 1944.

Effects of Close Air Support = TNA WO 291/976, *Military Operational Research Report No. 34: The Effects of Close Air Support. Part I—Medium and Heavy Bombers*, 1946.

Fighter/Bomber Tactics = TNA AIR 40/304, *Fighter/Bomber Tactics, December 1943–1944*, 1944.

[Gardner], *December Report* = NARA M1944, RG 239/0067, MFAA Field Reports, HQ Region 3 AMG [Maj. Paul Gardner], *December Report of the Division of Fine Arts*, 10 January 1944.

[Gardner], *Division of Fine Arts* = NARA M1944 RG 239/0067, MFAA Field Reports, HQ 5th Army AMG Region 3 [Maj. Paul Gardner], *Division of Fine Arts and Education*, 1 November 1943.

[Gardner], *November Report* = NARA M1944 RG 239/0067, MFAA Field Reports, HQ Region 3 AMG [Maj. Paul Gardner], *November Report of the Division of Education and Fine Arts*, 1 December 1943.

[Hammond—Maxse], *Memorandum* = TNA FO 371/37330/24, HQ AMG [Capts. Mason Hammond and F.H.J. Maxse], *Memorandum: Activities of Advisers on Fine Arts and Monuments, AMGOT*, 5 November 1943.

List of Monuments in Italy = NARA M1944, RG 239/0098, American Defense–Harvard Group, Committee on the Protection of Monuments, *List of Monuments in Italy* (June 1943).

Lists of Protected Monuments: Sicily = NARA M1944, RG 239/0064, MFAA Field Reports, ACC/AMG Sub-Commission for Monuments, Fine Arts and Archives, *Lists of Protected Monuments 1: Regions of Sardinia & Sicily*, [c. March 1944]

Lists of Protected Monuments: Campania = NARA M1944, RG 239/0064, MFAA Field Reports, ACC/AMG Sub-Commission for Monuments, Fine Arts and Archives, *Lists of Protected Monuments 2: Regions of Apulia, Calabria, Campania and Lucania*, [c. March 1944].

Lists of Protected Monuments: Lazio = NARA M1944, RG 239/0064, MFAA Field Reports, ACC/AMG Sub-Commission for Monuments, Fine Arts and Archives, *Lists of Protected Monuments 3: Regions of Lazio and Abruzzi-Molise*, [April–May 1944].

MAAF, Ancient Monuments of Italy = TNA AIR 8/638 and AIR 8/639, Headquarters Mediterranean Allied Air Forces, *Ancient Monuments of Italy: Aerial Photographs*, 23 February 1944 (2 vols.).

[Maxse], *Report for August* = NARA M1944, RG 239/0067, MFAA Field Reports, AMGOT HQ [Capt. F.H.J. Maxse], *Report for the Month of*

August in the Department of Fine Arts and Monuments, 11 September 1943.

MFAA Final Report: General = TNA T209/30/1, Headquarters Allied Commission, Sub-Commission for Monuments, Fine Arts and Archives, *Final Report: General*, 20345/0/MFAA, 1 January 1946 [pp. 3–55 of the downloadable pdf].

MFAA Final Report: Sicily = TNA T209/30/1, Headquarters Allied Commission, Sub-Commission for Monuments, Fine Arts and Archives, *Final Report: Sicily*, 20345/1/MFAA, 20 November 1945 [pp. 60–86 of the downloadable pdf].

MFAA Final Report: Apulia, Lucania, Calabria = TNA T209/30/1, Headquarters Allied Commission, Sub-Commission for Monuments, Fine Arts and Archives, *Final Report: Apulia, Lucania, Calabria*, 20345/2/MFAA, 1 September 1945 [pp. 87–102 of the downloadable pdf].

MFAA Final Report: Campania = TNA T209/30/1, Headquarters Allied Commission, Sub-Commission for Monuments, Fine Arts and Archives, *Final Report: Campania*, 20345/3/MFAA, 25 November 1945 [pp. 103–33 of the downloadable pdf].

MFAA Final Report: Lazio = TNA T209/30/1, Headquarters Allied Commission, Sub-Commission for Monuments, Fine Arts and Archives, *Final Report: Lazio*, 20345/3/MFAA, 5 December 1945 [pp. 134–70 of the downloadable pdf].

MFAA Pompeii and Herculaneum = NARA M1944, RG 239/0067, MFAA Field Reports, Allied Control Commission, Sub-Commission for Monuments, Fine Arts and Archives [Capt. F.H.J. Maxse], *Pompeii and Herculaneum*, 17 April 1944.

[Morey], *Outline of a Lecture* = NARA M1944, RG 239/0015, Correspondence, [Charles Rufus Morey], *Outline of a Lecture on the Protection of Cultural Treasures* [c. October 1943].

NWAAF, Air Intelligence Weekly Summary No. 44 = TNA AIR 23/7452, Headquarters Northwest African Air Forces A-2 Section, *Air Intelligence Weekly Summary* No. 44, 11 September to 17 September 1943.

OIS: Operations and Intelligence Summaries (see Appendix B)

OPSUM: Operations Summaries (see Appendix B)

ORB: Operations Record Books (see Appendix B)

RAF Narrative, vol. 1 = TNA AIR41/34, *R.A.F. Narrative (First Draft): The Italian Campaign 1943–1945*. Volume 1, *Planning and Invasion to the Fall of Rome* (1950).

RAF Narrative, vol. 2 = TNA AIR41/58, *R.A.F. Narrative (First Draft), The Italian Campaign 1943–1945:* Volume 2, *Operations June 1944–May 1945* (1956).

RAF Narrative, vol. 5 = TNA AIR41/43, *R.A.F. Narrative (First Draft): The RAF in the Bomber Offensive against Germany:* Volume 5, *The Full Offensive, Feb. 1943–Feb. 1944* (1950).

Report on Operation Strangle = TNA AIR 23/6332, Headquarters Mediterranean Allied Tactical Air Force, *Report on Operation "Strangle": 19th March–11th May 1944*, 24 July 1944.

Roberts Commission, Special Meeting = NARA M1944, RG 239/0010, Correspondence, *Minutes of a Special Meeting of the American Commission for the Protection and Salvage of Artistic and Historic Monuments in Europe*, 8 October 1943.

USAAF Combat Chronology = *US Army Air Forces in World War II: Combat Chronology, 1941–1945*. Compiled by Kit C. Carter and Robert Mueller. Washington, DC: Center for Air Force History) <https://www.afhra.af.mil/Portals/16/documents/Studies/101–150/AFD-090529-036.pdf>

War Room Monthly Summary = TNA AIR 22/343, [British] War Room *Monthly Summary of Mediterranean Air Command Operations*, September 1943.

Wheeler, *Antiquaries Paper* = TNA T209/19, Mortimer Wheeler, *Summary of Paper on Archaeology in the War Zone: Facts and Needs*. Society of Antiquaries [London], Thursday 13 January 1944 [pp. 47–63 of the downloadable pdf].

Wheeler, *Preservation* = TNA T209/19, Mortimer Wheeler, *Preservation of buildings, collections, etc., of artistic or archaeological importance in occupied territories: Notes resulting from first-hand experience with the 8th Army in Africa and the 5th Army in Italy*. 28 November 1943 [pp. 63–65 of the downloadable pdf].

Zuckerman, *Report* = TNA AIR 23/1516, Professor Solly Zuckerman, *Air Attacks on Enemy Rail and Road Communications in Italy and Sicily: Professor Zuckerman's Report* (1943).

Introduction

In August and September 1943, over 160 bombs hit the ancient site of Pompeii, dropped by aircraft of the British Royal Air Force (RAF), Royal Canadian Air Force (RCAF) and United States Army Air Force (USAAF) (Figures 1 and 2).[1] At the time, this evoked relatively little discussion or complaint, perhaps unsurprising given the scale of the human tragedy enveloping the world at that time. It also received little contemporary or subsequent popular or scholarly attention compared, for example, to the well-known and widely discussed bombing of the Benedictine Abbey of Montecassino some six months later. Amedeo Maiuri, the wartime archaeological superintendent for Campania, in whose remit Pompeii lay, described the bombs that hit the site as, 'most merciful' ('misericordiose') because the damage was less than might have been expected.[2] A similar view is taken in contemporary Allied reports that acknowledge damage was widespread, but suggest that 'the total of significant destruction is limited. The effect on the general appearance of the ruins . . . is almost negligible.'[3] Modern scholars typically take a less sanguine view, and from any perspective, damage to one of the world's best-known and most important heritage sites (then as now) is, and was, regrettable (Figure 3).[4]

The bomb damage to ancient Pompeii finally received its scholarly due in 2006, with the publication of Laurentino García y García's *Danni di guerra a Pompei: Una dolorosa vicenda quasi dimenticata* ('War damage at Pompeii: A tragic event almost forgotten'). In this rigorous and fascinating study, the author documents and assesses the damage done to the site largely by analysis of contemporary photographic evidence from the archive of the Soprintendenza Archeologica di Pompei.

This book makes no attempt to replicate García y García's detailed assessment of the damage, although a summary derived from Allied documentation produced at the end of the war is provided in Appendix A. Instead, it is a study in history, heritage and cultural property protection, a key aim of which is to set the bombing of Pompeii in context to explore wider questions relating to the treatment and protection of heritage sites in conflict zones that remain relevant to this day. I believe that the experiences of the

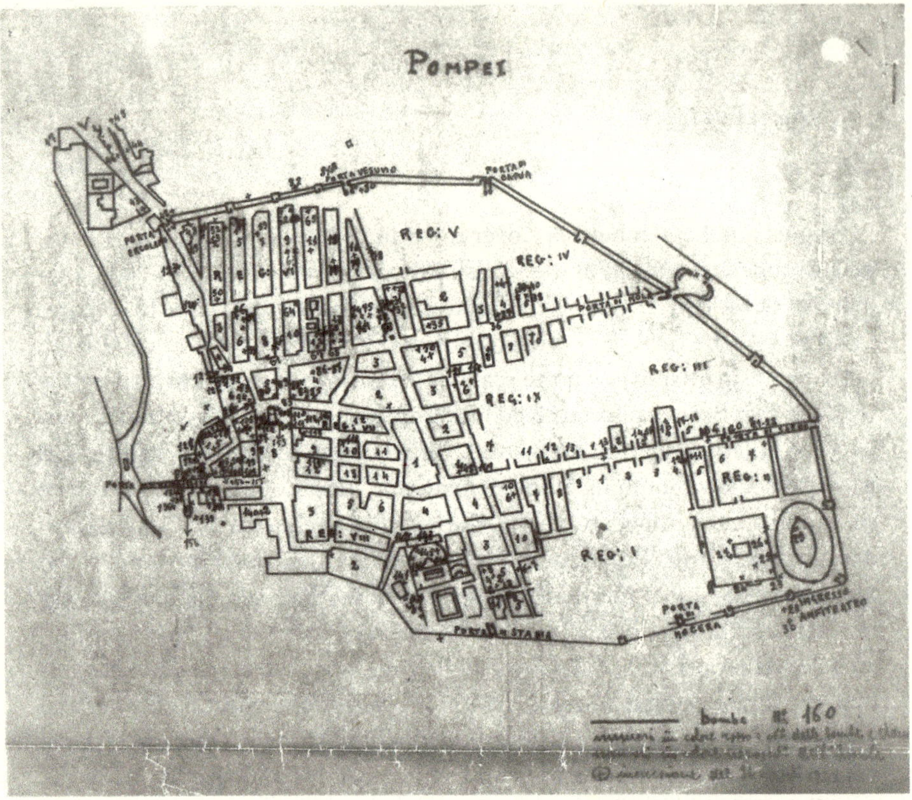

Figure 1: Contemporary plan showing locations of bomb damage at Pompeii, produced by Italian staff and included in NARA M1944, RG 239/0067, MFAA Field Reports, Allied Control Commission, Sub-Commission for Monuments, Fine Arts and Archives [Capt. F.H.J. Maxse], *Pompeii and Herculaneum*, 17 April 1944, p. 2 [= Frame 153].

Second World War are of great value in developing contemporary policies and practices for protecting heritage in war zones, and my engagement with modern military cultural property protection in recent years only reinforces that view.

The main contexts, themes, aims and issues in this book are as follows:

MILITARY

To understand the bombing of Pompeii in its military contexts, I have undertaken a detailed forensic and technical study based on contemporary wartime documentation. The operation is of inherent military interest for

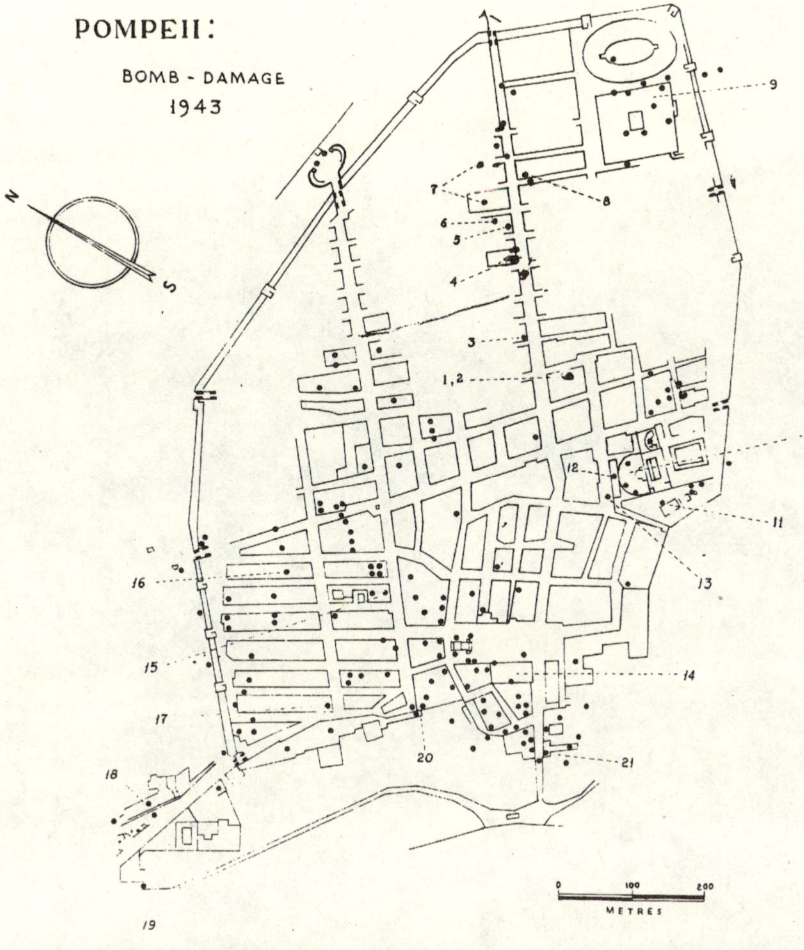

Figure 2: Contemporary plan showing locations of bomb damage at Pompeii produced as 'Pompeii: Bomb-Damage 1943' for MFAA *Final Report: Campania* = NARA M1944, RG 239/0075, MFAA Field Reports, Headquarters Allied Commission, Sub-Commission for Monuments, Fine Arts and Archives, *Final Report: Campania*, 20345/3/MFAA, 25 November 1945.

a number of reasons. It was an Allied effort that employed unusually varied bombing techniques and equipment for interdiction in a fast-changing situation with much at stake. My study includes assessment of the (hitherto poorly understood) planning and targeting decisions that led to the bombing that damaged the site, including the tactics employed and their accuracy. It is clear from this analysis that most of the damage to ancient

Figure 3: Contemporary photograph showing bomb damage to the House of Epidius Rufus, IX.1.20. British School at Rome photographic archive, Ward-Perkins collection, wpwar-0056.

Pompeii was accidental, resulting from bombing of nearby transportation targets in a bid to weaken German counter-attacks against the September 1943 Allied landings in the Gulf of Salerno. I also address and refute some alternative explanations for the bombing advanced at the time which sometimes recur even in more recent accounts.[5]

These issues form the focus of Part One of the book. Chapter 1 investigates damage to the site before the Salerno landings in September 1943, and Chapter 2 damage inflicted after those Allied landings on mainland Italy. Chapter 3 evaluates the military context in which the bombing took place (the 'why?') and Chapter 4 the methods and tactics employed (the 'how?') that explain much of the damage. Chapter 5 examines the military effectiveness of the bombing, considers whether it was necessary in military terms, and analyses it in terms of contemporary and subsequent Laws of Armed Conflict. Chapter 6 considers the origins and motivations of the other explanations of the bombing that arose at the time.

THE EVOLUTION OF ALLIED WARTIME HERITAGE PROTECTION POLICIES AND ORGANISATIONS

At the time of the bombing of Pompeii, the Allied Monuments, Fine Arts and Archives organisation (the MFAA 'Monuments Men') already existed. I examine the evolution of this organisation to show why it had no mitigating effect on the bombing near Pompeii. The focus of its activity at that time was on protection of heritage in areas occupied by ground forces, not on operational planning or limiting damage done by air forces, with which the organisation had little contact. However, other issues (poor initial organization, lack of authority) meant that even the occupation duties originally envisaged as the MFAA's main activities did not go well when the Allied liberated Naples in October 1943. However, autumn 1943 to spring 1944 was an important period of change in the MFAA's effectiveness. I consider how the lessons learned at this time led to changes that increased that effectiveness in many respects, but also highlighted deficiencies that were never overcome, in great part due to the exigencies of 'total war'.

This is a major focus of Part Two. Chapters 7 and 8 examine the origins and development of, respectively, British and US military cultural property protection (CPP) policies, practices and 'cultural intelligence' up to the time of the bombing of Pompeii, while Chapter 9 investigates the lack of

CPP input into contemporary air force planning, and its consequences for damage to heritage sites not just at Pompeii, but in Benevento, Naples and Rome. Chapter 10 sets out the measures taken in early 1944 by the Mediterranean Allied Air Force to mitigate such damage, and their successes and limitations.

DEFINING AND BALANCING 'MILITARY NECESSITY' AND 'MILITARY CONVENIENCE'

In his letter to Allied commanders of 29 December 1943 on the subject of heritage protection, Eisenhower (as Allied Commander-in-Chief, Mediterranean Theatre) stated, 'Nothing can stand against the argument of military necessity. That is an accepted principle. But the phrase "military necessity" is sometimes used when it would be more truthful to speak of military convenience or even of personal convenience.'[6] This is a central theme that runs throughout the book. Thus, in Part One (Chapter 5) I examine the bombing of Pompeii against definitions of military necessity employed in wartime laws of armed conflict as well as against some factors (such as proportionality) proposed before 1943 but only established in law after the Second World War. On that basis, I conclude that under the prevailing circumstances, it is unlikely that damage to Pompeii could have been prevented, even had more effective CPP policy existed at the time, although it should at least have provoked discussion and consideration of the principles at stake in that bombing—discussion that, in fact, never took place. There existed a conceptual void, with CPP not even admitted into the planning process. I also conclude that the damage was not disproportionate to the aims of the bombing. It would be very difficult to provide cultural property with complete immunity in wartime, although that does not mean that attempts to protect it are pointless.[7]

The theme of military necessity (along with the development of Allied CPP policy and practice) is taken up again in Part Three. In Chapters 11 and 12, I contrast the bombing of Pompeii with a case study of evident 'military convenience', namely the British military requisition of the Museo Nazionale di Napoli (National Museum of Naples) from 17 November 1943 to 29 June 1944. The deficiencies in Allied CPP practice in Naples, their identification, and responses to them (Chapter 13) highlight contexts in which military cultural property protection could, and can, be immediately and straightforwardly effective.

HISTORICAL LESSONS FOR CONTEMPORARY PRACTICE?

I hope and believe that a distinctive feature of this book is that it acknowledges the value of historical lessons for contemporary cultural property protection. The effectiveness of Allied wartime heritage protection was subjected to quite thorough and critical self-evaluation on a number of occasions and in a number of ways, both in the course of the war itself and in the immediate post-war period. For example, the deficiencies revealed at the time of the occupation of Naples (set out in Part Three) gave rise to a Commission of Enquiry held by military authorities in Naples, and a full written report with recommendations and detailed reports reflecting on failures as well as successes were written at the very end of the war.[8] Wartime experiences fed into the creation of the 1954 Hague Convention on the Protection of Cultural Property in the Event of Armed Conflict, which, with its subsequent protocols, remains the primary international legislation on this subject.[9] However, much of the experience of heritage protection from the Second World War was forgotten. The heritage protection lessons of the Second World War were also largely forgotten by the US and British armed forces.[10] Monuments officers, invariably wartime volunteers rather than regular soldiers, were demobilised, many resuming or beginning distinguished careers in academia, museums and galleries. Much of the documentation they produced remained restricted, and in the UK at least, unavailable before the 1970s, largely due to bureaucratic inertia rather than any particular sensitivity. There was little career advantage to be gained from heritage protection for British or US officers in Cold War armed forces. In Germany, envisaged as the principal theatre of any future European conflict, heritage protection was the preserve of the civilian authorities.[11] Eurocentric outlooks, perhaps, meant that the cultural heritage of Cold War theatres of conflict such as Malaya, Korea and Vietnam was not accorded the same importance as that of Europe in the Second World War.[12]

Besides the memoirs of some wartime monuments officers, most of the post–Second World War literature relevant to this study dates to the 1990s and later, much of it motivated more or less directly by destruction of cultural heritage during the break-up of Yugoslavia and subsequent conflicts in the Middle East.[13] Broadly speaking, this literature can be divided into work that addresses historical aspects of cultural property protection, and work that focuses primarily on the contemporary situation.

The historical literature relevant to this topic in turn comprises several strands defined by focus, intended audience and nationality, emerging largely independent of one another. Lynn H. Nicholas's rigorous, scholarly and fascinating book *The Rape of Europa* provides an important starting point, and includes a valuable examination of the impact of the Italian campaign on cultural heritage and the evolution of the Allied Monuments, Fine Arts and Archives organisation among its many riches. Ilaria Dagnini Brey's 2009 study *The Venus Fixers* in many ways builds on the precedent set by Nicholas's work, within a narrower frame and with equal scholarly rigour. Robert M. Edsel's 2007 *Monuments Men* did much to spread the story of the MFAA among a wider audience, and, of course, served as the basis for the 2014 George Clooney film of the same name which, despite some historical and cinematic deficiencies, made the existence of the organisation more generally known.[14]

Researchers in both Italy and Germany have engaged in productive exploration of their own countries' involvement in the destruction, preservation and restoration of cultural heritage in the Second World War. Italian scholars have produced a range of detailed local studies of these issues, as well as wider-ranging publications such as Lorenzo De Stefani's 2011 edited volume *Guerra, monumenti, ricostruzione: Architetture e centri storici italiani nel secondo conflitto mondiale* and Carlotta Coccoli's 2017 monograph *Monumenti violati*.[15] German scholars have also examined issues of cultural property protection in Italy in the context of wider re-examination of art and scholarship under National Socialism, including the activities of the Kunstschutz and the German academic institutes in Rome and Florence.[16]

In British (and UK published), scholarship, little attention has been paid to the Monuments, Fine Arts and Archives organisation of the Second World War in its own right, although the topic of war damage has been studied in the context of studies of bombing and post-war reconstruction. Nicola Lambourne's 2001 *War Damage in Western Europe* examines the devastating impact on cultural heritage of strategic bombing, especially in Britain and Germany, and more recent work has examined cultural dimensions of bombing in Italy and France, too.[17]

Today the protection of cultural property in conflict zones is certainly perceived as a more pressing issue than it was 30–50 years ago. A first draft of this introduction was begun in a week that saw the destruction by Daesh (the 'Islamic State'/ISIS/ISIL) of the Temple of Baalshamin at Palmyra, and revised as UK armed forces take measures to re-establish the cultural property protection capabilities that were lost after 1945. The protection or destruction of heritage sites and other forms of cultural property has been a factor not only in the current Syrian and Iraqi conflicts, but also in internal conflicts and outside interventions in places like Mali, Afghanistan, Libya, Egypt and the former Yugoslavia. The 2003 US-led invasion of Iraq showed that Western armed forces, at least, had little knowledge of the experiences of, and lessons learned by, the 'Monuments Men' of 1943–1945.[18] These events have, unfortunately, made cultural property protection a much more prominent issue, and this is reflected in the wide range of scholarly literature on the topic that has been published over the last decade.[19]

However, very little of what has been written draws explicit and practical lessons from the historical and the contemporary aspects of military cultural property protection. Notable exceptions to this are articles by Laurie Rush, whose 2012 study 'Cultural Property Protection as a Force Multiplier in Stability Operations' shows that procedures established over 70 years ago are still useful and relevant to modern military personnel, even on a detailed tactical level, such as in the securing and occupation of historic buildings and other cultural sites;[20] and Ronald T.P. Alcala's 2015 'Babylon Revisited: Reestablishing a Corps of Specialists for the Protection of Cultural Property in Armed Conflict'.[21]

Many of the issues discussed in the wartime documentation relating both directly and indirectly to the bombing of Pompeii are still under discussion in modern military cultural property protection circles. These issues include the balance between protection and military necessity, the place of cultural specialists within military organisations and hierarchies, education of military personnel, the provision, distribution and formatting of information about cultural property within military organisations, relationships with local heritage specialists, the value of cultural heritage in post-conflict stabilisation, and how to address different causes of damage, including aerial bombardment, ground combat and occupation by friendly forces.[22] One particular issue in Second World War cultural property protection that goes beyond recent Western military experience is its practicality, and the assessment of military necessity and proportionality (see Chapter 5), in high-intensity and 'total' conflicts. Most recent Western experience has occurred in the context of what are sometimes characterised as 'wars of choice' and post-conflict stabilisation operations rather than in situations comparable to those of the Second World War. While the seriousness of these 'wars of choice' is not to be under-estimated, typically the stakes are lower (for intervening powers, at least) than they were for the Allies in the Second World War, and operational planning less time-constrained.

Thus, an aim of my research is to contribute to the development of contemporary policy and practice in cultural property protection as well as to present an analysis that is of inherent interest as a historical study.

One legitimate criticism of a study like this (and one often advanced in the context of cultural property protection) is that it appears to value buildings and other material items over human lives, both civilian and combatant. Sometimes that was the perception of victims of the Second World War, and from time to time the human dimension was overlooked in, for example, American museum directors' advocacy of 'open cities' (urban centres formally immune from military action—see Chapter 10) primarily as a means to protect art rather than people. This impression is reinforced by the emphasis on traditional forms of cultural property—monuments and fine art—in the Second World War. Baldoli and Knapp suggest, with considerable justification, that the debates about the protection of art at that time reflect the survival of an elitist 'Grand Tour' perspective that had little regard for the people who lived among the art and buildings; the same might be said for the US academic focus on 'Western civilization' that motivated and coloured some Allied planning and training efforts (see Chapter 8).[23] The bombing that damaged the archaeological site of Pompeii also killed civilians, while at the same time other civilians were being killed in bombing attacks on places such as Benevento, Eboli and Naples itself. There is considerable debate about the scale of civilian casualties in wartime Italy, but regardless, the numbers presented are still tragic in the ended lives they reflect. An estimate advanced in official sources is 3,100 dead for the Provincia di Napoli (to which Pompei belongs) up to 21 September 1943, while more recent research suggests this is a substantial underestimate, proposing a total of over 6,000 for 1943 alone.[24] At the same time, Allied and German military personnel (volunteers and conscripts alike) were dying in combat in the Salerno beachhead, and the possibility of saving Allied soldiers' lives there was one of the factors that led to the bombing that damaged Pompeii.

Buildings, art and other manifestations of tangible cultural heritage can, however, also play an important role in constructing and preserving identity and in rebuilding communities after conflict. While Second World War cultural property protection largely focused on a much more limited and traditional (and purely tangible) range of cultural heritage than would be recognised today, even then there was some recognition of its value to the people who lived around and among it. While, perhaps surprisingly to outsiders, the 19th-century Santuario della Madonna of modern Pompei (listed as a zero star heritage site in wartime MFAA lists, compared to the three stars of the archaeological site—see below, Chapter 8) was more important in symbolic terms to most locals than the archaeological site, the latter was a valuable source of employment and income for the local community as well as an important strand of the identity of many who worked there and lived nearby. Certainly Allied funds provided for the reconstruction of damage to the site after its liberation and entrance fees paid by Allied service personnel who visited the site as a leave destination provided employment and a substantial boost to the local civilian economy at a time of great austerity.[25] The protection of people and protection of heritage are not mutually exclusive.

PART ONE

The Bombing of Pompeii, August–September 1943

CHAPTER 1

'La prima tragica notte di Pompei'

24/25 August 1943

INTRODUCTION

In August and September 1943, over 160 Allied bombs impacted within the ancient site of Pompeii, dropped by aircraft of British, US and Canadian air forces. Part One of this study examines why those bombs were dropped and why they hit the ancient site, setting this event in the wider contexts of the war in Italy and Allied bombing methods and technology. I seek to demonstrate in detail that the damage to Pompeii was accidental, largely the result of Allied efforts to defeat a German counter-attack against their beachhead in the Gulf of Salerno, some 17 miles (27 km) to the south-east.[1]

Laurentino García y García's 2006 study of the damage to the site includes a day-by-day reckoning based on a near-contemporary document, the *Diario delle incursioni*, compiled (in its final form at least) on 8 February 1944 by Alfonso D'Avino, the Capotecnico (Head of Technical Services) of the site, and sent to Superintendent Amedeo Maiuri at the Soprintendenza alle Antichità di Napoli, the administrative body for ancient heritage in that area.[2] Apart from one outlying (but serious) instance of damage on the night of 24/25 August 1943, all the major damage is attributed to day and night air raids that took place between 13 and 20 September 1943, with some damage to outlying areas of the site continuing from 21 to 26 September.[3] The timing of these air attacks relates closely to the Allied landings in the Bay of Salerno that began on 9 September 1943.[4]

While the RAF had been bombing the Italian mainland since June 1940, Pompeii was not damaged to any great extent until shortly before the Allied landings on the Italian mainland, and most of the recorded damage to the site was done in the third week of September 1943, shortly after the Salerno landings.[5]

So why did bombs hit Pompeii? Did Allied bombers actually target the ancient site for some reason, and if not, what were they attempting to bomb? We can address these questions by comparing the dates of damage to the site provided in the contemporary archaeological documentation to contemporary air force documents, to investigate the stated targets of missions flown near Pompeii on those dates.

Table 1 summarises the information provided by the Allied air forces intelligence documents available in the UK National Archives and the archive of the US Air Force Historical Research Agency, with documented bombing missions and their stated targets mapped as closely as possible against the dates of damage to the site recorded in the *Diario delle incursioni*.[6] There are some discrepancies that are examined in detail later.

These bombing missions were undertaken by aircraft of the USAAF, RAF and RCAF flying from bases in Sicily, Algeria and Tunisia. The RAF and RCAF bombers were all Vickers Wellington twin-engine medium bombers employed in night bombing, except for a small number of American-built Douglas Boston light bombers used on two nights to drop flares to illuminate and mark targets for other aircraft. Some of the USAAF sorties were flown by Boeing B-17 Flying Fortress aircraft, four-engine strategic heavy bombers, while others comprised North American B-25 Mitchell and Martin B-26 Marauder twin-engine medium bombers, typically employed during the day, but also, under some circumstances, at night, as on 13/14 and 17/18 September.

Technical aspects of bombing tactics and equipment and their implications for the damage to Pompeii are considered later (especially in Chapter 4), but in the first instance it is worth examining a sample of the air force documentation in more detail, particularly as it relates to the nominated targets. As can be seen, with the exception of the outlying RAF night mission of 24 August 1943, the specified targets all relate to transportation, including roads, railways, intersections and bridges. There is no suggestion in this documentation that the ancient site of Pompeii was the intended target of any mission, and it is clear that the ancient site was struck accidentally, by aircraft aiming to bomb the transportation network around (and especially immediately west of) the modern town of Pompei.

The air force documentation relating to the missions in question was produced at a number of different command levels, from the headquarters (in Algiers) of the Allied North West African Air Forces that exercised overall command of the air forces in the theatre, through Group, Wing and Squadron headquarters down to (in some cases) individual bomber crews who wrote or typed reports on their missions or dictated them to a squadron intelligence officer.[7] These are for the most part prosaic documents

Table 1: Instances of recorded damage to the archaeological site of Pompeii mapped against known bombing missions nearby and their intended targets

Recorded instances of damage	Summary of corresponding missions and stated targets
24/25 August (night)	No. 236 Wing RAF, No. 331 Wing RCAF (48 Wellington bombers) 'Torre Annunziata marshalling yards and steelworks'
13 September (day)	310th Bombardment Group USAAF (36 B-25 bombers) 319th Bombardment Group USAAF (35 B-26 bombers) 'Road junction at Pompeii'
13/14 September (night)	First mission: Nos. 231, 236, 330 Wings RAF, No. 331 Wing RCAF (91 Wellingtons) 'Road east of Pompeii' Second mission: No. 326 Wing RAF (3 Bostons) dropping illuminating flares for 12th Bombardment Group USAAF (23 B-25) and 340th Bombardment Group USAAF (12 B-25) 'Pompeii road junction'
14 September (day)	97th Bombardment Group USAAF (34 B-17 bombers) 'Crossroads west of Pompeii' 99th Bombardment Group USAAF (37 B-17 bombers) 'Torre Annunziata'
15 September (day)	310th Bombardment Group USAAF (48 B-25) 'Torre Annunziata road junction'
15/16 September (night)	Nos. 231, 236, 330 Wings RAF and No. 331 Wing RCAF (123 Wellingtons) 'Pompeii road/rail junction'
17/18 September (night)	First mission: No. 326 Wing RAF (3 Bostons) dropping flares for 12th Bombardment Group USAAF (10 B-25) and 340th Bombardment Group USAAF (10 B-25) 'Pompei road/rail junction' Second mission: 114 Squadron (No. 326 Wing) RAF (3 Bostons) dropping illuminating flares for 12th Bombardment Group USAAF (24 B-25) 'Torre Annunziata road junction'
19 September	[none recorded]
20 September	301st Bombardment Group USAAF (17 B-17) 'Torre Annunziata road SE'
21–26 September 1943 (minor damage to outlying parts of the site)	Armed reconnaissance, harassing attacks and close support of ground troops

recording routine details, and were secret, for internal rather than for public consumption.[8] Thus there is no reason to believe they are deliberately misleading as to the targets that crews were ordered to bomb or thought they had bombed. However, given the inherent inaccuracy of bombing in 1943 (discussed in Chapter 4) and the problems of assessing bombing results and damage, it is very likely that some reports are mistaken in their assessment of what the bombs actually hit.

POMPEII'S FIRST 'NIGHT OF TRAGEDY', 24/25 AUGUST 1943

The first damage to Pompeii was caused on the night of 24/25 August 1943. The mission that caused it was unique in two respects among those examined here. For one, it was the only such mission before the Allied landings at Salerno on 9 September. It was also the only instance of damage to Pompeii caused by truly strategic bombing, directed against railway marshalling yards and the steelworks at nearby Torre Annunziata.

The contemporary *Operations and Intelligence Summary* (*OIS*) of Headquarters, Northwest African Air Forces, produced as a summary of that night's activities, makes no mention of Pompeii, ancient or modern, as a target. However, one entry (for Mission no. 577) details an RAF/RCAF attack targeting the railway marshalling yards and steelworks near Torre Annunziata.[9] These were to the south-east of the town of Torre Annunziata itself, with the steelworks only c. 1.5 km from the west edge of the ancient Pompeii, and the adjacent marshalling yards even closer (see Figures 4–6). Undoubtedly bombs intended for these targets hit the archaeological site in error due to navigational errors and poor accuracy, despite the contemporary assessment (in the *OIS*) that bombing was 'well concentrated'.

> '[Mission] No. 577 night 24/25 August: Torre Annunziata marshalling yards and steelworks. 48 Wellingtons of 236 and 331 Wings dropped 56.5 tons [57.4 tonnes] of mixed bombs between 2202 and 2217 hrs from 7/10,000 feet. Many bomb bursts. 3/6 fires were seen in target area. Bombing was well concentrated and a 4000 lb bomb was seen to fall near the steelworks. No encounters. 1 a/c [aircraft] is missing, 2 a/c returned safely.'

Essentially the same information is provided by documents produced at Group and Wing level.[10] The lowest level of documentation, the records of

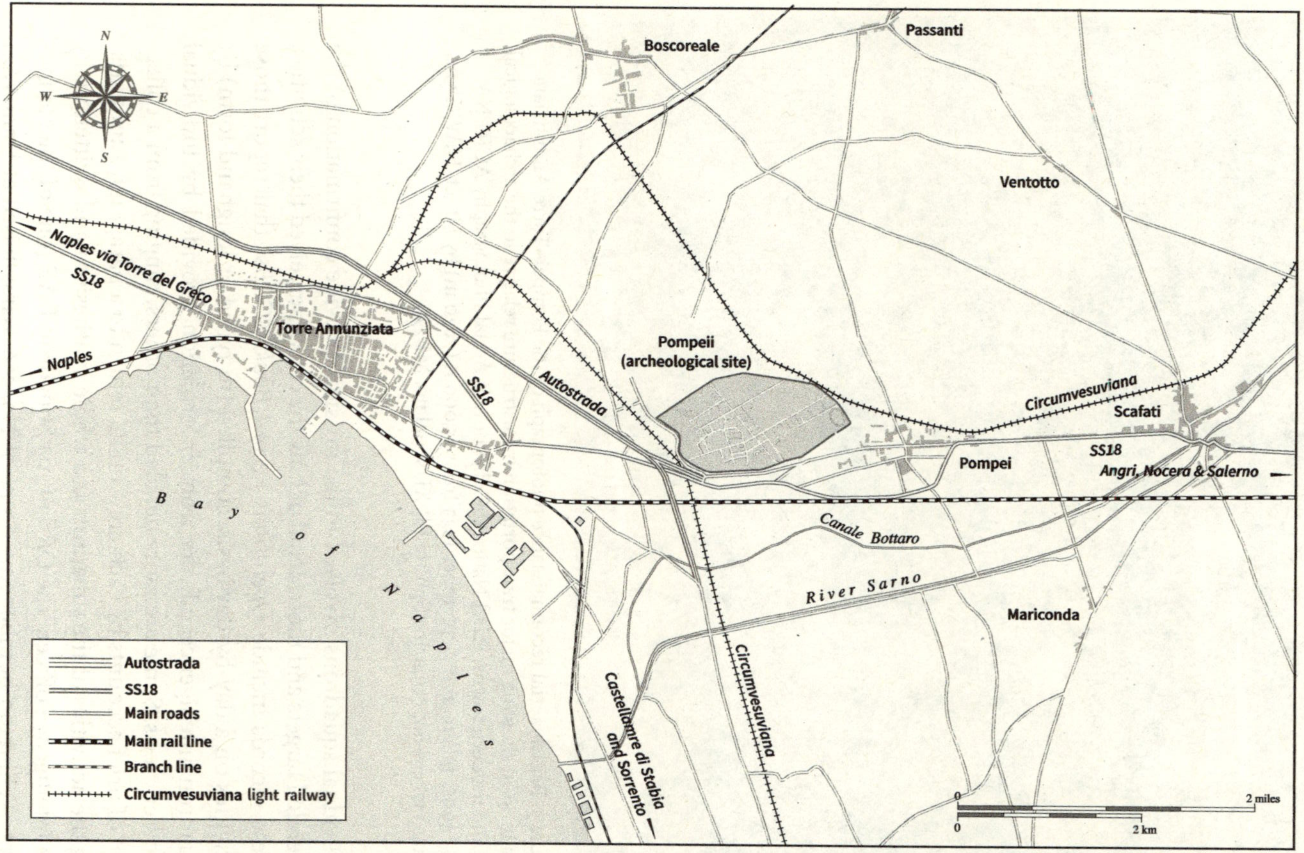

Figure 4: Map of the Pompei–Torre Annunziata area in 1943, showing major transportation infrastructure relative to the archaeological site and modern towns.

Figure 5: British aerial reconnaissance photograph of the Pompei–Torre Annunziata area in 1943, showing major transportation infrastructure relative to the archaeological site and modern towns. [UK] National Collection of Aerial Photography ACIU NA 0685 4006, taken on 18 September 1943 from 25,000 ft (7620 m) by Flt. Lt. H.W. Clyne, flying Vickers-Supermarine Spitfire PR XI, serial no. MB779.

individual squadrons involved in the mission, provide confirmation of the intended targets and more detail of how the crews perceived their activities. These records include *Operations Record Books* (*ORB*s) that report those activities on a day-by-day basis, compiled (in typed or longhand form) by squadron intelligence officers from information provided by individual bomber crews. Some are more detailed than others, ranging from a collection of brief accounts by each crew on its return to a paragraph summarising the activities of the squadron as a whole synthesised and written up by the intelligence officer. The *ORB* of 104 Squadron RAF (one of the component Wellington bomber squadrons of No. 236 Wing, based at Hani West airfield near Kairouan in Tunisia) is one of the latter kind.[11]

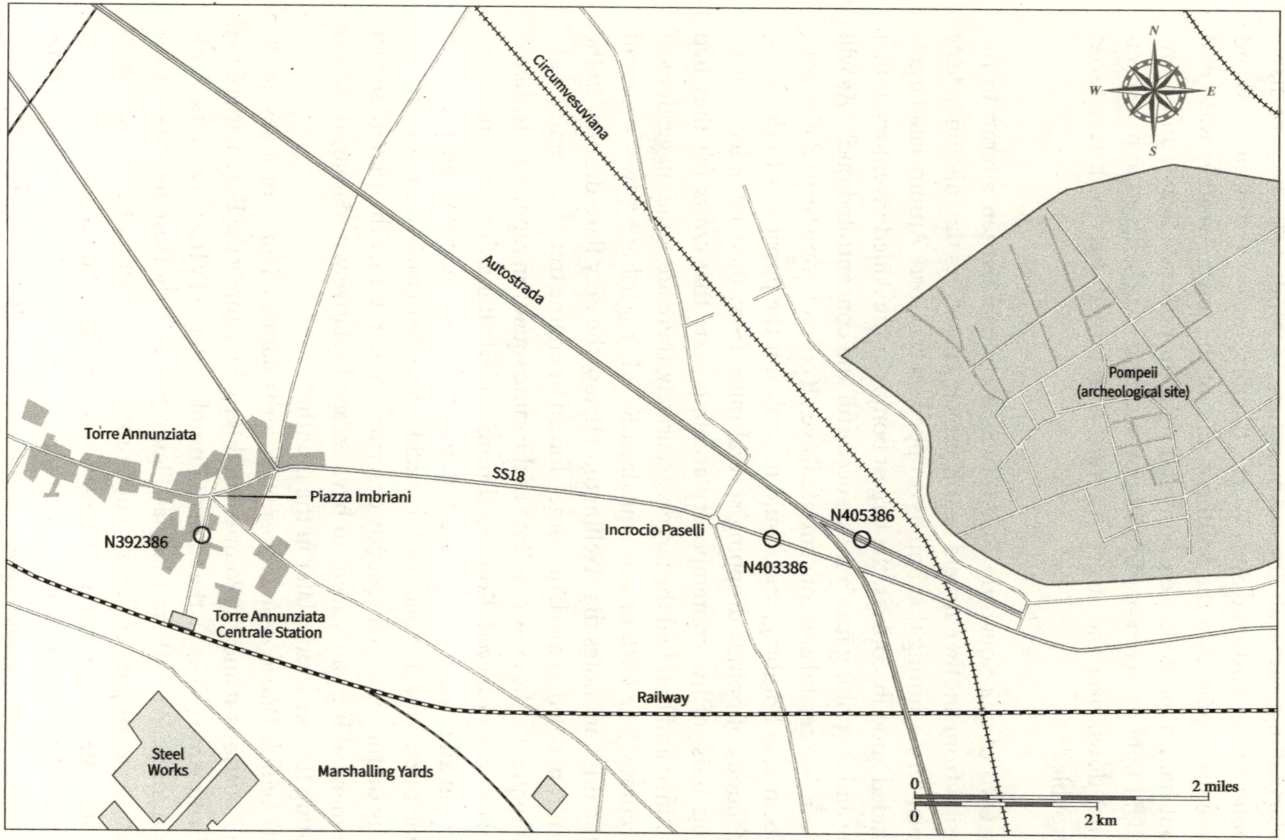

Figure 6: Detail of map of the Pompei–Torre Annunziata area in 1943 showing main targets of bombing attacks including the road/rail intersections immediately west of the archaeological site of Pompeii, and the Piazza Imbriani, steelworks and marshalling yards at Torre Annunziata. The N- numbers denote grid references specified as aiming points in contemporary air force documentation.

> '24th August: Aircraft of the Squadron were detailed to operate on the Marshalling Yards at Torre-Annunziata. Aircraft with help of flares bombed the Yards and Steel Works, bombing was well concentrated and one fire reported in the Southern part of the town. Weather was good but hazy, Opposition encountered light to moderate heavy, and a few night fighters. Aircraft "U" did not return to base believed to have been shot down over the target. Aircraft "A" returned early with rear turret trouble.'[12]

The *ORB* of 424 Squadron RCAF (which contributed ten aircraft to the mission from another airfield near Kairouan) describes the mission in very similar terms, noting that bombs dropped on the Torre Annunziata targets included 4000 lb 'cookies', the largest bombs in the Allied inventory at that time and describing it as 'a most successful and concentrated raid'.[13] As will be seen, 'successful and concentrated', even if correct, were very relative concepts in 1943 bombing, and would not rule out the possibility (indeed, the likelihood) of bombs dropping several miles from their intended targets. While most of the contemporary accounts state that crews felt they had identified and bombed the targets accurately, there are some suggestions of inaccuracy. The *ORB* of 420 Squadron RCAF, contributing twelve aircraft to the mission, notes that Wellington HE569, the only flare-dropper in the squadron, failed to mark the target, forced by engine trouble to return early. Consequently the crew of HE973 of the same squadron reported 'vis(ibility) by flares not observed. Bombed through cloud after 2 dummy runs'. Some crews in all squadrons reported that they had been unable to see their own bomb bursts due to cloud, and so unable to confirm their accuracy. The visibility on the night is frequently described as 'fair' rather than 'good'. In fact the marshalling yards seem to have escaped relatively undamaged, necessitating further attacks later in the month.[14]

D'Avino's *Diario delle incursioni* records damage (some of it severe) in four locations at ancient Pompeii on this night, namely the Forum, the Casa di Trittolemo (VII.7.2), the Casa di Romolo e Remo (VII.7.10) and the Antiquarium near the Porta Marina (Figure 7), all fairly close together in the south-western part of the site and commensurate with a few bombs inaccurately placed or drifting off-target from the Torre Annunziata area rather than a deliberate attack on ancient (or even modern) Pompeii.[15] Nevertheless, according to Maiuri, *Radio Londra* (the BBC Italian service) responded to reports of the damage by stating that the intended target had been a Ger-

Figure 7: The reconstructed Antiquarium (upper right, with white porch) and Porta Marina (left) at Pompeii today (author's photograph).

man headquarters in a hotel near the Porta Marina. There is no evidence at all in the RAF documentation to support this claim, and the possible motives for it are examined in Chapter 6.[16]

More bombs fell close to ancient Pompeii later that month without actually damaging the site, notably on 29/30 August, which saw daytime missions against Torre Annunziata flown by the USAAF as well as nighttime bombing by British and Canadian aircraft. The daytime mission was undertaken by 51 B-26 medium bombers of the 17th and 320th Bombardment Groups (USAAF), escorted by 40 P-38 fighters of the 1st Fighter Group (USAAF), provoking interception by an estimated 40–50 enemy fighters.[17] The night-time attack comprised 78 Wellington bombers of Nos. 231, 236 and 330 Wings RAF and No. 331 Wing RCAF.[18] Reports of both the day and night missions mention cloud causing problems in bombing, and the accidental damage caused beyond the intended target area included a hit on the transformer room of the Circumvesuviana railway, causing an electrical failure that forced services to terminate at Pompei Villa dei Misteri station.[19] However, the next report of damage to the ancient site in the *Diario delle incursioni* comes on 13 September, by which time Allied armies had landed in the Gulf of Salerno to establish a presence on the Italian mainland.

CHAPTER 2

'Everything we could put into the air'

Pompeii and the Salerno Beachhead, 13–29 September 1943

Much more extensive damage was done to ancient Pompeii, by many more bombs, in the third week of September 1943. Again, investigation of Allied air forces documentation provides a clear picture of the intended targets of the missions that caused that damage, and again, there is no indication in any of this that the ancient site of Pompeii was ever a target in its own right, despite some contemporary claims to the contrary (discussed in Chapter 6). As in August, Pompeii was bombed accidentally, by aircraft attacking other nearby targets of more obviously military importance. In this period the missions were interdiction rather than strategic bombing, targeting transportation nodes and routes with the aim of slowing and preventing the build-up of German forces counter-attacking the Allied landings in the Gulf of Salerno—a counter-attack that very nearly inflicted a disastrous defeat on the Allies on the mainland of Italy.[1]

13 SEPTEMBER 1943

The *Diario delle incursioni* records 35 instances of damage to the site during the day (25) and night (10) of 13 September, a period of exceptionally intense Allied air activity in the vicinity of ancient and modern Pompeii resulting from a crisis in the Salerno beachhead.

13 SEPTEMBER (DAY, USAAF)

The daytime missions that damaged Pompeii were conducted by USAAF medium bombers, specifically 36 B-25s of the 310th Bombardment Group, and 35 B-26s of the 319th Bombardment Group. While the *OIS* describes the target as 'ROAD JUNCTION AT POMPEII', more detailed reports compiled by the two Groups engaged refer to the target or targets as 'road junction of Torre Annunziata' (310th) and 'road junction SE of Torre Annunziata' (319th).[2] The contemporary mission reports also indicate that bombing was conducted in good visibility in the early evening, from somewhat higher altitudes than usual for US medium bombers, employing 100 lb bombs, relatively small weapons dropped in large numbers to smother road and rail targets and vehicles using them.[3]

It is clear from these accounts that the aiming point for the 319th Bombardment Group at least was the road intersection at the Piazza Imbriani on the south-east (Pompeii) side of Torre Annunziata, between the SS18 road (to Salerno via modern Pompei) and the main railway line (see Figure 6). As we will see, this intersection, distinctive and visible from the air, was a frequent aiming point for bombers targeting this area, and lay only c. 1.4 km from the archaeological site of Pompeii. The details provided in the 319th Bombardment Group records indicate that bombs spread along the road (presumably the SS18) at least as far east as Pompeii, and some of these undoubtedly caused the damage to the site.[4] Mission photographs of 310th Bombardment Group certainly show bomb strikes on the archaeological site, mostly to the west and north of the Forum (Figure 8).[5] A contemporary plot of bomb strikes from this attack produced by intelligence officers of the 310th from mission photographs indicates some 64 bomb strikes within the wall circuit of the ancient site, most in excavated areas but some in the unexcavated area north of the Via dell'Abbondanza (Figure 9).[6] D'Avino's *Diario delle incursioni* reports 14 instances of damage to the site in an attack timed at 1700 hrs that day, and a further 11 in an attack at 1730 hrs, all on the western side of ancient Pompeii.[7]

13/14 SEPTEMBER (NIGHT, RAF/RCAF)

The main bombing attack of that night (between 2122 and 0005 hrs, 13/14 September) was conducted by 91 Wellingtons of the RAF's Nos. 231, 236, 330 Wings and No. 331 Wing RCAF, dropping a total of 163.75 tons (166 tonnes) of bombs from altitudes of 5000 to 9000 ft (1524–2743 m), the specified target being 'Road east of Pompeii', rather than the roads west of the town attacked in the daytime mission.[8] The orders passed down from No. 205 Group to its constituent Wings give the objective of the mission as 'To disrupt road communications for 5 miles immediately East of POMPEI'.[9]

The target was selected and attacked at relatively short notice due to the emerging crisis on the ground in the Salerno beachhead (see Chapter 3).

Figure 8: Aerial photograph taken by a USAAF 310th Bombardment Group B-25 bomber while bombing near Pompeii on 13 September 1943, showing bomb strikes on the archaeological site. NARA RG 18, Box 1187, USAAF 310th BG, 13/9/1943, image 005.

The urgency of the situation is conveyed by the changing orders sent down from No. 205 Group to its constituent Wings in the course of the day.[10] The initial main target identified for the day (in Order B652) was a road junction between Sala Consilina and Atena, some 40 kilometres inland from Salerno. The stated aim of this original mission was to prevent the German 19th and 26th Panzer Divisions from linking up with forces opposing the Salerno landings as German forces withdrew from the south. That withdrawal was taking place in the face of the British 8th Army's advance after landing in Calabria on 3 September. Avellino, inland to the north of Salerno, was the initial planned target (in Order B653) for the rest of No. 205 Group. However, B652 was cancelled, and the 52 aircraft allocated to that mission were moved to the Pompeii target (B654) due to 'the presence of the HG [Hermann Göring] Division'. Finally, Order B654 was replaced by B655, which added the aircraft originally assigned to Avellino to the Pompeii mission, focusing the efforts of the whole Group in that area, with all of its 91 bombers.

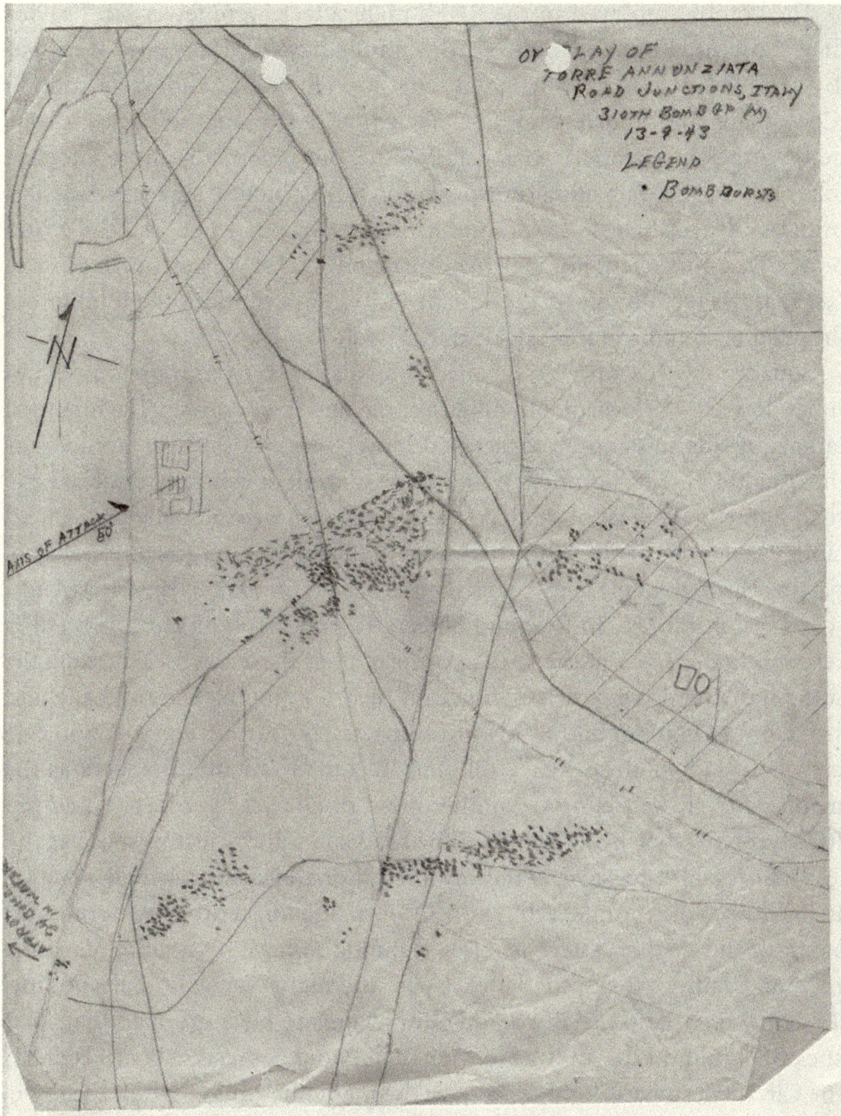

Figure 9: Contemporary plot of bomb strikes (marked as dots) for the mission on 13 September 1943, recorded from aerial photographs by an intelligence officer of the USAAF 310th Bombardment Group. The archaeological site is the hatched area on the east side of the image with the relatively low concentration of strikes. The greatest concentration of bomb strikes on this plot spreads from the Incrocio Paselli towards the coast and Torre Annunziata steelworks rather than the Piazza Imbriani. NARA RG 18, Box 1187, USAAF 310th BG, 13/9/1943, image 008.

The bombs employed in the RAF's night attack were fewer but heavier than those used by the USAAF earlier in the day. Typically they were 250 lb or 500 lb weapons, but included some 1000 lb bombs and a few 4000 lb 'Cookies' or 'Blockbusters', all less efficient at destroying 'soft' motor traffic than the small American 100 lb bombs, but potentially more effective for cratering and damaging transportation infrastructure such as roads and bridges.[11] Nevertheless, 'fewer' bombs is a relative concept, and the c. 160 bombs that hit ancient Pompeii over two months is set in perspective by the fact that the ten aircraft of 425 Squadron RCAF (a ninth of the total force) dropped 135 bombs in this attack alone.[12]

Squadron *ORB*s provide detailed information on this mission, sometimes down to the level of individual aircraft and their crews.[13] The intended targets of this mission are described loosely as 'road(s) near Pompei' or the 'road(s) east of Pompei'. While some aircraft specifically attacked the road immediately east of modern Pompei, attacks were actually prosecuted along the length of the SS18 road from modern Pompei towards Salerno, passing through or close to towns such as Scafati (c. 3 km to the east), Angri (c. 5 km), Pagani (c. 10 km) and Nocera (c. 12 km—see Figure 10). *ORB*s report bombs aimed at the road at or near all of these towns. For example, some individual crews of 70 Squadron record bombing the road 3–7 and 5–7 miles (4.8–8 km and 8–11.2 km respectively) east of Pompei, and two crews of 425 Squadron RCAF (aircraft 'B' and 'S') mention Nocera as the main focus of their efforts. Another crew, of aircraft 'T' of 425 Squadron RCAF, reports aiming its bombs at the road and railway just west of Pagani. The main Naples-to-Salerno railway line runs parallel and particularly close to the SS18 at that point. Wellington 'O' of 70 Squadron dropped bombs just south of the road at Angri, its crew claiming to have hit a junction of the road and railway there, the latter, again, the main Naples-to-Salerno line. The crew of aircraft 'M' of 70 Squadron claims to have dropped their first stick of bombs on the 'railway just north of Pompei', presumably (if correct) the Circumvesuviana light railway, as the main line runs south of the town.

Opposition over the target was negligible, with (according to 424 Squadron) 'no flak or S/L [searchlights] from the target', although there was some anti-aircraft fire in the Naples area. The 104 Squadron *ORB* mentions 'several reports of night fighters, no interceptions', while one Wellington of 420 Squadron 'reported a JU 88 [Junkers 88 night fighter] approaching dead astern', but it broke off its attack when fired upon.

All accounts agree that visibility was good, both because of the full moon

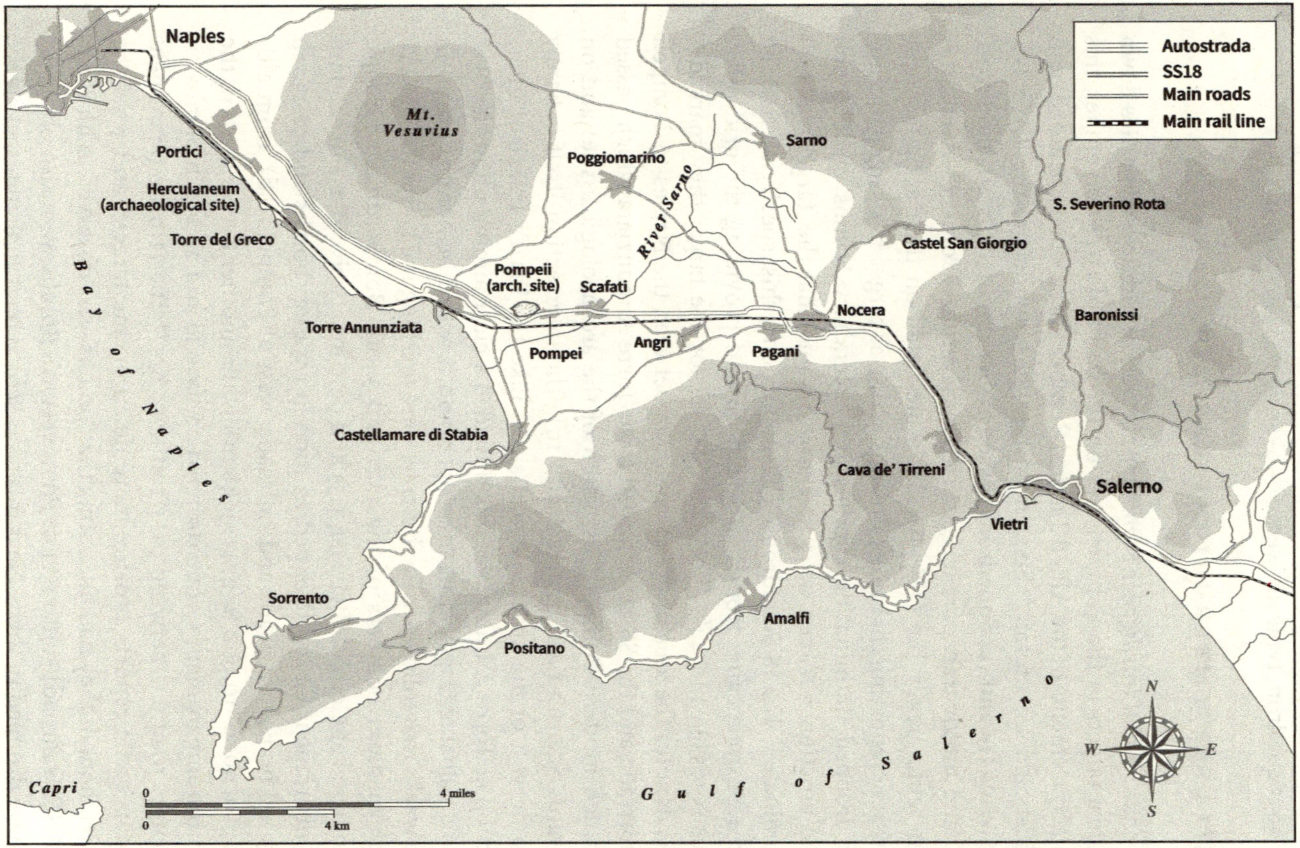

Figure 10: Map showing the Pompei–Torre Annunziata area and its transportation infrastructure relative to Naples and Salerno.

and illumination by flares.[14] Bombing altitudes, reported individually only for 425 Squadron, typically were 6000–8000 ft (1829–2438 m).

13/14 SEPTEMBER (NIGHT, RAF AND USAAF)

Operations and Intelligence Summary 206 reports additional sorties flown against targets in the Pompeii area on the night of 13/14 September, this time by elements of the Allied Tactical Bomber Force which included both British and US aircraft.[15] Sixteen Boston light bombers of the RAF's No. 326 Wing (18 and 114 Squadrons) based at Gerbini in Sicily attacked road, rail and motor transport targets 'in San Severino—Pompei—Avellino—Benevento area'.[16] The *OIS* provides more detail on their activities near Pompeii, reporting that three Bostons acting as target-marking pathfinders dropped illuminating candles and incendiary bombs on 'Pompeii road junction' between 0045 and 0104 hrs and that the 'target was well illuminated'. The 18 Squadron *ORB* supplements this, specifying that the three Bostons came from that squadron and providing the grid reference N405386 (40°44′54″ N, 14°28′48″ E) for the target they marked.[17] This denotes the area of the intersection between the Naples-to-Pompeii autostrada and the SS18 main road from Torre Annunziata which passed through modern Pompei (just south of the archaeological site) and on towards Salerno (see Figures 6 and 10). The intersection itself is barely 200 m west of the archaeological site.[18] Like the Piazza Imbriani intersection at Torre Annunziata, this provided a clear aiming point that was also a valuable target in its own right, and it would be bombed again in the weeks that followed. The Bostons were marking the target for USAAF B-25 medium bombers of the 12th and 340th Bombardment Groups, also based at Gerbini. Between 1153 and 0215 hrs, twelve B-25s of the 12th Bombardment Group dropped 63 1000 lb (454 kg) bombs and 52 250 lb (113 kg) bombs on roads and railroads 'west of Pompei (old)' from altitudes of 9000–10,000 ft (2743–3048 m), while another twelve B-25s of the 340th Bombardment Group dropped 26 1000 lb and 23 250 lb bombs on 'Pompei road jct.' between 0114 and 0124 hrs.[19] The 12th Bombardment Group sortie reports provide more detail on the targets, and what the crews thought they had hit, noting that 'bombs were observed to hit roads and RR [railroad] southwest of Pompei (old). Bombs were also observed to have dropped in town. Near miss was scored on bridge in target area'.[20] The RAF 18 Squadron *ORB* refers to '2 good fires at POMPEI 0305 [hrs]', presumably started by one of the earlier attacks and noted by one of its Bostons passing on a later armed reconnaissance sortie.

While, as in August, ancient Pompeii was not the intended target of the bombing on 13 September, nevertheless some bombs hit the site. The *Diario delle incursioni* lists 25 instances of damage caused during the daytime raids, and 10 during the night.[21] The greater number of instances of damage during the day and their relatively scattered distribution on the west side of the site reflects the greater number of bombs dropped by the USAAF, but still only 25 impacts on the site for the dropping of c. 1600 100 lb bombs.[22] While the damage was more wide-ranging than on 24 August, nevertheless it was almost entirely confined to structures in the Forum area and Regions VI and VII on the western side of the site. The instances of damage from the night attack were quite closely clustered around the Forum and a little to its east (VII.IV.62 and VII.IV.59, both on the north-west side of the insula, and VII.X.9, further to the south and east). This was probably the result of the 12th and/or 340th Bombardment Group attacks on targets close to the west side of the site, whose relative inaccuracy is suggested by the statement 'bombs were observed to have dropped in town' in the 12th Bombardment Group's *Sortie Report*. Otherwise this damage may have been caused by one or two RAF aircraft dropping part of their bomb load short of their intended targets east of the site, as the bombers typically turned in across the coast from the west to approach their targets (see below, pp. 59; 62).

14 SEPTEMBER 1943 (DAY)

The *Diario delle incursioni* records 19 instances of damage to the site, catalogued as occurring during the night of 14/15 September, between 3 and 5 am. In fact, no significant bombing near Pompeii is recorded in the air forces' documentation for that night. However, there were substantial attacks during the day, specifically the first use in the immediate area of four-engine B-17 Flying Fortress heavy bombers.[23] Was there really no damage caused to the site by this daytime attack (certainly later B-17 missions damaged the site), or did the confusion caused by the bombing lead D'Avino to attribute such damage to the subsequent night?[24]

The *OIS* records two discrete missions in the area, by the 97th and 99th Bombardment Groups respectively. The former attacked the 'crossroads west of Pompeii', with 34 B-17s dropping 408 500 lb bombs from 15,800 ft (4816 m) at 1031 hrs.[25] The targets attacked are specified more precisely elsewhere in the *OIS* as 'road intersection and bridges 500 yds [457 m] west of town' and 'road junction 1500 ft [457 m] SW Pompeii hit at junction'. Probably this was the same intersection of the autostrada and the SS18 attacked by the combined RAF/USAAF mission in the early hours of 14 September. A Northwest African Air Forces weekly intelligence summary for this period includes a photograph showing daytime bombing of the autostrada/SS18 intersection (Figure 11). The photograph is undated, but given the dates covered by the report, it probably depicts this mission on 14 September.[26] The distance 500 yards/1500 ft given in the OIS does not secure identification of the target as it depends on the definition of the western limit of 'Pompei'/'the town' at the time. Contemporary aerial photographs (see Figure 5) show that the western limits of the modern town, extending along the SS18, overlapped the archaeological site, but without the suburban sprawl that now characterises the area and effectively connects modern Pompei to Torre Annunziata. 'The town' may well denote the archaeological site in this context anyway, as it was a clearer landmark from the air at that time than the modern town. Another aiming point for bombing on 20 September may have been the prominent road junction some 300 metres further west (40°44′55″ N, 14°28′35″ E, Figure 6), known as the Incrocio Paselli or Croce Pasella, on the modern boundary between Torre Annunziata and Pompei. This was certainly heavily damaged by bombing by 15 September and sufficiently distinctive to serve as an aiming point.[27] In practical terms, given the proximity of the two intersections and the limitations of 1943 bombing methods and accuracy, the distinction was largely theoretical, as the *OIS* goes on to state: 'Bomb strike photos show road intersection and bridges 500 yds [457 m] west of town well covered in area 400 yds [366 m] square', so damage was wide-ranging. The *OIS* and the *97th Bombardment Group Mission Report* refer to damage to roads and overpasses in the target area, and the *Mission Report* mentions a 'south target', a 'NW target' and a 'southern overpass' without identifying each individually.

Just four minutes later, the B-17s of the 99th Bombardment Group attacked targets further west, around Torre Annunziata, focusing on 'highway, overpass, intersection'—again, road interdiction rather than the steelworks and marshalling yards that were the primary targets of the 24 August RAF Torre Annunziata mission.[28] While the *OIS* does not provide more precise details, the intersection may have been the Piazza Imbriani road junction already attacked on 13 September, and attacked again on 17/18 September. This lies just 300 m north of the main railway line at Torre Annun-

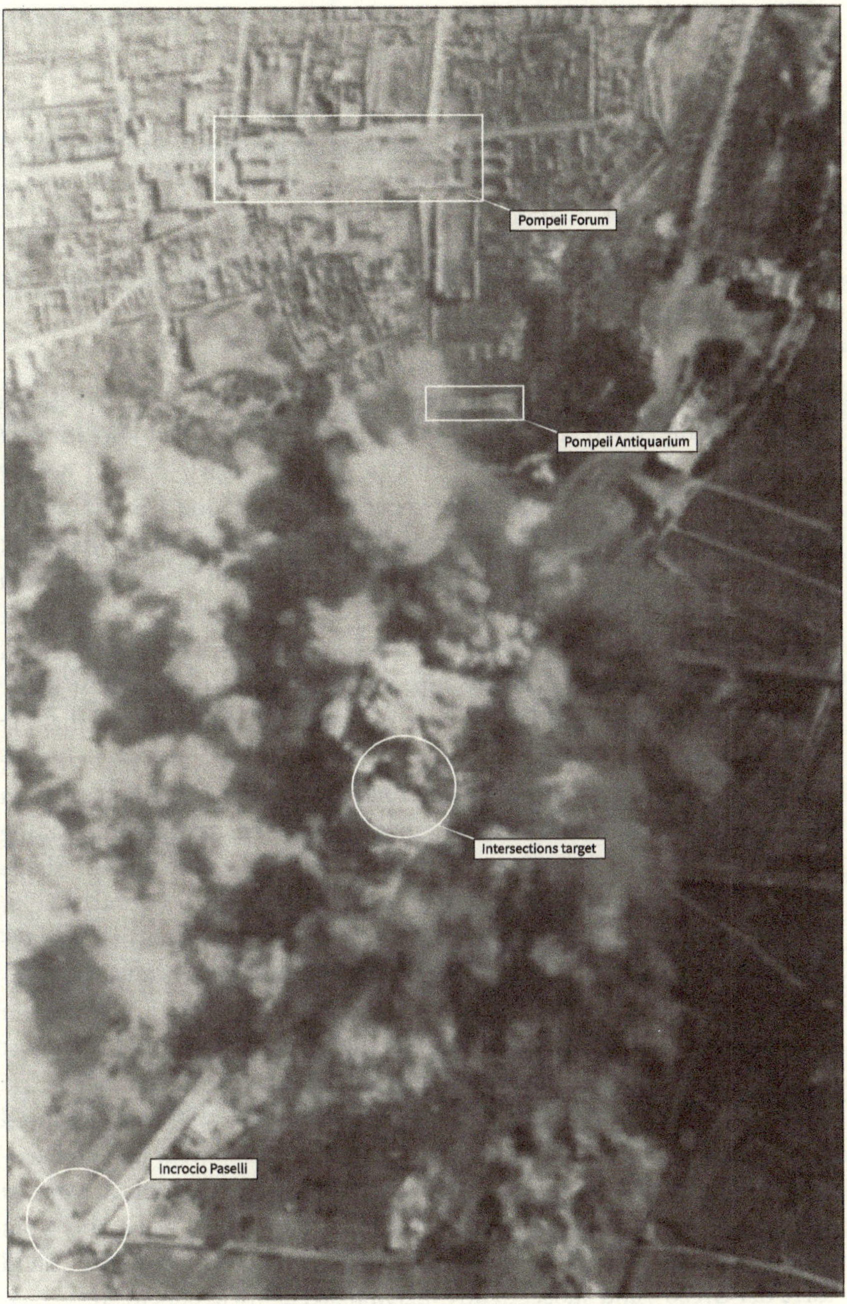

Figure 11: Contemporary aerial photograph captioned 'Pompeii Catches Hell Again', probably depicting the USAAF B-17 attack of 14 September 1943. The main target is clearly the area of the intersection of the autostrada and SS18, although smoke and dust are encroaching on the archaeological site, with the Forum area clearly visible at the top of the frame. The Incrocio Paselli (not under attack at this time) is visible in the lower left corner, and the diagonal line cutting across the lower right corner is the Naples-Salerno railway line. Reproduced from TNA AIR 23/7452, Headquarters Northwest African Air Forces A-2 Section, *Air Intelligence Weekly Summary* No. 44, 11 September to 17 September 1943, p. 28.

ziata Centrale station, with its marshalling yards to the east. The bomb damage report for this day in the *OIS* emphasises damage to railway lines as well as roads from Torre Annunziata to Pompeii, and from Torre Annunziata to Castellamare di Stabia, as does Zuckerman's contemporary report on the effectiveness of interdiction in the Italian campaign.[29]

15 SEPTEMBER 1943 (DAY)

The *Diario delle incursioni* records no significant damage to the site during the daytime on 15 September, although it is clear that Allied aircraft were active in substantial numbers in its vicinity, particularly around nearby Torre Annunziata. The *OIS* for the day again refers to the area's transportation infrastructure (and the vehicles using it) as a target for bombers of the Northwest African Strategic Air Force.[30] Forty-eight B-25s of the 310th Bombardment Group dropped 53.25 tons (48 tonnes) of bombs on 'Torre Annunziata Road Junction' at 1505 hours from altitudes between 8000 and 12,500 ft (2400–3800 m). The *OIS* reports 'bomb strike photos show many hits on road junction and four radiating roads. Direct hits on marshalling yards near POMPEII'. These accounts, along with a contemporary USAAF photograph (Figure 12) show that the road junction was, again, the Piazza Imbriani intersection at Torre Annunziata, and the railway marshalling yards were those between it and Pompeii. The photograph shows a large cloud of dust and smoke rising from the intersection, with a second, smaller cloud on the railway nearby to the south-east. Contemporary accounts indicate that some bombs from this attack also hit the modern town of Pompei, and a contemporary bomb plot of the attack is annotated '24 bombs in Pompei', without distinguishing between the modern town and the ancient site.[31] In addition, and apparently for the first time, fighter-bombers and dive-bombers of the Tactical Air Force were also employed against ground targets in the Torre Annunziata area.[32] It was in this context that archaeological superintendent Amedeo Maiuri, attempting to cycle from Pompei to Naples, was struck in the foot by a machine-gun bullet, presumably from strafing fighters, at Ponte della Gatta/Viúli (between Torre Annunziata and Torre del Greco), and subsequently hospitalised at Torre del Greco.[33]

15/16 SEPTEMBER (NIGHT)

The next recorded instances of damage to ancient Pompeii occurred that night, when a force of 123 Wellington bombers of Nos. 231, 236, 330 and No.

Figure 12: Contemporary aerial photograph showing the Piazza Imbriani area of Torre Annunziata under attack by the USAAF 310th Bombardment Group, 15 September 1943. NARA RG 18, Box 1190, USAAF 310th BG, 15/9/1943, image 001.

331 Wings RAF and RCAF dropped '240 tons [244 tonnes] of mixed bombs [ranging in weight from 250 to 4000 lb, 113 to 1814kg] at 2157–2357 hrs from 2500–10000 ft [760–3050 m]' on targets described as 'Torre Annunziata and Pompeii road', undoubtedly the SS18.[34] The aims and targets of the mission are set out in more detail in the orders produced by No. 205 Group for circulation to the Wings:

> 'The enemy's communications must be hampered, cut and destroyed. . . . [The aim is] [t]o disrupt enemy road communications between TORRE ANNUNZIATA and POMPEI and to block the roads in those towns by dropping "BLOCKBUSTERS" [4000 lb bombs] on them.'[35]

The No. 205 Group *ORB* is more specific about the targets:

> 'The targets were roads between TORRE ANNUNZIATA and POMPEII. . . . Special attention was paid to the road junctions and bursts were also reported on railways in the target area.'[36]

The *OIS* account states:

> 'Main bomb concentration was on road junction w. of Pompeii but a bridge between Torre Annunziata and Pompeii was also hit. Some 4000 lb bombs fell on Torre Annunziata. No encounters and no losses. Defences over target negligible.'

This mission saw a large concentration of aircraft operating in a relatively small area, and it is hardly surprising that the 424 Squadron *ORB* records congestion over the target. Otherwise bombing conditions are mostly described as good, with minimal opposition, although some crews' reports mention targets obscured by dust and smoke. The details provided in the individual squadron *ORB*s make it very clear that, in fact, roads, railways and bridges from Pompeii westwards to Torre Annunziata and the coast were targeted, with some squadrons focusing their efforts on the Torre Annunziata area. However, the vicinity of Pompeii, particularly the cluster of road and rail intersections and overpasses just west of the ancient site, clearly was hit very hard, with targets identified and bombed very close to the site. The individual crew reports of the 70 Squadron *ORB* are particularly specific about this, and refer to the ancient site as a navigational landmark, with targets identified relative to it. For example, Wellington 'T' 'aimed at road and rail crossing just west of Pompei ruins', Wellington 'A' 'Crossed W. side of Pompei ruins . . . [dropped bombs] across road junctions near railway just west of Pompei ruins'.[37]

Even 4000 lb (1814 kg) 'cookies', the largest bombs in the RAF inventory at that time, were dropped in the modern town of Pompei, close to the site. Aircraft 'V' reports the flash from its own 4000 lb bomb 'in centre of Pompei town' as well as another 4000 lb bomb flash seen in the same area; and the 40 Squadron *ORB* records 'One 4000 lb bomb burst on the roads and houses on the west side of POMPEII'. Under these circumstances, it is hardly surprising that structures in the modern town were damaged and destroyed, and civilian casualties inflicted.[38] The *Diario delle incursioni* attributes eighteen instances of damage to the ancient site on the night of 16 September (i.e., presumably 15/16 September as discussed in n. 34 on p. 35 above).[39] Unsurprisingly, given the concentration of bombing to the west of Pompeii, most of the recorded damage (fourteen instances) was in Regions V and VI, on the west and north-west of the site.

16–18 SEPTEMBER 1943

No damage to the site is recorded in the *Diario delle incursioni* during the daytime on 16 or 17 September, and this corresponds with the air forces' documentation of the intense aerial activity further south, closer to Salerno itself, rather than around Pompeii and Torre Annunziata. The next major attack on targets close to ancient Pompeii took place on the night of 17/18 September, presumably the *Diario*'s 'VII Incursione (notturna)'.[40]

17/18 SEPTEMBER (NIGHT)

In many respects the bombing on the night of 17/18 September followed the pattern established on 13/14 September, with RAF Bostons serving as pathfinders to mark targets for USAAF medium bombers.[41] The Northwest African Air Forces *OIS* for that night records that three Bostons of No. 326 Wing (from 114 Squadron) marked the 'Torre Annunziata road junction' for 24 B-25s of the 12th Bombardment Group whose bombs all 'fell in the target area across road and railroad'; and another three RAF Bostons (from 18 Squadron) marked 'Pompeii road/rail junction' for 10 B-25s from each of the 12th and 340th Bombardment Groups, dropping a total of 30 1000 lb, 54 500 lb (227kg) and 66 250 lb bombs.

Again, the 12th Bombardment Group's *Sortie Reports* provide more detail on the missions.[42] The aim of the mission is described as 'to bomb the town of Pompei' and 'individual bombing of Pompei'. While at first glance this implies that the town itself was the target, in fact the map grid reference given (N405386) is almost the same as that provided for the night of 13/14 September, again denoting the intersection (less than 300 m west of the archaeological site) of the Naples-Pompeii autostrada with the SS18 road to Salerno.[43] Bombing was conducted from 0422 to 0430 hours from 7500–10,000 ft (2300–3050 m) by nine aircraft of the 434th Bombardment Squadron (an additional aircraft, of the 83rd Bombardment Squadron, did not complete the mission—see p. 92 below) dropping 54 500 lb and 34 250 lb bombs.

The Torre Annunziata targets are variously described in the *Sortie Reports* of the three squadrons involved as 'road and railway at Torre Annunziata', 'rd. intersection and rr.[railroad] E of Torre Annunziata' and 'road and railroad junction at Torre Annunziata', but the grid reference for the aiming point provided is the same in each case, namely N392386 (40°44′55″ N, 14°27′52″ E). This is less than 100 m south of the prominent Piazza Imbriani intersection targeted on 13 (and perhaps 14) September and also just 150 m north of the main railway line at Torre Annunziata Centrale station with its marshalling yards to the east. This concentration of transportation infrastructure explains why the *Sortie Reports* refer to both road and railway targets. As already noted, this aiming point lay only c. 1.4 km west of the archaeological site of Pompeii. The bombing was conducted just before 0400 hrs from altitudes of 7500 to 10,500ft (2500–3200 m) with good visibility and no anti-aircraft fire in the target area. A total of 14 1000 lb, 118 500 lb and 48 250 lb bombs were dropped, and the squadrons' reports claim that all fell across the target and within the target area.

Seven instances of damage to the site are recorded as the 'VII Incursione—18 settembre (notturna)' in the *Diario delle incursioni*.[44] These were clustered in two locations, four damage sites on the Via delle Tombe and the Villa of Diomedes just north-west of the ancient town walls, to be expected given the location of the intended target, with the three others further to the south and east, affecting the Triangular Forum, Theatre and Samnite Palaestra. These two clusters perhaps reflect damage done by partial bomb-loads of two aircraft.

SEPTEMBER 18–20

At this point it becomes very difficult to correlate the *Diario delle incursioni* exactly with the air force records, as the former notes 10 instances of damage as a result of the 'VIII Incursione—19 Settembre' and another 12 from the 'IX Incursione—20 Settembre (notturna)' while the latter do not record any major attacks on targets in the vicinity of Pompeii except the daytime mission of 20 September (below). The stresses and difficulties of recording damage at Pompeii during the bombing itself or immediately afterward may have led to errors in D'Avino's account, or errors may have been introduced between the bombing and the writing-up of the final versions in January–February 1944.[45] Furthermore, substantial but perhaps less-focused Allied air activity continued in this area through this period, and the site may have been damaged by such activity on the nights recorded. For example, the *ORB* for 18 September of 18 Squadron RAF, one of the Boston-equipped light bomber squadrons of No. 326 Wing records armed reconnaissance 'of roads leading to the Battle area', mentioning towns such as Torre Annunziata, Sarno and Nocera. Since Allied fighter-bombers were now also operating in this area, their attacks on transportation targets nearby may have caused further damage. Finally, the recorded damage may have been the result of gross navigational errors, with bombs jettisoned or deliberately dropped by aircraft that (knowingly or otherwise) had failed to find their proper targets.

The distribution of damage on these occasions is interesting and potentially significant. For the 'VIII Incursione—19 Settembre' the damage points run in a line parallel to the Via dell'Abbondanza in Regions I, II, III and IX, which suggests a stick of bombs dropped by a single aircraft along the line of the road. This could have been sheer bad luck (a bomber jettisoning its bombs at random, or gross navigational error) or because an aircraft mistook the ancient road for a modern one. In contrast, the damage attributed to the 'IX Incursione—20 Settembre (notturna)' occurred in two discrete parts of the site, one around the amphitheatre on the east side, the other in the Porta Marina area on the west side.

20 SEPTEMBER (DAY)

The only documented major attack near Pompeii in this period took place during the day on 20 September. At 1331 hrs seventeen B-17s of the 301st Bombardment Group dropped 34.4 tons (31.2 tonnes) of bombs on 'Torre Annunziata road SE' from 20,200–21,200 ft [6157–6462 m]' while 'an additional a/c [aircraft] salvoed its bombs on highway E of Pompeii'. A further 14 B-17s of the same group bombed 'SW edge of Sarno'. [46] The *OIS* records direct hits on the highway near the Torre Annunziata marshalling yards, but also on the main railway line 'S of Old Pompeii cutting the line in 3 places'. The *Narrative Mission Report* of the 301st Bombardment Group provides more detail, including the type of bombs used (all 250 lb GP [General Purpose]) and observations on the perceived success of the bombing.[47] The bombing at Sarno was judged to be 'well-concentrated', while at Torre Annunziata it was described as 'a little more scattered', but two road junctions and a highway bridge were claimed destroyed.[48] The aircraft that 'salvoed its bombs on the highway E of Pompei' was considered to have scored direct hits, although its precise target (presumably the SS18 road) is unstated.

A USAAF mission photograph labelled '20-9-43 -13:23 . . . Hwy Junct—TORRE ANNUNCIATA [sic]' (Figure 13) certainly shows smoke/dust, and apparently bomb strikes, in the ancient site, mostly in the south-west corner (the area from the Porta Marina to the east side of the Forum is completely obscured), but also in Region VI, further north.[49] One of the Region VI bomb strikes in this photograph is clearly in the vicinity of (or even on) the House of the Faun (VI.12.2). *The Diario delle incursioni* does not record damage to this house on any date, even though it was certainly severely damaged at some point in the bombing, emphasising the (understandable) problems with the contemporary records.[50] Otherwise, as already noted, the *Diario delle incursioni*'s 'IX Incursione—20 settembre (notturna)' records 8 out of 12 instances of damage in the amphitheatre or palaestra, in the south-east corner of the site. If this is actually an erroneous record of damage inflicted during the daytime, it perhaps reflects the bombing of the highway to the east and the railway to the south recorded in the air force records for the daytime USAAF mission. The other four instances of damage recorded for 20 September (again, attributed to the night in the *Diario*) were in the south-west corner of the site, as might be expected from the daylight attack on the intersection just west of the site and the photograph cited above.

21–26 SEPTEMBER

The *Diario delle incursioni* briefly notes some damage done in this period to outlying areas of Region VIII, the Porta Marina and Insula Occidentale (all in the south-west corner of the site), and the amphitheatre and palaestra (south-east). Again, there are no reports of major bombing attacks near Pompeii in the air forces' records at this time, although missions continued to be flown in the area on a smaller scale. For example, the *ORB* of the RAF's No. 326 (Light Bomber) Wing records for

> 'Night Sept 21/22nd . . . six aircraft were delegated to harass movement on road Torre Annunziata–Nocera with the object of creating road blocks.'[51]

This road is the SS18 passing immediately south of ancient Pompeii, so bombs dropped by these aircraft and others conducting armed reconnaissance in the area may have caused the damage. On the following night (23/24 September), two Bostons of 12 (South African Air Force) Squadron dropped a few 250 lb bombs in Torre Annunziata and to the north-east of the town, towards Pompeii.[52]

As Allied ground forces advanced westwards, direct support of ground

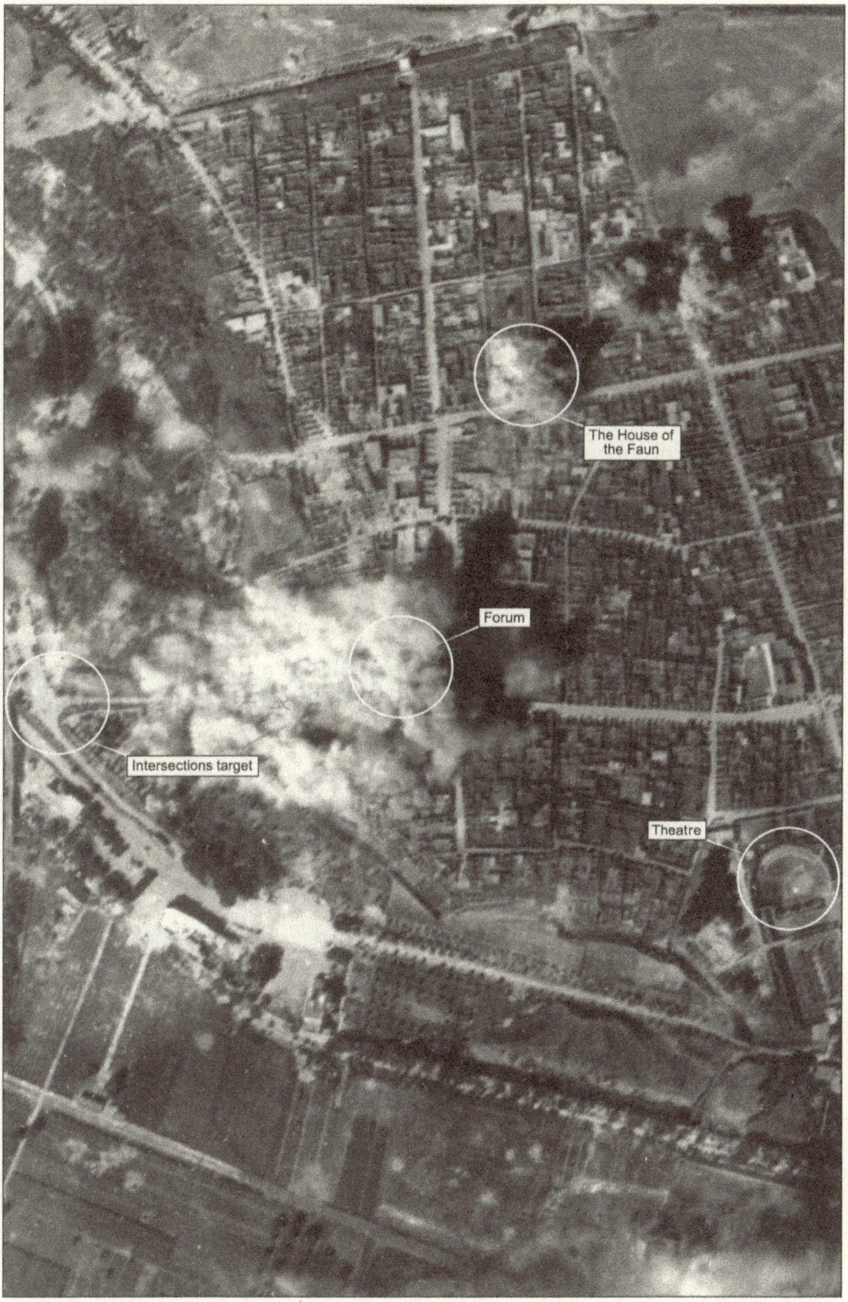

Figure 13: A USAAF mission photograph documenting part of the B-17 attack of 20 September 1943. The main concentration of dust and smoke is over the Forum and immediately west of it on the archaeological site, but there is also evidence of scattered bomb strikes further north-east in Region VI, including the vicinity of the House of the Faun (VI.12.2). NARA RG 18, Box 755, USAAF 301st BG, 20/9/1943, image 001.

troops by air forces may also have caused damage to the site. The USAAF *Combat Chronology* for 23 September, for example, records

> 'Planes of NATBF [North African Tactical Bomber Force] and XII A Spt Cmd [12th Air Support Command] attack motor transport, roads, railways, town areas, gun positions, and T/Os [targets of opportunity] in areas of San Severino Rota, Avellino, Sarno, Torre Annunziata, Aversa, Nocera, Resina, Serino, Pompeii and Camarella.'[53]

Similarly medium bombers and fighter-bombers bombed targets around Nocera and Sarno on 25 and 26 September, although the weather was deteriorating by this time and this grounded elements of the Allied air forces on some days towards the end of the month.[54]

29 SEPTEMBER 1943

Allied ground forces entered the modern town of Pompei, and the archaeological site, on 29 September, bringing an end to the damage inflicted on the site by bombing.[55]

CHAPTER 3

Why Was Pompeii Bombed?

It is very clear from the contemporary documentation examined above that the archaeological site of Pompeii was not deliberately attacked by Allied bombers, but was struck accidentally by bombs intended for other targets nearby. Those targets were mostly transportation infrastructure—nearby roads, railways and their intersections and bridges.

Nevertheless, the question of why and how these targets came to be bombed remains, and more specifically how some of the bombs came to hit the archaeological site. The bombing near Pompeii must be examined in a number of broader contexts. One such context is the wider military situation. Whether or not the cultural value of the site itself was considered at the time, the decision to bomb the intended transportation targets nearby certainly was not a casual one. As will be seen, it was taken at a time of particular crisis in the execution of Operation Avalanche, the Allied landings in the Gulf of Salerno, and events in the Salerno beachhead must be considered to judge the urgency of the air operations near Pompeii (see Chapter 5).[1]

Another military context relates to operational and technical aspects of the bombing. If ancient Pompeii was not the intended target of the bombing, how and why did bombs intended for other targets end up hitting the site? Finally, it is important to evaluate the alternative explanations for the bombing circulated and widely reported at the time, namely that the site was bombed deliberately because of the alleged presence of German troops there (Chapter 6). While these alternative explanations are strictly 'incorrect', they persisted long after the events, and shed important light on contemporary attitudes towards heritage in total war, popular misconceptions about bombing, and issues of memory and authority in historical evidence.

WHY POMPEII?

Examination of maps and aerial photographs (see Figures 4, 5, 6, and 10) makes it clear why Pompeii was the focus of so much transportation-related bombing at the time of the Salerno operations, as it was (and to a great extent, still is) a key node in the road and rail transportation system of the area, particularly between Naples (and so central and northern Italy) and Salerno. In 1943 the main road route from Naples to Salerno was the autostrada (highway) from Naples to Pompeii, opened in 1929.[2] At an intersection immediately west of the archaeological site of Pompeii, this autostrada merged with the Strada Statale 18 (SS18) from Torre Annunziata, at that time the main road to Salerno. The SS18 then skirted the south edge of the archaeological site and continued through the modern towns of Pompei, Scafati, Angri, Pagani and Nocera Inferiore, crossing the plain to the south and east of Vesuvius. From Nocera, the SS18 continued through the mountains by way of Cava de' Tirreni to the coast at Vietri, immediately west of Salerno. Alternatively, at Nocera Inferiore traffic could branch off to the north-east through Castel S. Giorgio and S. Severino before turning south towards Salerno via Fisciano, or south-east on other roads.

Other roads connected Naples with Castellamare di Stabia (the location of an important naval dockyard) and Sorrento. One road branched off the autostrada and crossed the SS18 on a bridge just west of Pompeii, near the point where the autostrada merged with the SS18. Another road to Castellamare and Sorrento met the SS18 further west, in the Piazza Imbriani area of Torre Annunziata.

This area was (and still is) important in terms of railway communications too. The main line from Naples to Salerno emerged from the narrow corridor between Vesuvius and the sea at Torre Annunziata. Torre Annunziata Centrale station is c. 200 metres south of the Piazza Imbriani road intersection (so c. 1.6 km west of Pompeii), and just to the east were marshalling yards and a junction with the branch line down the coast to Castellamare di Stabia. The importance of Torre Annunziata as a railway node was recognised and discussed at some length by Zuckerman in his wartime study of aerial interdiction in the Italian campaign.[3] From Torre Annunziata, the main railway line ran east, parallel to the SS18, passing some 240 m south of the Pompeii autostrada/SS18 junction as well as skirting the southern edge of the archaeological site (again, in places no more than 240 metres away) and the modern town of Pompei. The railway continued roughly parallel to the SS18 all the way to Salerno.

Thus the autostrada, the SS18, the roads to the Sorrento peninsula and the main railway from Naples to the south all converge in the area between Torre Annunziata and modern Pompei after emerging from the narrow corridor between Vesuvius and the sea into the plain south of the volcano. In addition, two lines of the Circumvesuviana light railway passed very close to the ancient site, with the Naples-Castellamare line along the west side of the excavations, and the Naples-Poggiomarino line skirting the north-east corner. There were numerous bridges immediately to the west and south-west of the ancient site, and these served as useful aiming points as well as important targets in their own right. This convergence of autostrada, SS18 and Circumvesuviana with its rail and road bridges, and the main railway line just to the south, was both important and prominent, and so was singled out as an aiming point. Given the limited accuracy of 1943 bombing techniques (Chapter 4), aiming at such a concentration of targets increased the probability of hitting something of military value. It constituted what in modern military terms would be described as a 'high payoff target'. Likewise, the Piazza Imbriani intersection just east of Torre Annunziata provided a prominent aiming point as well as a cluster of valuable targets, with the main railway line just to the south and marshalling yards to the south-east. Traffic through this area potentially could be restricted or halted by the destruction of bridges, cratering of roads and railway lines and also by blocking roads through towns with rubble.[4]

García y García suggests as a hypothesis that 'the real target' of the bombing that damaged ancient Pompeii was the nearby SS18 road and the railway.[5] In fact this is more than a hypothesis, as the evidence of the Allied air forces documentation clearly demonstrates this was the case. However, García y García's explanation of why bombs aimed at this target hit the ancient site shows some naivety regarding the limitations of bombing in 1943, as will be shown later.

POMPEII AND OPERATION AVALANCHE—THE SALERNO LANDINGS

As noted above, the bombing of targets close to the ancient site of Pompeii in September 1943 was not the result of routine military activity. It formed part of the response to a severe crisis in the Salerno beachhead, and the bombing of Pompeii must be considered in its wider military context, which was exceptional.[6]

The US 5th Army, composed of 10 (British) Corps and 6 US Corps, came ashore in Italy on the morning of 9 September 1943, with Salerno itself near the northern (largely British) end of the beachhead, and the Greco-Roman site of Poseidonia/Paestum towards the southern (US) end of the beachhead. The initial landings met with relatively light opposition, and that solely from German forces, the Italian armistice with the Allies having been announced on 8 September. However, it is notable that ancient Pompeii was not damaged by bombing until four days later (13 September), when a German counter-attack began that severely threatened the existence of the beachhead.

Already on 12 September, both General Alexander, commander of 15th Army Group, and Lieutenant-General Mark W. Clark, commander of 5th Army, were concerned over the progress of 'Avalanche' (the code name for the invasion). They noted the beachhead's lack of depth and the slow build-up of forces ashore and predicted that a heavy German counter-attack was imminent.[7] The Germans had responded to the initial landings by building up a substantial force to stage such a counter-attack.[8] This counter-attack, or rather series of counter-attacks, began on 13 September and the Allied situation did not truly stabilise until 16 September. The crisis caused was severe, leading to fears for the very survival of the beachhead, and the bombing of ancient Pompeii must be viewed in the context of this crisis.

Shortly after noon on 13 September, German forces attacked the vulnerable boundary between the US 36th and 45th Infantry Divisions along the River Sele, overrunning two US infantry battalions, the 1st/157th Infantry and 2nd/143rd Infantry. The Germans reached the junction of the Sele and its tributary the Calore, less than five miles from the sea, early the same evening. The situation was critical for 6 US Corps, as the slow build-up of forces (largely due to the limited quantity of suitable shipping) meant there were no fresh reserves to contain the attack. As the British Official History records,

> 'At this obstacle [the junction of the Sele and Calore] the [US] 158th and [US] 159th Field Artillery Battalions, firing over open sights; part of [US] 636th Tank Destroyer Battalion; drivers, cooks and clerks from the Army command post; and anyone else whom Walker [General Fred L. Walker, commander of the US 36th Infantry Division] could scrape together; stopped the enemy. Except for this stout-hearted American handful there was no-one else between the Germans and the sea. The outlook seemed very bleak for the Americans and dazzling for the Germans.'[9]

The artillery units were equipped with howitzers with a maximum range of over ten kilometres, and normally were deployed some distance behind the front line, supporting troops with indirect fire. They would engage the enemy at close range by direct fire over open sights only in a dire emergency. Likewise the 5th Army command post should have been well to the rear, and the scraping together of normally non-combatant troops from that headquarters demonstrates how deeply the Germans had penetrated into the beachhead, as well as the lack of available reserves. In response to the crisis, Clark ordered his staff to prepare plans for evacuation of the beachhead. On the night of 13/14 September, two battalions of the US 504th Parachute Infantry Regiment, previously ear-marked for other operations in Italy, parachuted into the beachhead as emergency reinforcements. On the following night, a further 2,100 men of the US 505th Parachute Infantry Regiment were dropped into the beachhead.[10]

The situation in the 6 US Corps sector stabilised somewhat throughout 14 September. However, the Germans had also built up a northern counter-attack force opposite 10 (British) Corps near Salerno, including the Hermann Göring Division. Its attacks were launched throughout 15 and 16 September, but ultimately were defeated by the severely stretched British 45th and 56th Divisions. By the evening of 16 September there was some confidence among the Allied commanders that the beachhead was secure.[11] At about the same time, German commanders took the decision to break off their attacks and establish a defensive line across the Italian peninsula both to prevent further casualties by continuing the battle, and to contain the British 8th Army which had advanced north from Calabria and was now close to linking up with the Salerno beachhead. The withdrawal began on 18 September, the initial intention apparently being to hold the Salerno area as a pivot for the rest of the German army to gradually withdraw north and east. However, Allied forces broke out of the beachhead, and an offensive by 10 (British) Corps, begun on the night of 22/23 September, captured a bridge over the Sarno at Scafati on 28 September and held it against a German counter-attack. Allied troops entered Pompei on the same day, reached Torre Annunziata on 30 September, and Naples on the morning of 1 October.[12]

THE ALLIED AIR FORCES' PERCEPTIONS OF THE CRISIS

García y García correctly sets most of the damage in the general context of air activity against 'the ferocious counter-attack of the German panzer-grenadiers that threatened to drive the Allies into the sea' and the subsequent breakout.[13] However, he places insufficient emphasis on the level of crisis and the urgency involved, something that comes through very clearly in the contemporary air forces documentation. For example, the *War Diary* of the USAAF 319th Bombardment Group presents the events of 14 September in particularly dramatic terms:

> 'Major Holzapple prefaced briefing in the morning by reading a Twelfth Air Force notice to the effect that the Allied troops on the Salerno bridgehead were in a desperate, touch-and-go battle to hold on to their strip of beach. Crew members present listened in grim silence as he announced we would be employed against German roads in support of our infantry and that extra effort was needed from everybody.'[14]

The 340th Bombardment Group's *War Diary* is equally dramatic, but somewhat less formal:

> '14 [September]: Busy day today with 60 sorties in the Salerno area. The Americans are in a highly critical situation there, so bad it appears all available air power is being thrown in.'
>
> 15 [September]: We had 58 more sorties in the Salerno area today. The money is really on the line in that crap game! The situation is still critical but it begins to look as if we'll pocket all the funds.'[15]

British sources understandably tend to emphasise the role of Montgomery's (British) 8th Army in operations on the ground. The 8th Army had landed in the Calabrian 'toe' of Italy on 3 September, and was advancing towards the Salerno area in the face of a German delaying action, hindered by terrain and demolitions. The British documents at the time of the German counter-attack frequently portray the 8th Army as a relief force for the embattled Salerno beachhead.[16] For example, the orders generated at No. 205 Group and passed on to the Wings) characterise the situation in the following terms:

> ***14 September***
>
> 'A hard struggle in Italy is taking place between our forces on the SALERNO strip and the enemy, who is endeavouring to link up his

southern army [i.e. the forces delaying 8th Army to the south] with the Hermann Goering Division on the west shin bone.'

15 September

'The struggle for the SALERNO BRIDGEHEAD is reaching new peaks of fury. The enemy's communications must be hampered, cut and destroyed. The 8th Army is on its way North.'[17]

While this strategic context of the missions flown is sometimes reflected in the RAF Wing *ORB*s, understandably it is less clear in documentation produced by the squadrons, with their limited access to the wider picture and greater focus on the detail of day-to-day operations.[18] One notable exception is the *ORB* of 104 Squadron RAF, which is unusually narrative and wide-ranging in content (probably reflecting the personality of its intelligence officer) compared to the laconic and to-the-point information presented by the other squadrons:

'14 September: The Squadron was called on to play an important part in the battle of Italy, the 5th Army were forced to give some ground in face of fierce enemy opposition in the Naples area, the 8th Army were pressing up from the toe of Italy as fast as possible in an attempt to relieve the pressure on the 5th Army.'

'15 September: It was learnt that the 8th Army were continuing their upward drive towards the Naples area, once again the Squadron were called on to blast the enemy road communications.'[19]

As shown in Chapters 1 and 2, accounts of operations in the Pompeii area provided in RAF squadron *ORB*s emphasise that their targets were road and rail infrastructure, and their aiming points and bomb strikes are described in terms of their location relative to fixed transportation structures such as roads and bridges. Nevertheless, the reports of squadrons and individual crews sometimes mention what was actually on the roads targeted and its relevance to the strategic situation. There are references to the Hermann Göring Division. This was concentrated to the north around Naples and the Gulf of Gaeta at the time of the Salerno landings, and redeployed through Torre Annunziata and modern Pompei to arrive in the Salerno area on 10–

13 September, where it faced the British 46th Division and the Commando and Ranger units holding the northern end of the beachhead.[20] It played a key role in the second phase of the counter-attack against the beachhead, on 15–16 September. The particular threat it posed to British ground forces explains its prominence in RAF *ORBs*, even though other German units (such as 15th Panzer Grenadier Division) were moving south by the same routes. The presence of the Hermann Göring Division was the primary justification given in the orders from No. 205 Group for the hurried changes of target implemented on 13 September, and the *ORB* of 142 Squadron for its mission on the night of 13/14 September refers to 'the coast road near Pompeii down which the Herman [sic] Goering Division was reported to be moving.'[21]

There are a few general references to armoured vehicles as targets, but their presence is largely assumed rather than observed.[22] The sporadic references to observed targets on the roads are mostly to motor transport (M.T. or M/T), trucks potentially carrying troops or supplies. Records of the daytime missions of 310th Bombardment Group on 13 and 15 September refer to substantial numbers of M/T spotted around Torre Annunziata and Pompei and heading eastwards, towards the Salerno battlefield, and claim hits on some of the vehicles.[23] On the night of 13/14 September the crew of Wellington bomber 'O' of 70 Squadron mentions 'Two M.T. vehicles seen here [on road 3–7 miles east of Pompei] but not hit', while the crew of Wellington 'L' reports targeting 'stationary transport in a close bunch just off the road. Bursts among M.T. Fire started.'[24] The *ORB* of No. 231 Wing records on the night of 15/16 'some M.T. reported around road junction', presumably the road junction just west of Pompeii that was an important target for that night's mission. However, these mentions of specific vehicular targets are always secondary to the references to fixed transportation infrastructure. There are no references at all to deployed or leaguered troops or vehicles as primary targets either in the vicinity of modern Pompei or in the archaeological site itself. From 13 to 16 September, at least, Allied air forces were targeting the build-up of German reinforcements and supplies to the Salerno beachhead primarily by slowing their movement through damaging and destroying the road and rail transportation system on which they moved.[25]

The perceived severity of the crisis at Salerno from 13–16 September is emphasised by the scale of the Allied aerial response, with even strategic bombers such as B-17s and Wellingtons, previously employed against targets such as airfields and railway marshalling yards throughout Italy, diverted to essentially battlefield interdiction tasks and even close support of ground forces in the beachhead itself. The scale of aerial activity in immediate support of land forces in the Salerno area increased significantly from 13 September, when the German counter-attack began. As Molony notes, the Allies had three possible responses to the counter-attack.[26] One was to hurry the advance of the 8th Army from the south to relieve the beachhead, and the second was to speed up seaborne reinforcements from North Africa. In practical terms, neither of these was possible within the time available, leaving the third option, the stepping-up of air and naval support. Naval gunfire support of ground troops played an important role in the defence of the beachhead, but it was air power, with its speed and flexibility, that was viewed as the swiftest and most effective response. Molony summarises this effectively in the British Official History:

> 'The air's outstanding contribution was when Mediterranean Air Command used the flexibility, speed and range of aircraft to switch almost all its bombers to the tactical role and concentrated a great number of aircraft against a small area.'[27]

Contemporary documentation emphasises the rapidity with which key elements of the air force could be switched from strategic targets to more immediate support of the beachhead. The *OIS* for the nights immediately before the German counter-attack of 12 September records the RAF Wellingtons attacking more distant strategic targets, including an airfield at Viterbo (night of 7/8 September), marshalling yards at Grosseto (9/10 September) and an airfield at Frosinone (night of 11/12 September). However, extracts from contemporary Northwest African Air Force diary entries for 11 to 15 September 1943 show that targeting shifted rapidly in response to the situation on the ground at Salerno:

> 'There was a strong German counter attack developing against the central bridgehead so all available Strategic air force was put on enemy concentrations and supplies.'

> 'Targets were vital road junctions surrounding the bridgehead in order to impede supply and reinforcement of the enemy. The railways were already blocked by previous raids.'

> 'The entire effort was directed to close support of the ground forces, in the main [i.e. "for the most part"] roads, railways now being ineffective. The object was to block the roads behind the Germans retreating in Calabria and in front of those moving to counter attack at Salerno.'
>
> 'Targets were the main roads from Naples to Salerno.'[28]

The Northwest African Strategic Air Force's demand to No. 205 Group on 14 September was for 'everything we could put into the air', and that night saw the Group's greatest effort of the Mediterranean campaign to date, with up to 126 sorties and 236.75 tons (240.5 tonnes) of bombs targeted at roads in the Battipaglia-Eboli area, the starting line for the German southern counter-attack.[29] However, on the following night (15/16 September), the bombers of No. 205 Group flew another mission on a similar scale, with up to 127 Wellingtons delivering 240 tons of bombs, this time (as discussed on pp. 34–36) against targets in the Pompeii and Torre Annunziata area.[30] It is hardly surprising that the *ORB* of 424 Squadron for that night described the airspace over the target area as 'congested'.[31] No. 205 Group was only able to assemble so many aircraft because of an emergency decision taken to retain the three Canadian squadrons of No. 331 Wing in the Mediterranean when they had been earmarked for return to the UK within days.[32] This is another indication of the gravity of the situation and the speed at which it developed. The scale and extent of the wider aerial response to the counter-attack is illustrated by the orders sent to No. 231 Wing by No. 205 Group on 14 September, when it flew its maximum-effort night-time mission against the Battipaglia-Eboli area.[33] These summarise other activity by heavy and medium bombers in the region on that day:

> 36 Fortresses [B-17] on POMPEII HIGHWAY
> 36 Fortresses [B-17] on TORRE ANNUNCIATO [sic] HIGHWAY
> 72 Fortresses [B-17] and 60 Mitchells [B-25] on BATTIPAGLIA
> 60 Mitchells [B-25] on EBOLI
> 36 Marauders [B-26] on AVELLINO ROAD JUNCTION
> 36 Marauders [B-26] on ACILETTO [= Auletta?] ROADS AND BRIDGES

Besides these bombers, fighter-bombers flew a further 573 sorties on 14 September, and other missions were flown during the night of 14/15 September.[34] The US Army Official History records that 9000 tactical air force sorties were flown during the first nine days of the Salerno operation, over 5000 of which were on 14 to 16 September.[35] As the references above show, the Pompei area was neither the sole nor principal target of Allied air activity at this time. García y García's claim that the Allies engaged in 'carpet bombing in all areas of Campania' at this time suggests this was essentially indiscriminate.[36] It wasn't, in intent or aim at least, but given the technical limitations of bombing accuracy in 1943, for the inhabitants of some areas, it might as well have been true. The towns of Eboli and Battipaglia 'were all but obliterated', as in that area the targets were not just roads and railways but also German troop concentrations.[37] Benevento, a crucial node on the alternative inland road and rail route from Naples to Salerno, whose position was in many respects analogous to that of the Torre-Annunziata-Pompei area, also suffered severely.[38] However, when the failure of the German counter-attack became evident on 16 September, much of the strategic air effort was shifted back to more distant transportation targets and the categories of strategic targets against which it had been employed before 12 September.[39]

CHAPTER 4

Bombing Conditions, Tactics and Accuracy

The bombing that damaged Pompeii was unusual in the variety of methods and equipment concentrated against such a small target area in such a limited time period. The mission of 24 September 1943 was purely strategic, launched against strategic targets (steelworks and railway yards in Torre Annunziata) at a time when there were no Allied ground forces in mainland Italy, using night bombing tactics typical of the RAF at that time of the war, albeit with equipment somewhat inferior to that used in northern Europe against Germany. The other missions, conducted after the Salerno landings on 9 September, were essentially interdiction operations on the edge of the immediate battle area, some of them employing equipment and tactics normally used for such missions (the US medium bombers flown by day and night), others using weapons and tactics more typical of strategic bombing (the RAF by night with Wellington medium bombers, and USAAF daytime missions with B-17 heavy bombers).[1] All of the techniques used had advantages and disadvantages in military terms, and, certainly in 1943, all of them suffered from limitations of accuracy that might lead to accidental damage beyond the intended target area, such as that which damaged ancient Pompeii.

BOMBING CONDITIONS

The initial strategic operations against Torre Annunziata that caused accidental damage to Pompeii were conducted under generally favourable, but not perfect, conditions of weather and opposition. The *Operations Record Book* of 104 Squadron reports that the weather on the night of 24/25 August, the first occasion on which Pompeii was damaged, was 'good but hazy'.[2] The waning moon rose some three hours after bombing was over, providing poorer visibility for targeting but protection from enemy defences. Nevertheless, as already noted, 104 Squadron lost a single Wellington bomber, designated 'U', presumed shot down over the target area, perhaps by one of the enemy night fighters observed.[3] There was also some anti-aircraft fire (flak), recorded as 'moderate [and] inaccurate . . . both light and heavy mostly from S. of the town [Torre Annunziata]. Quite a number of S/L [searchlights] operating from scattered points but mostly from the North of the town.'[4]

While the daytime and night missions of 29/30 August against Torre Annunziata are not recorded as causing significant damage to ancient Pompeii, the difficulties encountered then emphasise (by contrast) the generally good conditions encountered when bombing the same area in September. There was cloud cover on 30 August, so even during the day the fall of many bombs was obscured. While the night mission (with no moon) encountered only slight to negligible flak, nevertheless, one Wellington bomber went missing. The day mission, flown by USAAF B-26 bombers escorted by 40 P-38 fighters, encountered an estimated 40–50 enemy fighters, and one P-38 was shot down.[5]

The problems of 30 August serve to highlight the very favourable conditions under which the September bombing was carried out, both in terms of weather and visibility, and in terms of (largely absent) opposition. The full moon was on 14 September, and a number of the mission reports around this date mention moonlight as a help in identifying the target.[6] Weather and visibility are for the most part recorded as good.[7] US reports on daytime conditions also emphasise the good visibility.[8] There are occasional references to ground haze, although invariably this is specified as having little practical impact on bombing accuracy.[9] However, the sheer numbers of bombers attacking targets around Pompeii on the night of 15 September caused some problems. Besides the congested airspace mentioned above, the concentrated bombing threw up clouds of smoke and dust from the ground that reduced visibility.[10]

By mid-September, opposition to Allied air activity in the Pompei area was negligible to non-existent. Reports of RAF missions flown on 13/14 September record no flak (anti-aircraft fire) from the target area itself, but a few inaccurate guns firing from the coast and from Naples.[11] On the night of 14 September the Wellington bomber piloted by Flying Officer Cheek of 40 Squadron reportedly machine-gunned the road east of Angri, 5 km east of Pompei, from 1500 ft (457 m).[12] This was a remarkably low altitude for an aircraft the size of a Wellington in the face of even modest anti-aircraft or small arms fire, demonstrating the lack of opposition. On the night of 13 September, one of 114 Squadron's Bostons was held by a searchlight for just under five seconds, and there were a few reports of aircraft presumed to be enemy night fighters in the area, but only one exchange of fire, and no Allied losses.[13] By the night of 15 September, opposition of all kinds was reported as negligible to non-existent.[14] Certainly by 14 September, Allied fighters and fighter bombers were operating in substantial numbers in daylight as far north as Torre Annunziata, achieving local air superiority that provided protection for the bombers from German fighter activity.[15]

Thus, overall, the conditions under which the Allies bombed targets near Pompeii ranged from favourable to extremely favourable. The site itself was visible and recognisable not just during the day, but also, to some crews at least, by night, and some seem to have used it as a navigational landmark. For the most part, the problems of locating the target area that had dogged Allied bombing accuracy in the poor visibility and weather conditions of northern Europe were not a factor in Campania in August-September 1943.[16] On the surface, it seems plausible to echo García y García's incomprehension that ancient Pompeii was damaged even by daytime bombing.[17] However, he gravely underestimates the technical limitations of bombing in 1943, which meant that aiming bombs at even a clearly visible target did not necessarily mean those bombs would hit that target.

BOMBING TACTICS AND ACCURACY

The equipment and methods employed in the bombing that damaged ancient Pompeii in 1943 were diverse. USAAF B-17 heavy bombers bombed during the day, as did USAAF B-25 and B-26 medium bombers using different tactics. RAF/RCAF Wellington medium bombers bombed at night, also using significantly different methods, and other USAAF medium bombers bombed targets marked by RAF aircraft at night employing tactics similar to those of the Wellingtons. These differences affected accuracy in a number of ways. However, one issue common to all of them was the difficulty of striking even a visible target accurately with the equipment available in the Mediterranean in 1943. Bombs do not simply fall vertically from the bomber dropping them on to a target immediately below it. The factors that need to be considered when aiming a bomb at a visible target are the height, the heading and speed of the aircraft (since at first the bomb travels on the same heading and at the same speed as the aeroplane dropping it), wind speed and wind direction, and the ballistic performance of the bomb. Bombers used bombsights of varying types and accuracy to assess these factors to calculate a point at which bombs should be released to hit a particular target visible on the ground, but even minor variations or unpredictability (some of which were inevitable) in any of these factors at altitude might produce large errors on the ground.[18] Consideration of the tactics, techniques and technology employed by the different air forces involved is crucial to understand why and how ancient Pompeii came to be bombed.

USAAF HEAVY BOMBERS, BY DAY

As noted above, some of the attacks against targets near Pompeii were conducted by B-17 heavy bombers of the 97th and 99th Bombardment Groups (14 September) and 301st Bombardment Group (20 September). The attacks were conducted in daytime from altitudes of 15,800 ft (4815 m; Pompei crossroads, 14 September), 21,200 ft (6461 m; Torre Annunziata, 20 September), and 20,200 ft (6157 m; Sarno, 20 September). A photograph (Figure 14) taken during the 20 September attack against Torre Annunziata targets gives a vivid impression of the altitude from which these attacks were carried out, showing as it does a cluster of bombs falling away from the aircraft towards targets that appear both very distant from the bombing aircraft and very close to one another. The distance between the Piazza Imbriani intersection and the Pompeii intersections (in the top right-hand corner) is less than half the width of the frame.

In theory such attacks, even from high altitudes, could have been extremely accurate as these bombers were fitted with the Norden M-9 bombsight, a sophisticated tachometric sight that employed an analogue computer and autopilot to relate and apply the variable factors affecting bomb delivery during a run in from a visible navigation point, the Initial Point (IP). In the pre-war and early war period, much was made of the accuracy of the Norden sight, with extravagant claims by its manufacturers such that as it could hit a target 15 ft^2 (1.39 m^2) from an altitude of 30,000 ft (9114 m) without difficulty.[19]

In reality, under combat conditions, USAAF bombers using the Norden M were unable to achieve anything like such accuracy even against visible targets. USAAF bombing accuracy, particularly in northern Europe, was extensively studied using operational research methods. A detailed study of Eighth Air Force bombing missions in northern Europe between 1 September and 31 December 1944 provides accuracy data for B-17 and B-24 bombers bombing from a mean altitude of 21,000 ft (6400 m) in 'Good to fair visibility—no cloud cover, no haze, and no smoke'.[20] While there are some differences between the conditions under which this data was generated

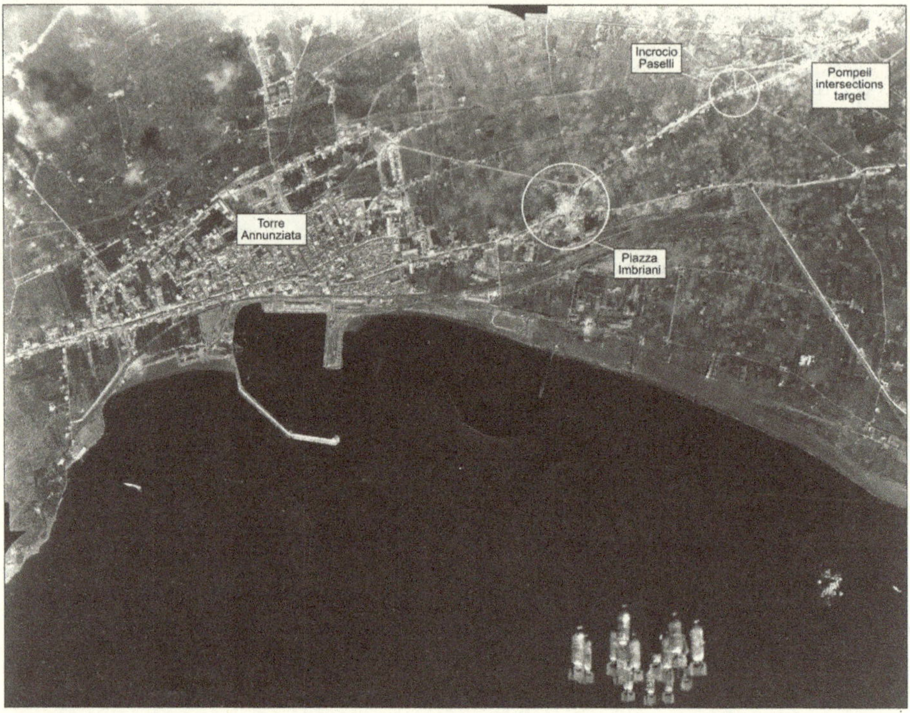

Figure 14: This mission photograph taken from a B-17 of the USAAF 301st Bombardment Group gives a vivid impression of the altitude and distance from the target at which the bombs were actually dropped. Both probable targets—the Torre Annunziata Piazza Imbriani intersection and the Pompeii intersections—appear both very distant from the bombing aircraft and very close to one another, to the point where it is unclear which is under attack. NARA RG 18, Box 755, USAAF 301st BG, 20/9/1943, image 003.

and those under which targets near Pompeii were bombed, Table 2 gives some idea of the levels of accuracy that might be achieved under normal combat conditions in similar visibility.[21]

Thus, for example, 17.6% (100%–82.4%) of bombs dropped in good to fair visibility on a target visible to the bombardier fell more than a mile (1609 m) from their aiming point. Given that three intersections near Pompeii used as aiming points for bombing lay less than a mile from the archaeological site, this data makes it clear that some damage to the site was likely and to be expected whenever bombs were aimed at them. Applying this data to those three aiming points (the autostrada/SS18 intersection;

the Piazza Imbriani at Torre Annunziata and the Incrocio Paselli), we can calculate very roughly the proportion of bombs that might be expected to hit the archaeological site when aimed at them. The percentages generated (by the method set out in Appendix C) are 4.53% (intersection of Naples-Pompeii autostrada and SS18), 2.91% (Incrocio Paselli) and 0.32% (Torre Annunziata, Piazza Imbriani).

Table 2: Percentage of bombs hitting within a specified distance of the aiming point

1000 ft (305 m)	½ mile (845 m)	1 mile (1609 m)	3 miles (4282 m)	5 miles (<8047 m)	More than 5 miles (>8047 m)
30%	64.9%	82.4%	91.5%	92.2%	7.8%

These are, in fact, low estimates, as they assume an even distribution of bombs in all directions around the aiming points when in fact the pattern of bomb strikes would have been elongated along the line of flight.[22] Typically this was west to east, crossing the coast near Torre Annunziata towards Pompei and beyond along the line of the SS18 main road, approaching the target on an eastward or north-eastward heading.[23] This would have led to a significantly higher percentage of bombs hitting the archaeological site than predicted by a simple even distribution. Nevertheless, the even distribution does at least provide a baseline minimum figure. To examine a specific example in more detail, on 14 September, 17 B-17s of the 97th Bombardment Group dropped 408 500 lb bombs on an intersection west of Pompei.[24] If we interpret this as the intersection of the autostrada and SS18, on the basis of the Eighth Air Force data we might expect a minimum of 18 bombs (11 if the aiming point was the more distant Incrocio Paselli) to have struck the ancient site along with, perhaps, another single bomb from the 99th Bombardment Group's near-simultaneous bombing of the more distant Torre Annunziata intersection.[25] In fact the *Diario delle incursioni* lists 19 instances of damage to the site on 14–15 September.[26]

The varied tactics, methods and technology employed by other elements of the Allied air forces in bombing targets near Pompeii also influenced their accuracy, sometimes positively, some negatively.

USAAF MEDIUM BOMBERS, BY DAY

In general, medium bombers operating by day were more accurate against tactical targets than heavy bombers bombing in daylight, primarily because they bombed at lower altitudes, but also because they bombed in tighter 'boxes' and (typically) in smaller formations.[27] The bombing on 13 September by the B-25 and B-26 bombers of 310th and 319th Bombardment Groups was conducted from 9300–12,000 ft (2835–3658 m), while the mission of 15 September (310th Bombardment Group, B-25s) was from 8000–12,500 ft (2438–3810 m), all substantially lower than the B-17 missions considered above. However, other factors made their bombing potentially less accurate and more likely to cause accidental damage beyond the immediate target area. These factors included less advanced bomb sights than those of the B-17s, the limitations of bombing in boxes 'on leader', and the fact that on this occasion (unusually) the mediums bombed in larger formations than the B-17s and also dropped more (but smaller) bombs, increasing the probability of overshoots hitting the site. For example, on 13 September 36 B-25s of the 310th Bombardment Group dropped over 800 100 lb bombs and 35 B-26s of the 319th Bombardment Group also dropped 100 lb bombs on transportation targets between Torre Annunziata and the archaeological site of Pompeii.[28] On 15 September the 310th Bombardment Group dropped 369 300 lb bombs on the Torre Annunziata road junction. The more bombs dropped, the higher the probability of some going astray, and even a 100 lb bomb could do substantial damage to the archaeological site.[29]

Typically USAAF medium bombers bombed in daytime in 'boxes' and 'on leader', at the prompting of a formation leader sighting the target. The boxes typically were close groups of 6 aircraft that flew to the target area in formation so as to be able to defend themselves more effectively, with (often) three boxes combining to produce Squadron or Wing formations of 18 or 24 aircraft. Within each box, the 6-plane flight flew in two elements of 3, typically with no more than 25 ft (7.62 m) between aircraft in each element, with the second element c. 25–50 ft (7.62–15.25 m) above or below the first to avoid its propeller wash. Only the box leader's aircraft would actually use a bombsight to aim at the target, the other five releasing their bombs when they saw the formation leader release his.[30] Boxes typically were arranged in staggered or echelon formations for defensive purposes, and might bomb with two boxes side-by-side or with individual boxes bombing in trail, depending on the target.[31]

These tactics introduced a number of inaccuracies of various kinds.[32] First, there was the possibility that the leader might drop his bombs at the wrong point, for human or technical reasons. In September 1943, B-25 bombers (and most or all B-26s) were equipped with less accurate bombsights than the Norden M-9 used in the B-17. Dale J. Satterthwaite, a B-25 pilot in the 340th Bombardment Group, recalls that they used the British Mark IX unstabilised course-setting bomb sight, a 1939 version of a First World War design, which he describes as 'crude' and 'basically a protractor'. They did not receive Norden bomb sights until late February 1944.[33] The Estoppey D-8, another unstabilised sight, but 'very simple to use', was also used in B-25s until it was discontinued, to be replaced by the Norden from October 1943.[34]

The formation and spacing of bombers also caused a degree of spread in the bomb strike pattern. The absence of significant opposition (as around Pompeii) made it easier to maintain tight formations that improved the overall accuracy of bombing. Bombing with boxes side-by-side spread the pattern perpendicular to the axis of the bomb run, while bombing with the boxes in trail spread the pattern along the axis of the bomb run. The positioning of boxes, along with timed delays between the elements bombing, could also be used deliberately to attack dispersed-area targets on the one hand, or 'corridor' targets such as roads and railway lines on the other. The use of numerous smaller bombs such as the 100 lb weapons employed against the junctions west of Pompeii on 13 September suggests that the intention was to achieve such a spread rather than precise attacks against individual bridges (for example—which would only be significantly damaged by precise hits from heavier bombs). Similarly the 'walking' of sticks of bombs along the roads between Torre Annunziata and Pompeii observed during the medium bomber missions of 13 and 15 September was undoubtedly militarily desirable. But area or 'corridor' attacks potentially generating a spread of bombs a mile and a half long along the axis of attack were risky when the ancient site of Pompeii lay only 1500 m (0.93 miles) beyond the aiming point along that axis.[35] And even against point targets such as bridges, the greater accuracy of medium day bombers over heavy bombers was only a relative one, with significant inaccuracies remaining and substantial risk of accidental damage in proximity to a heritage site like Pompeii.[36]

RAF/RCAF NIGHT BOMBING TECHNIQUES AND ACCURACY

As previously documented, some attacks close to ancient Pompeii that caused damage to the site were conducted at night by Wellington bombers of the RAF and RCAF. These missions were on the night of 24/25 August (against Torre Annunziata), the night of 13/14 September (against SS18 east of Pompeii) and the night of 15/16 September (against roads and bridges between Pompeii and Torre Annunziata). RAF bombers flying night missions navigated to their targets individually (although along a prescribed route) and aimed their bombs individually, so a great extent their accuracy depended on the skill and experience of individual crews.[37]

The route followed by RAF/RCAF crews from their airfields in Tunisia to bomb targets near Pompeii on the night of 15 September is specified in orders from No. 205 Group as 'CAP BON–PONZA–IS[C]HIA (SOUTHABOUT NAPLES (avoiding NAPLES and SALERNO)–TARGET. RETURN SAME ROUTE'. Individual crews' reports frequently note these specific navigational landmarks, along with the island of Capri, and indicate that they then identified and crossed the coast near Torre Annunziata.[38] Approaching the target area from the coast, most crews acquired and bombed their targets heading roughly west to east, parallel with SS18 and the main railway line (like the USAAF B-17s, above), with consequent risk to the ancient site if they overshot targets to the west of it (night of 15/16 September), or bombed early when approaching targets east of the site (night of 13/14 September).

Aircraft took off from their bases individually at slightly staggered times, to arrive at the target within a prescribed time slot. Not all the documents provide this information, but the 37 Squadron *ORB* (for example) does. Thus on the night of 13/14 September, the 8 Wellingtons of that squadron that bombed east of Pompeii took off between 1834 and 1845, and returned between 0100 and 0137 (although not in the same order they took off). On the night of 15/16 September, bombing just west of Pompeii, sixteen aircraft took off between 2000 and 2018, landing back at base between 0220 and 0316. Orders from No. 205 Group established the times slots within which aircraft of a particular Wing were to bomb, as set out in Table 3 below (37 Squadron formed part of No. 231 Wing).[39]

Table 3: Bombing times allocated to component Wings on RAF/RCAF bombing missions

13/14 September		15/16 September	
No. 331 Wing	2150–2200	No. 330 Wing	2200–2230
No. 231 Wing	2200–2220	No. 236 Wing	2230–2300
No. 236 Wing	2230–2300	No. 331 Wing	2300–2330
No. 330 Wing	2300–0030	No. 231 Wing	2330–0001

In theory these times would give average concentrations of 66 (for 13 September) and 64 (15 September) aircraft per hour over the target. These were relatively low densities compared to northern Europe, but high for the Mediterranean, particularly the opening of the 13 September mission, with 32 Wellingtons of No. 331 Wing scheduled to be over the target in a 10-minute time slot, for a very high average hourly density of 192.[40] The average hourly density during No. 331 Wing's 30-minute slot on 15 September was also high (86 aircraft per hour), explaining the references to congestion over the target in the 424 Squadron *ORB* discussed above. Actual bombing times are rarely reported, although the *ORB* of 420 Squadron RCAF for the 24 August attack on Torre Annunziata gives individual actual bombing times reported by ten crews ranging from 2202 to 2220 (with a mean of 2210) for an allocated bombing time ('B Hour') of 2200.[41]

The clear conditions, proximity to the coast and the use of flares to illuminate targets (see below) meant that few crews seem to have had difficulty locating the target area, and their accounts almost invariably specify that individual targets were bombed visually.[42] A very few accounts indicate difficulties, so (in a unique recorded example) 420 Squadron RCAF Wellington HE973 had to bomb through cloud on its third run over the target (Torre Annunziata) on the night of 24/25 September, and congestion over the target area on the 15/16 September meant that some aircraft of 424 Squadron 'had to make up to four runs before dropping their load'.[43] Otherwise, when individual crews' accounts survive, they almost invariably claim to have bombed accurately, although one ('R' of 70 Squadron, bombing west of ancient Pompeii on 15/16 September), acknowledges 'slightly overshot'.[44] Some bombers salvoed their bombs in a single stick, others report dropping them in up to five separate sticks, increasing the spread, potentially more effective in cratering road and rail routes and destroying traffic, but also more likely to cause accidental damage besides their intended targets.

As noted above, the British and Canadian bombers used illuminating flares on night missions in the vicinity of Pompeii, and the light from these flares was one of the most memorable aspects of these attacks for Italian civilian observers on the ground.[45] Target illumination and marking techniques had been in use by the RAF both in northern Europe and the Mediterranean since early in the war (see Figure 15), evolving into the sophisticated methods employed in the bombing of Germany by No. 8 Group, the Pathfinder Force, from August 1942.[46] However, the use of flares to illuminate targets near Pompeii was relatively unsophisticated, without the radio

Figure 15: A Wellington IC bomber T2508, 'LF-O' of 37 Squadron in Egypt in 1941. The Latin motto painted on it, *Defaecamus luces purpuras* ('We shit purple lights'), alludes to its flare-dropping role. © Imperial War Museum (CM 407).

navigation aids used against Germany or the complex choreography and 'layering' of flares, incendiary bombs and high-explosive bombs employed there. For the missions examined here, methods and timing of illumination were decided at Wing headquarters rather than coordinated at Group level or above.[47] The *ORB*s suggest that typically a single aircraft from each squadron (or equivalent) carried flares, and that the task was spread around the squadron rather than being assigned consistently to particularly skilled or experienced crews.[48] While the evidence is fragmentary (different *ORB*s provide very different levels of detail), it suggests that each Wing designated one aircraft to illuminate at the beginning of the Wing's 'B' (bombing time slot) and another to take over part-way through the slot, with take-off times allocated accordingly.[49]

How sufficient continuous illumination was maintained is unclear. There is very little evidence of the detailed tactics employed by the illuminators, as most *ORB*s merely indicate that flares were dropped by the aircraft in the course of the mission. The only relevant exception is the

420 Squadron RCAF *ORB* entry for the bombing of Torre Annunziata on 29 September, which reports for Wellington HE414 'Bomb load 38 Illuminators dropped 0058 at 8000', implying they were all dropped at the same time rather than at intervals.[50] However, the 750,000 candlepower (9.5 million lumen) 4.5" flares employed burned for only 3–4 minutes each, which seems insufficient to maintain continuous illumination with just two illuminators over the target for a 30-minute bombing slot. Likewise it is unclear whether flares were dropped as clusters (the Cluster Projectile 270 lb No. 1, Mk. 1 with seven flares was normal, with a burning time of 7–8 minutes) or individually.[51]

Nevertheless, sufficient continuity seems to have been maintained throughout all the missions. The general quality of illumination is reported in very positive terms by almost all crews whose individual accounts are preserved, and its continuity in particular is singled out by some.[52] There are only a few references to problems. On the night of 13 September, with No. 231 Wing illumination conducted by two aircraft of 37 Squadron (and none from 70 Squadron), some 70 Squadron crews reported problems:

> 'w': 'Set course from Ischia and picked up mole at Torre Annunziata. Illumination which started at 21:35 hrs had died out before road could be bombed.'
>
> 'L' 'While aircraft was over Ischia illumination and photo flashes seen over target. This had died out by the time aircraft reached target.'[53]

'W' and 'L' perhaps arrived over the target area just too late to benefit from the illumination (visible on their approach) provided for other Wings' earlier bombing, but too early for their own (No. 231 Wing) bombing slot of 22.00–22.30 hrs. This was perhaps compounded by illumination for the latter beginning five minutes late, since the crew of 'P' reports: 'Target easily distinguished under good illumination which started 22.05 hrs'. Also on the night of 13 September, one of the two flare-droppers of 40 Squadron returned before reaching the target with torn fabric, although there is no indication this caused particular difficulties for the mission as a whole.[54]

In general, the perceived accuracy of the placement of the flares (and the bombing accuracy achievable as a result) is praised by the bombing crews, with only a few problems highlighted. For example, the report by the crew of Wellington HE522 'B' of 425 Squadron RCAF (*ORB* 15/09/43) states:

> 'Target identified in light of flares close to target but not quite over it.'

'G' of 40 Squadron RAF (*ORB* 24/09/43) records:

> 'Illumination late and father [sic] off target but possible to see moles and road-formation N. of target.'

Of course, there is an element of circularity in the bombing crews' judgement of the accuracy of the flare-dropping, given that it depended on their awareness of their own position, but the combination of moonlight (on 13/14 and 15/16 September) and artificial illumination meant that visibility was generally good enough to relate the position of the flares to the topography visible on the ground.

General indications of bombing altitudes are given in the *OIS* accounts of the missions. For example, the targets of 13 September were bombed from 5000–9000 ft (1524–2743 m), and those of 15 September from 2500 to 10,000 ft (762–3048 m).[55] A few squadron *ORB*s provide more detail on this, with, for example, 425 Squadron RCAF reporting bombing altitudes ranging from 6000 to 8000 ft (1829–2438 m) on 13 September and 4500 to 5300 ft (1372–1615 m) on 15 September. The lower altitude for the later mission may reflect the lack of opposition in the target area. Such bombing altitudes were typical for Wellingtons. As a point of comparison, the February 1942 attack on the Renault factory at Billancourt near Paris, a (relatively) precise attack conducted by a high proportion of Wellingtons in clear conditions against weak defences, was flown at 1000–4000 ft (305–1219 m) for the initial illuminators and main force) and 4000–6000 ft (1219–1829 m, the rear force).[56] That attack was considered a great success, but even so, its accuracy was judged in terms of the number of aircraft that bombed within a mile of the centre of the factory.[57]

The bombsight in use on No. 205 Group's Wellingtons in September 1943 typically was the unstabilised 1939 vintage Mk. IX course-setting bombsight, a basic development of a 1917 design (Dale Satterthwaite's 'protractor', also used in USAAF B-25s—see above).[58] A contemporary analysis of what is described as 'pinpoint bombing by night' (specifically by RAF light bombers, but undoubtedly more widely relevant) states:

> 'Even where flares are used to illuminate the target, the "spread" of a night bombing pattern must be considerable as each aircraft bombs individually and very often at quite considerable intervals of time. So that the effectiveness of this type of bombing against anything but an "area" as distinct from a "pinpoint" target is very doubtful.'[59]

The immediately post-war *British Bombing Survey* data for April to July 1943 (against targets in Germany) shows an average density of just under 20% of bombs hitting within a square mile of the aiming point.[60] Given 1942–1943 methods and technology, and the proximity of transportation targets to the ancient site of Pompeii (some considerably closer than a mile), it was to be expected that some bombs would hit the ancient site due to minor variations in their release, ballistics and winds. If anything, it is surprising that so few bombs hit the archaeological site on these occasions.

USAAF MEDIUM BOMBERS, AT NIGHT

The final bombing tactic considered is a relatively unusual one involving aircraft from both major Allied nations, namely USAAF medium bombers bombing at night against targets marked by RAF Boston light bombers. On the night of 13/14 September, 3 Bostons of 18 Squadron marked with illuminating candles (i.e., Target Identification Bombs [TIs]) and incendiary bombs the junction of the Naples-Pompeii autostrada with SS18, which subsequently was bombed from 9000–10,000 ft (2743–3048 m) by 12 B-25s from each of 12th Bombardment Group and 340th Bombardment Group. This tactic was repeated on the night of 17/18 September, when 3 Bostons of No. 326 Wing marked the distinctive Piazza Imbriani 'Torre Annunziata road junction' for 24 B-25s of 12th Bombardment Group bombing from 7500–10,500 ft (2286–3200 m). The same night 3 Bostons again marked the Pompeii autostrada/SS18 intersection, for 10 B-25s from each of 12th and 340th Bombardment Wings, bombing from 7500–10,000 ft (2286–3048 m). Besides the joint Allied nature of the operation and the units involved, the key difference from the night bombing conducted by the Wellington squadrons is that the marking for these missions was done with TIs and incendiaries, both of which were primarily ground markers, rather than the flares used by the Wellingtons, which illuminated the target area from the sky. On the 13 September mission the Bostons of 18 Squadron dropped a total of six 250 lb TIs and 540 4 lb incendiary bombs, and on 17 September 48 30 lb and 540 4 lb incendiaries, on each occasion marking the intersection of the autostrada and the SS18. The aircraft of 114 Squadron also used a mix of 30 lb and 4 lb incendiaries to mark the Torre Annunziata road junction on 17 September.[61] It appears that parachute flares were not used on this mission, although 'non-delay' TIs, if used, would have had a sky-marking effect as they ignited immediately on leaving the aircraft.[62]

Similar combined missions, with British pathfinders marking for USAAF medium bombers at night, had already taken place in North Africa as early as the summer of 1942, with Wellingtons as well as Albacore naval aircraft dropping flares for B-25s of 12th Bombardment Group targeting transportation and supply infrastructure.[63] Bostons of 18 and 114 Squadrons had already performed a pathfinder role for 12th Bombardment Group against airfields at Sciacca in Sicily, and carried out a number of similar attacks elsewhere in Italy.[64] Presumably the rationale for this arrangement was that British crews were more specifically trained and experienced in night-time navigation than the American crews, whose primary role was day bombing. In contrast to the day bombing missions flown by the USAAF (and like the RAF Wellington missions), the night attacks were flown individually rather than in formation boxes, with each crew navigating to the target area and aiming its bombs individually.[65] The factors determining accuracy were largely similar to those applicable to RAF night bombing missions, although the bombing altitudes documented for the 12th and 340th Bombardment Groups are somewhat higher than those of the RAF operating around Pompeii (but lower than the USAAF daytime medium bombers). Much depended on visibility and the accuracy of marking, and as noted already, the sky was clear with moonlight on those nights. Bombing crews' reports on the quality of marking are positive, including 'very well lit up by white incendiary "X" pattern' for the Torre Annunziata road junction attack of 17/18 September.[66] The bomb-aiming equipment and the skill of individual B-25 crews was also a crucial issue. Like their day-flying counterparts, the 12th and 340th Bombardment Groups were not yet equipped with the Norden M sight (indeed, the Norden was essentially ineffective at night anyway), but with less sophisticated sights, such as the Mark IX used in the RAF Wellingtons, and the Estoppey D-8.[67]

CONCLUSION

A very wide range of technologies and tactics was employed in bombing targets near the ancient site of Pompeii, ranging from night bombing by RAF Wellington crews who navigated to and identified their targets individually, to daytime bombing by US heavy and medium bombers bombing in formation. The bombing was carried out with little opposition in good visibility that meant that many or most crews could identify key landmarks in the target area, potentially including the archaeological site, even at night when the target area was illuminated by flares. However, the fact that the archaeological site was visible could not be expected to prevent it being damaged. Fundamentally all the bombing tactics employed in 1943 had inherent inaccuracies. The decision to bomb targets so close to the site meant that it was almost inevitable that some bombs would hit it. If anything, given the levels of accuracy achievable at the time, it is surprising that more bombs did not strike the site.

CHAPTER 5

Judgements of Success, Military Necessity and Legality

With the partial exception of the missions against Torre Annunziata on the night of 24/25 August, when the steelworks were attacked as a strategic target, the principal objective of the bombing that damaged Pompeii was to support the Allied land campaign in Italy by attacking transportation routes for German troops and supplies. This took on particular urgency when the counter-attack against the Salerno beachhead began on 13 September. Given that 1943 standards of bombing accuracy meant accidental damage from attacks so close to the archaeological site was almost inevitable, did the military advantage achieved by those attacks make the damage worthwhile, and hence proportionate (see below) given the urgency of the situation set out in Chapter 3?[1] How successful was the bombing in military terms? These are complex question to address. Of course, ultimately the German counter-attack against the Salerno beachhead was defeated and Allied forces there both linked up with the British 8th Army advancing from the south, and broke out to the north, entering Naples on 1 October 1943. Had the counter-attack forced the evacuation of the beachhead, even if the invasion of Italy had been salvaged by the advance of 8th Army from the south, it would have been a very serious setback to Allied operational plans, prestige and confidence, not to mention the casualties, loss of equipment and other practical ramifications it entailed. However, ultimately the Salerno beachhead held, so the issue under discussion here is how significant a part did the bombing play in the ultimate operational success? This is a difficult question, given the numerous factors that contributed to the successful defence of the beachhead, and it is impossible to reckon the importance of air interdiction in quantitative terms, but some qualitative analysis is possible.

Many of the contemporary reports compiled at squadron level (such as RAF *ORB*s) include general comments about crews' perceptions of their accuracy, occasionally referring to hits on specific types of target. For example, the *ORB* of 40 Squadron RAF for the night of 15 September reports

'One 4000 lb bomb burst on the road and houses on the west side of POMPEII'.[2] However, these reports are perhaps unreliable in the confidence they express, given the difficulties of observing damage accurately under combat conditions.

Interpretation of photographic intelligence, both strike and post-strike, permits rather more objective damage assessment. Vivid evidence of both the successes and the inaccuracy of the bombing is provided by a photograph taken by a Spitfire PR XI of the RAF's 682 (Photo Reconnaissance) Squadron on 18 September 1943 (Figures 5 and 16). Damage to the transportation infrastructure revealed by detailed examination of that photograph includes cratering on SS18 (Figure 17, no. 1), two complete breaks in the elevated section of the Naples-Pompeii autostrada just east of where it crosses SS18 (Figure 17, no. 2), and a partial break immediately over SS18 (Figure 17, no. 3).[3] Craters are also visible on the main Naples-Salerno railway line just south of Pompeii (Figure 18) and on the railway line and marshalling yards south and east of Torre Annunziata's Piazza Imbriani (Figure 19). However, the same images also show vast numbers of bomb craters spread across the open countryside and (more difficult to see) in residential areas and the archaeological site of Pompeii, demonstrating the general inaccuracy of the bombing even when directed against highly visible aiming points. Very many misses were inevitable to achieve relatively few hits on the intended targets.

The Allied Northwest African Air Forces' *Operations and Intelligence Summaries* include assessments of the effectiveness of previous days' operations under the regular daily heading 'BOMB DAMAGE', drawn from a range of sources including the crews' reports, photo reconnaissance evidence and other intelligence.

OIS 205, for 13 September, filed immediately before the first attack near Pompeii, provides a baseline:

> 'Pompei: No damage is noted to roads or railway.'[4]

After that, the reported damage mounts:

> (*OIS* 206, 14/09/43): 'Pompeii. The RR line to Torre Annunziata and Castellamare is cut in two places. One line to Salerno is cut in 4 places, while the other line is damaged by blast. The road to Castellamare and Naples is cut, but the road to Salerno remains passable though damaged.'

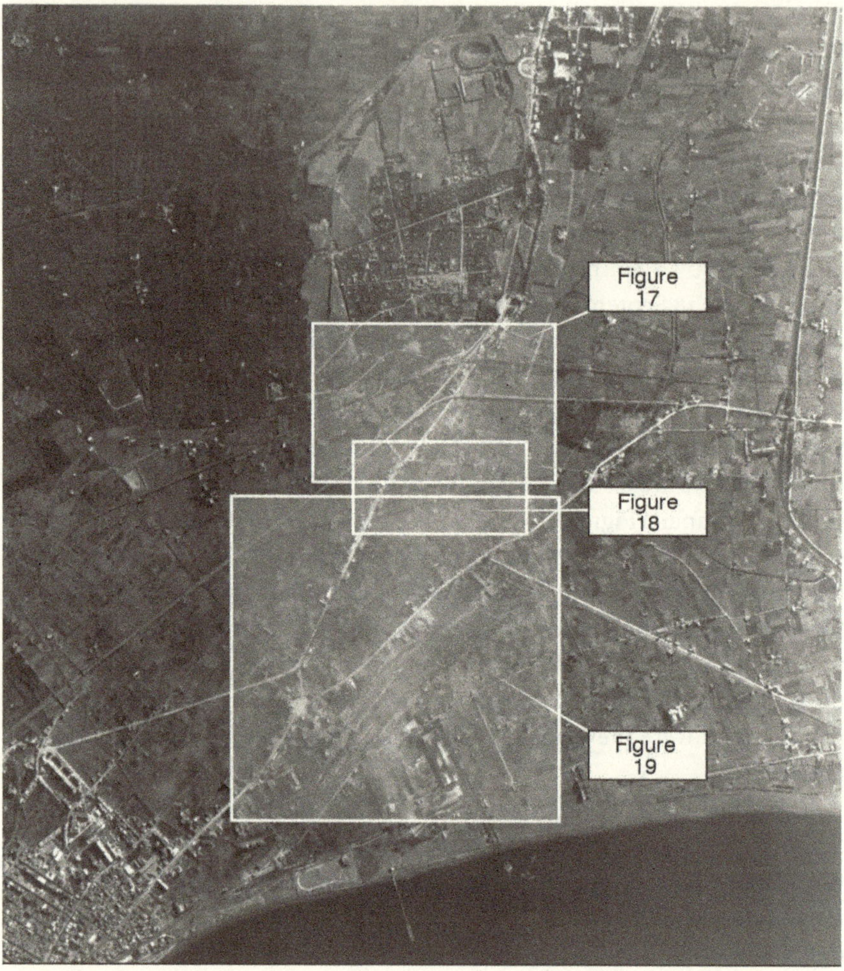

Figure 16: RAF aerial reconnaissance photograph of the Pompei–Torre Annunziata area taken on 18 September 1943, with areas depicted in detail in Figures 17–19 marked. [UK] National Collection of Aerial Photography ACIU NA 0685 4006.

(*OIS* 207 15/09/43) 'Torre Annunziata. The RR lines to Castellamare, Salerno, Naples and Cancello are all cut by direct hits. The highway to Naples NW of the town is blocked and the roads to Castellamare and Naples are severely damaged. In the marshalling yards, severe damage is noted to tracks and rolling stock. . . . Pompeii. The RR line to Torre Annunziata and Castellamare still appears blocked.'

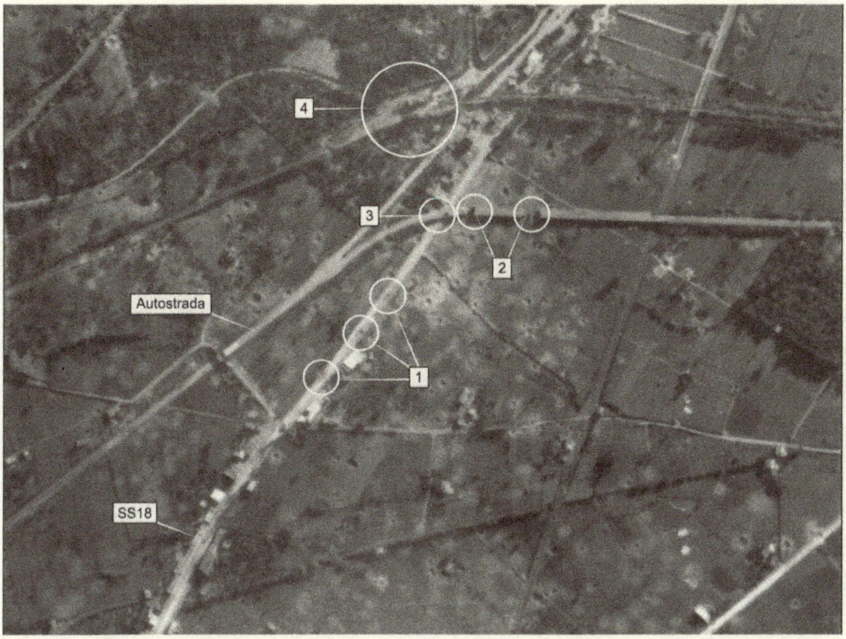

Figure 17: Detail of Figure 16, showing damage to the transportation system (as well as heavy cratering in open countryside) around Pompei. 1 indicates cratering on the SS18 road, 2 marks complete breaks in the autostrada overpass, 3 is a partial break in the autostrada overpass immediately over the SS18 road and 4 marks damage to the Circumvesuviana light rail line. [UK] National Collection of Aerial Photography ACIU NA 0685 4006.

> (*OIS* 211, 19/09/43) 'Pompeii: The RR line to Cancello and Castellamare di Stabia remains cut. The northern road remains blocked.'

Professor Solly Zuckerman's contemporary report on the effectiveness of the bombing against the railway system also draws heavily on interpretation of bomb damage imagery (although the disruption of German operational mobility that the bombing was planned to achieve would not have been visible in its entirety from battle damage imagery). Zuckerman's analysis of damage in the Torre Annunziata area starts with the RAF attack on the night of 24/25 August, which he notes damaged primarily the steelworks rather than the railway marshalling yards, although in the course of subsequent attacks by day and night on 29 August

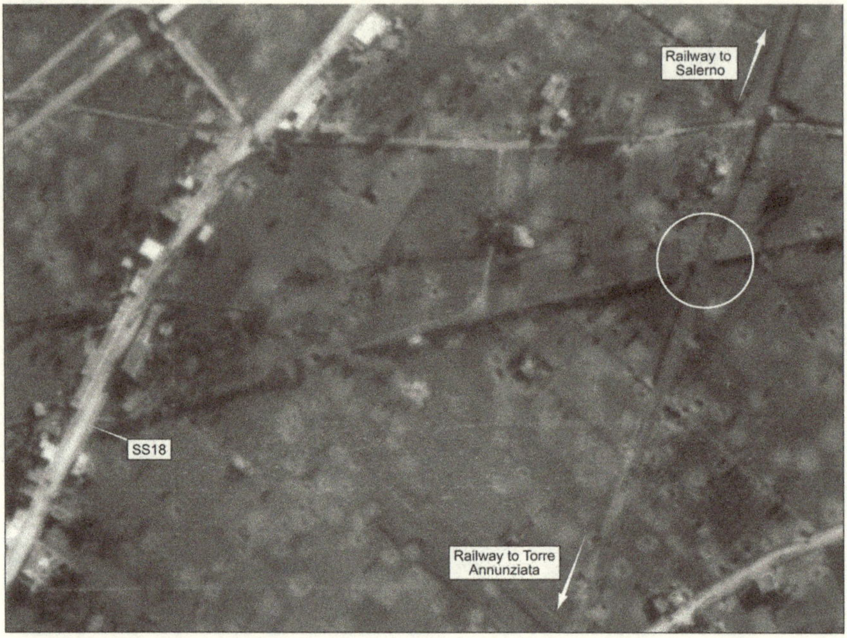

Figure 18: Detail of Figure 16, showing damage to the transportation system (as well as heavy cratering in open countryside) around Pompei. This shows cratering of the main Naples-to-Salerno rail line. [UK] National Collection of Aerial Photography ACIU NA 0685 4006.

> 'considerable damage was done in the marshalling yards and much rolling stock was destroyed—partly by fire. . . . The line to Salerno at the east end of the marshalling yard was blocked and the appearances suggested that the track to Naples was also impassable. On September 3 it was clear that the line to the north was still blocked, but that repairs were taking place in the marshalling yards and on the tracks to Naples.'[5]

This last point emphasises that railway tracks could be repaired, and, Zuckerman notes, on 8 September (the eve of the Salerno landings)

> 'Photo-cover . . . suggested that the lines on both sides of [Torre Annunziata] had been re-opened.'

Thus bombing resumed, and as a result of the B-17 attacks against Torre Annunziata and Pompeii

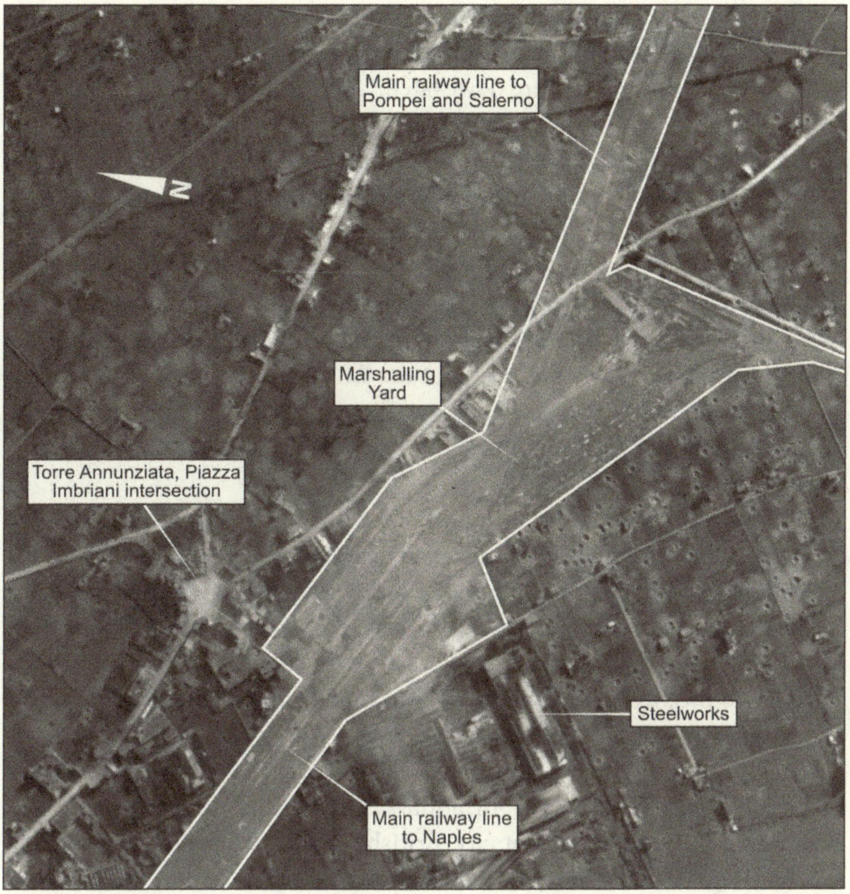

Figure 19: Detail of Figure 16, showing damage to and around the marshalling yards, main rail line, steelworks and Piazza Imbriani in Torre Annunziata. [UK] National Collection of Aerial Photography ACIU NA 0685 4006.

> 'the lines to Salerno were again blocked, as also was the main road towards the south-east [i.e., the SS18] . . . judging from photo-cover, it is clear that all traffic through this town [Torre Annunziata] was effectively stopped as from September 14 and 15.'

Finally, by 25 September

> 'Photo-cover showed that the whole railway area had been considerably disrupted and that the lines to Salerno, Naples and Cancello, as well as

> the main roads out of the town [Torre Annunziata—so including the SS18 towards Pompeii], had all been cut. Rolling stock and the tracks in the marshalling yards were devastated.'[6]

Accounts by observers on the ground confirm that much damage was done to the transportation infrastructure. Archaeological superintendent Amedeo Maiuri's account of his activities at this time emphasises the difficulty of travel between the different areas under his responsibility, which included both Pompeii and the city of Naples. This difficulty was caused partly by German roadblocks and requisition of motor vehicles and petrol after the armistice of 8 September, but the damage he describes on his bicycle trip through the Incrocio Paselli and Torre Annunziata on 15 September clearly was the result of bombing.[7]

> 'We passed through piles of rubble, dead horses, smashed doors. . . . The main road through Torre Annunziata was unrecognisable amidst the heaps of stone and the tangle of electrical wires. It was hit just a few hours after our passing. The last house, that of my poor sick and paralysed friend Luigi Jacono, fortunately was still standing. Outside the town, in the sweet September sun, we could ride more freely and calmly.'

As Allied ground troops advanced into Pompei and beyond, the impact of the bombing on the transportation system was apparent to them too. As his unit passed the ancient city, British Captain Peter Freeman of 1/7th Queen's Regiment noted that the cluster of road and rail routes just beyond it had received considerable attention from Allied bombers (and also that some of the bombs had fallen on the ruins, producing 'instant excavations').[8] Pesce, drawing on contemporary accounts, emphasises the extent to which the bomb damage that originally had impacted German operational mobility now acted, along with German demolition and rearguard actions, to slow the British advance along the main road towards Naples.[9] This was certainly true as far as Torre del Greco, although access to the autostrada at Pompeii was judged particularly bad, hardly surprising given that it was the aiming point of many of the attacks. Freeman notes that progress along SS18 from Sarno through Pompei to Torre Annunziata was equally difficult. A contemporary photograph (Figure 20—see also Figure 21) shows British Army vehicles on the SS18 by the autostrada overpass just west of Pompeii.[10] Rubble lies in the road, along with a hastily filled crater, and the overpass itself is cratered and partially collapsed. Certainly substantial damage was done, and as Zuckerman states,

> 'If the measure of air attacks on enemy rail and road communications is taken as the destruction of the means of communication, then the offensive carried out against rail targets in Sicily and Southern Italy must be regarded as an outstanding success.'[11]

Of course, in reality, the true measure of military success in this context was the impact that the visible destruction had on the fighting on the ground and on the Germans' overall operational mobility, their ability to reinforce and re-supply. There are occasional claims of specific operational success presented in Allied squadron and group documentation. For example, the *ORB* of 40 Squadron for 15 September states 'It is noteworthy that advances by our troops followed this and other Wellington attacks on road targets in the battle area.'[12] Such claims are inadmissible as evidence in the absence of wider analysis, because their primary aim was to enhance unit morale, and it is unclear on what evidence, if any, they were made. However, contemporary intelligence reports from higher-level headquarters make similar claims. The Allied Force Headquarters *Weekly Intelligence Summary* for the week ending 18 September 1943 claims

> 'The enemy's lines of movement and supply were subjected to heavy and sustained bombing and strafing. . . . Allied command of the air and the sea thus prevented the enemy from exploiting his temporary advantages on the ground and made it impossible for him to counter the continued build-up of our own forces. . . . Temporary ground superiority was severely limited by Allied command of the air and the shore-line, and the initiative boldly seized on 12 September had by 15 September begun to pass to the Allies.'[13]

In the published British inter-service Official History, Molony paraphrases and quotes (translated) captured documents emphasising the tactical impact of Allied air power in the battle, particularly on German movement.[14] Nevertheless, Zuckerman continues,

> 'If, however, the measure of success were taken as the complete cutting and blocking of the railway lines and roads, then the offensive could be

Figure 20: Photograph taken shortly after the liberation of Pompei, showing British army personnel and a carrier vehicle on the SS18 road under the autostrada overpass. The hole in the autostrada seen from the air in Figure 17 (3) is clearly visible, as are rubble and hastily filled craters on the SS18. ©Imperial War Museum (NA 7459).

> regarded as partly failed in its purpose. There is little indication that the attacks prevented the enemy from moving from place to place within the limits imposed on him by the capacity of transport at his disposal.'[15]

This is literally true—Allied airpower was certainly not able to impose a *complete* block on the movement of German ground troops to and from the Salerno area. However, it was not a matter of *absolute* success or failure. A complete block is unlikely to have been the objective of the bombing, which rather sought to achieve as great a degree of attrition, dislocation and disruption ('friction') on German ground forces as the Allied air forces were

Figure 21: The autostrada/SS18 overpass depicted in Figure 20 as it is today (author's photograph).

able to achieve. Undoubtedly the bombing of transportation targets near Pompeii contributed to this friction as the interdiction reduced the tempo of the counter-attacks and hence their effectiveness. It may have played a part, for example, in forcing the Germans to delay their northern counterattack against the British sector of the beachhead, preventing its close coordination with the southern counterattack against the Americans.

The general success (or otherwise) of aerial interdiction in the earlier part of the Italian campaign (essentially to the end of 1943, including the aerial response to the counter-attack at Salerno, with its activity around Pompeii and Torre Annunziata) is reflected and analysed in Solly Zuckerman's contemporary report focusing specifically on this aspect of the campaign, and subsequently in the execution and recording of Operation Strangle, the later programme of interdiction to support the Allied advance on Rome in the spring of 1944.[16] In some respects, the conduct of Operation Strangle drew on Zuckerman's conclusions derived from his analysis of the early part of the campaign, but there were some notable differences of emphasis. Zuckerman's judgement of the qualified success of earlier air operations forms part of his argument that the Italian rail network could most effectively be targeted by destroying rolling stock and repair facilities at certain specific key rail centres.[17] He may have tended to underplay the success of air interdiction in the southern Italian campaign to strengthen his argument for such a more focused approach later in Italy and then in Normandy.

In practical terms, interdiction of lines of communication could be achieved in a number of ways. These included

1. Cutting and blocking of railway lines themselves and the bridges carrying them.
2. Damaging main roads by cratering (to slow motor transport by forcing it to divert off-road or onto minor roads), most efficiently at intersections where multiple roads converged; damaging and destroying road bridges; and blocking roads with rubble by destroying adjacent buildings
3. Destroying the means of transport—locomotives, rolling stock and motor transport.

None of this was simple. Trains and motor vehicles, while vulnerable, were difficult to find and hit as individual targets, and trucks, at least, were numerous and thus easy to replace. Roads and railway lines were relatively difficult to hit, and damage to them could be repaired fairly quickly. Bridges were even more difficult to hit and difficult to damage, but took longer to repair.[18] The effect of blocking roads depended to a great extent on the location of the blocks, because in open country (for example), they could easily be bypassed without operationally significant delay. However, Zuckerman argues that bombing of towns (particularly smaller, congested ones) to block roads passing through them could be operationally effective, especially if the bombing was heavy (he mentions the use of 4000 lb bombs) and in situations 'when every moment may be vital'—in other words, when any effect on operational tempo might be significant.[19] All of these factors (urgency, roads passing through congested towns like Pompei and Torre Annunziata, and the use of 4000 lb bombs) were applicable to the bombing around Pompeii. While some commanders and analysts (including Zuckerman) later advocated focusing on particular elements of the transportation system in Italy and elsewhere as 'panacea' targets, the Allied bombing around Pompeii and Torre Annunziata seems to have targeted all these different facets of the transportation system. This was an acknowledgment of the difficulty of damaging one or the other sufficiently to affect the land campaign by itself, given the technical problems of bombing (particularly accuracy against 'pin-point' targets) at the time, although without necessarily rationalising it in those terms.[20] The Pompeii–Torre Annunziata area was an obvious target for such an approach because of the concentration of different types of targets in a relatively small area—roads, railways (which passed through or near urban centres and natural confines), rail marshalling yards, intersections, bridges, and the traffic they carried. The diversity of targets explains the variety of bombs used, from 4000 lb LC (i.e., Light Case—with a high proportion of high-explosive filling to metal case for blast effect) that would destroy buildings and perhaps damage bridges with a near-miss, to 100 lb bombs that would destroy motor transport and cause some cratering of roads and railways. The proximity to the sea, the urban centres and intersections aided bomber navigation and the intersections and bridges provided clear aiming points.

Despite the evidence of damage done to the transportation system, it is very difficult to weigh the contribution of the bombing around Pompeii to the Allied victory at Salerno against the damage done to the archaeological site (and other accidental and collateral damage, to civilian lives and property) in quantifiable and comparable terms to establish proportionality. From a heritage-protection perspective, it is easy (but anachronistic) to argue with the benefit of hindsight that *any* damage to the site was unacceptable.[21] However, it is unlikely that Allied commanders would have avoided bombing near a heritage site, even with the virtual inevitability of some damage, in a situation as urgent as that developing at Salerno on 13 September 1943, when air power was seen as one of the very few responses that could be delivered rapidly. At the time, the bombing was judged to be necessary, and proportionate. For reasons discussed in detail in Part Two, the nascent Allied Monuments and Fine Arts organisation had little or no contact with the air forces at this time, primarily due to its initial focus on protecting sites in occupied territory. Consequently, there seems to have been no discussion or consideration of the implications of bombing so close to such an important heritage site, and certainly that discussion should have taken place. On the other hand, it is unlikely that such considerations would have had a significant effect on the ultimate decision to bomb. The rules of engagement for bombing targets in or close to heritage sites developed later (in 1944), when the Monuments, Fine Arts and Archives Sub-Commission *did* liaise with Mediterranean Allied Air Forces Headquarters, remained quite permissive and explicitly prioritised assessed military necessity over the protection of cultural sites.[22] Given the urgent circumstances of the counter-attacks at Salerno, it seems unlikely that even with a more robust Allied monuments protection organisation in place, bombing near ancient Pompeii would have been prevented.

Nor were there many alternatives to the methods and tactics that *were* actually employed. In theory, more use could have been made of more accurate daytime tactical air power instead of the medium and heavy bombers that were actually used—often at night. In particular, the USAAF had over 100 single-engine A-36 'Invader' or 'Apache' dive-bombers in the Mediterranean theatre, an early specialised version of the famous P-51 Mustang fighter.[23] Their dive brakes meant they could employ steep diving attacks to deliver their two 500 lb bombs more accurately than larger bombers bombing in level flight, or other fighter-bombers employing shallow dive attacks.[24] In theory, such tactics and equipment might have made it possible to destroy bridges in the Pompeii area selectively, with less accidental damage to the archaeological site as well as fewer civilian casualties. In reality, however, this was impractical. Until the Allies established airfields within the Salerno beachhead itself, the A-36s were among the few fighter aircraft with sufficient range to fly defensive patrols over the beachhead from bases in northern Sicily, and so initially they were committed to such missions.[25] However, even if these aircraft had not been required for other duties, missions in the Pompeii area would have been at the very limits of their range from Sicily, or perhaps beyond it when carrying bombs. A-36s were not properly established on bases within the Salerno beachhead until 16 September, and their movement to those bases was actually delayed by the German counter-attacks, further emphasising that they could not have given an effective emergency response to those counter-attacks. Another problem with A-36s in this context was that even a direct hit from a 500 lb bomb—the heaviest carried by an A-36—was unlikely to destroy even a relatively minor bridge.[26]

Another *theoretically* possible adjustment to reduce damage to the archaeological site was to change the direction from which the bombers approached their targets. As noted above (pp. 59; 62), both US and British bombers mostly bombed targets near Pompeii on a roughly west-to-east heading, having used Capri as a navigational landmark to turn in across the coast and running in to the targets along the Sarno valley. This approach potentially spread bombs along the axis of flight, and the fact that the archaeological site lay just beyond the targets on that same axis increased the probability of accidental hits on the site if bombers and their bombs overshot the targets. In theory, approaching the targets on a north-to-south heading instead of west to east would have reduced that risk. In practice, however, this was not possible. Approaching from the south would have taken bombers close to the Allied fleet in the Gulf of Salerno, creating a severe risk of casualties from friendly naval anti-aircraft fire. As noted above (p. 62n.38), bombers were ordered to take an indirect, western route to the target area specifically to avoid this risk. Also, the target area is masked from the south by the mountains of the Sorrento peninsula, the Monti Lattari, with Monte Faito, due south of Pompei, rising to 1131 m. A run in from the south over these mountains would have been difficult (and potentially dangerous) to fly, and would have hidden from view the targets themselves and identifiable features around the targets for most of the approach, affecting the accuracy of bomb-aiming. Immediately to the north of the targets lies Vesuvius, rising to a height similar to that of Monte Faito, and beyond that, the defended area of Naples, neither of which could be overflown without significant risk. In reality, the west-to-east approach to the targets was the only practical one.

While the Allied Monuments, Fine Arts and Archives Sub-Commission provided no input into the decision to bomb near ancient Pompeii in August and September 1943, with the benefit of hindsight it did provide a verdict of sorts on the bombing in its immediate post-war summary and conclusions. In a section entitled 'VI. Damage from the Air: Allied Precautionary Measures' the author writes

> 'Some of the earlier destruction does indeed appear to be out of proportion to the military results achieved. The lower half of Benevento was pulverized when there were barely fifty Germans in the town. . . . For lack of specific targets the Castelli Romani were on several occasions indiscriminately bombed on the chance of killing the Germans quartered therein. Viterbo was smashed with a total loss of 8 Germans and 2000 civilian Italians to create a road-block which could be cleared in half an hour by a bull-dozer. *The two hundred bombs dropped on Pompeii, quite apart from any damage done, were two hundred wasted bombs.*'[27] [my italics]

In a very literal sense this was true. The bombs that hit ancient Pompeii were 'wasted' because they were aimed at targets elsewhere, and there were no enemy troops on the site to be hit (see Chapter 6). It is unclear whether this interpretation reflects the author's intended meaning. In context, he seems to be making a retrospective point about the deliberate bombing of particular places, either (1) to target enemy troops presumed to be stationed in them (Benevento, the Castelli Romani) or (2) in ineffective attempts at interdiction (Viterbo)—in each case conducted without proper consideration of their impact on cultural heritage. The author may have considered the situation at Pompeii analogous to (1) if he thought it was bombed because Allied forces considered German forces to be present on the site itself (discussed in Chapter 6). In that case the bombs were 'wasted' either because there were (in fact) *no* German troops on the site, or otherwise because the bombs were ineffective in killing them.[28] The case of Pompeii was analogous to that of Viterbo (2) in that it involved interdiction and blocking of routes, although at Pompeii the routes ran close to the heritage site, whereas at Viterbo they ran through the historic core of the city. Another possible interpretation of this comment is that the writer considered the bombs wasted because the interdiction of routes close to Pompeii was unsuccessful. In this case, it is unclear on what basis he formed that judgement or (as a monuments officer) on what basis he was qualified to make a judgement regarding military effectiveness. However, his conclusion may also reflect (in a general sense) contemporary preferences for more specifically targeted interdiction efforts, such as those against railway rolling stock and repair yards advocated by Zuckerman, which were to some extent taken up in the subsequent air planning for the advance on Rome and the Normandy campaign, emphasising systematic attack on rail targets rather than the sporadic blocking of roads represented by the example of Viterbo.

MILITARY NECESSITY, LEGALITY, PROPORTIONALITY

The basis of international law relating to the treatment of historic sites and buildings in 1943 was Hague Convention (IV) 1907, *Regulations*, Article 27, which states 'In sieges and bombardments all necessary steps must be taken to spare, as far as possible, buildings dedicated to religion, art, science, or charitable purposes, historic monuments . . . provided they are not being used at the time for military purposes'.[29] Thus heritage sites were to be protected from damage in war, but that protection was not absolute ('as far as possible . . . provided they . . .'). Hague Convention (IV) 1907 provided the legal underpinning for regulations on the protection of historic buildings reflected and quoted in the British War Office *Manual of Military Law* (1929, reprinted 1939), which formed the basis of the subject for British forces during the Second World War, and in its US equivalent, the 1940 War Department *Basic Field Manual FM 27-10: Rules of Land Warfare.*[30] The *Manual of Military Law* emphasises,

> 'Edifices for which inviolability is thus claimed must not be used at the same time for military purposes, as, for example, for officers [sic] and quarters, or for signalling stations or observation posts. If this condition is violated, the besieger is justified in disregarding the sign.'[31]

However, the *Manual of Military Law* also acknowledges the difficulty of avoiding damage to such buildings and states that accidental damage was a grey area:

> 'Hague Rules 27. The introduction of long range artillery, aircraft &c. makes it difficult to ensure immunity for such buildings, but they should not be bombarded deliberately.'

It acknowledges that technological changes during and after the First World War and the increasing difficulty of separating 'military' and 'civilian' in modern war had made aspects of Hague (IV) 1907 anachronistic.[32] Fundamentally, the damage caused to Pompeii would have been legitimate on the grounds of military necessity under prevailing laws of armed conflict had German forces made any military use of the site. The rules of engagement distributed to Mediterranean Allied Air Forces in *The Ancient Monuments of Italy* in February 1944 echo this principle, stating,

> 'If a town is in the actual zone of military operations on the ground, and is occupied by the enemy, no restrictions whatever are to be applied. The sole determining factor will be the requirements of the military situation.'[33]

However, the Germans appear *not* to have made military use of the site itself (see below, Chapter 6), which takes its legality into that grey area of accidental (and collateral) damage acknowledged as problematic by the *Manual of Military Law.* The transportation infrastructure that formed the intended target of the bombing was a civilian object, but nevertheless a legitimate military target under the terms of the 1907 Hague Convention, as it undoubtedly was in military use by German forces. As Roger O'Keefe notes, under the terms of Hague Convention (IV) 1907, 'no positive rule compelled a belligerent to ask whether the military need to destroy a lawful target outweighed the damage likely to be caused to cultural property'.[34]

With the benefit of hindsight, we can also weigh the bombing that damaged Pompeii against principles of international law that were *not* in force in 1943, but, again, we see that even if held to these (anachronistic) standards, the Allies could have made a strong claim of military necessity and even—a new criterion—proportionality.

The Hague Draft Rules of Aerial Warfare were created in 1923 by a Commission of Jurists appointed by the 1922 Washington Conference on the Limitation of Armament, but were never binding. They sought to impose more restrictive and nuanced constraints on aerial bombardment in response to the experiences of the First World War and the technological developments that had occurred since 1907.[35] Article 24 (1) states that aerial bombardment is only legitimate when directed at a military objective, defined as 'an object of which the destruction or injury would constitute a distinct military advantage to the belligerent' and further defined in Article 24 (2) to include 'lines of communication or transportation used for military purposes'. Certainly the transportation infrastructure around Pompeii was a military objective under those terms. However, Articles 24 (3) and (4) went on to set limits on incidental casualties and damage to civilians and civilian property (including cultural property) in a way that Hague Convention (IV) 1907 did not, requiring bombardment of military objectives to take into consideration proportionality—whether the importance of the military objective was proportionate to the risk to civilian lives and property.[36] Article 24 (3) forbade bombardment even of *military* objectives when these were not in the immediate neighbourhood of land operations if they could not be bombarded 'without the indiscriminate bombardment of the civilian population'. Article 24 (4) states that bombardment of cities, buildings or similar entities 'in the immediate neighbourhood of the operations of land forces' is legitimate 'provided there exists a reasonable presumption that the military concentration is sufficiently important to justify such bombardment, having regard to the danger thus caused to the civilian population'. However, a strong argument could be made that in the circumstances applying in September 1943, the bombing near Pompeii was 'in the immediate neighbourhood of the operations of land forces', and was necessary (given the importance of the mission to disrupt the German offensive) and proportionate (given the nature of the German target, its proximity to civilians and civilian property, and the means available to achieve the effects required).[37] While the failure to adopt the Hague Air Rules as binding meant that this concept of proportionality had no legal standing during the Second World War (and thus no conceptual basis in contemporary military doctrine), it *was* adopted in the 1977 Protocol I to the [1949] Geneva Conventions, and so applies to its signatories when engaged in targeting now.[38] Article 57 (2) requires combatants to take precautions in their means and methods of attack to avoid or at least minimise damage to civilian objects (which include heritage sites), and also to refrain from attacks that are likely to cause incidental damage 'which would be excessive in relation to the concrete and direct military advantage anticipated'.

Contemporary UK armed forces' targeting documentation provides an example of how modern western armed forces seek to adhere to international humanitarian law in targeting.[39] Explicitly citing Protocol I to the Geneva Conventions, 'Principles of Lawful Targeting' takes into consideration 'Military Necessity' (employment of 'only that degree and kind of force, not otherwise prohibited by the law of armed conflict, that is required to achieve the legitimate purpose of the conflict'), 'Humanity' (inflicting no more injury or damage than necessary to accomplish a legitimate military purpose), 'Distinction' (avoiding or at least minimising incidental damage to civilians and civilian objects in attacking military objectives—sites of cultural significance are specifically mentioned) and 'Proportionality' (ensuring that incidental damage is not excessive 'in relation to the concrete and direct military advantage anticipated'). Another section (Annex 3B8) focuses on prevention or minimisation of accidental and collateral damage by means of weapons selection, timing of attacks and integration of collateral damage estimation into the targeting process.[40] Modern discussions of necessity and proportionality inevitably require consideration of factors such as the nature of the conflict, mission imperative (the commander's intent), the means and precision with which the attacker is capable of acting (including, but not limited to, physical force), and situation awareness predicated on intelligence (in the sense of what the attacker knows about the capability, intent and disposition of the enemy relative to the target, any related civilian objects, and their immediate surroundings).[41]

We can apply these concepts to the circumstances relating to the bombing of Pompeii. Such an analysis is, of course, anachronistic and in some senses unfair to those who had to make the relevant decisions, under stressful circumstances, at the time. Bearing that in mind, however, these later concepts do provide valuable tools of analysis.

THE NATURE OF THE CONFLICT

The damage caused to ancient Pompeii occurred in the context of a high-tempo global war in which the survival of nations was at stake. At an operational level, the military action that led to the damage was taken to prevent the failure of an inherently risky and important operation (the Salerno landings) against a sudden and unexpectedly successful counter-attack. The time constraints on planning and responding dynamically to the German counter-attack limited Allied planners' options.[42] The massive use of air power to interdict German reinforcement and supply was one of the few effective options available. For these reasons, the risk of damage to the site (and, perhaps, the actual damage inflicted) might have been considered proportionate to the urgency of the situation and the risk of failure.[43] However, a different judgement would be more appropriate in the context of a modern 'war of choice' in a less immediately urgent situation, with, perhaps, more options available in terms of tactics and weapons, and more planning time available. However, a war of higher intensity, such as that envisaged in Cold War Europe, would be much closer on the spectrum of conflict to the circumstances in which Pompeii was damaged.

THE PRECISION WITH WHICH THE ATTACKER IS CAPABLE OF ACTING

As discussed above, the Allies could argue that they attacked in as precise a manner as possible under the circumstances, and that the inherent general inaccuracy of bombing in 1943 was the problem, not the particular methods and equipment employed against targets near Pompeii. For the most part that bombing was conducted in good visibility using the best methods and equipment available in the Mediterranean theatre of war, at specific aiming points outside of and beyond the heritage site. It was not indiscriminate, although bombing so close to a heritage site was bound to damage it. The course of action taken, as it happens, was proportionate, although proportionality and distinction in respect of cultural property were not explicitly part of the doctrine that led to it.

Once it was accepted that the use of air interdiction was necessary against those targets, there were no practical alternatives that would have been more accurate. The possible use of fighter-bombers (particularly USAAF A-36 dive-bombers) has been discussed above, but as noted, their numbers, the ranges involved and the urgency of the situation would have made their use impractical. Similarly, alternative approaches to the target might have been considered, but probably would have been rejected for reasons discussed above. In a modern context, however, the availability of precision-guided weapons (for example) would make it more difficult for an attacker to justify the use of unguided weapons so close to a heritage site and any consequent damage to the site.

INTELLIGENCE

The Allies correctly assessed that road and rail routes close to ancient Pompeii were being used to carry combat supplies and reinforcements to the counter-attack against the Salerno beachhead, and targets were selected accordingly. While they may have had some information that small numbers of German forces (primarily anti-aircraft artillery) were deployed very close to the archaeological site, there is no evidence they ever specifically targeted those forces (see Chapter 6). Even if the Allies did make an (incorrect) assessment that German troops were deployed or quartered on the site itself, it is clear that the site was not deliberately targeted anyway.

MILITARY USE OF 'IMMEDIATE SURROUNDINGS'

While air forces bombing near a cultural site might incur responsibility for damage to that site, what about the responsibilities of the defenders? As already seen, Hague Convention (IV) 1907, Article 27, stated that that military use of a historic site or building removed its protected status, but there is no implication that military activity *close to* such a site was in any way problematic. However, the 1923 Hague Air Rules paid more specific and nuanced attention to historical monuments as a distinct category of protected civilian object than did Hague 1907. While Article 25 of the Air Rules essentially reiterated the protection offered by Hague 1907 to 'historic monuments' alongside hospitals and other educational and cultural institutions, Article 26 of the Air Rules singled out a special category of 'monuments of great historic value'. It proposed that countries might specify (by diplomatic notification in peacetime) such monuments for special protection, and that this protection might apply not *just* to the monument itself, but also to a zone of up to 500 m in width from the periphery of the monument. In some ways this special protection anticipated the formal status of 'Special Protection' provided for in the 1954 Hague Convention and the 'Enhanced Protection' of its Second Protocol (1999).[44] If the 1923 Hague Air Rules had been accepted as binding, the archaeological site of Pompeii would have been an obvious candidate for special protection under Article 26, and a number of the targets bombed by the Allies lay within such a 500 m zone. Had that zone been respected, some (but not all) of the bomb damage to the site would have been prevented. On the other hand, this special protection came with the requirement that the monument and the zone around it be completely demilitarised.[45] Thus, if the Hague Air Rules had been observed by Germany in 1943 (another level of hypothesis), they also would have forbidden German military use of the transportation infrastructure immediately around Pompeii. Similar restrictions apply to centres granted Special Protection under the 1954 Hague Convention, which specifically includes transit of military personnel and material as forbidden military use.[46]

CONCLUSION

Under the circumstances prevailing at the time, it seems unlikely that the September 1943 bombing near Pompeii and the consequent damage to the ancient site would have been prevented by the existence at that time of a more effective and robust Allied Monuments, Fine Arts and Archives organisation. In fact, as discussed in Part Two (especially Chapter 9), in September 1943 that organisation's responsibilities emphasised protection on the ground of heritage sites in occupied territories, and did not envisage (or include) input into planning air operations. It is probable that, even had the existence of the heritage site been taken into consideration in the planning process, the urgency of the situation at Salerno and the political and military importance attached to the landings' success would have led to perceptions of military necessity outweighing protection of the site, and the decision would have been taken to bomb. Once that decision was made, given the limitations of bombing accuracy in 1943, little could have been done to avoid damage to ancient Pompeii. Such a decision would have been defensible under then-existing laws of armed conflict, and even could have been argued to satisfy the requirement of proportionality, had the Hague Air Rules been binding at the time, such was the urgency and importance of the military situation.[47]

However, that is not to say that the Monuments, Fine Arts and Archives organisation, or the measures taken to improve its effectiveness in early 1944 (see Part Three), were pointless even in these circumstances. A key aspect of the attacks near Pompeii is that the legality, morality and advisability (political, social, cultural) of bombing so close to a heritage site of world importance seem never to have been discussed as an aspect of their operational planning. While the existence of the archaeological site clearly was known in general terms to the Allied air forces and to individual bomber crews, nothing in the contemporary documentation suggests its location was considered when deciding to bomb or in planning the bombing. For example, none of the orders from higher headquarters (such as the RAF's No. 205 Group) preserved in the RAF *ORB*s warn crews about the site, and none of the Northwest African Air Forces' *Operations and Intelligence Summaries* refer to Pompeii (in its broadest sense, including the modern town and transportation infrastructure nearby) as anything but a target. Even if (as I have suggested) the military circumstances were such that exactly the same decisions would have been taken even after a discussion in which a monuments officer alerted a senior commander to the importance of the heritage site, nevertheless, the important thing is that the discussion would have taken place.[48] While even the 1954 Hague Convention does not protect heritage absolutely, and military necessity and enemy military use still provide legitimate grounds for military action directed near or at a heritage site, it does place a formal responsibility on commanders to consider cultural property as part of the planning process, and also on governments to provide appropriately trained personnel to contribute to that consideration. That was not the case in 1943, although the situation improved somewhat within a year, and provides valuable lessons for contemporary practice.

CHAPTER 6

'The Germans were encamped on the site and allied aircraft were obliged to treat it as a military objective'

Alternative Explanations for the Bombing of Pompeii

It is very clear from the contemporary documentation analysed above that Allied air forces never sought to bomb the ancient site of Pompeii in its own right, and that the bombs that damaged it were intended for other targets nearby and hit the site in error, causing accidental damage. While the term 'Pompeii' is used in the documentation to denote the general target area, it is clear from the details provided that the intended targets were in and around the modern town of Pompei and not on the ancient site. Indeed, the ancient site is only mentioned in its own right on a very few occasions, typically as a landmark by which other targets were identified. One *apparent* reference to intentional deliberate bombing of the ancient site of Pompeii is misleading, and also reflects an attack against one of the transportation targets. It refers to the combined RAF/USAAF mission on the night of 17/18 September 1943.[1] One aircraft of the US 83rd Bombardment Squadron was supposed to bomb the Pompei targets but returned to base early due to IFF (Identification Friend or Foe) equipment failure. Its crew's sortie report describes the aim of the mission as 'bombing of old city of Pompei, Italy', implying that the archaeological site was targeted. In fact the map grid recorded (N403386) shows that the sortie's actual target was the same autostrada/SS18 junction west of ancient Pompeii targeted by other 12th Bombardment Group aircraft that night. The ancient site was used as a general identification feature to help crews locate their aiming points rather than being a target in its own right. The only other *apparent* reference to intentional bombing of the site comes in the 70 Squadron RAF *ORB* for the mission of the night of 15/16 September that states that the Wellington bomber identified as 'E' 'aimed across road running through

Pompei ruins. Some bursts seen no results'.[2] Given the particular targets specified for the mission, the 'road running through Pompei ruins' was probably the SS18 as it passed through the modern town along the south edge of the site rather than a road on the site itself. The *ORB* shows other 70 Squadron crews using the ancient site as a landmark in reporting their bombing that night (see p. 36).

Nevertheless, while the bombing was actually taking place, and then in the months after Pompeii came under Allied control, stories circulated that the site had been targeted deliberately because German troops were quartered on it, or alternatively, because the Allies *mistakenly* thought that German troops were there when they were not. These stories appear in a range of sources reflecting the opinions of essentially two broad groups: Italian civilians, and Allied service personnel and journalists visiting the site. However, there is some evidence of cross-pollination between the two groups. These explanations for the bombing re-emerged in the post-war memoirs of some of the participants, and still appear in scholarly and popular works about wartime Pompeii from time to time.

These various accounts are most effectively examined in the order in which they are claimed to have taken place, although in many cases their publication date was significantly later, and so potentially subject to the distortions in recollection that are so common in participant accounts of historical events.

C. 25 AUGUST 1943, RADIO LONDRA

As noted above, the first occasion on which damage was done to the ancient site was the night of 24/25 August 1943, in the course of an RAF attack on the railway marshalling yards and steelworks at nearby Torre Annunziata. However, in his 1956 memoir, *Taccuino napoletano* (further discussed below), the archaeological superintendent Amedeo Maiuri recounts that at the time of the bombing, a broadcast of the BBC Italian service Radio Londra expressed regret for the damage, but justified it with the claim that a German headquarters had been quartered in the Albergo del Sole hotel, close to the Porta Marina in the south-west corner of the site where most of the damage took place.[3]

The broadcast's apparent claim that the damage to the site that night was collateral damage to the targeting of a nearby German headquarters is implausible. Even if the German headquarters had existed (and Maiuri states it did not), the Allied air forces' documentation relating to the planning of the mission makes no reference to it as a target.[4] Also, given the inaccuracies of bombing at the time (see Chapter 4), Allied air forces would not have been able to target a single building with even a reasonable hope of hitting it, especially at night. Undoubtedly the damage to the site was caused by a few stray bombs intended for the targets near Torre Annunziata.

The reported Radio Londra explanation, if an accurate recollection, may have been created and propagated by British sources to counter negative stories about damage to the site in the Italian and international press, essentially invoking military necessity due to German military 'use'.[5] I can find no reference to this alleged targeting of a German headquarters in other English-language broadcasts or media, while a London *Times* article of 26 August 1943 reported and discussed the previous night's bombing solely in terms of targets at Torre Annunziata, with no mention of Pompeii.[6] On the other hand, the damage to the ancient site was reported in contemporary Italian and German media.

It seems likely that the message—that damage to the heritage site was caused in the course of an attack against a German military target—was tailored and propagated specifically for Italian audiences. Concern about Italian public opinion critical of cultural property damage caused to heritage sites by Allied forces is well attested in contemporary evidence, notably the proceedings of the later Allied military Commission of Enquiry (the Collier Commission) in Naples.[7] While Radio Londra avoided the overtly propagandistic content of 'black' radio stations and print sources, its large audience in Italy, its ability to respond to Italian press reports, and the anecdotal nature of much of its programming made it an effective medium for shaping Italian interpretations of the damage.[8]

13–26 SEPTEMBER 1943: NEWSPAPER REPORTS IN ALLIED COUNTRIES

As we have seen, this was the period when most bomb damage was caused to Pompeii, as accidental damage caused by attacks against transportation targets near the ancient site. These attacks were intended to help disrupt the dangerous German counter-attacks against the Salerno beachhead that began on 12 September 1943 by interdiction of reinforcements and supplies in transit along their main supply route past Pompeii. There are many reports of bombing in this area in contemporary British and US newspapers, and all of them refer to the targets as road and rail routes rather than the archaeological site.[9] It is unsurprising that these newspaper accounts correspond with the official documentation, since these were based on official communiqués rather than independent sources. However, the similarities at least imply that there was no manipulation of the official account before its dissemination, in contrast to what seems to have happened with the Radio Londra report discussed above.

C. 15 SEPTEMBER 1943, MEMOIRS OF AMEDEO MAIURI

Maiuri's memoir *Taccuino napoletano* records that there was a widespread belief among the local civilian population that the archaeological site of Pompeii was occupied by German troops at the time of the Allied bombing. Maiuri himself states that this was incorrect, but he thought that the Allies believed it to be true, and so deliberately targeted the site to attack its supposed German garrison. *Taccuino napoletano*, while published in 1956, is presented as Maiuri's contemporary diary of wartime events. His first discussion of the reasons for the damage to ancient Pompeii comes among observations on German resistance to the Salerno landings, in an entry dated 4 September 1943.[10] He writes of Allied activities,

> 'News gathered by bad informants must have led the [Allied] military headquarters to believe that Pompei was a fortified camp and that the ruins were hiding armed men and munitions. Some small group of visitors or deserters surprised on the Theatre steps by reconnaissance flights undoubtedly provided confirmation of that belief. Another factor . . . was our own unfortunate use in those days of reinforced concrete and *eternit* [corrugated cement with asbestos fibres] for roofing [excavated Roman] buildings in the New Excavations, making them look like barracks. In this way a myth was created that Pompei had become a German strongpoint. The myth spread and grew, to the point that that in my pained stupor I even heard it repeated, by a young Red Cross nurse at the hospital in Torre del Greco when I was being treated there. Therefore it was not a surprise when the first American correspondent told me as justification of the bombing, that their headquarters had been informed, with certainty, that a whole German armoured division was encamped in the ruins.'[11]

The reference to Torre del Greco is clarified in a later entry, relating to Maiuri's wounding in an Allied air attack on 15 September 1943 while he was travelling from Pompeii to Naples, and his treatment at the hospital there:

> 'Once I had been recognised and treated on the operating table, the doctors and Red Cross nurses expressed disbelief that I had come from Pompei. Wasn't there a German division in the excavations there ready to resist the Anglo-American forces that had landed at Salerno? From their stupefied astonishment at my imprudence [of having been in Pompei] and from the false news circulating in the rear areas, I understood the unfortunate reason why those 160 bombs fell on the blameless ruins of Pompei.'[12]

Thus Maiuri's explanation was that the ancient site of Pompeii was bombed deliberately by the Allies because of their (mistaken) belief that it was occupied by German troops. He suggests that this belief was the result of untrue stories passed on by 'bad informants', presumably Italian civilian sources, as well as misinterpretation of aerial reconnaissance intelligence, with individual Germans and small groups of visitors mistaken for a garrison, and the restored roofing of ancient buildings misidentified as modern military structures. The date at which these views were held by local civilians is unclear, but the implication of Maiuri's account is that they were current by 15 September, when he was admitted to the hospital at Torre del Greco.

On 2 October 1943, the day after Allied troops entered Naples, Associated Press correspondent Relman Morin visited Maiuri in the city's National Museum. By then, the recuperating superintendent was lodging in the museum to protect it, and Morin interviewed him there. Their discussions included the museum itself and the fate of other heritage sites in Naples, but Maiuri also expressed his views on why Pompeii had been bombed. Again, he clearly believed that the site had been targeted deliberately, but mistakenly so:

> 'the tragic irony of the bombing of Pompei was that the Germans had never actually encamped inside the famous excavated city. [Maiuri] said they were only in the vicinity.'[13]

29 SEPTEMBER 1943: ALLIED CORRESPONDENTS AT THE LIBERATION OF POMPEII

As British troops entered Pompeii on 29 September 1943, driving out the German rear guard, Canadian BBC correspondent Matthew Henry Halton recorded a report for radio transmission, on the archaeological site itself.[14] It is clear from the recording that combat was still going on nearby.

> 'And early today I was able to enter Pompeii—you can hear the sound of enemy guns—with one of the first British units. . . . I speak now from Pompeii. I speak actually from the ruins of the Roman amphitheatre, nearly 2000 years old. I am standing on the high wall of this amphitheatre. It was used by the Germans as a gun position, with the result that we had to bomb it, and there is a gaping bomb crater right in the middle of the arena.'

On the same day, the American Associated Press correspondent Relman Morin filed a report from the site to be published a few days later in a number of US newspapers.[15] He stated,

> "The Germans had been using the ancient amphitheatre as a camp ground and the marks of their tanks and trucks were plainly visible all around the ruins. The amphitheatre itself was damaged by bombs and shells.'

Morin repeated this claim in the 2 October 1943 (publication date) report of his interview with Amedeo Maiuri in the National Museum of Naples.[16]

> *'EVIDENCE OF GERMAN VEHICLES*
>
> What appeared to be the unmistakable evidences of German military vehicles and tanks were visible inside the ruins last Wednesday [29 September] when this Associated Press correspondent was there. However, they may have been made since Maiuri's last visit.'

There is no other clear evidence that the archaeological site was actually occupied by German forces, and a report by another US correspondent present at the liberation of the site merely refers to German troops having been 'around' the ruins rather than in them.[17] Even if the site was occupied by German forces, nothing in the air forces' documentation relating to the bombing suggests the Allies were aware of it (or even incorrectly assessed it as such), let alone deliberately targeted it.

According to Maiuri, whose account shows that he was on the site regularly until his departure and wounding on 15 September, actual German military dispositions near (but not on) the site included an anti-tank gun under the bridge carrying the autostrada over SS18, a bridge which was actually targeted by Allied air attack (and hit—see Figure 20), but as part of the transportation infrastructure; an anti-aircraft battery along the road linking the Villa of the Mysteries to the Porta Marina area; and some trucks parked in the area between the piazza outside the Porta Marina and the parking area outside the amphitheatre gate.[18] The contemporary diary of local inhabitant Franco d'Alessandro refers to an unsuccessful 15 September petition from the modern town of Pompei to Colonel Scholl, commander of German forces in the Naples area, requesting him to 'move the batteries of field guns and concentrations of troops away, since the city had no anti-aircraft defences'.[19] However, this undoubtedly relates to the modern town rather than the archaeological site.

An RAF aerial reconnaissance photograph taken on 18 September 1943, in the time period when most of the bomb damage to the site was caused, shows no indications of vehicles or other military activity on the site, although its resolution is good enough to identify some motor vehicles elsewhere, on the road network around the site and beyond.[20] It is possible that some German forces entered the site temporarily at some point between c. 15 September (when Maiuri left) and Morin's arrival on 29 September, particularly as their rear guard withdrew through the area in the days before its liberation. The vehicle tracks cited by Morin may have reflected temporary parking of German vehicles in the amphitheatre area (one of the few parts of the site open enough for vehicle traffic, and mentioned by both Morin and Halton), particularly given Maiuri's report of trucks parked near the amphitheatre gate. Alternatively, they may have been left by Allied military traffic, since as Wheeler's account (below) shows, Allied vehicles were present on the site by 30 September at the latest. But, again, it should be emphasised that none of the Allied air forces' documentation (*Operations Record Books*, *Operations and Intelligence Summaries*) give any indication that they were aware of a German military presence on the site, let alone targeted it.

Another US correspondent who sought to explain the bombing was Herbert L. Matthews, of the *New York Times*. He, too, entered Pompeii with the first British troops, and his initial report for the newspaper states that '[Pompeii] was severely bombed. The Germans were in and around it for weeks'.[21] However, in a conversation in New York seven months later, with Francis Henry Taylor, director of the Metropolitan Museum of Art and a member of the Roberts Commission, and monuments officer Colonel Henry C. Newton, Matthews suggested

> 'The ruins were bombed in the belief that the Germans were using the ruins as a bivouac area and also for the storage of trucks and military material. . . . Dr. Maiuri, curator of the National Museum in Naples, made a personal investigation as soon as he had heard of the bombing and was told by the guards and the people in the vicinity . . . that there were no Germans in the ruins whatsoever but that they were in the general area.'[22]

Matthews's accounts show a shift away from the initial claim presented by other Allied correspondents and military personnel that the site *was* occupied by German troops, to the story, exemplified elsewhere by Maiuri, that it had been bombed because the Allies incorrectly *believed* it to be occupied by the Germans. Matthews, like Morin, subsequently met and spoke to Maiuri in Naples, and as an Italian speaker undoubtedly heard accounts from other Italian civilians. The shift in his explanation suggests he was influenced by Maiuri or other Italian contacts, and furthermore, that whatever evidence he had seen or heard of the alleged German occupation in Pompeii itself was not strong enough for him to continue in that belief.

30 SEPTEMBER 1943, MORTIMER WHEELER'S VISIT TO THE SITE

Another account of the site at the time of its liberation comes in the 1955 memoir of Mortimer Wheeler, an important figure in the development of British archaeology both before and after the Second World War, and also in the origins of Allied military cultural property protection.[23] In September 1943, Wheeler was a Royal Artillery brigadier commanding an anti-aircraft brigade. He reminisces, in a characteristically stagy account, looking back on a visit to Pompeii on the evening of 30 September:[24]

> 'More than six years previously in the dusk I had thrust my military caravan into the Amphitheatre gate of Pompeii as far as a new bomb-crater would allow me, and all night long that same Vesuvius had leered at me with an inflamed Cyclopean eye. At dawn I had walked into the city, a little gingerly, preceded by a sapper who thrust a bayonet ever and anon into the suspect soil. The reconstructed two-storey houses of the *nuovi scavi* [New Excavations] had been bombed with satisfactory nicety by our fellows up above: not their fault—they had been told that a German armoured division was "in Pompeii", and the map writes POMPEII across the blackened mass of the old city, whilst the insignificant modern townlet on the main road is merely *Pompeii*.'[25]

Clearly Wheeler held this view by December 1943, since a memo written by him at that time suggests that, in general, mitigation of damage caused to monuments by bombing was impossible,

> 'although at least one instance occurred recently (at POMPEII) where informed advice would not only have prevented the gratuitous destruction (mostly by bombing) of most of the ancient Roman city but might have aided the war effort by diverting the attack to the intended target (to the modern town of the same name).'[26]

Wheeler cited the damage to Pompeii (and his views on its cause) in advancing his arguments for more vigorous measures to protect monuments when he was back in London in December 1943, including to an All-Party Amenities Group in Parliament on December 6.[27] The New Excavations (the eastern part of the Via dell'Abbondanza), while damaged, certainly were not the main focus of bomb damage, although this was a widespread perception at the time.[28]

At first glance, it is tempting to take Wheeler as an authority on the reasons for the bombing because of his association with Allied wartime heritage protection, even though his explanation is one attested nowhere else. However, his military duties at the time meant he was far from the headquarters that planned the bombing, and there is no particular reason why he (or even any monuments officers serving at the time—see below, p. 102, on Fred Maxse) would have been aware of the 'real' explanation of the damage. Furthermore, this anecdote, perhaps more entertaining than instructive, accords well with Wheeler's critical and irascible attitude (demonstrated in contemporary documents, see Chapter 7) towards Allied headquarters and their failure to protect cultural heritage.

16 October 1943, Memoirs of Spike Milligan

Soon after the liberation of the site, Pompeii became a regular destination for Allied military personnel on leave. An early documented visit was that by Terence 'Spike' Milligan, a gunner (later lance-bombardier) in 56 Heavy Regiment, Royal Artillery, on 16 October 1943. In his wartime memoirs (first published in 1978), he recounts,

> 'I discovered that the Americans had actually bombed it! They believed German infantry were hiding in it! Not much damage had been done, museum staff were already at work trying to repair it. Bombing Pompeii!!! Why not the Pyramids, Germans might be hiding there?'[29]

While the comic hyperbole is obvious, and his account was published long after the event, Milligan's theme that the site was bombed (but by the Americans) because it was German-occupied (or rather, because the Allies believed it to be German-occupied) recurs, and corresponds well with the explanations advanced by other contemporary visitors.

c. 9 November 1943, 'Damage at Pompeii. British Officer's Account', in the *Times* [London]

On 9 November, a few weeks after Milligan's visit, the *Times* of London published an account attributed to a contemporary military visitor to the site, repeating the notion that Pompeii had been bombed because it was occupied by German troops:

> 'We have received from a British officer, who recently visited Pompeii, an account of the damage done to the place during September, when the Germans were encamped on the site and allied aircraft were obliged to treat it as a military objective. The following is a summary of damage observed . . .'[30]

12–15 APRIL 1944, ITALIAN STAFF AT POMPEII TO CAPTAIN F.H.J. MAXSE OF THE ALLIED MONUMENTS, FINE ARTS AND ARCHIVES SUB-COMMISSION

In the months after the bombing and liberation of Pompeii, Allied officers of the Monuments, Fine Arts and Archives Sub-Commission began inspection visits to the site to liaise with local antiquities service staff (including Maiuri) over its repair and re-opening, and to inspect work funded from Allied sources. One such visit, to Pompeii and Herculaneum (12–15 April 1944), was written up on 17 April 1944 by British monuments officer Captain Frederick H.J. Maxse (Royal Sussex Regiment—see Chapter 7). Perhaps surprisingly, Maxse relied on local Italian staff for an explanation of the damage. He reports,

> 'From the evidence given by the custodian and other personnel who witnessed the bombings it would appear that the object was to destroy a German Command Post in the Albergo [hotel] near the Porta Marina and the concentration of bombs round the Museum and the Forum suggests the likelihood of such an aim. There were a few German tanks near the Villa dei Misteri, but the only German troops inside the old city were visitors. There was no concentration of troops within the old city . . .'[31]

This echoes Maiuri's account of the Radio Londra broadcast, unsurprisingly, since Maiuri directed the staff on the site, they shared the experience of the bombing, and they undoubtedly discussed it. While Maxse doesn't specifically cite Maiuri as his source, Maiuri was certainly present for part of the visit, as Maxse records that he was taken to Herculaneum by the superintendent on 15 April. This anecdote is interesting in that it confounds our expectations of authority, as a British Army officer relies on local Italian civilians to explain damage inflicted by the officer's own air force. However, as with Wheeler, there is no reason why Maxse, a very junior officer within the institutions of Allied military government, would have had any special insight into the bombing. Indeed, even the 1946 final report of the Monuments, Fine Arts and Archives Sub-Commission describes the bombing of Pompeii as a mystery: 'There were no doubt reasons, but they have never been released.' That was true at the time, but the archival materials available today make those reasons quite clear.[32]

CONCLUSIONS

Thus we can observe the development of an alternative explanation for the bomb damage to ancient Pompeii in several different strands, from several different sources. The earliest is the Radio Londra broadcast of c. 25 August 1943, claiming that it was collateral damage resulting from an attack on a German military headquarters near (but not on) the archaeological site. There is good reason to believe that this story was created centrally by British sources specifically for Italian consumption, as propaganda implicating the Germans in the damage. This explanation was also recounted to Fred Maxse in the following April.

Next came a belief among local Italian civilians that German troops had occupied the archaeological site and that the Allies were bombing it deliberately to target those troops. If the chronology of Maiuri's memoir can be trusted, this story was in circulation by 15 September 1943, two days after the bombing began. Maiuri himself believed a variation of this explanation, namely that the Allies had bombed the archaeological site because they *incorrectly* believed it to be occupied by German troops. He clearly held this belief at the latest by 2 October, when he stated it in his interview with the journalist Relman Morin.

It is entirely plausible that the claim of German occupation of the site originated as Allied propaganda, spread deliberately to shift responsibility for its damage from the Allies onto the Germans, implicitly branding them as barbarous for using a heritage site for military purposes and so exposing it to damage.[33] While the idea that deliberately targeting a heritage site is more legitimate than accidental damage seems strange, as noted above, the key legal distinction in the 1907 Hague Convention was based on enemy occupation and consequent judgement of military necessity. Enemy occupation of an historic building or heritage site cancelled its protection from targeting, whereas collateral and accidental damage, at that time, constituted more of a grey area. Furthermore, a claim of deliberate targeting also masked (from both friendly civilian opinion and the enemy) the relative inaccuracy of contemporary Allied bombing.[34] Such a story might have been disseminated by another Radio Londra broadcast that (like so many others) happens to remain undocumented. Alternatively, this explanation of the bombing may have originated locally, among Italian civilians, perhaps as an embellishment and adaptation of the original Radio Londra broadcast relating to the bombing of 24/25 August, developed to explain the scale of Allied aerial activity in the Pompeii area from 13 September and/or the level of German military traffic on the roads around the site. Certainly the local civilian population came up with other stories relating to the bombing that owed nothing to Allied propaganda.[35]

The next strand emerges with the arrival of Allied correspondents and military visitors after the liberation of Pompeii. Again, we see claims that the site had been bombed deliberately because it was occupied by German troops (Halton, Morin, and the *Times* report of 9 November) or bombed deliberately because it was believed (incorrectly—echoing Maiuri's own view) that ancient Pompeii was occupied by German troops (Wheeler, Milligan). The latter view reflects the cynicism about intelligence and the competence of headquarters often found lower down in the military hierarchy. Again, this may reflect propaganda disseminated from London to justify the damage to the site. On the other hand, there is very little evidence of centralised creation or propagation of such a narrative, and the stories appear to originate at grassroots level in Pompeii itself. Even the *Times* report of 9 November cites an anonymous military visitor to Pompeii as its source for the explanation. While theoretically it is plausible that the Allies could have spread such a story, it seems more likely that correspondents and military visitors heard the explanation from locals and spread it among themselves, or that it emerged independently among those correspondents and military visitors trying to explain the damage and other marks of military activity visible to them.[36]

PART TWO

'Our Common Task'

CHAPTER 7

British Military Cultural Property Protection, from Cyrene to Syracuse

INTRODUCTION

As already noted, by the time Pompeii was bombed, an organisation established specifically to protect heritage and cultural institutions—what would become the Monuments, Fine Arts and Archives Sub-Commission, the 'Monuments Men'—already existed within Allied military government structures. The first official monuments officer, Captain Mason Hammond of the USAAF (a pre- and post-war Harvard University professor of ancient history and Latin), had arrived at Syracuse in Sicily as adviser on fine arts and monuments at the end of July 1943, some three weeks after Allied forces invaded the island.[1] Hammond set to work immediately, submitting his first report on local monuments on 2 August 1943 to the chief civil affairs officer in Sicily, British Major-General Lord Rennel of Rodd.[2] At about the same time, Hammond moved on to Palermo, where he established his base. On 6 September he was joined by his British counterpart, Captain F.H.J. ('Fred') Maxse. Despite their very limited resources (primarily lack of transport, a recurring problem for monuments officers in Italy), Hammond and Maxse undertook a series of inspection tours of monuments in Sicily on which they wrote reports. They liaised with the Italian antiquities and fine arts officials (with whom they enjoyed extremely good relationships) and with Allied military government officers who dispensed funds for repair activities.[3]

Despite the existence of this organisation, it had no discernible influence on the bombing in the vicinity of Pompeii in August and September 1943, nor much on the initial Allied occupation of mainland Italy (including Naples) through October to December 1943. There were a number of reasons for the organisation's deficiencies, most of which had their roots in its origins. In the first instance it was conceived as an organisation to protect monuments and fine arts in Allied-occupied areas rather than in enemy-occupied areas or in the battle area itself, and for this reason there was no initial liaison with Allied air forces command structures, a crucial factor in the bombing of Pompeii. This initial conception also affected the perceived role of monuments officers as an element of military government to be kept well to the rear of forces engaged in combat, rather than actively involved in the planning or execution of combat operations and their immediate aftermath. In 1947 Lt. Col. Sir Leonard Woolley could look back on the priorities and duties of the MFAA and list them as:

1. To preserve historic buildings, works of art and historical records, which 'could only be done by furnishing the ground and air forces with information as to the location of such monuments'.
2. To conserve monuments when they passed into Allied occupation.
3. To record German damage to monuments and art.

However, this was clearly a later rationalisation, based on the duties the MFAA eventually performed.[4] At the outset, role 2, protection of monuments in Allied-occupied areas, clearly was envisaged as the primary one, by the British at least, and provision of information to the air forces was not undertaken systematically or effectively. In great part, the expansion of the role was a result the problems encountered in Campania in the autumn of 1943 and subsequent review and reform that took root (albeit with mixed success) in 1944.

The aim of Chapters 7–8 is to examine the Second World War origins and development of the Monuments, Fine Arts and Archives organisation from its diverse roots, both military and civilian, British and US. This will introduce the structural factors that lay behind the organisation's deficiencies in autumn 1943 as manifested in the bombing of Pompeii and subsequent problems in Naples.[5] Chapters 9 and 10 then focus specifically on the relationship between the 'Monuments Men' and Allied Air Forces before and after the damage to Pompeii. Part Three examines the requisition and occupation of the National Museum in Naples as a case study of the wider problems encountered in Naples and as a clear case of what Eisenhower characterised as 'military convenience'. These problems of military requisition and occupation of historic buildings and cultural institutions should have been (and eventually were) prevented by effective cultural protection policy and practice, while the judgement of military necessity and the technical limitations that led to the bomb damage at Pompeii were less likely to have been outweighed by cultural protection considerations.

'WHAT THE ENGLISH DID IN CYRENAICA'

Even before the onset of World War Two, British military law as manifested in the War Office *Manual of Military Law* (1929, reprinted 1939) acknowledged a duty to protect historic buildings and cultural institutions so long as they were not used by an enemy for military purposes, as established by the terms of Hague Convention (IV) 1907.[6] However, no specific mechanisms or personnel were in place at the beginning of the war to ensure British military compliance with this body of international law, and it was not a high priority. For example, while nominal attempts were made to avoid the bombing of private property (i.e., civilian objects) in Germany early in the war, the level of achievable accuracy (far worse in northern Europe at that time than in Italy in September 1943) ensured that those attempts *were* purely nominal, and cultural sites in Germany (as in Britain) were destroyed and damaged by strategic bombing. No special restraints were placed on bombing policy to avoid damage to cultural sites (see Chapter 9), and, as we shall see, initially at least, few measures were put in place to protect museums and sites under British military control. Those that were realised were largely at the initiative of a few committed individuals rather than examples of the effective functioning of higher policy and planning. These factors in turn had implications for the lack of Allied cultural protection measures at the time of the bombing near Pompeii.

The first significant British military occupation of enemy territory came in February and March 1941. After defeating Italian forces in eastern Libya, British and Australian forces occupied the Italian colonial territory of Cyrenaica, with its important archaeological sites and collections at Cyrene, Apollonia, Tolmeta and Tocra. However, this occupation was short-lived, and a joint German-Italian counter-attack drove the British out and re-occupied the area in April 1941. Subsequently the Italian Ministero della Cultura Populare published a substantial illustrated book of propaganda, *Che cosa hanno fatto gli Inglesi in Cirenaica* ('What the English did in Cyrenaica').[7] Under headings such as 'Bestialità brittanica' ('British beastliness'), 'Città spogliate' ('Looted cities'), and 'Peggio delle belve' ('Worse than wild animals') were allegations that British and Australian forces had raped and murdered civilians in the occupied territory, mistreated Italian wounded, and looted, damaged and destroyed private houses, churches, mosques and hospitals. Among the photographs (captioned, but without detailed discussion in the text) were four that purported to depict damage inflicted on the museum at Cyrene by British and Australian troops. Three show broken pottery and statue fragments alongside intact sculptures, while the fourth shows graffiti on the museum walls.[8] The accusations (and attributions) of damage undoubtedly were exaggerated and distorted for propaganda purposes, something that was emphasised in a subsequent (1943) statement by the British Under-Secretary of State for War Arthur Henderson.[9] However, there was still some substance in the accusations, as admitted in a report by future monuments officer Major John Ward-Perkins after Cyrenaica was re-occupied by British forces at the end of 1942 (see p. 113).[10] The apparent damage in Cyrene and its exploitation for propaganda purposes raised concerns in the War Office in London that led to Sir Leonard Woolley being consulted for the first time on archaeological matters. Woolley was a well-known and important pre-war archaeologist, best known for his 1922–1934 excavations at the site of Ur in Iraq, an important factor in his knighthood in 1935. He was employed in another capacity in the War Office in 1941, initially with the rank of major. However, the consultation on archaeological issues became more official and more frequent, leading to his appointment as full-time archaeological adviser to the director of Civil Affairs at the War Office as a lieutenant-colonel on 1 November 1943.[11]

WHEELER AND WARD-PERKINS IN NORTH AFRICA

The next period of British occupation of Italian colonial territory came after the second battle of El Alamein in Egypt (October 1942), when the 8th Army had driven back Axis forces into Libya and eventually Tunisia, re-occupying Cyrenaica (November 1942) and taking control of Tripolitania (January 1943) with its important ancient sites of Lepcis Magna and Sabratha. Publically (and retrospectively), Under-Secretary of State Henderson claimed that British authorities had taken precautions to prevent damage to antiquities by British forces in Tripolitania and Cyrenaica during both occupations.[12] Woolley's post-war report states that before El Alamein, instructions had been sent to the British Army's deputy chief civil affairs officers for Cyrenaica and Tripolitania to take measures to preserve any archaeological sites that came under British occupation. Consequently, Woolley records, when Cyrene was re-occupied, the museum was secured and guards set on it.[13]

However, other evidence presents a less positive picture, and suggests that no significant preparations had been made to protect heritage sites, especially in Tripolitania, and what measures were taken were done at the local initiative of Lieutenant-Colonel Mortimer Wheeler, a Royal Artillery officer with extensive pre-war archaeological experience, who was there on active service at the time.

Wheeler had been a major in the Royal Artillery in the First World War, and was an important figure in the development of British archaeology both before and after the Second World War. He was director of the National Museum of Wales from 1924, and (with his wife Tessa Verney Wheeler) directed the excavation of important Roman sites such as the legionary fortress at Caerleon. He was keeper of the London Museum from 1926, and (again with Tessa Verney Wheeler) established the University of London Institute of Archaeology, which opened in 1937. Subsequently the Wheelers excavated at Verulamium and Maiden Castle. In 1944 he was appointed director-general of the Archaeological Survey of India. He was knighted in 1952, and was a central figure in the media popularisation of archaeology in the UK through his appearances in the popular TV panel quiz *Animal, Vegetable, Mineral?* as well as specifically archaeological programmes.

Wheeler was in North Africa in 1943 commanding 42nd (Light Anti-Aircraft) Regiment, Royal Artillery. He was what Lydia Carr, the biographer of his wife Tessa Verney Wheeler, describes as 'a man of overwhelming personality', 'aggressively male', in many respects egotistical, with 'a sharp tongue, and he did not censor himself'. As a commanding officer, he was something of a martinet. We have little detailed evidence of his role in protecting monuments in North Africa besides his own words, and one may suspect that he sometimes overstates his own role and importance. But undoubtedly his energy ('daemonic'; 'extraordinary and concentrated'), self-assurance, and tendency to take charge were valuable in this context. His friend and biographer Jacquetta Hawkes described it as 'exactly the kind of undertaking he relished, with its combination of archaeology and soldiering, the chance to exert authority, impose order to get something done, all under intense pressure'.[14]

In notes for a subsequent lecture (13 January 1944) to the Society of Antiquaries of London, Wheeler wrote of Henderson's parliamentary statement on monuments in Cyrenaica and Tripolitania:

> '*Reply dishonest.* [Wheeler's emphasis]. I don't impute personal dishonesty to the distinguished Secretary of State for War, but I do impute falsification on the part of those who supplied him with information. . . . On

> my entry into Tripoli I . . . found that no steps whatever had been envisaged for the protection of the libraries, buildings and sites of historical value in Tripolitania. . . . In Africa, in spite of spurious reassurances from on high, *NO* official steps whatever were taken to preserve any part of our cultural heritage.'[15]

While Wheeler's depiction of the situation was undoubtedly overstated (he himself admits, for example, that he would have been oblivious to any activities under way to protect museums and monuments in Cyrenaica as he passed through), self-centred and often indiscreet, it was probably closer to reality than Henderson's bland statement to Parliament.

Wheeler's own accounts describe how he became aware of the problem in January 1943 on the advance into Tripolitania, and, during a lull in his military duties after the entry into Tripoli, took the initiative to visit some of the key sites in the province along with his friend, archaeological colleague, and subordinate officer in the regiment, Major John Ward-Perkins.[16]

Ward-Perkins had been an assistant at the London Museum under Wheeler in 1936, and had undertaken excavations in his own right, notably of the Roman villa at Lockleys in Hertfordshire. He was appointed chair of archaeology at the Royal University of Malta in 1939, but returned to England to enlist in Wheeler's regiment, in which he served until 1943. He subsequently served as an MFAA officer in Italy (see Part Three), and after the Second World War, as director of the British School at Rome, was a key figure in the development of British archaeology in the Mediterranean.[17]

There followed what Wheeler described as 'a characteristic exemplification of British . . . improvisation'.[18] In Tripoli itself he and Ward-Perkins found that the office of the Italian archaeological authorities attached to the museum had been robbed of its cameras and its records dispersed, and so they prevailed upon senior officers to secure it (apparently unsuccessfully, as it was broken into a second time).[19] At Lepcis Magna, Wheeler reports, the small museum had been ransacked, the RAF was in the process of establishing a radar installation on the site, and graffiti and general wear and tear were inflicted on the site by both 'the momentarily idle troops of a famous division' and the local civilian population. The archaeologists' response was to post "Out of Bounds" notices around the site and to direct 'the vague attention of the military police' to them; to give impromptu lectures to the troops there; to persuade the RAF to locate the radar installation elsewhere; and to arrange with the local town major (the British military officer responsible for quartering troops and similar matters) to post a military sentry outside the museum.[20] The final stage in Wheeler's involvement was a visit to Sabratha (2 February 1943), where he and Ward-Perkins encountered Gennaro Pesce, the Italian colonial Inspector of Antiquities for Libya, with all his Italian staff, who had withdrawn westwards with the retreating Italian forces. Between them they drafted regulations providing for the return of the Italian inspectors to their sites and the re-appointment of Arab custodians to work under them.[21] This provides an early example of the effective cooperation between military cultural protection personnel and local officials that characterised MFAA operations in Italy.

Wheeler then left to resume his primary military duties in the Royal Artillery. However, aside from an interval commanding their old regiment at the battle of Mareth (southern Tunisia, late March 1943) when Wheeler had moved up to command a brigade, Ward-Perkins remained seconded to the British Military Administration on monuments duties for about four months in total, until August 1943.[22] In that time he effectively reconstituted the Italian antiquities organisation in Libya (with its Italian and Arab staff) to the point where it could significantly contribute to the protection and conservation of the major sites. He produced an impressive series of reports that not only dealt with the pressing and practical issues of site protection, but also considered the possible futures of archaeological research in both Tripolitania and Cyrenaica. While the reports' main focus was the protection of the major classical urban sites, they do include some discussion of (for example) Roman rural sites and also (albeit as a relatively minor part) record bomb damage to historic Arab houses and mosques.[23] The reports also suggest that protective measures met with mixed success. For example, what Ward-Perkins describes as the sole instance of damage to a 'first class monument' in Tripolitania, namely to the frieze and one pilaster of the Arch of Septimius Severus at Lepcis Magna, occurred in June 1943, after the custodians had been put back in place. Both Lepcis Magna and Sabratha suffered low-level damage from troops quartered nearby that Ward-Perkins describes as 'considerable and cumulatively serious', which potentially exposed British forces to both enemy propaganda and domestic and neutral criticism.[24] In August 1943 Ward-Perkins was invalided to Cairo, but he returned to monuments duties in Italy in December 1943, and spent the rest of the war in that role.

In his January 1944 report to the Society of Antiquaries, Mortimer Wheeler claims that the protection of monuments in Libya essentially collapsed once Ward-Perkins had left. Woolley, on the other hand, suggests a relatively smooth transition of responsibilities to others within the administration. The reality is likely to have been somewhere between the two, with Wheeler by then out of direct touch with events, cynical after his experiences in Italy (see below, pp. 116–21) and dramatising the situation to win support from his civilian audience for more effective measures; Woolley's account is a bland official one, masking the practical difficulties encountered on the ground. While undoubtedly overstated, Wheeler's picture is, again, is perhaps closer to reality than Woolley's.[25]

The key themes and outcomes of this initial British military engagement with cultural property protection are that it was, fundamentally, a largely grassroots and entirely military undertaking; that it focused on the protection of heritage sites under occupation rather than affecting planning for combat or bombing; that it undoubtedly influenced Ward-Perkins's later practical approach to monuments protection in Italy; and that it affected the way Wheeler presented the issues and problems to civilian authorities in London on his return towards the end of 1943.

The British population had been mobilised to a very great extent by the end of 1942, particularly males of military age, and even males of above normal military age, especially men with previous military experience, typically from the First World War. Thus Wheeler (commanding a unit in combat) and Woolley (in the War Office) were 53 and 63 years of age, respectively. Ward-Perkins was 32 (relatively young for a British monuments officer), Major P.K. Baillie Reynolds (the first director of the MFAA Sub-Commission in Sicily and Italy) was 48, Maxse was 38 and Captain Edward Croft-Murray 36.[26] All of them had relevant civilian experience, since the scale of national mobilisation meant a very wide range of occupations was represented in the wartime British armed forces. The length of time Britain had been at war also meant that British monuments officers invariably had several years of military service in other capacities before their involvement with wartime heritage protection. For these reasons it is hardly surprising that British initiatives in this area emerged from the Army (but not at a senior level among regular officers) and tended to work within familiar military structures.[27]

Ward-Perkins's and Wheeler's activities in North Africa were aimed fundamentally at protecting sites on the ground and under British military occupation. Their concerns did not affect the planning of operations, particularly not air operations, and Ward-Perkins's reports make hardly any reference to bombing at all, besides listing some bomb damage to buildings in Tripoli. All this reinforced the existing perception of heritage protection (such as it was) as an aspect of military government and civil affairs. Their engagement with the local (Italian, colonial) archaeological authorities also prefigures the emphasis Ward-Perkins placed on their role and importance in the course of his Italian experience, and the similar emphasis placed on military cooperation with local civilian authorities in the 1954 Hague Convention.[28]

'IT WAS MY INTENTION TO GO STRAIGHT TO THE PRIME MINISTER': WHEELER'S LOBBYING IN LONDON

Mortimer Wheeler had returned to his official military duties in February 1943 and during the Tunisian campaign (March–May 1943) moved up from command of his own regiment to that of the 8th Army's anti-aircraft brigade as a brigadier. He then commanded 12th Anti-Aircraft Brigade in 10 (British) Corps (part of the US 5th Army) for the Salerno landings in September 1943. He left Italy on 8 November 1943, spending four months in London before setting out to become director-general of the Archaeological Survey of India.[29] In that time, he engaged with the issue of protecting cultural heritage against war damage on three more occasions: in the planning of the Allied invasion of Sicily; in his experiences in Italy, including his visit to Pompeii (see Chapter 6, above); and in lobbying for more effective protection on heritage during his stay in London in November 1943 to February 1944. The first two are considered in their wider contexts below, but it is worth evaluating Wheeler's lobbying activities at this point, as they reflect his experiences in Africa and Italy and reinforce the idea of military cultural property protection as something relating to occupation duties rather than the planning of operations and particularly air attack.

Wheeler was lobbying for the development of centralised, coherent and regular British military cultural protection efforts as early as June 1943. According to his autobiography, he contrived a meeting in Cairo to discuss the issue with Lord Harlech (William Ormsby-Gore—a politician with strong archaeological interests, known to Wheeler from the establishment of the Institute of Archaeology in London), who was en route to London from his post as high commissioner to South Africa. Wheeler also records that in June 1943 he wrote to the president of the Society of Antiquaries of London (described by Wheeler, rather extravagantly, as 'the titular head of all archaeology'), of which Wheeler himself was a Council member, setting out a scheme for 'a small but properly-thought-out organization for the preservation of works of art and antiquity in newly occupied European territories'.[30] Wheeler later claimed that on his return to London

> 'It was my intention to go straight to the Prime Minister and lay the matter before him. Unfortunately Mr. Churchill had chosen the moment to discuss less important matters with Mr. Roosevelt and Mr. Stalin in other parts of the world, and I had therefore to content myself with going to the War Office and discussing the matter with the Permanent Under Secretary of State and the Directorate of Civil Affairs.'[31]

While clearly there was humorous intent in his reference to Churchill's absence at the Teheran Conference, Wheeler's self-confidence was such that he may actually have considered trying to take his views to the prime minister. At any rate, he did present his views to an All-Party Amenities Group of members of the House of Commons and House of Lords on 6 December at the invitation of Conservative member of Parliament E.H. (Edward) Keeling, himself a RAF Volunteer Reserve officer. He also discussed the issues over lunch on 9 December with Pierson Dixon, principal private secretary to Foreign Secretary Anthony Eden. This lobbying provoked a flurry of correspondence between interested parties including Keeling, Secretary of State for Air Sir Archibald Sinclair, Deputy Prime Minister Clement Attlee, J.G. (James) Mann (director of the Wallace Collection) and Sir John Forsdyke, director of the British Museum, circulating copies of a report Wheeler had written in November presenting his views on the preservation of historic buildings and collections in the war zone.[32] Then, on January 13, Wheeler gave a paper entitled *Archaeology in the War Zone: Facts and Needs* to Fellows and visitors at the Society of Antiquaries of London.[33]

There are degrees of overlap between Wheeler's June 1943 letter, the November 1943 report and the January 1944 paper. All draw on, and to a greater or lesser extent recount, his own experiences in North Africa and Italy. Wheeler envisaged an organisation of archaeologically qualified officers (lieutenant-colonels or majors) serving under a War Office archaeological adviser of sufficient rank and authority (a brigadier) to make personal contact with senior commanders in the field. Each officer would be assigned to a particular geographic district (he gives 'Tripolitania and Cyrenaica', 'Sicily and Calabria' and 'central Italy' as examples), and that officer would 'enter . . . with the foremost troops' as a forward element of military government, with a small staff (typically one or two clerks), a car (transport was a recurring problem for monuments officers in Italy) and able to draw on half a dozen or so military police ('essential'). The district officer would institute measures according to a prepared scheme to protect against 'wilful, unnecessary and unintelligent damage' by occupying troops and civilian looting; reconstitute and reorganise the relevant local heritage authorities; and (mentioned in the November and January documents) supervise initial repairs to damaged structures. District officers should be chosen not just on the basis of technical knowledge, but also 'their *energy* and power of dealing with men'.[34] Rigid distribution of officers to geographical regions or districts was initially practiced by the MFAA in Italy, and this was a problem when urgent needs for personnel were actually focused in just one or two areas, such as Naples. Subsequently this was changed to a more flexible, task-organised structure (see Part Three). The size of the area Wheeler suggested a single officer might supervise was probably unrealistic, and derived from the fairly benign situation he had encountered in North Africa. On the other hand, Wheeler recognised the dangers to heritage in the initial phase of occupation and the need to have the district officer 'enter . . . with the foremost troops'. Failure to have MFAA specialists in the forefront of military occupation was a significant problem in Naples (again, see Part Three).

However, Wheeler's recommendations also show development in his thought from June 1943 to January, particularly the attention he pays to damage by bombing. In part this must have been brought about by his own changing responses to different forms of war damage encountered in different parts of the Mediterranean theatre, but also due to discussions with others in London for whom bomb damage to heritage was a particular concern (see below, Chapter 9). Wheeler's June 1943 letter on the topic envisages his organisation as concerned solely with occupation duties, and has nothing to say about damage in combat or bombing at all. The November report presents damage as occurring in three stages. 'The immediate wake of an attack' and 'the subsequent period of occupation' are the second and third stages respectively, but the first stage is characterised as caused 'particularly by bombing, during the preparation of an attack'. Clearly this reflects the differences between Wheeler's experiences in North Africa, on the one hand, and in the Naples area, where bomb damage had been extensive, on the other. Nevertheless, Wheeler is sceptical about how often monuments officers might (or should?) be able to intervene against perceptions of military necessity in such instances—'it will obviously be impossible, normally, to vary the military plan to save a monument of art and antiquity'. However, he notes, from time to time 'some damage can be obviated in the planning of an operation, if good reason can be shown from an authoritative source'. He goes on to cite his erroneous explanation for the bombing of Pompeii (see Chapter 6 above), implying that a suitably qualified officer could have pointed out the map-reading error that, he believed, had caused it.[35]

Wheeler's Society of Antiquaries paper (January 1944) goes much further in its discussion of bombing. This time the stages of conflict in which damage might occur are characterised as four: strategic bombing, tactical bombing and shelling, the attack, and the aftermath. Wheeler states that 'whilst it is obviously impossible to hamstring our attack by forbidding the flattening of important objectives whatever their historical or artistic importance, occasions will arise when some mitigation of unthinking, blind destruction is perfectly feasible'. He refers to the then-recent (December 1943) bombing of railway targets in Padua, and argues that if such attacks were carefully planned, it might be possible to bomb a railway line 'equally effectively a mile or two further off'.[36] Undoubtedly Wheeler's increased attention to bombing was the result of his discussions with Keeling and others who had been focusing primarily on this issue since September 1943 or earlier. Indeed, the notion that information provided by heritage experts might enable the air forces to modify their targeting to avoid historical structures without adverse operational effects is a recurring theme in their correspondence.[37] Given his scheme for distribution of officers by district, it is not clear whom Wheeler envisaged providing this input into planning air operations. However, in the January paper he argues that Italy might need 20 officers, more personnel than implied by the November report. Ultimately in Italy a strict distribution by administrative regions would have required about 14 monuments officers, so 20 allowed for some supernumeraries, who might have served with army and air forces headquarters in a planning function.[38] Wheeler also makes the point that Italian authorities had taken largely effective precautions, particularly in situ, to minimise bomb damage.[39]

Of course by January (and even in November), Wheeler knew that a War Office structure for protection of heritage in war zones had been established, with Woolley (with whom he had some contact) as archaeological adviser, but of a lower rank than Wheeler felt necessary; and that 'two or three other officers of lesser rank' (initially Maxse and Baillie Reynolds) had also been sent out to Italy. In his paper he urged the Fellows of the Society of Antiquaries to support these personnel. On the other hand, he also emphasised the need to lobby Parliament and for political support for the monuments and fine arts organisation's work at the very top, from Churchill himself and the Cabinet, something which never emerged with the clarity he felt necessary. Finally, Wheeler urged that the military organisation 'must be left free to operate *without a trail of committees or commissions behind it. Choose the right men*, check up on them from time to time, but don't hamper them with a lot of useless clutter in the form of committees' [Wheeler's emphasis].[40] This reflected Wheeler's own military experience and preference for vigorous action, although there was a certain irony in that some of his correspondents and listeners would lobby for, and serve in, such a civilian committee, the Macmillan Committee, later that year.

PLANNING FOR SICILY

Back in June 1943, before his participation in the Salerno landings and subsequent return to England, Wheeler had briefly engaged with the issue of cultural protection for the Allied invasion of Sicily, which began on 9/10 July 1943. According to Wheeler's account, he had been sent to a headquarters in Cairo engaged in planning the operation, where he encountered Lieutenant-Colonel Lord Gerald Wellesley, a former diplomat, architect and Surveyor of the King's Works of Art who was to be senior civil affairs officer for Catania after the invasion. Wellesley supposedly knew nothing of any precautions to protect monuments in Sicily, and Wheeler's account makes great play of his own efforts to secure a copy of the Baedeker travel guide to Sicily as a starting point without undermining the secrecy of the planned invasion.[41]

However, Wheeler exaggerates for dramatic effect, as such planning was certainly undertaken, regardless of whether or not he knew about it. The military government plan prepared by General Alexander's (15th Army Group) planning headquarters in June 1943 includes a page of recommendations regarding monuments and *General Administrative Instruction No. 8* on the topic for distribution to (non-specialist) civil affairs officers.[42] The summary opens by stating,

> 'It is the policy of AMGOT [Allied Military Government of Occupied Territories] to insure by every means at its disposal that local archives, historical and classical monuments and objects of art shall be preserved.'

It goes on to note that the Allied chief civil affairs officer in Sicily, British Major-General Lord Rennel of Rodd, would be advised by one or more specialist antiquities and fine arts officers on his staff (ultimately these would be Hammond and Maxse), that purchase and export of 'classical objects of art' by military personnel or others were to be prohibited, that civil affairs officers (in general, rather than the specialists in particular) would advise tactical officers on cultural sites to be placed out of bounds, and that museums and similar sites should be closed and only re-opened with AMGOT consent after appropriate security arrangements had been made. *General Administrative Instruction No. 8* includes a definition of 'monuments': any site, building or structure, public, ecclesiastical or private 'whose historic, cultural, artistic, traditional or sentimental value render its protection and preservation a matter of public interest', including ruins, museums, libraries, churches, memorials, palaces and the like. It also provides for civil affairs officers to inspect monuments to report damage and make provision for repair; to take precautions (notices, guards and similar) to protect monuments from damage or defacement by military personnel or civilians and to ensure that the perpetrators of any such damage be punished by appropriate authorities. It also indicates that civil affairs officers should submit reports through military channels to the chief civil affairs officer for the use of the advisers on Fine Arts and Monuments.

In addition to this, *AIM Planning Instruction No. 12* on civil affairs in Sicily (produced by the same headquarters and dated 14 June 1943) was earmarked for wide distribution to combat formations as well as civil affairs specialists. This included prominent references to the protection of monuments and cultural institutions, noting that both the British and American governments 'have set great store on the preservation and security of ancient monuments' as counter-propaganda to (alleged) German mistreatment of such things. Besides repeating some of the provisions already noted in the military government plan, the planning instruction included an attached sheet of 'DO's and DON'T's' intended for wider distribution. These exhorted officers and men (as appropriate) to 'respect public and private property'; to post guards on public buildings including museums to prevent looting; not to allow or turn a blind eye to 'looting, theft or trafficking in money, works of art or valuables'; and not to 'destroy, or allow to be destroyed or removed, archives, documents or books'.[43]

These planning documents were supplemented by brief lists of historic buildings included in the 'Works of Art' section of the *Sicily Zone Handbook* produced in June 1943 by the [British] War Office Directorate of Civil Affairs, for Allied Military Government use. This listed just 13 historic buildings and sites in seven locations on the island, including Palermo, Syracuse, Agrigento and Segesta.[44] The Zone Handbook Lists were significantly shorter than the US 'Harvard Lists' and 'Frick Maps' (see Chapter 8), and unlike them, made no attempt to rank sites on their importance.

Finally, *A Soldier's Guide to Sicily* of 17 pages was produced by Mediterranean Expeditionary Force Headquarters in June 1943, and was intended (at least) to be distributed to every officer. This is brief but wide-ranging in its content, covering the history, topography, climate and people of the island, and addressing practical issues such as language and occupation currency. A few pages, however, also contain very basic information on antiquities and historic architecture in the towns.[45]

Mortimer Wheeler also recounts that while he was in Cairo, he received an indication that

> 'Two Americans, whose names meant nothing to us, were, somewhat vaguely as it seemed, going to keep an eye upon the churches, temples and collections of Sicily. We glanced sceptically at one another, admitting however that the Americans were at any rate half a move ahead of us.'

One of those Americans was, of course, Mason Hammond, who had already made a substantial contribution to Allied preparations, including drafting of *General Administrative Instruction No. 8*.[46] There were many problems with Allied monuments protection in Sicily, but they were not caused by the fact that only Mortimer Wheeler had foreseen the issue. The main problems were the low priority accorded to the issue, limited resources, and failure to implement the provisions and legal protections that already existed, particularly with regard to military discipline. All of these recurred early in the invasion and occupation of mainland Italy. In particular the AMGOT plan foresees many basic activities for the protection of heritage being undertaken by non-specialist civil affairs officers, when in practice they were too busy to provide for these duties that inevitably fell to the (also) overstretched specialist monuments and fine arts advisers. But perhaps the worst problem was the continuing focus on protection as a facet of occupation duties, without proper liaison with air forces' operational planning, since the vast majority of damage to heritage in Sicily was bomb damage to historic churches and buildings in the towns.[47]

BRITISH CIVILIAN ENGAGEMENT WITH CULTURAL PROPERTY PROTECTION: THE MACMILLAN COMMITTEE

Despite the interest in protecting cultural heritage in British museum and political circles apparent in late 1943, at the time of Wheeler's lobbying in London (above), much of it in response to the damage caused to cultural sites in Italy by bombing (see Chapter 9), there was never a real British equivalent of the US civilian committee, the Roberts Commission, that was so prominent in American cultural property protection initiatives (discussed in Chapter 8). The closest equivalent was the Macmillan Committee, which was created nearly a year after the US commission, and was much more limited in its influence and role.

Named for its chair, Lord Macmillan, this was more correctly the British Committee on the Preservation and Restitution of Works of Art, Archives and Other Material in Enemy Hands, and was established on 8 May 1944. Many of its members were museum directors and similar people who had been involved in the late 1943 discussions preceding and relating to Wheeler's lobbying. Included were J.G. Mann of the Wallace Collection, Sir Kenneth Clark (National Gallery), Sir John Forsdyke (British Museum), Sir Eric Maclagan (Victoria & Albert Museum), historian Professor G.M. Trevelyan and the 7th Duke of Wellington, whom we last met as Lieutenant-Colonel Lord Gerald Wellesley with Mortimer Wheeler in Cairo. Wellesley had inherited the title on the death of his nephew, Henry, 6th Duke of Wellington, at Salerno in September. While the Macmillan Committee was envisaged by some as a British counterpart to the Roberts Commission, its terms of service specifically limited its activities to post-war restitution issues. While its members sometimes sought to extend their remit to issues like pre-emptive protection and bomb damage that were certainly discussed at their meetings (see Chapter 9), such interests were limited by the terms of service.[48]

CONCLUSION

While this chapter has taken us away from the bombing that damaged Pompeii both geographically and chronologically, it contributes to setting that damage in the wider context of wartime cultural property protection. One important theme emerges that goes some way towards explaining the lack of consideration paid to protecting the archaeological site of Pompeii in attacking targets nearby. British military cultural protection policy initially was envisaged as an activity to be undertaken in occupied territories, primarily to protect heritage sites from damage and looting by troops and the local civilian population. This was the focus of the early activities by Wheeler and Ward-Perkins that in turn influenced planning for the occupation of Sicily and the Italian mainland. Thus, at the time of the damage to Pompeii, cultural protection considerations played no role in the planning of operations, either on land or (of particular importance to Pompeii) in the air. The following chapter focuses on the development of American cultural property protection in parallel with the British activities just discussed.

CHAPTER 8

The Development of US Wartime Heritage Protection, 1942 to September 1943

The development of US efforts to protect heritage sites and cultural institutions in European (and later global) war zones took a rather different path from those of the British. While the latter emerged to a great extent in-theatre and at the initiative of archaeologists already serving in the British Army, the former began at the top, among politicians and leading figures in the nation's museums, arts and culture. In the US, civilian committees played an important role in developing and supporting military efforts, initially the Harvard Group—American Defense and the Committee of the American Council of Learned Societies (ACLS) on Protection of Cultural Treasures in War Areas. In June 1943 (but announced publically only in August), the 'Roberts Commission' (the American Commission for the Protection and Salvage of Artistic and Historic Monuments in War Areas) came into being.[1]

In many respects, the activities of these groups provide a model for how civilian academics might support military cultural property protection, especially by providing information as 'cultural intelligence'. However, they also show up some misunderstandings, relating, for example, to the format in which that information was provided.

THE CREATION OF THE ROBERTS COMMISSION

Correspondence relating to the development of a civilian commission in the US was exchanged between individuals connected with the National Gallery in Washington DC in late 1942, with its director David E. Finley Jr. and chief curator John Walker proposing the establishment of such an organisation to Chief Justice Harlan Stone, who was a trustee of the gallery. On 8 December 1942, Stone wrote to President Franklin D. Roosevelt, citing the discussions at the National Gallery and consultation with William Bell Dinsmoor Sr. (a Greek archaeology professor at Columbia University) and Francis Henry Taylor, director of the Metropolitan Museum of Art in New

York, and enclosing a memo with recommendations on the structure and remit of the commission. Roosevelt responded on 28 December, expressing his appreciation of the initiative taken by the National Gallery in formulating 'this interesting proposal', which he passed on to the Joint Chiefs of Staff and other government agencies for comment. Further response came in April, when Roosevelt conveyed the view of Admiral Leahy (chairman of the Joint Chiefs of Staff) that 'while this undertaking does not appear to promise any military advantage', the Joint Chiefs would direct military commanders 'to give the Committee every practical assistance that does not interfere with their military operations'. The president also noted that former New York State governor Herbert H. Lehman, now the US State Department's director of foreign relief and rehabilitation operations, was in favour.[2] In June 1943 a lengthy letter to the president from Secretary of State Cordell Hull, recommending the establishment of the committee along the lines proposed by Walker and Stone, brought it closer to reality, and in July, potential members were solicited to serve.[3] However, the commission did not meet for the first time (in the National Gallery, in Washington DC) until 25 August 1943, when the existence of 'the American Commission for the Protection and Salvage of Artistic Monuments in Europe' was publicised in a press release (the 'in Europe' of its title changing to 'in War Areas' in February 1944, when the Far East came into its remit).[4]

That press release characterises the commission in rather general terms as 'a channel for communication' between the government and civilian experts 'in a position to furnish information and services relative to the work of the Commission', but specifically refers to its function in coordinating existing volunteer committees (such as the ACLS Committee and the Harvard Group—see below) and creating subcommittees for 'the collection of material which will be of special value to the Army in its military operations'. Earlier statements regarding the commission's potential functions, such as Cordell Hull's June 1943 letter to the president (in turn based on concepts originating at the National Gallery in late 1942), take a rather different perspective. Hull's letter emphasises the commission's role in providing the Army General Staff with appropriately qualified personnel ('museum officials and art historians') 'so that, so far as is consistent with military necessity, works of cultural value may be protected in countries occupied by armies of the United Nations'. Like initial British efforts, the emphasis was on preventing damage caused by occupation of territory by friendly forces rather than, for example, by Allied bombing of enemy-held territory.[5] The production of lists of art and monuments to be protected is not specifically mentioned here, although the fact that the commission was tasked with coordinating volunteer committees (the Harvard Group, the ACLS Committee) that were already doing so presupposes it. Nor is protection against bombing particularly mentioned, although the Army Air Force was among the intended recipients of these materials, which suggests that the commission's members had this in mind, although they regularly (and justifiably) expressed concern over whether these were actually reaching the Air Force and in use for their intended purpose.[6] By the end of the war, a retrospective account of the Roberts Commission's functions included 'to prepare materials relevant to the protection and salvage of artistic and historic monuments, such as lists of those monuments, maps for the use of Civil Affairs Officers and the USAAF', although at the time Pompeii was bombed in August and September 1943, its ability to influence air forces and bombing was more problematic (see pp. 142–45; 161–65).

The two principal civilian volunteer committees that came to be coordinated by (and to some extent, subsumed into) the Roberts Commission were the Harvard Group—American Defense and the ACLS Committee.

HARVARD GROUP—AMERICAN DEFENSE

While the Harvard Group–American Defense came into being as early as 1940, its principal activities for the protection of European art and monuments developed in March 1943, when it established a subcommittee in response to requests from the US Army's Office of the Provost Marshal General for information about art and monuments that might need protection from war damage. The subcommittee's members were Paul J. Sachs (of Harvard's Fogg Art Museum), Hugh O'Neill Hencken (curator of European archaeology at the Peabody Museum) and W.G. Constable (curator at the Boston Museum of Fine Art).[7] The group's primary activity was production of geographical lists of monuments and other cultural heritage to be protected, for submission to the War Department for distribution to, and use by, U.S. armed forces. A 1945 report on the history of the group (read and approved by Sachs) states that 61 scholars with special knowledge of the areas covered were contacted and provided information in response. It is clear from other evidence that this was done at least partially by questionnaire. Burke (the author of the 1945 report) describes how:

> 'each list was prepared by individuals or groups with special knowledge of the countries concerned, and includes material not to be found in guidebooks. Throughout, special care was taken to include material which for any reason is treasured or revered by the local population, quite apart from any general historical or artistic interest.'

The first set of the group's 'Harvard Lists'—of Sicily—was sent to the War Department on 12 June 1943.[8]

The excavated site of Pompeii is included in the 'Harvard List' for the Region of Campania.[9] The Campania 'Long List' comprises 27 typescript pages with 316 sites, monuments and cultural institutions in 105 locations throughout the region, 60 of the entries being in the city of Naples itself. The list includes churches, palaces, castles, monasteries, museums and galleries, libraries and archives, ancient remains and sites of various kinds, scientific institutions, catacombs and cemeteries, theatres, villas, arches, towers, seminaries and public statues. These were assigned star rankings reflecting their importance as perceived by the scholars who compiled the lists, from *** (three-star—most important) to zero-star (important enough to be on the list, but less important than other listed monuments).[10] The compilation of the 'Harvard Lists' for Italy was directed by Doro Levi, an Italian Jewish scholar of classical archaeology who had emigrated in 1938 to the US, based initially at Princeton University's Institute for Advanced Study. He was assisted by other émigré scholars and Americans with expertise and experience of Italian archaeology and art history, including the Roman archaeologists Marion E. Blake, who had returned to the US from the American Academy at Rome on Italy's entry into the war, Herbert Bloch, and Karl Lehmann.[11] Pompeii was one of only seven three-star monuments (so 'of extreme importance') in the Campania lists that also include 37 two-star, 72 one-star and 200 zero-star entries.[12] The entry for the archaeological site is characteristically brief:

> '*** Ancient Pompeii. The most famous ruins of a Roman town, buried during the eruption of Mt. Vesuvius in 79 A.D., now largely excavated. Museum within excavations.'

Besides the ancient site, the list also includes the 19th-century 'Santuario' (Chiesa della Santuario della Madonna del Rosario) in the modern town adjacent to the site, arguably of greater importance to both the local and national identity of modern Pompei at that time than the Roman city, and also the Museo Vesuviano and observatory on the slopes of the volcano outside the town. Both of these were zero-star monuments. The ancient Pompeii entry also appears in a condensed version of the Harvard Group list, the *Short List of Monuments: Italy*, and subsequently (after the bombing of Pompeii) these served as the basis for, and overlapped with, a range of other documentation used by Allied armed forces, including the so-called Zone Handbook Lists and formal printed Civil Affairs handbooks.[13]

THE ACLS COMMITTEE

The Committee of the American Council of Learned Societies (ACLS) on Protection of Cultural Treasures in War Areas ('the ACLS Committee') met in full for the first time in New York on 25 June 1943, the result of a decision made by the executive committee of the ACLS in January of that year. That committee voted to allow Columbia University's Professor William Bell Dinsmoor (president of the Archaeological Institute of America, who worked primarily on Greek temple architecture) and Charles Rufus Morey (a Princeton scholar of early Christian art) to co-opt additional members.[14] With Dinsmoor as chair, the ACLS Committee eventually included Sumner McKnight Crosby, a Yale University professor specialising in French medieval architecture; Francis H. Taylor, director of the Metropolitan Museum of Art; David E. Finley (National Gallery); Archibald Macleish (Librarian of Congress); Solon H. Buck (National Archives); and Horace Jayne (a curator of Far Eastern art at the Metropolitan Museum). The committee's activities were funded by a grant from the Rockefeller Foundation, and it was based in the Frick Art Reference Library in New York, whose facilities were provided for the committee's use from July 1943 by its founder, Helen Clay Frick. Dinsmoor, Crosby and Morey were core members of the committee who worked at the Frick on a regular basis, along with (largely unnamed) technical staff and volunteer researchers.[15] Scholars named as contributors to the committee's work include Gisela Richter, curator of Greek and Roman art at the Metropolitan Museum, and Doro Levi, who also contributed to the Harvard lists.

The ACLS Committee's general function is defined in contemporary documents as 'to be of assistance in the conservation of the cultural material in war areas during and after the war', and prominent among its more specific aims in those early documents is the recommendation to the Civil Affairs Division of the War Department of individuals with specialist knowledge of cultural heritage who might serve as 'cultural officers'. However, that particular function was soon subsumed under the Roberts Commission's roles, and, alongside its activities to educate and train civil affairs officers in cultural matters (see below) the most distinctive products of the ACLS Committee were its 'Frick Maps'. These maps recorded the locations of cultural sites on a regional and town-by-town level, keyed in to concise lists of those sites. They complemented the Harvard Lists, and used the same star ranking system. They drew on card indexes compiled from a combination of sources, including the Harvard Lists, questionnaires sent to scholars (like those used by the Harvard Group), and publically available sources such as Baedeker and Touring Club Italiano guidebooks (see below). Their coverage of Italy was complete by early August 1943, with 162 maps of Italian cities or sites, 17 of which were in Sicily. Multiple photostat copies of each map produced by the committee (3 of each for Sicily, 6 of each for Italy) were sent initially to the Civil Affairs Division in Washington, DC—for forwarding to appropriate military headquarters and personnel. Ancient Pompeii, for example, was included in the 'Naples Suburban-East' map sheet, the outline of the site blocked out in the bottom corner of a map that covered a much larger area in the environs of Naples, including all of Mount Vesuvius. This is clearly based directly on the Touring Club Italiano's contemporary map of the eastern suburbs of Naples (Figures 22 and 23).[16] Ancient Pompeii is listed by name in the accompanying text, with its three-star ranking and a grid reference that keys its location to the map.[17] By January 1944, the ACLS Committee had produced a total of 59 regional maps (with 34 in production) and 345 city maps (with 109 in preparation) for 13 European countries.[18] At the same time, the committee began work on maps for China, Indo-China, Japan, Korea and Thailand under the direction of Horace Jayne. The original photostat maps subsequently were incorporated into printed atlas volumes supplementing lists of cultural sites in US Army Civil Affairs handbooks.

Despite all the emphasis on scholarly participation in the production of the ACLS maps, and on expert and precise knowledge of the heritage recorded (particularly in accounts produced for journalists and the general military community), much of the information provided came from publically available sources. The report on the ACLS committee's activities for July 1943 mentions the use of contemporary (up to 1940) Touring Club Ital-

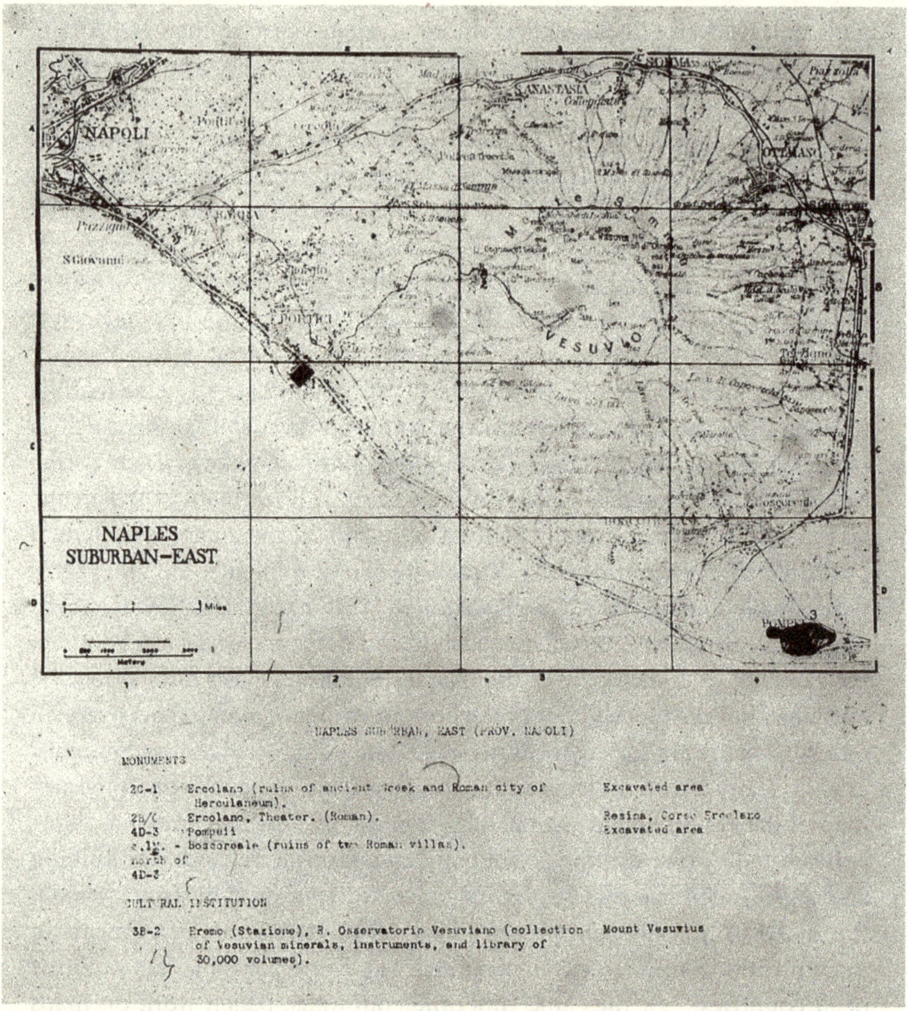

Figure 22: The 'Naples Suburban-East' sheet of the ACLS 'Frick Maps', showing the ancient site of Pompeii as the small inked area in the lower right corner. NARA M1944, RG 239/0156, 'Maps Showing Areas to Be Spared Destruction/Europe: Hungary-Italy', *Naples Suburban-East.*

iano (TCI) guidebooks. It also states that the 'Frick Maps' were produced by screening the original maps with tracing paper, on which monuments were marked and numbered in black, with the addition of grid lines, a scale and north arrow as necessary. This is certainly visible in the maps themselves. For example, the Frick Map of Pozzuoli clearly originated as a photostat of the TCI map 'Pozzuoli e la Solfatara' (Figures 24 and 25). Most of the his-

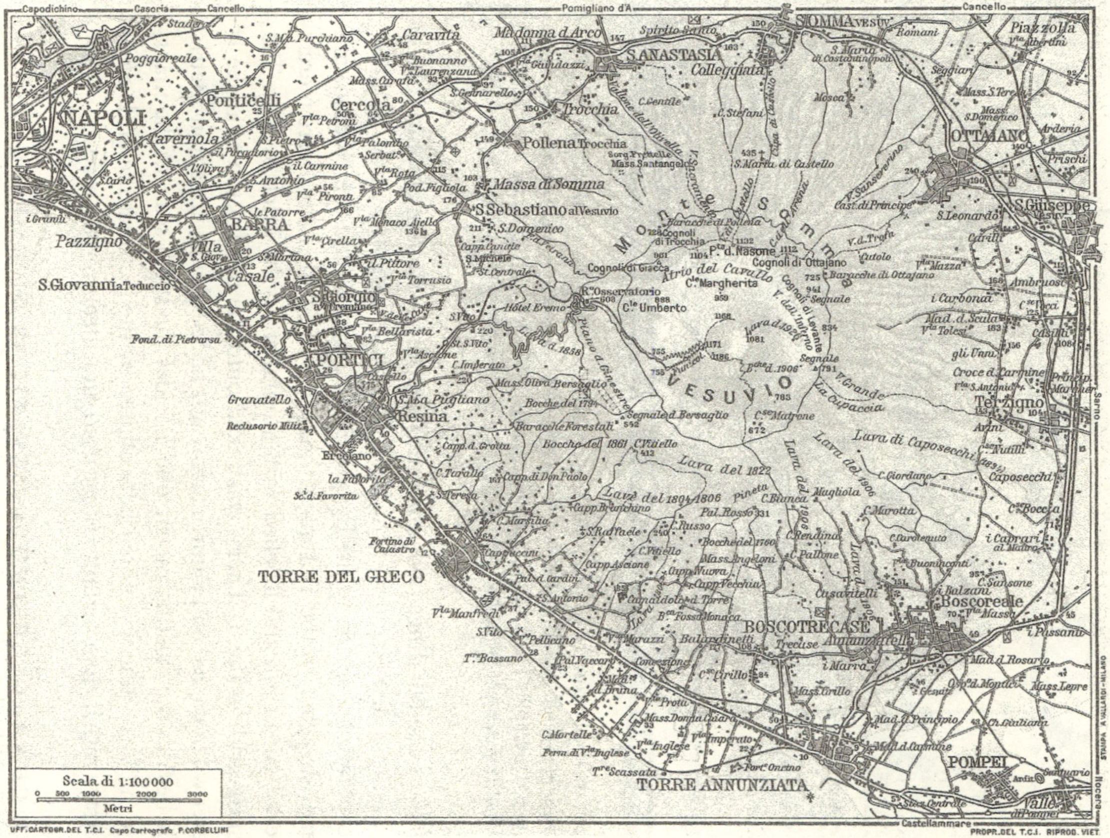

Figure 23: The 1927 Touring Club Italiano map showing the area east of Naples, with Pompeii in the bottom right corner, clearly used to provide the base of the 'Naples Suburban-East' sheet of the ACLS 'Frick Maps'. Touring Club Italiano, *Guida d'Italia: Italia meridionale.* Vol. 2: *Napoli e dintorni* (Milan: Touring Club Italiano, 1927), between pp. 384–85 (out of copyright).

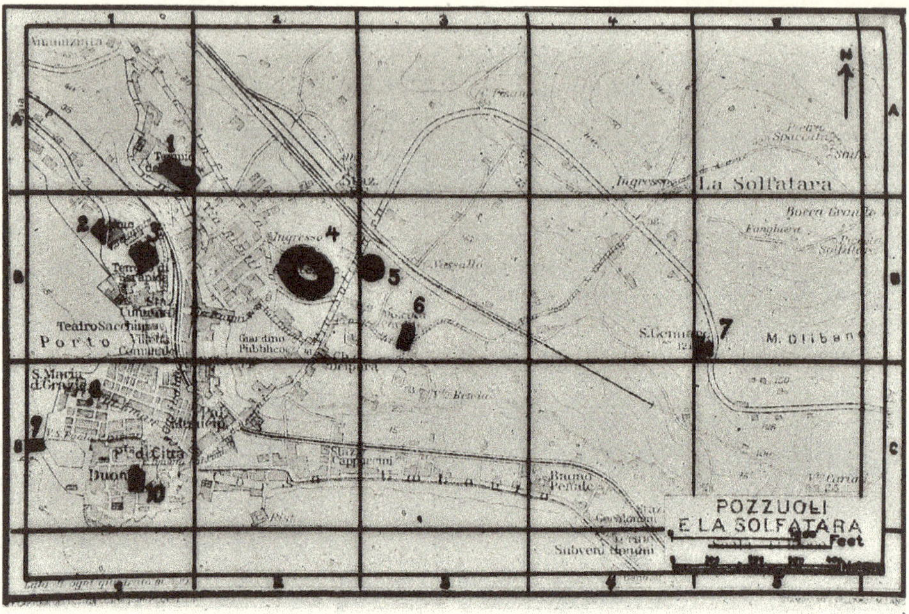

Figure 24: The Pozzuoli e la Solfatara sheet of the ACLS 'Frick Maps' with cultural sites blocked out in ink, including the larger Roman amphitheatre (4) and the Macellum (3, 'Tempio di Serapide'). NARA M1944, RG 239/0156, 'Maps Showing Areas to Be Spared Destruction/Europe: Hungary-Italy', *Pozzuoli e la Solfatara*.

toric sites and buildings (including the larger of the Roman amphitheatres, the 'Tempio di Serapide'—actually a Roman *macellum* market building incorporating a shrine to the Egyptian god Serapis—and the Duomo) are already depicted on the TCI map. These and a few other sites were merely blocked out in ink and labelled with a number on the Frick overlay. The existing grid on the TCI map was inked onto the overlay too to make it clearer when copied and a north arrow was added along with a non-metric scale besides the existing metric one. Besides the small scale of the maps, their military value was potentially limited by the fact that the grids were arbitrary rather than tied into those used on Allied military maps.

THE CHARACTER AND MOTIVATIONS OF AMERICAN ACADEMIC AND POLITICAL CONCERN

But why was the protection of European culture so important to American scholars, museum directors and politicians who were so distant from the

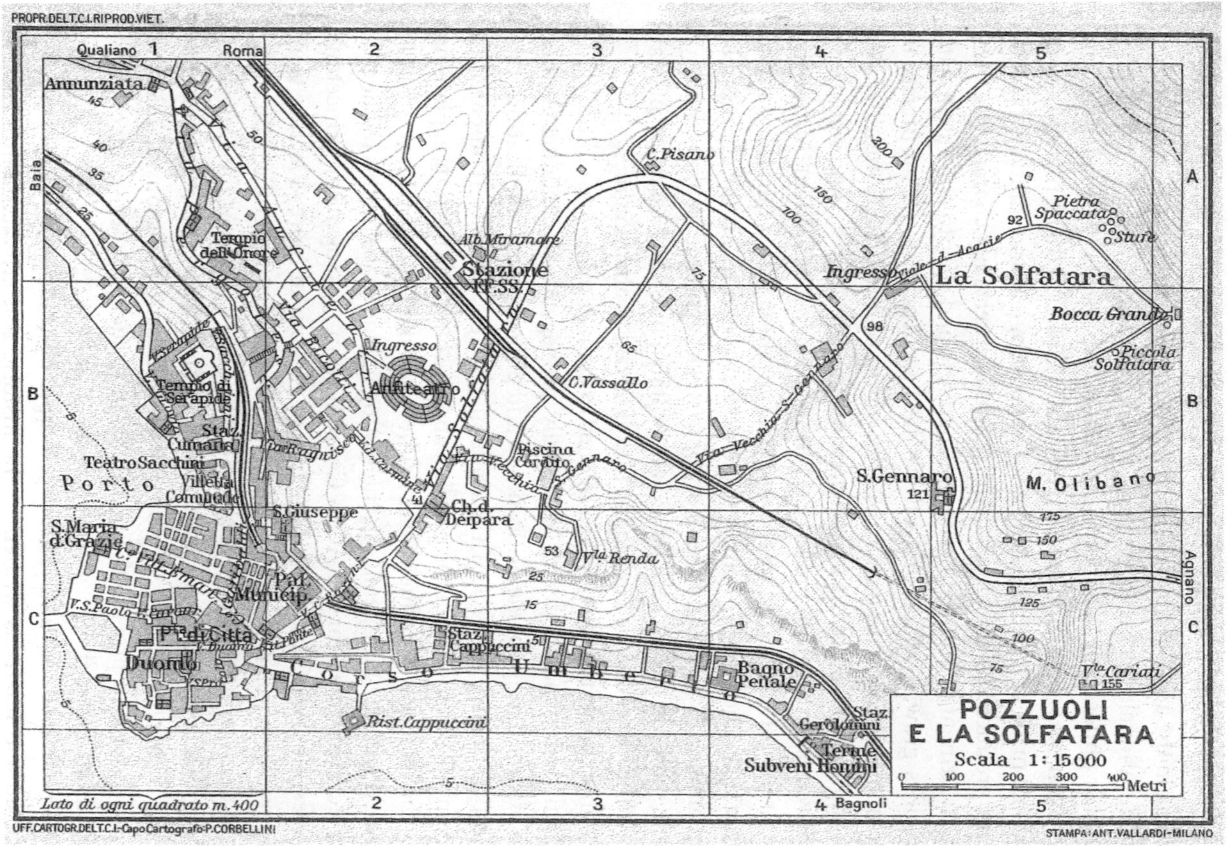

Figure 25: The 1927 Touring Club Italiano map showing Pozzuoli e la Solfatara, clearly used to provide the base of the corresponding sheet of the ACLS 'Frick Maps'. Touring Club Italiano, *Guida d'Italia: Italia meridionale.* Vol. 2: *Napoli e dintorni* (Milan: Touring Club Italiano, 1927), between pp. 336–37 (out of copyright).

theatres of war? What motivated these concerns and activities in the upper echelons of US cultural and even political life?

Unsurprisingly, given its origins among practical archaeologists already serving in the army in the field or in the War Office in London, much of the British rationale for heritage protection in 1943 was pragmatic rather than moral or philosophical, largely for counter-propaganda (particularly in the aftermath of Cyrene) and (to Wheeler and Ward-Perkins) a matter of professional pride and competence, both archaeological and military.[19] Documents produced by the US civilian committees certainly characterise German treatment of cultural heritage as barbaric and seek to contrast it with the Allies' growing role as protectors of heritage. For example, the preface to a pamphlet prepared in 1943 by Charles Morey of the ACLS Committee, for distribution to US politicians, opens with the uncompromising statement, 'This war is a struggle to preserve civilization against barbarism'. A covering letter sent out to scholars by the ACLS Committee with a questionnaire to gather their knowledge of cultural sites in Europe contrasts the committee's own aims with 'German threats of some weeks ago to leave not a stone of Rome standing if they were forced out of Italy [and] their assertion of May 9 that they would leave Greece in ruins if forced to abandon it'.[20]

While the attitudes expressed by the US civilian movers of cultural protection policy included such essentially propagandistic statements, they also include a range of idealistic, moral and philosophical justifications that reflect distinctive features of US academia, society, and also (compared to Britain) its distance from the conflict, and go some way towards explaining why the issue was so influential at a time when the United States was barely engaged with the European war. Interesting light is shone on this by the text of a lecture written for the ACLS Committee in 1943, again by Princeton's Charles Morey. In January to March 1944 versions of Morey's lecture were delivered by scholars across the US to military government officers in training at the wartime military government training schools, at the University of Virginia, Boston University, the University of Chicago, Harvard, the University of Michigan, Pitt, Stanford, Western Reserve, Wisconsin, Yale and Northwestern, to provide them with an introduction to the protection of 'cultural treasures'.[21]

Morey introduces and justifies his topic by stating 'the history of civilization and liberty is written in the historic and artistic monuments of Europe to whose conservation the President's commission [the Roberts Commission] is dedicated'. There follows a very condensed overview of

'Western civilization', a model of history and culture constructed for, and propagated by, numerous contemporary American university survey classes and textbooks.[22] Such Western civilization classes ('a characteristically American invention') had their roots in the late 19th century but grew in importance during the First World War as American university teachers sought to emphasise cultural connections with European democracies along with common concepts of citizenship and citizen education. Such approaches were particularly to be encountered in SATC (Students Army Training Corps) 'War Issues' courses taught to university students undergoing military training on campus, whose peak in popularity lay between the First and Second World Wars. Consequently 'Western civ.' classes were a standard component of the university experience for most educated Americans by 1943. In contrast, British tertiary education at the time was much more specialised, and lacked such broad surveys of European art and culture. Classics, for example, as a university subject, was heavily linguistic in emphasis and typically included little ancient history or art in the undergraduate syllabus. On the other hand, the availability in public libraries of much-reprinted popular books such as J.C. Stobart's *The Grandeur that Was Rome* (first published in 1912 but readily available in later editions until the 1970s) provided a popular equivalent for interested British readers.[23]

Morey's lecture text presents some key themes of 'Western civilization'. Greece introduced 'the rational habit of mind which has been the norm of thinking in the Western world', Italy spread 'classic culture' and kept it alive in the 'dark period' of the early Middle Ages, then gave us the Renaissance revival of learning and science. Medieval France 'organized and codified the Christian faith', leaving us Gothic cathedrals as a tangible reminder. After inveighing against German vandalism and looting, Morey presents the rhetorical centrepiece of his justification for cultural protection:

> 'Our obligation to preserve the cultural monuments of Europe is a heavy commitment weighted not alone by altruistic considerations, but by self-interest as well. The culture of Europe, manifest and recorded in its monuments, works of art, archives and libraries, is the fountain-head of civilization in the Western hemisphere, and what damage it suffers in this war will be felt in one way or another by ourselves, for generations to come. The time has passed when America was a mere cultural colony of Europe, but the traditions we have inherited from across the sea are still alive and working among us, crushed though they be by Nazi tyranny

> in Europe itself. They are alive and working not only by reason of the European origin of the founders of our republic, but also because every immigrant family and refugee has brought and brings some reinforcement to the European heritage on which American civilization is built.'

Thus, in Morey's view, American culture, as part of a wider Western culture, is directly descended from the European past. However, now it is not a 'mere cultural colony' of Europe. America now serves as the refuge and protector for the culture of that European past. Furthermore, the cultural contributions of 'immigrants and refugees' of European origin (so, ordinary people, not just the founding fathers of British origin) have made American culture something new and unique, and conversely, all these different American peoples have a stake in protecting European culture threatened by the war.

The argument that the material remains of European culture were, in some sense, a common heritage of mankind is not unexpected, and the idea that cultural heritage is common to all humanity remains an important justification for its protection.[24] However, Morey also emphasises the importance of the physical manifestations of culture to national and cultural identities, another important strand in contemporary thought about cultural property. Poland and the Poles are held up by Morey as a particular example, in as much as they have a distinctive culture manifested in buildings, arts and archives that have enabled it to survive despite the repeated foreign occupations of the past. It provides a clear and relevant example for Morey's audiences, given Poland's central position in the war's origins and in the light of the substantial Polish expatriate community in the US. Morey goes on to make the more general point that even things 'that would not seem important to a foreigner' (i.e., that are not necessarily recognised as cultural heritage from a universal perspective) may be important on a local level, a view tentatively expressed, but moving towards a more inclusive, less universalising definition of cultural property more familiar from modern discussions.[25]

The relationship between identity and cultural heritage is developed further in a document produced by the American Defense–Harvard Group for the use of the US Army's Military Government Division. It makes the point that as Allied armies enter countries previously occupied by the enemy, they will establish order and provide for material needs. 'But they must also create with the peoples of such countries relations of sympathy and understanding designed to create confidence and a sense of security; [and] restore the foundations of their cultural life' by protecting those peoples' tangible cultural heritage. This, the document argues, will have the practical benefit of improving relations between the occupying armed forces and the peoples whose countries they occupy and will 'develop an atmosphere favourable to the adoption of peace treaties'.[26] Thus, protection of cultural heritage can be pragmatic (as part of post-conflict reconciliation) in military and political terms, as well as moral. According to the Harvard Group document, 'too much emphasis cannot be laid on the occupying authority's working in cooperation with the local population'. Besides improving relations with the population of the occupied country, local heritage administrators and personnel are presented as crucially important in practical terms for the protection and restoration of heritage during the occupation, a theme also emphasised by Morey in his military government lecture.[27]

The early documents produced by the US civilian commissions also discuss at some length what exactly they should be helping to protect. As might be expected from groups with 'cultural treasures' and 'artistic and historic monuments' in their titles, traditional categories of tangible cultural heritage dominate their discussions. Morey's ACLS military government lecture notes define 'cultural treasures' as including

1. Churches.
2. Houses, palaces and chateaux.
3. Monuments (a broad category, incorporating commemorative monuments, ancient structures and archaeological excavations, buildings of historic or artistic interest, open-air art, and monumental fountains).
4. Cultural institutions (including museums, university buildings, libraries, archives, and scientific collections and laboratories).[28]

Apart from a few photographs specifically depicting war damage from the First and Second World Wars (Reims Cathedral, a London church, Benevento Cathedral), the slides listed to accompany the lecture would not have been out of place in an early to mid-twentieth century US university survey of Western art and archaeology, including the Palace of Knossos, the Arch of Trajan at Benevento, the Athenian Agora, the Victory of Samothrace, the Temple of Athena Nike on the Athenian Acropolis, the medieval French town of Carcassonne, Princeton University's excavations at Antioch, and an Athenian painted vase. However, there are suggestions, both in

Morey's lecture notes and in a questionnaire sent out by the ACLS committee to gather information from the wider scholarly community across the US, of wider definitions of cultural treasures, cultural heritage, and cultural property, including Morey's things 'that would not seem important to a foreigner but loom large in the affections of a European populace'. The specific examples he gives are parks and amusement places and 'relics of popular superstition like the Bocca della Verità', while categories in the questionnaire include 'folk art and costume' as well as non-Western (Islamic, Far Eastern) art.[29] However, these tentative moves towards a broader definition of what should be protected had relatively little impact on the later remit of monuments officers and the contents of lists supplied to them, which (unsurprisingly) remained substantially traditional and conservative compared with modern concerns.[30]

Churches figure prominently both as an organising category of cultural property in Morey's lecture notes and as individual monuments in the inventories produced by the US civilian committees and subsequently incorporated into Civil Affairs handbooks. However, there is some ambivalence as to whether they were to be valued exclusively or primarily for their historical value, or at least partly for their religious significance. Morey notes that churches are 'first among "cultural treasures" in the consciousness of the inhabitants of any European city or town', and the Roman Catholicism of Italy, and Italian and other (Polish, Irish) immigrant communities in the US, was surely a popular factor reinforcing arguments for the protection of Italian churches.[31] The religious aspect of churches in Rome and the Vatican was certainly the primary consideration when Rome was bombed in July and August 1943 (see Chapter 9), and Francis Spellman, then Roman Catholic archbishop of New York, was appointed a member of the Roberts Commission in October 1944 (replacing the recently deceased Alfred E. 'Al' Smith, former governor of New York and the first Roman Catholic to run for US president). The Allied monuments officers in Sicily reported as a problem the submission of numerous requests for the repair of '[churches] partly or wholly not of a monumental character', suggesting that they saw their function primarily as preservation on strictly historical rather than broader cultural (e.g., religious) grounds. While they concluded that the expenditure was nevertheless worthwhile because the churches were potentially 'an important element in public morals and in preventing further deterioration', they argued that the funding might come from other sources channelled through senior civil affairs officers rather than those earmarked for the repair of specifically historic buildings.[32] Likewise in April 1944, monuments officer Colonel Henry C. Newton (himself a Roman Catholic and an architect of Roman Catholic churches in the US) expressed concern that the US media over-emphasised the religious significance of Rome, arguing that 'the saving of the historical monuments and the art and culture of Europe *is definitely not a religious issue*'.[33]

While the emphasis lay on Europe and European cultural heritage, in the first instance this was partly, at least, for practical reasons. The American civilian committees' initiatives gathered momentum as the campaign in North Africa was coming to a close, land warfare and territorial occupation by US forces was still a very limited feature of the Pacific theatre, and it was clear that Allied forces would soon seek to occupy territory in Europe. However, in February 1944, the Roberts Commission changed its full title to 'The American Commission for the Protection and Salvage of Artistic Monuments in War Areas', rather than '. . . in Europe' as, under its aegis, the ACLS Committee began to produce materials to support protection of cultural property in the Far East, led by Horace Jayne.

MASON HAMMOND: THE FIRST US MONUMENTS OFFICER

Developments in the US armed forces took place in parallel with the civilian activities discussed above rather than as a direct result of them. Part Two of this book began with the deployment of Harvard professor and USAAF Captain Mason Hammond to Sicily. Hammond's journey to Sicily had begun in May 1943. In the very same letter that Secretary of State Hull sent to President Roosevelt on 21 June 1943 recommending the creation of the Roberts Commission, he informed the president of the creation at the School of Military Government at Charlottesville of a section of specialist officers to advise commanders in the field 'as to the locations of, and the care to be given to, the various artistic and historic objects in occupied territory'.[34] Thus an initial US military cultural property protection capability, while perhaps responding to general concerns expressed by academics and politicians, had in fact been created within the expanding US armed forces themselves, without any direct input from the civilian commissions that saw their functions as including recommendations of suitable personnel for precisely such roles.

Initially the US War Department had approved, in May 1943, the creation of an Office of Adviser on Fine Arts and Monuments to the Chief Civil Affairs Officer of Allied Military Government of Occupied Territories, with an establishment of a lieutenant-colonel and a major. However, Mason Hammond was the first such officer to be appointed. Hammond was already serving with the rank of captain in Washington DC in the Army Air Forces Headquarters A-2 (Current Intelligence Section). He was initially sent by air to AFHQ at Chréa in Algeria on 21 May 1943, then on to the Military Government holding centre at Tizi-Ouzou (also in Algeria). Hammond there played an important role in preparing for the invasion of Sicily (including the drafting of *General Administrative Instruction No. 8*—see above) before his eventual deployment to Sicily itself in July 1943.[35] The first Hammond heard of the Roberts Commission's creation was in a 14 August clipping from the *New York Times* that reported its establishment. He had no direct contact with the commission before September 1943. He wrote to David E. Finley in response to a letter from Finley that had been forwarded to him by the War Department.[36] Hammond noted 'we have had some evidence of your activity in cultural maps etc. sent through', but that they were only just beginning to arrive, and were needed in much greater numbers. He also advised that the documentation provided

> 'should not be prepared simply from guidebooks but checked by people who have been there, as I find the guide-book descriptions wholly inadequate in forming true judgement on the importance of a building—not every bit of mediaeval work in a church wall makes it an inestimable treasure and local enthusiasm often exalts secondary things into primary.'

CHAPTER 9

Pompeii's Legacy? Aerial Bombardment and Cultural Heritage in Italy, 1943–1945

Undoubtedly the greatest deficiency of Allied wartime cultural property protection in 1943 was its failure to address the issue of aerial bombardment, which ultimately was the primary cause of damage to cultural heritage throughout the Second World War, including, of course, the damage to Pompeii.[1] As already noted, there is no evidence whatsoever that the proximity of the archaeological site of Pompeii was even considered in the planning and execution of bombing missions nearby in August and September 1943, except inasmuch as it served as a navigational marker. The reasons for this failure were essentially twofold. The first was the initial (and particularly British) perception of cultural property protection as something relating to military government and occupation rather than operational activity and planning; the second relates to the accuracy of bombing at the time, including a degree of British (military) realism about what could (or rather, could not) be achieved, and American (civilian) naivety about the accuracy of so-called 'precision' bombing. Eventually, in early 1944, cultural property protection *did* become a formal component in the planning of some Mediterranean Allied Air Forces' operations, and its inclusion as a consideration in missions conducted against targets near Florence, Siena and Venice in 1944–1945 was rightly held up as an example of effective MFAA influence in the organization's post-war reports.[2]

However, even with the incorporation of cultural property protection into operational planning in 1944, the targeting protocols formulated were permissive and emphasised military necessity over protection of heritage. As already noted, there is no particular reason to think Pompeii would have suffered any less under similar circumstances a year later. On the other hand, a year later, the existence of the adjacent heritage site would at least have been considered as part of the operational planning process. As a parallel, the historic and religious status of the Benedictine Abbey at Montecassino was certainly considered before a decision was taken to bomb it in February 1944, but ultimately military necessity was judged to outweigh those factors, rendering its destruction proportionate in the context of available means and methods. And certainly strategic bombing against urban and transportation targets in Italy, France, Austria and Germany continued throughout 1944 until the end of the war with little or no serious consideration given to protection of cultural property. This was a tacit admission that even as bombing accuracy improved, it was still not accurate enough to avoid damage to and destruction of historic buildings; yet again, assessments of military necessity meant that those targets would be bombed regardless.

The origins of British military cultural property protection, with their emphasis on protection of historic buildings and institutions in occupied areas, have been set out in some detail already. This was certainly the approach taken in the planning documents created for the invasion of Sicily and then of the Italian mainland, which lay firmly within military government structures rather than operational planning, of air forces or otherwise. This was also the role emphasised in early correspondence between Cordell Hull and President Roosevelt.[3] However, the U.S. civilian committees expressed concerns about the effect of bombing from an early stage, and, for example, while most copies of the ACLS maps were sent to the Civil Affairs Division of the War Department, some were earmarked for direct distribution to the Army Air Forces. The question of whether those maps were reaching their intended destination and whether they were being used effectively is one that recurs in correspondence and discussion between the Roberts Commission and U.S. military authorities, with the latter responding in the affirmative.[4]

Certainly contemporary U.S. newspaper accounts of USAAF bombing raids against Rome in July and August 1943 gave an impression of extremely precise bombing planned with the aid of clear documentation specifically provided to crews to prevent damage to the Vatican and other church buildings. *New York Times* correspondent Herbert L. Matthews participated in the briefing and flew on the mission of 19 July 1943, and reported:

> 'Each crew member was carefully briefed. Photographic air maps of Rome were given to everyone participating in the raid. On them four places were marked in white squares with the notation "must on no account be damaged."'
>
> 'St. John Lateran was a mile and a half away. With precision bombing there was no possibility of coming anywhere near that "Mother Church" of the Catholic world.'[5]

Nevertheless, the church of San Lorenzo fuori le Mura *was* damaged by the bombing (on 14 July), as were two sections of the third-century AD Aurelianic Walls.[6] And looking back at the mission in a *Harper's Magazine* article in May 1945, as the war in Europe was ending, even Matthews told a rather different story:

> 'I attended the final briefing and I distinctly recall that, at this last pre-mission briefing, bombardiers were not warned of the presence of the Basilica of San Lorenzo. I knew what care had been taken by the Air Command to avoid damage to the four main basilicas of Rome and the Vatican buildings. However, the plain truth is that high-altitude bombing had not then reached and probably never will reach the point of perfection where it can be guaranteed that no damage will be done to a structure so close to the target area as San Lorenzo was to the marshalling yards that were destroyed.'[7]

Matthews was even more candid in a private conversation on 24 April 1944 with Francis Taylor of the Roberts Commission and Colonel Henry C. Newton, notes on which were kept in the commission's archive. Newton recorded that Matthews had flown on the mission and attended the pre-flight briefing:

> '"but no one there could point out anything for anyone" (these are his very words).'[8]

Clearly the media presentation of USAAF bombing of Rome as being so precise that damage to culturally significant buildings could be prevented was a carefully managed fiction. It was motivated primarily by Rome's religious significance, to allay concerns among Roman Catholic civilians and members of the US armed forces. However, this public position, that US precision bombing, combined with maps delineating the location of historic buildings and cultural institutions, could prevent their destruction, was still being maintained in October 1943 when the scale of damage caused by bombing to cities such as Palermo, Naples and Benevento (Figure 26), as well as Pompeii, was readily apparent. A story on (and by) the Roberts Commission, written for distribution to the press by the US Office of War Information, claimed

> 'The commission of scholars is also supplying the Army with maps that designate clearly the areas in each city where no bombs must fall lest a

Figure 26: The cathedral at Benevento, virtually destroyed by Allied bombing in the same air-interdiction campaign that led to the damage to the archaeological site of Pompeii. British School at Rome photographic archive, Ward-Perkins collection, wpwar-0061.

> famous fresco or a great church be damaged. These maps are studied in briefing rooms by crews of United States bombers before going out on bombing missions over European cities.'[9]

As at Pompeii, damage to cultural sites visible to Allied troops and correspondents was sometimes explained away with stories that blamed the Germans and sought to maintain the fiction of precision bombing. For example, a December 1943 story about the Monuments and Fine Arts organisation for the Italian theatre edition of *Stars and Stripes* (the newspaper for US military personnel) claimed that the virtual destruction of the medieval church of Santa Chiara in Naples (Figure 27) had been caused by a German officer who parked his armoured cars in front of the church. The story given is that those Germans had opened fire on American aircraft heading for the port, and they had responded by bombing the German troops, damaging the church in the process.[10] The idea that bombers might even notice such limited small arms fire, let alone attempt to respond to it, betrays a complete (and probably deliberate) misunderstanding of the (in)accuracy and (in)-flexibility of Allied bombing, comparable to the Radio Londra story that the British had bombed Pompeii when aiming at a nearby German headquarters, and Maiuri's naïve and fruitless attempt (see p.103n.34) to signal bombers away from Pompeii.

Concern about damage to cultural heritage caused by bombing in Italy at this time is evident in the minutes of an October 1943 meeting of the Roberts Commission, at which Dinsmoor claimed 'We finished [i.e., destroyed] the most important excavations of Pompei. I am told there is nothing left' and Finley referred to 'the destruction of Naples' as the likely future fate of other cities in Italy. Nonetheless, the views expressed at this meeting suggest a continuing faith among its members in the combination of American precision bombing and the ACLS Frick maps as a means to prevent damage to cultural property. The problems, they suggest, lie with the British. Finley reported that he had asked Assistant Secretary of War McCloy about the use of the Frick maps. McCloy had in turn passed the query on to Major-General John H. Hilldring of the Civil Affairs Division, who

> 'said informally . . . that the only hole in the system was the British Bombing Command, which they do not reach. The British do not do precision bombing, but night bombing, and the maps would not be very useful.'[11]

Figure 27: The (originally 14th century) church of Santa Chiara in Naples after its virtual destruction by Allied bombing and the consequent fire. British School at Rome photographic archive, Ward-Perkins collection, wpwar-0054.

In reality, as we have seen, American 'precision' bombing was nowhere near as precise as its exponents claimed, and there is no evidence (or reason to believe) that the USAAF daytime missions against targets near Pompeii (for example) caused any less accidental or collateral damage than RAF night missions.[12] Nor is there any indication that the USAAF was using the Frick maps in the planning or execution of missions. Matthews's account of the briefing for the Rome missions refers to aerial photographs rather than maps of the target area, with only four religious sites marked on them rather than the range of cultural property indicated on the Frick maps. Even if these had been available and used, the small-scale and rather cluttered nature of what were essentially guidebook maps undoubtedly would have limited their value to crews bombing cities from altitudes of 5000–6000 metres even in good visibility. The Roberts Commission's members' faith in the utility of the Frick maps for bombing betrays a widespread naivety regarding the realities of contemporary bombing tactics and accuracy.[13]

The British were under fewer illusions about the potential (and actual) impact of their bombing policies and tactics on cultural heritage. Certainly from September 1943 onwards, specific concerns had been aired about damage caused to historic buildings by bombing, both publically in Parliament and privately in correspondence by prominent individuals with personal and professional interests in heritage. As already noted, Conservative MP Edward Keeling and others had raised in Parliament the question of protecting historical monuments in Italy, in great part in response to the bomb damage in Campania.[14] Certainly the damage to Pompeii was one example specifically mentioned in related correspondence, based on Mortimer Wheeler's reports and interpretation of that damage.[15] Furthermore, Woolley's advisory role at the War Office had been noted, and there were suggestions that 'some connoisseur' should serve in a parallel role as adviser to the Air Ministry (which had responsibility for the RAF). War Office major and art historian Anthony Blunt is one individual who recurs in contemporary correspondence as a possible candidate for the position.[16] There are also references to lists of monuments recommended for protection submitted to the RAF, but it is unclear how these lists related to others in circulation at the time (see below).[17] Growing awareness in 1941 of the inaccuracy of RAF strategic bombing of Germany had led the British to abandon any regular attempt at what the Americans were calling 'precision' bombing in favour of a strategy of area bombing of cities.[18] Bombing methods that could not guarantee to hit a factory or industrial complex could hardly be claimed as reliable in avoiding historic buildings and cultural institutions. In his comments on a draft statement entitled *The Protection of Cultural Monuments and Works of Art*, prepared by J.G. Mann, Sir Eric Maclagan observed,

> 'My own impression is that the Air Ministry will be less sympathetic than the W.O. [War Office.] Sir K.C. [Kenneth Clark] said Tedder was willing to cooperate; when the Bp.[Bishop] of Chichester sent in his memorandum some months ago I spoke to [Air Chief Marshal] Joubert, who took the line that almost any discrimination in favour of individual monuments was impossible in bombing from any altitude.'[19]

In fact, rather than merely unsympathetic, Joubert's attitude was realistic, reflecting the accuracy that was possible (or impossible) at the time. A political decision had been made to bomb Germany and German-occupied territories, and area bombing was the consequence of that decision combined with the level of accuracy technically and tactically possible at the time. Nor, perhaps, would British public opinion in general have accepted putting a brake on what was perceived and presented as militarily necessary. As J.G. Mann noted in a letter in September 1943,

> 'The idea of prolonging the war in order to save the architecture of Italy would shock the public and one would be reviled for it.'[20]

Even as the RAF's ability to bomb individual targets improved and perhaps surpassed that of the Americans under similar operational conditions, and even as it became a matter of stated policy to spare cultural property from bombing as much as possible, different standards were applied to strategic bombing than those employed in tactical bombing and interdiction.[21] Secretary of State for Air Sir Archibald Sinclair wrote (in July 1944, in the context of ongoing strategic bombing of Germany and tactical bombing and interdiction in Normandy):

> 'Buildings of archaeological, historic or religious importance are not attacked except when military objectives of extreme importance lie within them or near them. Such a case occurred at Cassino and to some extent at Caen; it is feared that this might happen again in other ancient towns if the enemy persists in fighting every step of the way across Europe. Such destruction is hateful but military necessity leaves us no choice. In all other cases we take what precautions we can to avoid damage to historic objects, though naturally all questions of this kind must be subordinated to the needs of operations.'

However:

> 'So far as Germany is concerned I am afraid similar precautions [to those employed in tactical bombing and interdiction in France and Italy] are impossible. There our bombing has been directed primarily against the whole system of industry and transport on which Germany depends for prosecuting the war. . . . It is impossible to try to protect a church or museum which lies among a complex of industrial targets and if we were to claim that we do so we should only discredit the value of our precautions elsewhere.'[22]

TEDDER AND ZUCKERMAN IN THE MEDITERRANEAN

Sir Eric Maclagan, cited above, alluded to 'Tedder [being] willing to cooperate'. British Air Marshal Arthur Tedder was commander-in-chief of Mediterranean Air Command (Mediterranean Allied Air Forces from December 1943), the joint headquarters commanding both British and US air forces in the theatre. From the autumn of 1943 Tedder played a personal role in establishing an (eventually) substantive liaison between MFAA and Allied air forces operating in Italy. In part, Tedder's interest in the issue may have been provoked by external concerns originating in the conversations in political and museum circles in London and discussions of the Roberts Commission in the US set out above.[23] It seems unlikely that the maps produced by the ACLS Committee and sent to the USAAF reached Tedder or anyone else with any campaign-level influence by October 1943, nor is there any evidence that a list of Italian historic buildings produced in Britain and sent on to Tedder by the middle of that month was ever used in practice.[24] Regardless of their origins, lists of monuments had no practical impact on the planning of air operations at this time, and this was recognised by the individuals concerned. In his 19 December 1943 letter to Archie Sinclair in which he criticised the damage to Pompeii, Keeling also contended,

> 'You told me of the lists supplied to the Allied forces in the Mediterranean with this aim [of preventing damage, including that caused by bombing] in view. We had, however, grave doubts (which you told me you shared) whether those lists achieved their purpose. At our meeting Brig. Wheeler . . . and the Duke of Wellington, who have just returned from Italy, told us that the lists were in practice dead letters.'[25]

Wheeler, with an axe to grind and no inside knowledge of operational air planning, was not the best source for this, but the claim was broadly true. However, autumn 1943 saw the first substantive moves towards liaison between the MFAA and Allied air forces.

On 8 November 1943, a meeting was held in Palermo between MFAA officers and Professor Solly Zuckerman, director of the Bombing Survey Unit ('Special Air Mission, North African Air Forces') analysing the results of the recent air interdiction campaign in Sicily and Italy. Contemporary MFAA reports suggest a Major Thompson on Zuckerman's staff requested the meeting, based on Tedder's personal interest in the topic.[26] Zuckerman's own account (published 40 years later) in contrast states it took place at the request of 'two Americans' (presumably including Mason Hammond) 'who, I believe, were attached to AMGOT', and who hoped Zuckerman might be able to alert Tedder to their concerns about bomb damage to historic buildings.[27] Zuckerman, whose reports on rail interdiction in Sicily and Italy have been cited at length in Part One, was an academic biologist of South African origin who became an influential adviser on bombing strategy to the British government and RAF.[28] According to the Sub-Commission's account of the meeting, Zuckerman was given a prioritised list of fifty cities in Italy 'which the Sub-Commission considers should be spared from aerial bombardment if military considerations allow,' along with plans of those cities indicating the locations of their principal monuments.[29] Later reports (below) suggest that the maps were copies of the ACLS maps, but the lists were not the complete Harvard lists—even the short version of the latter included some 223 cities and other locations containing cultural sites.

The paths of Headquarters Mediterranean Air Command (soon to be renamed Mediterranean Allied Air Forces) and the MFAA Sub-Commission did not cross again until early 1944, although in the meantime the former had been active and there had been notable developments. The MFAA learned of these developments purely by chance, when Major John Ward-Perkins (formally assigned to monuments duties in Italy in December 1943) was sent from Naples to undertake an inspection of monuments and fine arts in Foggia Province in Apulia (January 1944). While the rest of Apulia at this time lay within the remit of AMG Region II and was thus the responsibility of the monuments officer assigned to that region, USAAF Lieutenant-Colonel (and landscape architect) Norman T. Newton, Foggia province remained separate under the control of the civil affairs apparatus of British 8th Army.[30] By this time, the province was also the location of numerous important Allied bomber airfields and consequently many air force headquarters and personnel. Thus in the course of his visit Ward-Perkins encountered Squadron Leader Peter Shinnie, another young archaeologist who had excavated with Mortimer Wheeler at Maiden Castle before the war.[31] Shinnie, whose initial academic training had been in Egyptology, was serving as an RAF intelligence officer at Mediterranean Photographic Reconnaissance Command (MPRC) and had been assigned by Headquarters Mediterranean Allied Air Forces to compile information relating to historic sites and works of art in Italy. Through Shinnie, Ward-Perkins learned of air force activities relating to cultural property protection that had been underway since at least October 1943, although they had remained unknown to, and separate from, MFAA activities except for the encounter with Zuckerman the previous November.

Drawing on an initial report commissioned by Tedder himself and submitted in October 1943, Shinnie was now compiling an atlas of aerial photographs of central and northern Italian cities, annotated with the locations of, and information on, cultural sites in and near those cities. Shinnie had a full set of copies of the ACLS Frick maps, which presumably were the copies given to Zuckerman the previous autumn. However, he lacked the Harvard lists, and Ward-Perkins requested that he be sent a set as a matter of urgency. Ward-Perkins welcomed the work that had been done at MAAF, while bemoaning the duplication of effort caused by the fact 'that (once more) Higher Authority should have ignored the body competent to deal with such things', namely the MFAA.[32]

CHAPTER 10

'Any consequential damage is accepted'. Mediterranean Allied Air Forces Reforms, Successes and Failures in Cultural Property Protection, February 1944 to March 1945

THE MEDITERRANEAN ALLIED AIR FORCES 'BOMBING BOOK'

Shinnie's 'bombing book', as Ward-Perkins described it, was completed and distributed in February 1944 as *Ancient Monuments of Italy: Aerial Photographs*, under the signature of Brigadier Lauris Norstad, the US director of operations for Mediterranean Allied Air Forces. Copies were to be distributed to Group- and Wing-level formations as a matter of course, and used in briefing at lower levels as necessary. This atlas was substantially a product of the air forces themselves, although the MFAA *Final Report* notes that the Sub-Commission 'assisted informally in the final stages'.[1] The copy of the atlas preserved in the UK National Archives is divided into two volumes. Each comprises loose-leaf pages arranged in alphabetical order by city name, alternating aerial reconnaissance photographs marked with historic buildings and monuments with simple typescript lists of those buildings and monuments keyed to the photographs with numbers. Despite its title, the atlas included sites of all historical periods, not just those considered 'ancient' in a strict sense. Volume One (A–P) includes 36 cities, and Volume Two (R– Z) has 22, for a total of 58.[2] The cities vary both in size and number of cultural sites, and also the detail with which those sites are identified. The images of Florence (Figure 28) and Milan are both relatively high-altitude shots (from 28,000 and 29,000 ft [8534 and 8840 m] respectively, with an F6 lens) in which the city itself fills a relatively small proportion of the frame. No attempt is made to identify individual sites within the city. Instead, a large rectangle is superimposed on the historic centre of each, labelled '1–26' and '1–14' respectively, and so keyed in to the list of individual buildings. The image of Venice (Figure 29), in contrast, is much more detailed. The city itself overflows the frame of the photograph (taken from 24,000 ft [7315 m] with an F20 lens), and 25 cultural sites are marked and numbered individually. With the qualification 'This list is only a small selection of the city's major monuments', the typescript key includes San Marco and 15 other churches, seven *palazzi*, the Accademia and the Rialto bridge. This really is, however, a small selection compared with the Harvard lists and ACLS Frick maps. The 1944 US Army *Civil Affairs Handbook* that incorporated the Harvard Lists included 114 entries for the city of Venice.[3] The introduction to the atlas acknowledges this limitation, and refers to the Frick maps as sources of more complete information. Given that the atlas was produced by the air forces for their own use, presumably these aerial photographs were considered to be of greater practical value than the ACLS maps, and they certainly give a clearer indication of what would be seen by an aircrew than do the maps. Furthermore, the reduction in the number of monuments marked as protected de-clutters the imagery that the air forces personnel had to deal with, and introduced a greater degree of practicality and realism into the data.[4] However, just as Zuckerman noted of the maps, the crucial issue was whether the achievable bombing accuracy matched the precision of the information provided in the aerial photographs. The limited detail provided for Florence might be explained by the near-total prohibition on bombing the city expressed in the Preface to the atlas (below), but there was no such blanket ban on Milan (similarly lacking detail); the same prohibition did apply to Venice, however, which was depicted in much more detail.

RULES OF ENGAGEMENT

Just as important and interesting as the aerial photographs and lists themselves is the preface to the volume that sets out the restrictions on bombing the cities covered. They are as follows:

> 'Category "A". ROME, FLORENCE, VENICE, TORCELLO.'
>
> 'These towns are in no circumstances to be bombed without authority from this Headquarters [Mediterranean Allied Air Forces].'
>
> 'Category "B". RAVENNA, ASSISI, SAN GEMIGNANO [sic], PAVIA, URBINO, MONTEPULCIANO, PARMA, AOSTA, TIVOLI, UDINE,

Figure 28: Mediterranean Allied Air Forces aerial photograph of Florence, with cultural sites marked. From TNA AIR 8/638, Headquarters Mediterranean Allied Air Forces, *Ancient Monuments of Italy: Aerial Photographs*, 23 February 1944 (vol. 1).

GUBBIE [sic], VOLTERRA, SPOLETO, BORGO, SAN SPOLONE [?], ASCOLI PICENO (as ASCOLI, PICENO), COMO, PESARA, AQUILLA [sic] and the Dalmatian Coast towns of SPALATO and RAGUSA. The bombing of these towns which have at present no particular military importance should be avoided if possible. If however it is for operational reasons, considered essential that objectives in any of them should be

Figure 29: Mediterranean Allied Air Forces aerial photograph of Venice, with cultural sites marked. From TNA AIR 8/639, Headquarters Mediterranean Allied Air Forces, *Ancient Monuments of Italy: Aerial Photographs*, 23 February 1944 (vol. 2).

bombed, there should be no hesitation in doing so, and full responsibility will be accepted by this Headquarters.'

'Category "C". PISTOIA, MODENA, BRESCIA, CREMONA, ZARA, SIENA, PISA, PADUA, VERONA, BOLOGNA, AREZZO, ORVIETO, FERRARA, VICENZA, PRATO, VITERBO, CORTONA, PIACENZA, LUCCA, RIMINI, FRASCATI, BRACCIANO, PERUGIA, ANCONA. There are important military objectives in or near these towns which are to be bombed, and any consequential damage is accepted.'

No restrictions were imposed on the bombing of towns on the list or targets nearby if enemy-occupied and in the actual zone of military operations on the ground. In such cases 'the sole determining factor will be the requirements of the military situation'. This reflected the provision of Hague Convention (IV) 1907, *Regulations*, Article 27 in removing the immunity of cultural property in the event of military use. There were some restrictions on the bombing of towns outside the zone of military operations on the ground but even these restrictions were relatively permissive. Such towns were not to be bombed if obscured by cloud, but even then, if this cloud cover were temporary and less than 10/10, then 'it will be at the discretion of the formation leader whether he waits till the target is clear or not, and his discretion will not be questioned'. At night, targets in or near these towns were not to be attacked

'[iii] unless the actual target can be identified and markers placed with reasonable certainty. This is left to the discretion of crews and their decision will not be questioned, but it must be understood that in the towns listed there should be no question of releasing bombs "In the target area" when the actual target cannot be located.'

'(iv.) Other things being equal, the attack on targets near these monuments should be planned in a way to minimise risk of damage to them. However, it should be made quite clear to air-crews that the responsibility for such damage is accepted by this Headquarters and that its avoidance is not to be undertaken at the cost of increased risk to themselves. Unnecessary damage is of no advantage and should be avoided if that is possible without increased cost.'

There is also a reminder of the neutral status of Vatican City and other property of the Vatican State such as the Papal Domain of Castel Gandolfo. Churches in Rome were to be given comparable diplomatic immunity if possible. However, 'Although every care must be taken to avoid damaging these properties when a target is ordered to be attacked. . . . they will not be allowed to interfere in any way with the attack of military objectives'.

While adding the requirement of command authority at the highest level (MAAF) for bombing the culturally paramount sites of Rome, Florence and Venice, and urging the avoidance of damage to cultural heritage wherever possible, these rules of engagement continue to reflect the 1907 Hague Convention in that bombardment of historic buildings and similar was justifiable if these were used for military purposes.[5] There is a strong emphasis on the primacy of military necessity and that responsibility for damage to cultural property would be accepted by command rather than attributed to crews and formation leaders. The distinction between towns in the zone of military operations on the ground and those outside reflects the distinction between essentially strategic and tactical bombing underlying the unadopted 1923 Hague Air Rules (Articles 24 [3] and [4]) and the Rules of Engagement's prohibition on releasing bombs 'in the target area' perhaps reflects the Hague Air Rules' prohibition (Article 24 [3]) of 'indiscriminate bombardment' of even legitimate military targets outside the zone of military operations on the ground.

The final advance in air forces' treatment of cultural property was the establishment of formal liaison between the MFAA Sub-Commission in Italy and both strategic and tactical elements of Mediterranean Allied Air Forces, initiated in a meeting between Norstad and the sub-commission's director (Major Ernest T. De Wald) in March 1944. This came at a time when MFAA officers had finally been assigned to headquarters of the 5th (US) and 8th (Br.) Armies in Italy, marking a more general move towards integrating cultural property protection into operational and even tactical planning.[6]

From the perspective of cultural heritage, these measures were a significant improvement on the state of affairs that existed at the time of the bombing of Pompeii. Intelligence relating to important historic buildings and cultural institutions was now produced in a format designed by the air forces themselves to be useful to them in practical terms, and was appropriately disseminated. The importance of avoiding damage to cultural heritage had been accepted and underlined at the highest level of air force command in the theatre, Headquarters Mediterranean Allied Air Forces, in a signal sent out to all its formations (Signal SY.171 of 10 February 1944) whose importance was underlined by Norstad in *Ancient Monuments of Italy*.[7] These developments, along with the establishment of a liaison between the air forces and MFAA organisation, meant that cultural heritage could be taken into consideration in planning air operations. In contrast, when Pompeii was bombed, the ACLS maps, drawn from civilian guidebooks, while theoretically available to the USAAF, do not seem to have been properly distributed or used. In August-September 1943 there had been no liaison between the nascent MFAA organisation and the air forces, and, indeed, initially MFAA was not structured with a view to engagement in the planning of air operations. Nor, despite the restrictions set out in the 1907 Hague Convention, was there any explicit acknowledgment from higher levels of command or political structures that preservation of cultural heritage should receive serious consideration in the planning and execution of bombing missions.

SUCCESSES AND FAILURES: FLORENCE, VENICE AND BEYOND

Certainly the changes in Allied air forces' treatment of heritage sites was beneficial in a number of respects. The MFAA *Final Report* claims 'the results were proved in the brilliant precision raids on the marshalling-yards at Florence and Siena, and on the harbour area of Venice' and also refers to the protection of the Villa Nazionale at Stra as the result of effective liaison with the tactical air force.[8]

The marshalling yards at Florence and Siena were attacked as part of the rail interdiction campaign to support the Anzio beachhead and attempts to break through the Gustav Line/Montecassino position in the spring of 1944.[9] The Florence targets were particularly important because of the presence there of locomotive repair shops (key targets in Zuckerman's analysis) as well as locomotives and rolling stock, and due to the position of Florence in the rail net connecting the north (via Pisa and Bologna) to Rome. Despite this perceived military importance, the city's cultural importance underlined in the rules of engagement circulated with the *Ancient Monuments of Italy* made Florence a particularly sensitive target. Furthermore, the main target, the Campo di Marte marshalling yards, were close to the historic centre of the city, at their closest just 1.5 km east of the Duomo. In fact when Tedder's successor US Lieutenant-General Ira Eaker contemplated authorising bombardment of these marshalling yards, his British deputy Slessor referred the matter to Sir Charles Portal, chief of the Air Staff in London, and thence to the British War Cabinet Chiefs of Staff Committee of which Portal was a member. The minutes of the relevant meeting (1 March 1944) emphasise the military importance of the targets and note that 'it was proposed to employ only the most experienced and accurate bomber squadrons. . . . It would therefore be very bad luck if any of the really famous buildings were hit'.[10] The agreement of the Chiefs of Staff and the Air Staff was given on those conditions, and the minutes of the next day's meeting recorded that Churchill himself had written 'Certainly Bomb' against the minute.[11] The bombing went ahead, with missions flown against Florence's Campo di Marte and Rifredi marshalling yards (the latter c. 3.5 km from the Duomo) in March and (particularly) May 1944, and against Siena in April. These attacks employed exclusively medium bombers (USAAF B-26s are specified for some missions) bombing in daylight from lower altitudes and more accurately than heavy bombers, and with the benefit of greater experience and better bombsights than many of the crews who had bombed targets near Pompeii six months or so earlier.[12] Presumably they also made use of more detailed imagery than the rather cursory aerial photograph of Florence provided in the MAAF atlas, in which the targets are visible but major historical buildings are not marked individually. The attacks were successful in the sense that the targets were hit and damaged while no historic buildings were destroyed, although there were civilian casualties.[13]

The planning and execution of Operation Bowler, an air attack on German supply ships in the port of Venice (21 March 1945), did indeed include very careful and detailed consideration of the need to protect the city's cultural heritage. Discussion and planning of the operation had begun some two months earlier, and was only authorised by MAAF on the condition that bombing be undertaken in a restricted area, in visual bombing conditions, and by selected crews. Ultimately the mission was flown by Mustang and Kittyhawk fighter-bombers of No. 239 Wing of the RAF, composed of British, South African and Australian squadrons, supported by US (79th Fighter Group) P-47s suppressing anti-aircraft fire. Fighter-bombers employing dive-bombing attacks could bomb much more accurately than medium or heavy bombers, and the mission was successful both in military terms and because damage to cultural heritage was avoided.[14] On the other hand, it was hardly a typical use of air power, tactical or strategic, in the Italian campaign, even after the changes of February 1944, and the conditions were certainly very different from those under which Pompeii had been bombed in 1943. Time was available to plan the operation in great detail, contrasting sharply with the urgent conditions prevailing at the time of the Salerno landings. Using fighter-bombers was a realistic option for 'Bowler', as they were available in substantial numbers with experienced pilots, flying from airfields relatively near the target against non-existent air opposition. In contrast, as already noted, while the use of more precise A-36 dive-bombers against targets near Pompeii had been possible in theory, in reality it was impractical because of the distance between Pompeii and their initial bases in Sicily and the need to employ them in a fighter role against significant German air opposition over the Salerno beachhead. Also, some of the 'Bowler' fighter-bombers could carry 1000 lb bombs or rocket projectiles, both of which were more likely to damage or destroy their targets than the 500 lb bombs carried by the A-36s.[15]

However, the emphasis placed on these conspicuous examples of success in avoiding bomb damage to cultural sites tends to distract from the continuing damage inflicted by air attack even after the improvements of early 1944. On 2 February 1944, even as *The Ancient Monuments of Italy* was being finalised, USAAF B-25s bombing a road junction at Albano Laziale dropped five of their bombs in error on the nearby Papal estate at Castel Gandolfo.[16] As early as 11 March 1944, some of the bombs intended for railway marshalling yards in Padua, dropped by a force of over 100 USAAF B-17s, hit the historic centre of the town instead and struck the Church of the Eremitani, less than a kilometre to the south, destroying its 15th-century frescoes by Andrea Mantegna.[17] This was a three-star monument in the MFAA lists, although Padua as a whole was in Category C in the MAAF rules of engagement: 'There are important military objectives in or near these towns which are to be bombed, and any consequential damage is accepted'.[18] In both cases, intelligence regarding the location of the cultural site was available, and, at least in the case of Padua, presumably there was at least cursory consideration of the risks of bombing so close to cultural sites when the mission was planned (as required by the MAAF rules of engagement). Once it was accepted that the road junction (near Castel Gandolfo) and rail marshalling yards (at Padua) were legitimate military targets, the essential problem was, as at Pompeii, the inaccuracy of contemporary bombing technology and tactics.[19] Cultural sites in many Italian cities besides Padua were damaged and destroyed even after the changes to bombing policies promulgated in early 1944, including Treviso, Verona, and Vicenza, in many cases apparently due to bombing errors while targeting nearby transportation routes, similar to those near Pompeii.[20] On 3 March 1945, just a few weeks before Operation Bowler was executed in Venice and two months before the end of the European war, Allied bombing badly damaged the Roman Temple of Augustus at Pola in Italian Venezia Giulia (now Pula in Croatia), a one-star monument in Allied lists.[21] Beyond Italy, cultural sites in French cities, such as (to give just one example) the Église Notre-Dame in Saint-Lô (Samuel Beckett's 'Capital of the Ruins'), severely damaged by bombing on the night of 6/7 June 1944, suffered heavily from Allied bombing of the transportation system in preparation for Operation Overlord and then from tactical bombing as well as ground combat after the landings in Normandy.[22] Again, the location of the heritage sites was known and documented in reference materials like those used in Italy, but the limitations of contemporary bombing accuracy and the politico-military imperative for military success meant there was no question of protection of heritage sites taking precedence over perceived military necessity. Targets in Germany, of course, were subject to no such restrictions anyway, as already discussed.

The only thing that would have guaranteed the end of damage to such cultural sites was a politico-military decision either to cease bombing such targets completely, or to designate some centres as 'open cities' that would not be bombed and might serve as refuges for portable works of art. Such a decision was ultimately militarily and politically unacceptable, and it seems morally repugnant to spare some targets because of their cultural importance while civilians continue to be killed in the course of bombing others. Nevertheless, exactly such a policy was advocated by some, particularly in the Roberts Commission.

OPEN CITIES

After the first USAAF bombing mission against Rome in July 1943, Italian prime minister Badoglio declared the capital an 'open city', although this had little effect on either Allied or German treatment of the city at the time.[23] Hitler made various declarations implying that Florence was an open city, but the actual German treatment of the city up to August 1944 was ambivalent at best, and the situation was further complicated by advertised Allied intentions to make use of transportation facilities through the city after it was liberated.[24] The Roberts Commission correspondence shows two periods of particular interest in the possibility of an 'open city' in Italy, initially in October 1943 when the impact of Allied bombing in Sicily and the Naples area first became clear, and then again in the spring of 1944, after the bombing of Montecassino Abbey and at a time when Allied air forces were attacking the railway system of central and northern Italy.

The opening of this debate can be seen in a letter of 2 October 1943 from Vice-Chairman David Finley on behalf of the Roberts Commission, to Assistant Secretary McCloy. Citing the destruction at Naples (which he attributes to the Germans), Finley enquires whether US forces might take some 'affirmative action' to protect cultural heritage, such as establishing an open city to which portable art might be moved with the agreement of the Germans. Florence is proposed, with Assisi as an alternative, deemed potentially more acceptable because of its lesser strategic significance.[25] Consideration of the proposal continued in a special meeting of the Roberts Commission the following week, with military representation from Major-General Hilldring and McGeorge Bundy, later (1961–1966) US national security advisor, but then a junior intelligence officer. There was wide-ranging discussion of the damage caused by bombing in Italy, particularly Naples, and Pompeii is mentioned too. In the course of this, Finley noted 'the destruction of Naples' and asked whether a city such as Florence might be declared an open city. Chief Justice Roberts, the chair, responded that the War Department 'agrees in principle that we ought to open one or more cities in Italy'. Hilldring responded that Eisenhower had not objected (yet—see below), but overall the military men were sceptical. Hilldring himself stated 'if we said we wouldn't bomb art objects, we would be giving the enemy a great advantage', while Bundy maintained 'every time you tell a fellow you aren't going to bomb something, they are apt to put an ammunition dump there'. Bundy continued, 'It wasn't the practice of the Germans coming over England to spare anything, and they remember that'.[26] The subsequent written response from McCloy at the War Department expressed similar scepticism. His letter (23 October 1943) noted that while it was the policy of the armed forces to avoid damage to art as much as possible, declaring 'open cities' would be impractical without handicapping military activity, as most contained communications infrastructure that would be vital for future Allied operations.[27] Nevertheless, McCloy indicated that the War Department was exploring the possibilities of such a plan, and in fact had already passed on the suggestion to Eisenhower as theatre commander.

Eisenhower's responses were summarised in a 27 October 1943 memo from David Finley to members of the Roberts Commission.[28] While Eisenhower admitted the potential propaganda value of the idea and that it might be possible to spare such a city from bombing, he argued that it was not feasible in practice. Furthermore, Eisenhower suggested, collecting so much art in one location might even make it more convenient for the Germans to appropriate or destroy, and besides, Italians in German-occupied territory had no freedom to move the art to any open city that might be established.

There is no further consideration of this matter in the Roberts Commission's correspondence until the spring of 1944, when it re-emerges, perhaps provoked by news of the bombing near cities such as Florence and Siena, and the destruction attested in Padua and elsewhere. In the meantime, the fact that the Allies were no longer bombing the urban centre of Rome itself, along with the protected status of the Vatican, meant that they became, in effect, an undeclared open city for portable works of art evacuated from refuges in central Italy. Earlier in the war, museum collections from Rome itself had been dispersed to refuges in and around smaller towns in central Italy against the possibility of the Allies bombing the capital.[29] This process was reversed in late 1943, when not only were the Rome collections returned to Rome and the Vatican, where they were now considered to be safer, but collections were also sent there from 24 other towns in central Italy, some of which originally had been refuge locations themselves. Thus, for example, the Palazzo Vitelleschi museum in Tarquinia initially had served as a refuge for collections from Rome, but when these were returned to Rome, they were accompanied by 24 cases of the Tarquinia museum's own Etruscan collections that were to be sheltered in the capital's Villa Giulia Museum. The perception that Rome was now safer than Tarquinia proved correct, as the Palazzo Vitelleschi subsequently was badly damaged by tactical bombing.[30] On the other hand, collections from the city of Florence, evacuated earlier in the war to outlying refuges in its hinterland, mostly remained there, even though Allied restrictions on bombing the city actually made it safer than the outlying areas.[31] However, the Allies believed that these collections had, in fact, been returned to the city, something that later put them at significant risk when their dispersed refuges became caught up in ground combat west of the city in August 1944.[32]

In this case, some kind of open acknowledgment of, and agreement on, the de facto 'open' status of Florence might have benefited the protection of its cultural heritage. On the other hand, it would have caused a range of other problems, not all of them military. A Roberts Commission proposal for an open city in Italy for cultural heritage clearly went as far as the cardinal secretary of state in the Vatican, as shown by a memo forwarded by the general secretary of the National Catholic Welfare Conference to Huntington Cairns, the commission's secretary, on 4 May 1944.[33] The cover letter suggests that the commission had taken the initiative in contacting Vatican authorities about the issue through the NCWC in April. The cardinal deplored the aerial bombardment of cities and civilians in general terms, emphasising the humanitarian dimension, claiming that bombing had not been restricted to objectives of strictly military importance and pointing to the disproportionate relationship (as he viewed it) between the damage and slaughter it caused on the one hand, and the 'questionable military advantages' gained on the other. However, when it came to open cities, 'His Eminence calls attention to the numerous serious practical problems.' Among other issues, 'The designation of any one town or city would inevitably give rise to recriminations and complaints from other localities not thus favoured.' The Cardinal sets this in the specific context of local pride in cultural heritage, but given his emphasis on the humanitarian consequences of bombing earlier in the memorandum, it is likely that he was equally aware of the moral dilemma that would be provoked by designating a city 'open' to protect its cultural heritage while civilians in other cities continued to be killed and injured by bombing. Such a designation would be a very clear example of prioritising protection of art and buildings over protection of people, still a regular (and not unreasonable) criticism of attempts to protect cultural property in conflict zones.[34]

At any rate, the Roberts Commission's advocacy of an open-city policy was as unsuccessful in spring 1944 as it had been in autumn 1943. In response to Finley's letter of 19 April seeking an update on the military consideration of open cities begun the previous October, McCloy responded that the commission's queries had been presented to the theatre commander. However, he wrote, the commander (presumably British General Henry Maitland Wilson, who by this time had succeeded Eisenhower) had responded that for military reasons it was not possible to designate cities as 'open' or more generally to indicate particular places that would or would not be bombed at particular times.[35]

Open cities were advocated by the Roberts Commission for the last time in July 1944, and in the context of France rather than Italy. The inter-Allied Vaucher Commission in London, in response to damage to cultural heritage in Normandy and beyond caused by Allied tactical bombing and air interdiction of transportation systems, passed a motion calling on the air forces either to adopt more precise bombing methods or, in some unspecified way, to ensure 'that the tide of battle will be diverted . . . from the areas surrounding those architectural treasures whose importance to the cultural life of Europe as a whole is so outstanding as to admit of no argument'.[36] French members of the Vaucher Commission had secretly selected and designated 25 such 'architectural treasures' that were communicated to Dinsmoor (in London on Roberts Commission duties at the time) to be passed to the War Department in Washington DC. Presumably some sort of 'open cities' arrangement was envisaged, given that most of the monuments probably were in urban centres. The Roberts Commission resolved to support the Vaucher motion and pass it on to the secretary of war, but nothing came of it. The Vaucher Commission also forwarded their motion to the British Macmillan Committee in the hope of receiving support from that quarter, but the British organisation, while expressing sympathy with the aims of the motion, declined to forward it to British military authorities on the grounds that it 'would almost certainly be regarded as interfering in a purely military matter and as such could not be expected to receive consideration'.[37]

CONCLUSIONS

The accidental bombing of Pompeii, along with damage caused by bombing to other cultural sites in Campania in 1943, including the cathedral at Benevento and the church of Santa Chiara in Naples, provided an important point of discussion for academics, museum and gallery directors and politicians on both sides of the Atlantic with an interest in protecting cultural heritage in Italy. The MFAA organisation existed at the time this damage was done, along with documentation of the locations of cultural sites provided by the Harvard Group and the ACLS Committee. However, the lack of effective liaison with Allied air forces meant that cultural property protection was not taken into consideration at all in planning bombing missions against the targets close to Pompeii that led to the site being damaged. Even if the cultural protection issues *had* been evaluated, the urgent military situation under which Pompeii was accidentally bombed, the limitations of contemporary bombing accuracy and (perhaps) limitations of the documentation provided by the US civilian committees mean that even with more effective MFAA–air forces liaison, the bombing probably would have gone ahead regardless and damage would have occurred. Nevertheless, reports and discussion of the damage to cultural sites in Campania played a role in driving forward reforms in February and March 1944 to enhance the role of cultural property protection in the planning of air operations, exemplified by MAAF's *Ancient Monuments of Italy* atlas of aerial photographs along with the rules of engagement contained in its preface.

However, publicised successes at Florence, Siena and Venice notwithstanding, to a great extent these reforms were symbolic rather than practical. It was significant that cultural property protection was now recognised by Headquarters MAAF as a factor to be taken into consideration when planning air missions, that this necessity had been advertised to subordinate air force formations, and that cultural intelligence was available in a format that could be used in operational planning. Nevertheless, change invariably came up against the inaccuracy of contemporary bombing combined with politico-military imperatives against general restriction of bombing. While bombing accuracy against point targets had improved significantly by the end of the war, it remained essentially true that under normal conditions, the only way to guarantee *not* hitting a cultural site such as Pompeii or the Eremitani church in Padua was not to bomb at all, or at least not to bomb anything within several kilometres of the site. Such decisions would have generated other military and political problems that there was no appetite and no clear means to solve in 1944. On the other hand, conditions exist today that make those early 1944 advances in the field of cultural property protection potentially much more concrete and achievable. The greater precision of many air-dropped weapons (at least, those used by Western armed forces) is one factor. The use of information technology such as GIS-enabled cultural inventories and 'no-strike' lists makes it much easier to disseminate and use cultural intelligence than was the case with their predecessor, *The Ancient Monuments of Italy*. These combine to make protection of cultural property against damage from air attack a much more practical element in modern operational planning. Likewise, changes in international law from the 1954 Hague Convention onwards, and changing attitudes towards the protection of civilians and civilian objects in conflict, mean that military and political decision-making structures are potentially much more receptive to cultural property protection imperatives. Pro-active preparation and learning from past experience (including the Second World War) can only further enhance these developments.

MONTECASSINO

At this point, some brief discussion is required of the best-known and most widely discussed example of the destruction of cultural property in wartime Italy. While the Benedictine abbey of Montecassino has been mentioned in passing, there has been no specific discussion of the Abbey's destruction by Allied bombing in February 1944. The reason for this omission is that in many ways, the case of Montecassino was atypical of bomb damage to cultural sites in Italy, and certainly very different from Pompeii. Montecassino was not bombed in error, but was bombed deliberately and (mostly) fairly accurately. It was a known heritage site, easily located and identified, initially listed in MFAA documentation as a two-star site, but subsequently upgraded to three stars on account of the materials evacuated to there from other locations such as the Museo Nazionale in Naples.[38] A deliberate decision was taken to bomb the Abbey on the grounds of perceived military necessity after lengthy discussion that included consideration of its status as a cultural site (although much of the discussion related to its religious significance rather than its historical/artistic importance).[39] That judgement of military necessity might be challenged today (albeit anachronistically), and certainly the practical military problems caused by the reduction of the building to rubble might lead one to make another decision with hindsight. However, Montecassino does not provide a particularly useful or typical example of the success or failure of the cultural property protection developments explored in this chapter.

PART THREE

Military Convenience? The British Military Requisition and Occupation of the National Museum of Naples, 17 November 1943 to 29 June 1944

CHAPTER 11

Allied Cultural Property Protection from Salerno to Naples

A number of different factors potentially and actually cause damage and destruction of cultural property in conflict zones. Definitions of these vary in contemporary scholarly literature, but four were especially relevant to Italy in the Second World War.[1] These were deliberate damage by combatants specifically targeting cultural property as cultural property; incidental, accidental and collateral damage during combat (including bombing and artillery); damage by military or civilian looting; and damage by careless occupation and military use of cultural sites. Fortunately there were relatively few examples of deliberate targeted damage by combatants in Italy in the Second World War, although some of the clearest examples occurred in and near Naples and were advertised prominently in contemporary Allied accounts for their clear propaganda value.[2] The second category, incidental and accidental damage during combat, was the primary cause of damage to cultural heritage in Second World War Italy, mostly due to Allied bombing, as noted in numerous examples above, not least at Pompeii. The final two causes of damage relate primarily to contexts of military occupation, for which Allied monuments protection policies were originally envisaged and designed. Their prevention entails securing and policing cultural sites against potential looters, whether civilian or military, and ensuring that cultural sites are recognised and protected from potentially damaging occupation and use by one's own military forces. While cultural property factors relating to occupation and military governance had less impact than bombing in terms of the amount and severity of damage inflicted in the Second World War, they were addressed and dealt with quite effectively, in great part in response to negative experience in Naples.[3] And as damage caused by bombing, in particular, can today be potentially reduced by the combination of better cultural intelligence and more accurate targeting and weapons, conversely the damage caused by occupation and security issues becomes relatively more prominent and important. This was illustrated during the 2003 Coalition invasion of Iraq, in which little damage was caused to cultural heritage by Coalition forces in combat, including by bombing. The most serious (and in some cases best publicised) examples of such damage were caused by civilian looting exacerbated by Coalition failures to plan for and act to secure and protect cultural sites in the transition from combat operations to occupation, along with subsequent inappropriate or careless military use of some such sites.[4] The experience of cultural property protection in Naples in 1943–1944 provides valuable lessons in this area.[5]

While the bombing of Pompeii provided a case study in which perceptions of military necessity influenced and complicated cultural property protection, the 1943–1944 British military requisition and occupation of the Museo Nazionale (National Museum) of Naples perhaps provides a contrasting case study of what Eisenhower in his December 1943 letter (p. 192) characterised as 'military convenience'. In this case, which forms the central discussion of Part Three, an immensely important cultural institution was put at risk of damage for what was (according to contemporary judgement) no particularly pressing military reason, and played a central role in a subsequent military Commission of Enquiry (the Allied Commission of Enquiry Appointed to Investigate Damage Alleged to have been Caused to Real and Personal Property of Historical and Educational Importance in Italy, 28 December 1943 to 21 January 1944, otherwise known as the Collier Commission, after its chairman, the British Major-General A.L. Collier). Despite its limited remit, the Collier Commission was extremely influential in reinforcing command responsibility and establishing effective policies and procedures for securing and protecting historic buildings in Allied occupied territory, ensuring that such problems did not recur in Italy.

To understand the military occupation of the museum and subsequent events, it is useful to understand the cultural protection context in which they occurred. As already noted, preparations had been made for protection of historic buildings and cultural institutions before the Allied invasion of the Italian mainland, including 'Avalanche', the Salerno landings that began on 9 September 1943. For the most part, the provisions of the *AMGOT Plan for Sicily*, the civil affairs planning handbook for the occupation of Sicily, including *General Administrative Instruction No. 8* and *AIM Planning Instruction No. 12* that dealt with heritage sites (see pp. 119–21), were carried over into the equivalent *AMGOT Plan for Italy*. Extensive documentation of historical sites was available too, including the Harvard and ACLS materials and the British War Office Zone Handbook Lists incorporated into regional civil affairs handbooks such as No. 6, which covered Campania, although these were not as widely distributed as they might have been (see pp. 177–80). Alongside the provisions for closing and guarding historic buildings and cultural institutions specified in these documents, the 1907 Hague Convention (IV) (*Regulations*, Article 56) prohibited requisition of, or damage to, such buildings under belligerent occupation:

> 'The property of municipalities, that of institutions dedicated to religion, charity, and education, the arts and sciences, even when State property, shall be treated as private property. All seizures of, destruction, or wilful damage done to institutions of this character, historic monuments, works of art, science, is forbidden and should be made the subject of legal proceedings.'

This wording was reproduced in both the contemporary British *Manual of Military Law* and its US equivalent, *Rules of Land Warfare*.[6]

The specialist personnel to protect cultural heritage existed too. As we have already seen, Mason Hammond was in Sicily, and had been joined (6 September 1943) shortly before 'Avalanche' by Frederick Maxse. On 23 September, British Major P.K. (Paul) Baillie Reynolds, a pre-war archaeologist, was appointed acting director of the Sub-Commission for Monuments, Fine Arts and Archives, with its base in Palermo. Another officer with a monuments and fine arts background, Major Paul Gardner of the US Army, was assigned to the military government component of 15th Army Group for duty in Campania. Gardner was a First World War veteran who had studied art history and was the director of the Nelson-Atkins Museum of Art in Kansas City (MO) before he re-enlisted. He was nearly 50 years old in September 1943. However, despite all of these preparations, Allied protection of cultural heritage during the liberation and occupation of Naples went disastrously wrong from the outset.

By the time Allied troops entered Naples on 1 October 1943, there was a growing body of cultural property protection experience from Sicily to draw on. The lessons learned in Sicily in some respects anticipated the problems that would occur in Naples, although there was no easy way to communicate those lessons in time to anyone who could do anything about them, and to some extent, the experience in Sicily overlapped with and proceeded in parallel with what happened in Naples. Not until 24 October 1943 was Hammond able to summarise in writing what he and Maxse had learned, in a memo to Brigadier-General Frank J. McSherry, the US Army deputy chief civil affairs officer.[7] In it, Hammond emphasises that contrary to expectations held during the planning process, the reality of the occupation of Sicily had shown that ordinary civil affairs officers did not have time among their more pressing duties to undertake monuments and fine arts protection activities. In practice, most of these activities fell to the very few specialised monuments and fine arts officers on the ground, working closely with the re-activated local authorities. Hammond also stresses the importance of the first phase of occupation, as ground combat moved forward and reserve and administrative elements of Allied military forces took over an area.[8] Consequently Hammond advocates attachment of monuments officers to advanced elements of the military government apparatus within 15th Army Group and its subordinate Armies (5th US and 8th British) to place advisers 'more closely in touch with the initial phases of occupation' rather than merely within the rear components of AMG headquarters. In this way, Hammond argues, 'during the first, uncontrolled, days of the occupation' specialist officers could post off-limits signs and arrange for guards to be established if required, prevent unnecessary military requisition of historic buildings and limit civilian and military looting and damage caused by carelessness and ignorance. He also argues for the separation of education and fine arts duties. Initially these two aspects of military government had been combined in a single Allied sub-commission, based on the structure of the associated Italian civilian administrative units. As Hammond notes, however, their problems (which for education entailed the re-establishment of the Italian school system) were very different. For this reason, the Monuments, Fine Arts and Archives Sub-Commission became a separate entity within AMG on 24 October 1943. All of these issues would be encountered and raised again over the following months and reiterated not only in the MFAA's own reports, but also in those of Sir Leonard Woolley and Mortimer Wheeler, who came to hear of such recommendations.

THE ALLIED OCCUPATION OF NAPLES

Fifth Army's break-out from the Salerno beachhead and its advance on Naples were quite rapid, beginning on 22 September, reaching the town of Pompei late on 28 September, and Naples on 1 October.[9] The speed of this advance meant that in the first instance, at least, occupation of historic

Figure 30: Contemporary photograph of US Army personnel established in the archaic Greek 'Basilica' temple at Paestum, captioned 'A company of men has set up its office between the columns (Doric) of an ancient Greek temple of Neptune, built about 700 B.C.,' 22 September 1943, NARA online version, <https://catalog.archives.gov/OpaAPI/media/531170/content/arcmedia/media/images/43/1/43-0050a.gif> (accessed 16 July 2019).

buildings by Allied forces was not a serious problem, although a US signals unit had set up in the archaic Greek 'Basilica' temple on the archaeological site of Poseidonia-Paestum, close to the US landing beaches (Figure 30).[10]

The entry of Allied forces into the city of Naples was anticipated by the *quattro giornate*, the 'Four Days' (27–30 September) during which partisans harassed and hindered the German withdrawal through the city. Some lurid speculation appeared in the Allied press about the damage that the Germans were doing or might do to the city, including its historic buildings and collections. While the retreating Germans' destruction of Naples's civilian infrastructure was genuine and severe, reports on the damage to cultural heritage were speculative and exaggerated. *New York Times* correspondent Herbert L. Matthews interviewed Italian philosopher and former senator Benedetto Croce on the island of Capri (already occupied by Allied forces) on 26 September.[11]

> *'NAZIS TAKE ALL THEY CAN*
>
> From everything heard here, the Nazis, however, are not missing much. They are seizing what they can, including art objects, and destroying what they cannot take with them. . . . "Italian art treasures belong to the world, and it will be the world's loss if they are destroyed," Signor Croce said. "The Germans have nothing worthwhile to be destroyed in any sense comparable. They never had a true culture, except worship of force and strength."'

Other rumours reported in the press exaggerated the burning of the Royal Society library into the destruction of the entire University of Naples, and claimed, incorrectly, that the Palazzo Reale had been blown up and 'the beautiful San Carlo opera house had been burned and many palaces ransacked'.[12] Some later newspaper coverage continued to elaborate the theme of German barbarism, particularly in response to more detailed information on the burning of the Royal Society library. However, within a week or so of their arrival in Naples, correspondents (often citing Maiuri as their source) typically were presenting a more balanced and realistic picture of the situation, on the one hand reducing their emphasis on destruction by the Germans, and on the other acknowledging the heavy damage to historic buildings (especially churches such as Santa Chiara) caused by Allied bombing.[13]

Just as Mason Hammond argued on the basis of his experience in Sicily, for Naples too 'the first, uncontrolled, days' of Allied occupation were important for the treatment of historic buildings. There were a number of instances of looting, and of casual damage to, and uncontrolled military requisition and occupation of, historic buildings in the city. The most significant examples were the Palazzo Reale (Royal Palace) of Naples (Figure 31, Figure 32), which was on both Harvard and Zone Handbook Lists, and the University of Naples. The former, already damaged by Allied bombs, was occupied by a mix of British, US and French military detachments from 1 October 1943. The most valuable materials from the palace had already been evacuated, and German troops had occupied it briefly immediately before the Allied occupation, but the later Collier Commission of Enquiry (see pp. 194–97) held Allied troops responsible for appropriations and damage that including 1200 m^2 of silk brocade stripped from the walls of sixteen rooms, and oil paintings, furniture and clocks damaged or removed from the Palace.[14] While the commission concluded that 'no really valuable antique had been removed or damaged by Allied troops', in great part because these had been evacuated already, and that many of the removals (of furniture, in particular) were for military use elsewhere rather than personal looting for gain, nevertheless, as Colonel Edgar Erskine Hume, chief of AMG 5th Army, who had inspected the palace, testified,

> 'I have been told by many people in NAPLES that damage caused by Allied troops in the Palace was the subject of much adverse comment among people from all classes of [Italian] society and that sometimes there was the statement that "even the Germans did not do that."'[15]

American troops had taken over part of the University of Naples from 2–3 September and ransacked and looted its scientific departments. In his evidence to the subsequent Commission of Enquiry, Gardner reported that when he had visited the areas occupied by the American troops, in all those areas and rooms adjacent to their billets,

> 'there were evidences of an enormous amount of damage to collections of specimens, museum material, libraries, laboratory material and scientific instruments. Glass cases containing birds, other animals, mineral collections and samples of undersea life were broken open and the contents missing.'

Books had been pulled out of bookcases and heaped on the floor, and microscopes had been wrenched apart and their lenses removed. In this instance, it was possible to identify the particular unit of the men responsible for the damage—the US 82nd Airborne Division.[16]

Subsequently, officers responsible for overseeing the process of quartering Allied troops in the city claimed to know nothing of the provisions and resources established for the protection of historic buildings, neither the protections afforded by the 1907 Hague Convention, nor the specific regulations and guidelines drawn up by Allied civil affairs structures, nor the lists and maps that (in theory at least) were available to them. Giving evidence to the Commission of Enquiry in late December and January, first the British Naples Town Major, Major Huggan, asked if he had received lists of historic buildings, responded,

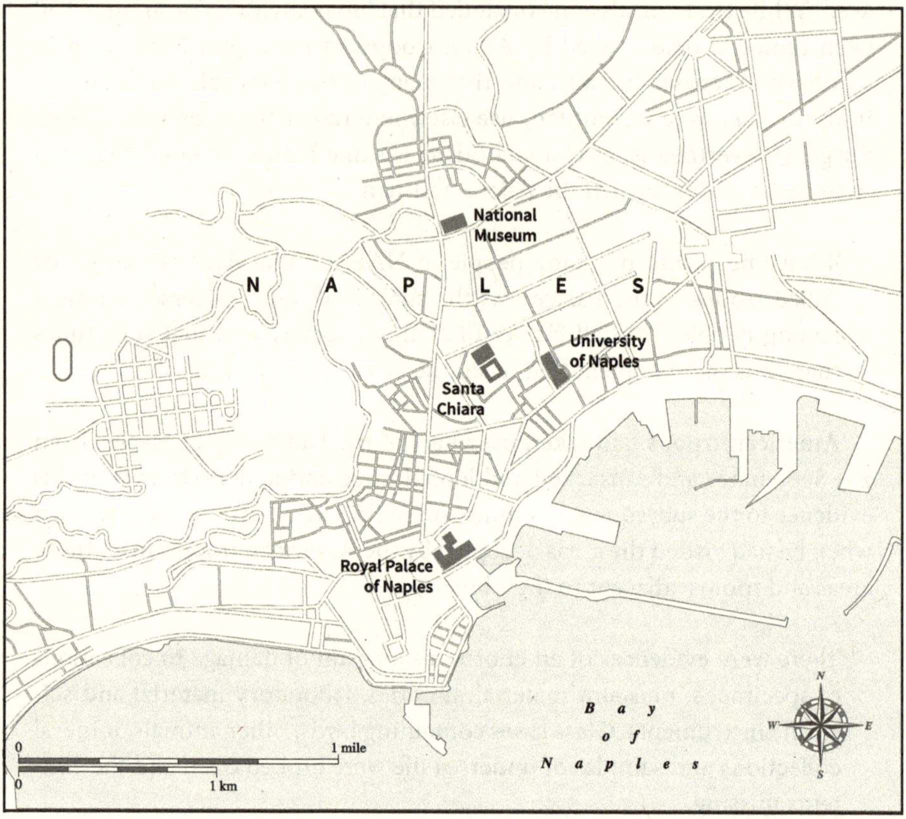

Figure 31: Map of Naples in 1943 showing key cultural sites discussed in the text.

A. No, I have never been given any such list until I was handed one by a member of the Commission about a fortnight ago.

Q. How are you expected to know what buildings are national monuments etc.?

A. Unless I or any other Town Major am given such a list by higher authority, we have to get the information as best we can out of any local guidebook we can find.

Q. Have you a copy of the British Zone Hand Book for Campania?

A. I have never seen this publication.'

Figure 32: The Royal Palace of Naples today (author's photograph).

Brigadier J.G. Bruxner-Randall, the British commander, 57 Area, stated

> no orders were received by me drawing attention to the necessity that [monuments] were not damaged by the troops. I did not receive any instructions either about the occupation of such buildings.
>
> Q. Were you given any lists of such places?
> A. No; it might have been a great help to have had a list of this sort given to me 2 or 3 weeks before my arrival here in NAPLES.'

Finally, Major Huggan's US equivalent, Lt. Col. Edward D. McCall of the Real Estate Section, Metropolitan Area, Peninsular Base Section [PBS], stated

> 'To my knowledge, there were no instructions issued naming historical monuments or buildings as such, prior to sometime around the middle of December [1943—shortly before the Commission of Enquiry commenced].'

McCall claimed he had received no instructions about the occupation of historic buildings by troops, and also noted that some cases had occurred even before his section had been set up to oversee requisition and billeting.[17]

Thus the provisions made by Allied armies to protect historic buildings from abusive military occupation before the invasion of Sicily, subsequently re-stated for mainland Italy, were initially ineffective in the occupation of Naples. Officers whose role was to oversee requisition and billeting claimed to know nothing even of the protections afforded historic buildings in the British *Manual of Military Law* or its US equivalent, nor of the protective measures required in the *AMGOT Plan for Italy* planning manual, nor of the lists of protected buildings in the *Zone Handbook* for Campania. Either the provisions and documents had been inadequately disseminated or advertised even to middle-ranking officers whose duties required knowledge of them, or they had chosen to ignore them for the sake of convenience, given that their superiors had not emphasised their importance.

Many of the reasons for these failures had been anticipated by Hammond and others on the basis of their experiences in Sicily, and were re-iterated and identified in later reports and enquiries. The sheer scale of occupying and consolidating control of Naples overwhelmed Allied civil affairs officers with more immediately pressing duties than protecting cultural property. Besides the size of the civilian population and the dire conditions in which much of it was living (and continued to live), Allied military personnel flooded into the city, a crucial port and base area for the logistical support of the advance on Rome.[18] One early consequence of this over-stretch of military government was that Gardner, the sole specialist monuments officer assigned to 15th Army Group/Region III at this time, reached the city only on 19 October, missing the first crucial days of the occupation. He had been sent instead to serve in the first instance as temporary civil affairs officer on the island of Ischia, performing general military government activities until he was released for Naples.[19] Even after he arrived there, Gardner's role as head of Section of Education and Fine Arts meant that much of his time and energy inevitably was devoted to rehabilitating the city's educational system. For the separation between fine arts and education established in Sicily at sub-commission level in Sicily had not affected Gardner in Naples. Mortimer Wheeler, characteristically dramatic, noted,

> 'Enquiry discovered on the staff of AMGOT at NAPLES a major, with one sergeant as his total staff, appointed to look after "Education and the Fine Arts"! "Education" included the immense task of reopening the Ital-

ian schools, and it will be appreciated that "Fine Arts" scarcely entered the picture.'[20]

Consequently, among the recommendations even in Gardner's first report from Naples (1 November 1943) was that the head of education and fine arts 'should arrive in any occupied area at the earliest possible moment', and also that the Division of Education and Fine Arts should be divided into its two component elements. This did not happen until 4 December, when another officer was appointed to take over Education.[21] Even in Gardner's absence, officers of Naples City Allied Military Government had sought to undertake basic measures to protect the city's monuments, but with little success. They had established initial contact with Italian museum directors, distributed 'off-limits' signs among them, and requested guards from the US 82nd Airborne Division for historic buildings, although there is no evidence that these were ever provided, and as noted, men of that unit were later judged responsible for damage in the university. AMG officers also made regular protests against requisition and occupation by military units of museums, libraries and other historical monuments.[22]

There were a number of reasons for the problems. As noted, at the subsequent enquiry, responsible billeting officers claimed to have no knowledge of the regulations established to protect historic buildings. However, some clearly were aware of restrictions on such requisitions, and advanced arguments of military necessity to counter AMG protests against occupation and damage. In December 1943, Brigadier Maurice Lush, who had been British chief civil affairs officer in Tripolitania at the time of Wheeler and Ward-Perkins's activities and would soon become vice president of the Allied Control Commission in Italy, wrote

> 'I am frankly shocked at the attitude of the [US] PBS and the [British] Area [57th] towards museums and ancient monuments in Naples, and I know that Hume has felt himself frustrated by the invariable and unanswerable reply that the action has been taken because of military necessity. . . . The uncompromising attitude with regard to fine arts shown by commanders, and the inevitable damage once troops are permitted to occupy such buildings, has left an even more painful impression. . . . I think you know how fully I realise the paramount importance of operations. But I am as anxious for the good name of the Allied Armies which, in Naples, is in danger of being tarnished.'[23]

Lacking clear direction on the importance of the issue from senior commanders, middle-ranking British and US billeting officers ignored the prohibition on the use of historic buildings when possible, and claimed military necessity when ignoring it was no longer possible. Certainly historic buildings were potentially attractive billets, as their size meant they could be used to house entire units, and their prestige and association with authority potentially enhanced their occupiers' authority. Besides (or in the context of) occupation of historic buildings, some individuals of lower rank, perhaps influenced by the attitudes of their commanders, stole and caused damage to cultural property for a variety of motives ranging from casual ignorance, vandalism and souvenir-hunting to the prospect of financial gain. This was essentially a disciplinary and educational problem. As the Collier Commission later noted to emphasise this point, damage and theft were not confined to buildings formally occupied by troops, but even buildings where 'off-limits' signs had been posted were broken into. In some cases, unsettled conditions meant that Italian custodians were absent from their usual places of work; in other cases, they were present, but lacked authority when faced with Allied military personnel.[24]

THE MFAA IN NAPLES

Even though Gardner arrived in Naples on 19 October, he was unable to effect much change until well into December. While continuing the activities begun by other civil affairs officers (liaising with Italian authorities, providing and posting 'off-limits' notices, protesting against occupation of historic buildings, undertaking inspections of occupied and damaged buildings and liaising with commanders of troops in occupation), Gardner was handicapped by his relatively low rank and consequently limited authority, and by administrative and organisational problems within the Allied cultural property protection apparatus. For while the Sub-Commission for Monuments, Fine Arts and Archives existed at this time with Baillie Reynolds as its own (acting) director, it had no formal responsibility for Gardner or for cultural heritage in Naples. The sub-commission was part of HQ AMG, its formal area of responsibility at this time restricted to Region I (Sicily) with its headquarters physically located in Palermo.[25] Gardner, on the other hand, was a civil affairs officer in AMG 15th Army Group/Region III, unable to communicate formally with Baillie Reynolds and other fellow monuments officers except indirectly through his own chain of command. Among other things, this restricted his initial ability to learn from the experiences of Hammond and others in Sicily. By December 1943, elements of HQ AMG had moved from Palermo to Naples, including individual MFAA officers such as Mason Hammond, who was joined by others such as USAAF Major Theodore Sizer (who in peacetime had been director of the Yale University Museum of Fine Arts), USAAF Lieutenant-Colonel Norman T. Newton, and Major John Ward-Perkins. However, it was not until 7 February 1944 that the sub-commission's headquarters (by this time essentially Baillie Reynolds) eventually reached Naples.[26] In the meantime, as Baillie Reynolds himself noted in early January 1944:

> 'The Sub-Commission has no authority in Campania; and will not for some time, and meanwhile damage is being done by one section of the army and another section created to prevent such damage is powerless to intervene. . . . If the protests of the Regional MFAA officer for Region 3, who has the rank of Major, are disregarded by military authority, he should be able to secure support for his contentions from the Sub-Commission for Monuments, Fine Arts and Archives. But the Acting Director of the Sub-Commission has no authority in Region 3, is himself a Major and is not even present with HQ AMG.'[27]

The low rank of Gardner and other monuments officers in Naples relative to other officers with whom they might come into contact and contention was a recurring issue. Even when British War Office Archaeological Adviser Sir Leonard Woolley, a lieutenant-colonel, came to Naples on an inspection visit in December, his arguments against requisition were ignored, in the short-term at least, although they may have contributed to the establishment of the subsequent Collier Commission. One of the recommendations advanced by Mortimer Wheeler, who was in Naples about the time of Woolley's visit, was for monuments officers of higher rank, with a brigadier as archaeological adviser, with authority to contact commanders directly.[28] This was never achieved, however. Most wartime monuments officers were captains and majors, with Colonels Geoffrey Webb, the British adviser to SHAEF (Supreme Headquarters Allied Expeditionary Force, in northwestern Europe) and Henry C. Newton (US Army) the highest-ranking specialist officers.

Regardless of the many difficulties Gardner faced in his first few weeks in Naples, they would only get worse. For on 17 November 1943, he received word from Maiuri that the Museo Nazionale was to be requisitioned for British military use.

CHAPTER 12

The Museo Nazionale di Napoli, Its Requisition and Consequences

The importance of the Museo Nazionale in Naples was recognised by its inclusion in all the Allied lists of protected monuments in the city, including the Zone Handbook and Harvard Lists, which rated it as a three-star monument, the highest category, and described it, with some justification, as 'the most important museum of classical antiquities in the world'.[1] Some of the sculpture, stone and bronze, had been excavated at Pompeii and Herculaneum, and the museum also contained the Farnese Collection, brought from Rome in 1787 by Ferdinand IV of Naples, a Farnese through his grandmother Elizabeth, the wife of Philip V of Spain. Other material from Pompeii included fresco paintings excavated in the 18th and 19th centuries, when it was usual to remove them from their contexts on the site for display. Besides hosting the archaeological material, at this time the Museo Nazionale also housed the city's most important collection of paintings, only subsequently (1950) transferred to the Museo di Capodimonte. This included Raphael's *Madonna of the Divine Love*, Titian's portraits of the Farnese family and his *Danae*, Artemisia Gentileschi's *Judith Slaying Holofernes*, Bellini's *Transfiguration of Christ*, and Breughel's *The Blind Leading the Blind*.[2]

However, by the time of the Allied liberation of Naples, some of the museum's contents had been evacuated to refuges elsewhere. In accordance with national policy to protect movable works of art from bombing in particular, Maiuri (as archaeological superintendent) and Dr. Bruno Molajoli (Maiuri's counterpart with responsibility for galleries) oversaw the packing and transfer of part of the collection to repositories outside the city, often located in what were themselves buildings of historic and religious importance. Thus, items from the National Museum, along with collections from other museums, galleries and churches in Naples, were dispersed to official refuges, including the Loreto Abbey at Mercogliano (Provincia di Avellino), the Abbey of SS. Trinità at Cava de' Tirreni (Provincia di Salerno) and (in particular) the Benedictine Abbey at Montecassino. In the case of

Figure 33: One of the inner courtyards of the Museo Nazionale di Napoli (National Museum of Naples, now the Museo Nazionale Archeologico di Napoli). The original British Army occupation plan envisaged establishing a field kitchen in one of the courts, although that idea was abandoned when the requisition did eventually take place (author's photograph).

the National Museum, the final stage of this evacuation took place only in September 1943, when the city had already suffered considerable damage from bombing and the Allied landings in the Gulf of Salerno were almost underway. According to Maiuri, the first consignment, of 60 crates containing, for the most part, precious items from the museum's archaeological collection such as gold, silver, glass, jewellery and ivory, was transported to Montecassino on 15 June 1943, and the final consignment, of sculpture, on 6 September. In addition, 45 cases of paintings from the museum were taken to the Abbey.[3] Orders for the September evacuation came directly from the Badoglio government in Rome, in response to the British 8th Army landings in Calabria on 3 September. Initially the evacuation was supposed to include marble sculpture such as the huge Farnese Hercules and the even bigger (but very fragmentary) Farnese Bull, but Maiuri argued against this on grounds of practicality and eventually moved only the bronzes, including famous and important pieces excavated in the 18th century from the Villa of the Papyri at Herculaneum. The remaining materials were protected either in situ, with sandbags and wooden frames, or in basement rooms.[4] After describing in his memoir his initial trip to Montecassino with the first consignment of cases, Maiuri added,

> 'When I departed, I felt like a great weight had been lifted from my shoulders. Now the most fragile and endangered part of the museum's collection was in safety. Who could have anticipated the deliberate and planned bombardment of the Abbey, repeated and total?'[5]

Besides the unanticipated risk to the evacuated materials at Montecassino, the Museo Nazionale itself lay in the midst of fighting during the *quattro giornate* (27–30 September). As previously noted, Maiuri had been wounded in an Allied air attack on 15 September, but returned to Naples on 28 September, and lodged in the museum while convalescing from his leg wound. He subsequently recounted that the museum lay at a key point on the Germans' retreat, and so fierce fighting took place around it.[6] On one occasion, partisans asked to deploy snipers on the museum's balconies but Maiuri refused curtly (*recisamente*), fearing this would expose it to German attack. On another occasion, partisans claimed that Fascist militia were firing at them from the roof of the museum and demanded entry to flush them out. Maiuri refused, but sent a member of the museum staff to check. He established that the firing was actually coming from a house nearby, and the partisans relented, leaving the museum, in Maiuri's words, 'rispettato come una Basilica e un Santuario in quelle dramatiche giornate' ('respected throughout those dramatic days as if it were a church or sanctuary').

The *quattro giornate* gave way to Allied occupation on 1 October 1943. Shortly after their arrival in Naples, US correspondents visited the Museo Nazionale and spoke to Maiuri, an obvious subject for interviews given American (in particular) concerns about damage to the city's heritage sites and Maiuri's fame beyond Italy as the excavator of Pompeii. As the journalists noted, damage to the museum was largely confined to broken windows, caused by blasts from nearby bombs, but the remaining sculpture was well protected in place. The superintendent discussed damage to other historic buildings at some length, but (initially at least) was secretive about the destination of the evacuated elements of the museum's collection, describing it only as 'a secret and sacred place'.[7] Eventually it became known that the 'secret and sacred place' was the abbey at Montecassino:

> 'The best pieces went to Montecassino, all but a few, with which Professor Maiuri could not bear to part. "A curator never wants to send his things away" he said unhappily. "If it were up to me, nothing would have left here, but orders came from Rome. It all went just a few days before the armistice. Once I heard the announcement, I stopped all new shipments." Those pieces that he had kept back included such world-famous pieces as the "blue vase" from Pompeii and the "Farnese Cup" of sardonica [sic]. It was pathetic to walk through the bare rooms, with all the empty frames on the walls.'[8]

For the most part, the Museo Nazionale was spared the traumas inflicted on other cultural sites such as the university and the Royal Palace, despite false claims in some quarters (for example, in the *Paris-Soir* newspaper published in German-occupied France) that the museum (including its collections from Pompeii) was being pillaged by the Americans, and despite proposals advanced to Maiuri from time to time from as early as 7 October, for the museum's requisition as a depot to accommodate troops in transit to the front. In one version of this story, Maiuri specifically refers to the museum's potential occupants as troops 'of colour' (so presumably African-American, French Moroccan or Indian troops), suggesting populist racist rumours rather than genuine plans to use the museum in that role.[9]

The condition of the Museo Nazionale was the very first subject addressed in Paul Gardner's first report after his arrival in Naples on 19 October. Like the journalists, he noted that there was no direct bomb damage to the building, although most of the windows were broken, and that much material, including the small sculpture, had been moved to safety, while the large sculpture had been sandbagged for protection. However, on all floors of the museum 'minor objects' remained in their display cases, and overall, Gardner estimated, about 75% of the collections remained in the museum. It was closed to the general public, but Italian civil government offices had been established on the first and second floors. Gardner concluded,

> 'The entire situation is very well controlled by competent Italian authorities. It is most strongly recommended that at no time will the museum be requisitioned for any military purpose.'[10]

However, less than three weeks after Gardner submitted this report, on 17 November, he learned from museum authorities (rather than through military channels) that a serious attempt was under way to requisition and occupy it as a British medical stores depot.[11]

Gardner immediately sent a memo deploring the threatened requisition to Colonel Hume. He outlined the plan to use a large part of the museum as the British Medical Corps No. 10 Base Depot. Forty personnel were to be billeted there to staff the depot (although Gardner noted there was a tendency to expand numbers to fill the available space once a building was occupied), and a field kitchen would be installed in one of the museum's courtyards. It was of particular concern that the layout of the building made it impossible to secure any one part of the building from troops for safe storage of the remaining collections. The risk of fire from the kitchen and inflammable stores was another concern. Gardner concluded in emotional and unmilitary terms that left little doubt regarding his feelings on the requisition:

> 'The Museum has the most important collection of classical and Roman sculpture in the world and the greater part of it is still in place in the building. Other sections are still installed with parts of the important painting and unique Pompeian collection. . . . I have seen too many historical monuments such as the Palazzo Reale, the Castel Nuovo, the Bibliotheca nazionale and the university reduced to a shambles by troops to foresee any other destiny for the Museo Nazionale. . . . I cannot protest too strongly against such a requisition. The continued requisitioning and pillage of historical monuments in Naples is furnishing just the type of propaganda that the Germans and Fascists use with telling effect. Further, once troops are quartered in the midst of one of the greatest collections of all Italy, I can not assume any responsibility for its safety.'[12]

Nevertheless, Gardner's protests were ineffective, and while the museum was not yet under full-scale military occupation at the beginning of December 1943, this was still planned, and preparatory work was underway. On 1 December, Sir Leonard Woolley, now officially the archaeological adviser to the director of Civil Affairs in the British War Office, arrived in Naples on an inspection visit. The issue of the National Museum was clearly the most pressing problem, and Woolley spent much of his visit engaged in meetings relating to it, summarised in a memo submitted to the chief civil affairs officer of 15th Army Group a few days later. Initially he met with Brigadier J.G. Bruxner-Randall, commander of [British] 57th Area. Bruxner-Randall held to the view that the occupation of the museum was 'a matter of urgent military necessity' for the storage of medical supplies, and that no other building was suitable for the purpose. His argument is not to be dismissed lightly. The provision of medical supplies to treat Allied wounded was, rightly, a high priority, and the museum had many advantages in terms of size, access and security. Few buildings of that size remained undamaged in Naples at that time. Woolley, who as a lieutenant-colonel was out-ranked by Bruxner-Randall, admitted 'that the museum is temptingly convenient' for its intended function and bomb damage meant that similar structures were not easily found. In response, Woolley sought to argue that this *particular* building was not indispensable, and in his subsequent written report, at least, Woolley noted that both American and British political authorities 'will require more justification for [the requisition of the museum] than is given by Brigadier Bruxner-Randall's arguments', casting doubt on his claim of military necessity.[13]

However, Bruxner-Randall remained unconvinced, and the following day he, Woolley, Gardner, and Maiuri met at the museum to discuss ways to mitigate the impact of military occupation on the museum and its contents. It was eventually conceded that the military personnel who were to work in the building would not actually live there, but in a nearby house, and only guards would be allowed in the museum at night.[14] Woolley returned to London a few days later, leaving his report on the requisition, arguing against it, warning of the potential for political agitation if it went ahead, pushing instead for complete evacuation of the building (including the Italian public works personnel already in occupation) and the museum's total closure as the logical alternative to occupation. Addressing matters of policy beyond the individual case of the museum, Woolley also proposed publication of a general order that no building on the *Zone Handbook* 'Works of Art' lists (which included the Museo Nazionale and the Palazzo Reale) should be used for military purposes without special permission, granted individually, from the commander-in-chief.

Despite Woolley's intervention, and despite a brief temporary lifting of the requisition on 18 December, full-scale occupation of the museum went ahead on 22–23 December. Maiuri describes the arrival of trucks loaded with medical supplies, the transformation of the galleries into a huge medical warehouse with crates 'piled higher than the statues' and a pervasive smell of disinfectant 'worse than a harbour quarantine station'.[15] And just a few days after Woolley's departure, even as Gardner was arguing against occupation of the museum, he also received word that the Bourbon Royal Palace at Caserta, 25 km north of Naples and partially occupied by Allied personnel since October, was to be fully requisitioned and occupied by Allied Force Headquarters (AFHQ), Eisenhower's headquarters controlling all Allied forces in the Mediterranean theatre.[16] The Royal Palace at Caserta was a two-star monument on the Harvard Lists, and also appeared in the Zone Handbook Lists. In his December report from Palermo MFAA Sub-Commission director P.K. Baillie Reynolds describes the planned requisition of the palace as 'particularly disquieting', noting that the MFAA Sub-Commission was itself responsible through HQ AMG to AFHQ 'and if that HQ itself takes action likely to damage monuments and works of art which it has a sub-commission to protect, the sub-commission's position becomes ridiculous'.[17]

However, also in December 1943, some combination of pressure from political and civilian circles in Washington DC and London, Woolley's intervention, and repeated protests from Gardner and other monuments officers eventually produced results.[18]

RESPONSES TO THE PROBLEMS CAUSED BY INADEQUATELY CONTROLLED MILITARY REQUISITION AND OCCUPATION OF HISTORIC BUILDINGS IN NAPLES

Mid-December 1943 saw the beginning of a sequence of events and communications aimed at ending the uncontrolled requisition and occupation of historic buildings in Naples and beyond, and damage to those buildings caused by looting and vandalism by military personnel. As noted, a framework of international law to protect cultural sites already existed, along with regulations established by the military government components of the Allied armies, specialised personnel, and appropriate documentation. The measures taken in December 1943 to spring 1944 in response to the problems encountered in Naples did not require radical changes to existing regulations. Rather, they sought to ensure effective observance and implementation of procedures that had already been established, by advertising them more widely, by making both commanders and their men aware of their responsibilities and by demonstrating the willingness of the Allied high command to enforce them as a matter of military discipline. At the same time, organisational and practical changes were promulgated to make the MFAA Sub-Commission more effective in protecting historic buildings in newly occupied areas. These proceeded in parallel with the air force measures discussed in the last chapter, and were carried forward throughout the rest of the war in Italy and into northwestern Europe.

Evidence for those reforms and changes are provided in seven important contemporary documents.

Major Paul Gardner to Brigadier-General Arthur W. Pence, Commanding General Peninsular Base Section, Monuments of *[sic]* Fine Arts and Cultural Institutions of Naples Occupied by Allied Troops, *20 December 1943*[19]

Gardner characterises this communication as 'complying with your request', suggesting that Pence had been alerted or pressured to engage with Gardner to obtain information relating to military occupation of historic buildings. Gardner's reply (this document) comprised a list of occupied buildings with brief notes on damage and problems caused. Those buildings are the Palazzo Reale of Naples, the Museo San Martino, the Castel Nuovo, the University of Naples and its agricultural college, the Palazzo Reale of Capodimonte and the Villa Floridiana museum. In some cases (Museo San Martino, Capodimonte and Villa Floridiana) Gardner describes the occupation as unproblematic. The Museo Nazionale di Napoli is not included because its full-scale occupation did not begin until a few days after the report was submitted.

HQ Peninsular Base Section, Circular Number 37, *20 December 1943*[20]

This routine circular covered a variety of topics relevant to officers of the US Peninsular Base Section and other officers using its services. This was the US base command responsible for the organisation and administration of Naples as a logistical base for Allied armies. One of several (unrelated) topics covered in this issue was 'Protection and Preservation of Historical and Cultural Objects in Italy'. This draws attention to the fact that 'Italy is a land of monuments, statues, works of art and objects of cultural and historical interest' and claims 'Germans have drawn the censure of the world by their gross theft and wanton mutilation of such things. The Allied Command has directed their preservation'. It goes on to remind commanders of the damage that could be done to historical buildings and objects by day-to-day careless use and souvenir hunting and that they must caution their men against causing such damage and take responsibility for protection and preservation.

This modest communication served to alert commanders to the more substantial measures taken later in the month. However, the fact that it covered the issue at all was a significant step forward given the problems that had occurred since October.

***Allied Force Headquarters, Office of the Commander-in-Chief,* Historical Monuments, *29 December 1943*[21]**

This letter, signed by Eisenhower as theatre commander-in-chief and addressed to all commanders, essentially advertised the will of the Allied high command to protect historical buildings and cultural institutions based on the principles and laws that already existed.

The preamble states:

> 'Today we are fighting in a country which has contributed a great deal to our cultural inheritance, a country rich in monuments which by their creation helped and now in their old age illustrate the growth of the civilization which is ours. We are bound to respect those monuments so far as war allows.'

A key middle paragraph acknowledged the paramount importance of military necessity ('If we have to choose between destroying a famous building and sacrificing our own men, then our men's lives count infinitely more and the buildings must go') but criticised the abuse of 'military necessity' arguments such as, perhaps, the one that Bruxner-Randall had advanced to Sir Leonard Woolley to justify the occupation of the National Museum in Naples.

> 'Nothing can stand against the argument of military necessity. That is an accepted principle. But the phrase "military necessity" is sometimes used where it would be more truthful to speak of military convenience or even of personal convenience. I do not want it to cloak slackness or indifference.'

The final paragraph places responsibility on higher commanders to determine from AMG officers the locations of historic buildings both in potential operational areas ('immediately ahead of our front lines'), highlighting the need to incorporate cultural property protection in planning operations, as well as in military requisition and occupation.

Allied Force Headquarters, General Orders Number 68, *29 December 1943*[22]

This document was sent out at the same time as Eisenhower's letter and provided the practical details to complement Eisenhower's general statement of policy. Section 1, under the heading 'Buildings', prohibits military use of any structure listed in the 'Works of Art' appendix to the British Zone Handbooks without the explicit permission of the commander-in-chief of 15th Army Group, British General Sir Harold Alexander. It also authorises commanders to put such buildings out of bounds, to secure them and place 'off-limits' notices and guards on them as necessary. Still under 'Buildings', it notes that AMG officers could provide supplementary lists of historic buildings 'of secondary importance' additional to the Zone Handbook Lists. Art galleries, religious buildings, and similar locations 'should not be occupied when alternative accommodations are available'. The second section of the order deals with looting, wanton damage and sacrilege, prevention of which is highlighted as a command responsibility, its gravity to be made clear to all Allied troops. The order was signed by Eisenhower's chief of staff, US Major-General Walter Bedell Smith.

Crucially this order did nothing to ensure the de-requisition and evacuation of buildings such as the Royal Palace of Naples and the National Museum that were already under (or marked for) military occupation.[23] Another controversial aspect of Allied *General Order* 68 was its emphasis on the British Zone Handbook Lists of historic buildings to determine what could not be occupied, and these were by no means comprehensive.[24] *Zone Handbook No. 6 Campania* included just 46 sites across all of Campania, 21 of which were in the city of Naples itself. In contrast, the Harvard 'Long List' included 316 sites, 60 of which were in Naples. The Harvard Lists, of course, also prioritised sites by assigning to them a star ranking, which the Zone Handbook Lists did not. However, the brevity of the Zone Handbook Lists made them more acceptable from a military perspective and potentially reduced resistance to their application, while setting a precedent for the acceptance of later and more complete inventories. In this sense, the Zone Handbook Lists served as a 'foot in the door' subsequently widened by addition of supplementary lists (77 sites in the Campania auxiliary lists in addition to the 46 in the *Zone Handbook*) and eventual replacement by the *Lists of Protected Monuments* (see below).[25] In theory, at least, the Zone Handbooks were more widely available than copies of the Harvard

Lists, although as seen above, officers responsible for overseeing billeting in Naples (for example) claimed to have seen neither.

Allied Commission of Enquiry Appointed to Investigate Damage Alleged to Have Been Caused to Real and Personal Property of Historical and Educational Importance in Italy *(The Collier Commission), Naples, 28 December 1943 to 21 January 1944*

This military Commission of Enquiry was established to enquire into, and where possible determine responsibility for, damage 'other than war or combat damage' by Allied forces in Italy, with particular reference to 1907 Hague Convention (IV) (*Regulations*, Article 56):

> 'The property of municipalities, that of institutions dedicated to religion, charity, and education, the arts and sciences, even when State property, shall be treated as private property. All seizures of, destruction, or wilful damage done to institutions of this character, historic monuments, works of art, science, is forbidden and should be made the subject of legal proceedings.'

Thus the terms of the commission were quite narrowly drawn to cover only buildings and other civilian objects in areas of Allied military occupation rather than, for example, the bombing that had caused the majority of the damage to historic buildings in Naples or elsewhere (Palermo, for example). However, its findings did squarely address the issues raised and problems and damage caused by military requisition of heritage sites, including the Royal Palace of Naples, the University of Naples and the National Museum. It also touched, albeit briefly, on sites outside Naples, including Pompeii. Taking as its starting point Woolley's 7 December report, *The Commandeering of the Naples Museum for Military Purposes*, the commission heard or took written statements from 40 witnesses, including Italian heritage authorities (notably Maiuri and Molajoli), Allied officers overseeing requisition and billeting, AMG officers, and MFAA representatives, including Gardner. It took place over 18 sessions between 28 December 1943 and 21 January 1944. As a result of its deliberations on this evidence, the commission made a series of recommendations regarding specific current problems and buildings, as well as wider policies and practice relating to the requisition and occupation of historic structures. Some of the recommendations regarding particular problems in Naples (the Museo Nazionale, the Palazzo Reale) were not acted on, straight away at least, but the wider changes proposed were largely promulgated through the spring of 1944 and were influential in preventing a repetition of the damage caused in Naples when the Allies liberated Rome in June 1944.

The Commission of Enquiry was chaired by British Major-General A.L. Collier, district officer commanding Headquarters 3 District, Central Mediterranean Force, and its other members were a US Colonel and a British lieutenant-colonel (each from their respective armies' claims services, that dealt with civilian claims for damaged property). US Major Theodore Sizer represented the MFAA Sub-Commission. Two British captains served as secretary and assistant secretary, and produced a detailed account of the proceedings some 120 pages long including transcripts of witness statements and copies of relevant documents.

As already noted, the commission examined the cases of the Palazzo Reale di Napoli and the university, and found that damage to both could certainly be attributed to Allied military occupants. However, safeguards against further damage had been introduced at the palace, and the Italian authorities expressed no objections to its continued occupation.[26] The cultural importance of the National Museum meant it formed the focus of much of the commission's business. The argument of military necessity that Brigadier Bruxner-Randall had made to Woolley was dismissed as weak, on the grounds that Naples was not in the fighting zone and other suitable accommodation was available for the medical stores depot. It was noted that neither the Germans nor the Italians had used the museum for military purposes, although they had asked Maiuri, accepting his refusal. In essence the commission characterised the occupation as Eisenhower's 'military convenience' rather than genuine military necessity as claimed by Bruxner-Randall.[27] Nevertheless, witnesses such as Gardner and Maiuri were asked how the museum could be made safe if its occupation were to continue (as it did). The agreements to billet military personnel in nearby houses rather than the museum itself and to arrange for their food to be cooked elsewhere were brought up as mitigating factors. The British Army would ensure a fire officer was on the premises at all times, allow daily inspections by the Italian custodians and would only hire existing museum staff to provide labour rather than civilians from outside who might steal from and damage the collections.[28] Despite all these precautions and Maiuri's admission that British troops had not actually caused any damage to the museum as yet, the commission's final recommendation was that the plan to use it as a medical store be abandoned, if only because continued occupation 'would have a political effect out of proportion to any actual damage or loss'.[29] Despite this recommendation, the full occupation of the National Museum went ahead as planned, and continued until 29 June 1944.[30]

Besides assessing the treatment of individual historic buildings in Naples, the commission's report highlighted the need for wider preparations for protection of monuments when Rome and Florence (in particular) were occupied, and made a number of recommendations ranging from general issues of policy to quite specific and detailed tactical advice. Allied armed forces should educate soldiers and commanders alike in their responsibilities to protect monuments and emphasise that this was first and foremost a matter of military discipline.[31] Messages to this effect might be contained in, for example, a pamphlet outlining the history and art of Italy, noting that the Germans viewed the latter as loot, while UN forces considered themselves its trustees. A new edition of the *Soldier's Guide to Italy* should include some 'strong paragraphs' forbidding pilfering, souvenir hunting and 'vulgar damage'.[32] The value of specialist MFAA personnel and their resources was emphasised as a source of advice and information. Lists and maps of cultural sites should be made available to the town majors and real estate officers who managed requisition and military occupation.[33]

On a tactical level, the Commission of Enquiry, like Hammond, Wheeler and Ward-Perkins's reports based on experience in the field, emphasised that the key time for MFAA activity was immediately after the battle moved forward and reserve and administrative echelons were taking over newly occupied areas and 'everything is in a state of confusion'.[34] Military units were to avoid partial occupation of historic buildings, which cast confusion over responsibility for unoccupied sections. If partial occupation were necessary, then commanders should block entrances into the unoccupied sectors and make appropriate use of passes and guards to ensure that unauthorised personnel would not loot or cause damage in unoccupied rooms. Occupation by mixed units and mixed nationalities was also to be avoided as this also confused responsibility for security and the disciplinary consequences of damage.[35] This was evident from the example of the Palazzo Reale di Napoli, initially occupied by US, British and French personnel. Most of these recommendations remain useful today in the context of military occupation and stabilisation activity. Preparation and education of military personnel remain key factors, as do acceptance of responsibility and enforcement of discipline by commanders. The detailed tactical lessons on how to occupy a historic building, if necessary, while protecting the building and its contents are still applicable in modern conflicts, as emphasised by Rush.[36]

Ancient Pompeii was one of the few sites beyond Naples also considered by the Commission of Enquiry. Maiuri noted that only minor damage had been done to the site by Allied military personnel from the time of its occupation, and most of that by soldiers who climbed the walls of the site when it was closed. In response, a joint US/British Military Police post detachment would be stationed at the site to reinforce the authority of the Italian custodians, and to patrol the site, particularly when it was closed. [37]

The Collier Commission and its recommendations gave rise to the production and dissemination of further communications establishing and forbidding activities that might damage historical buildings.

Headquarters ACMF, **Property of Historical and Educational Importance in Italy—Preservation of,** *17 February 1944*[38]

This order was sent to commanders of all formations and units by General Sir Harold Alexander, the commander-in-chief of 15th Army Group/ Allied Armies in Italy, and was clearly an initial response to the findings and recommendations of the Collier Commission. Like Eisenhower's letter of 29 December 1943, it emphasised the will of the Allied high command to protect historical buildings and cultural institutions based on the principles and laws that already existed. It notes that while the damage to historic buildings investigated by the commission had been exaggerated, a certain amount had nevertheless been inflicted by 'a few wilfully destructive individuals'. Every officer was directed to bring continually to the notice of those serving under him their responsibility and obligation to preserve and protect as much cultural heritage as possible under operational conditions.

Headquarters Allied Armies Italy (Administrative Echelon), **Administrative Instruction No. 10: Preservation of Property of Historical or Educational Importance in Italy,** *30 March 1944*[39]

This was also a direct response to the findings of the Commission of Enquiry, although in contrast to General Alexander's letter of 17 February (to which it alludes), *Administrative Instruction No. 10* provides detailed and practical instructions for the implementation of the commission's recommendations. The key contents of this document include:

Recognition that tactical considerations were paramount during fighting, but that most damage occurred between when the battle moves forward and when reserve and administrative formations assume complete control. Thus commanders must impose 'a rigid control' over any occupation of historic buildings.

That there was no complete ban on military occupation of any particular category of building except that churches were only to be used as temporary shelters for wounded 'in extreme necessity' (but not as casualty clearing stations or hospitals).

That a decision to occupy a listed historic building was to be taken only by an officer at the level of divisional commander or above, except in cases of extreme emergency during actual fighting.

That new inventories known as *Lists of Protected Monuments* would supersede the Zone Handbook Lists, and would include historic monuments, archives and 'artistic treasures' with the degree of their importance indicated by stars.

That complete copies of these *Lists of Protected Monuments* were to be held at Army-level headquarters, districts and bases. Relevant sections (relating to their areas of operations, occupation or administrative control) were to be distributed as a matter of course to corps, division and area headquarters as well as to the town majors (British) and real estate officers (US) who oversaw requisition and billeting. When planning the capture or eventual occupation of territory, the *Lists* were to be distributed down to battalion or equivalent level.

That no building designated a historical building in the *Lists of Protected Monuments* should be occupied if an alternative were available, or without the express written authority of an appropriate commander (i.e., at divisional level or above).

That if it were necessary to occupy a historic building, the commander should notify ACC/AMG as soon as possible and take precautions to prevent wilful damage. These precautions followed the recommendations of the Collier Commission, and included consulting responsible Italian officials when available, blocking internal doors, controlling entrances with passes and guards, and avoiding partial or mixed occupation.

That archives and collections of books and documents encountered by military personnel were not to be destroyed or dispersed casually.

Attention was drawn to the availability and authority of specialised monuments officers.

That repositories of stored materials—such as refuges to which art had been evacuated—might be identified in the course of operations, and were to be treated as starred monuments.

The order is signed by Major-General Sir Brian Robertson, who (as noted above, p.181n.23) had been unsympathetic to the plight of the Museo Nazionale. The inclusion of the detailed tactical recommendations of the Collier Commission and MFAA officers such as Hammond is particularly important, and, as Rush has shown, still valuable today.

The new *Lists of Protected Monuments* were a compromise between the Harvard Lists and the Zone Handbook Lists in terms of the number of sites included. As already noted, the Harvard List for Campania included 316 sites, whereas the *Zone Handbook* equivalent had just 46, plus 77 on the supplementary list, for a total of 123.[40] The comparable *Lists of Protected Monuments* had 155 sites. It might be expected that the *Lists of Protected Monuments* were created by expanding the Zone Handbook Lists with additional sites from the Harvard Lists, but this does not seem to have been the case. Forty sites in the *Lists of Protected Monuments*, mostly in the Avellino area, do not appear at all in the Harvard Lists.

The *Lists of Protected Monuments* do employ the Harvard system of ranking sites' importance with zero to three stars.[41] However, many of the same sites are assigned different rankings across the two sets of lists. While 115 sites appear on both lists, 43 of them are assigned different star rankings. In some cases (such as the Royal Palace at Caserta and Castel del Monte in Apulia—see below) the differences reflected changing circumstances and new information. In most cases, they seem to reflect differences of opinion. The *Lists of Protected Monuments* state that they were prepared and issued by the MFAA Sub-Commission, so its personnel may have adapted the existing rankings from the Harvard Lists and/or made use of data gathered by the British War Office Political Warfare Executive that prepared the Zone Handbook Lists. The *Lists of Protected Monuments* includes no information on the nature or importance of any site besides the star ranking, merely its name, province, and (an improvement on the earlier lists) a grid reference locating the town (but not necessarily the individual site) on the topographic maps in use by Allied armed forces.[42] The brevity of individual references made these lists more compact than the Harvard Lists, and this facilitated their production as small printed booklets, allowing for wider dissemination. Besides the lists, the booklets include, by way of a preface, General Alexander's letter of 17 February 1944, and the text of *Administrative Instruction No. 10* that indicates, among other things, how the lists themselves are to be used.

Allied Force Headquarters, **Preservation of Works of Art in Italy, *8 May 1944*[43]**

The Collier Commission had advocated production of a booklet outlining the art and history of Italy and contrasting German treatment of Italian cultural heritage with that of the Allies. Such a document was produced in May 1944. It included a forward by British General Henry Maitland Wilson, Eisenhower's replacement as Allied supreme commander in the Mediterranean, who, besides expressing the hope that the pamphlet will be read by all officers and men, states,

> 'In war, great damage to buildings, including churches and those of great historical value, has to be accepted when it is operationally unavoidable. To add to such destruction either by wanton action or through thoughtlessness is a crime against civilization.'

The other contents are essentially those suggested by the Collier Commission. There are sections addressing questions such as 'What Is a Work of Art?', 'What Is the Value of a Work of Art?', 'Why Is Italy so Rich in Works of Art?' and 'Is Art National or International?'. There were also claims that the Germans were systematically looting European art because Germany had to be supreme in art collecting as in everything else; that Germany attacked its enemies by attacking their cultural heritage (Poland is singled out here); and that art had a value as currency. It concludes with 'What You Can Do', exhorting its readers not to leave graffiti or take souvenirs; to treat historic buildings with respect; and to preserve any libraries and books that they encountered. Presumably with the fate of the University of Naples in mind, it also advocates the preservation of scientific collections and laboratories, noting that 'the man who gave you your torch-battery was an Italian scientist, Volta.' It concludes, 'Have you thought who, in the long run, pays for the damage you do?'

Overall the tone and style of the pamphlet are rather awkward and patronising, and the writer seems uncertain of the audience for which he is writing. The cover letter to a copy sent by John Ward-Perkins in Italy to Sir Leonard Woolley in London indicates that initially it was prepared as a British Army Bureau of Current Affairs (educational service) publication that subsequently was adapted for use by the MFAA Sub-Commission.[44] While Hilldring's cover letter to the Roberts Commission states it was prepared 'for wide distribution among the troops', surviving copies are typescript rather than printed, raising the question of how widely, ultimately, it was disseminated.

CHAPTER 13

Responses, Failures and Successes

The 1946 *Final Report* of the Monuments, Fine Arts and Archives Sub-Commission argues that *Administrative Instruction No. 10* of March 1944 'clearly defined the responsibilities of the Armies in respect of the cultural monuments of Italy and it established a machinery to control indiscriminate requisition'; it characterises the *Instruction* as the 'turning point of the Sub-Commission's fortunes' after its failures in Naples.[1] The *Instruction*, of course, was substantially driven and informed by the Collier Commission's recommendations, which in turn were provoked in great part by the requisition of the Museo Nazionale.

Certainly in many respects, the lessons learned from the occupation of Naples were successful in that the failures experienced there were not repeated elsewhere for the most part. In particular, planning for the occupation of Rome (below) benefited from that experience, although the six months available for its preparation while Allied armies were stalled below Montecassino were another important factor.

In the case of some historic buildings, military requisition and occupation remained a problem through part or all of 1944. As already noted, despite the Collier Commission's recommendations, the Museo Nazionale di Napoli remained occupied until 29 June 1944. Fortunately (or perhaps as a result of the agreed precautions) the occupation did no major damage to the building or its contents.[2] The Royal Palace of Naples also remained occupied. Repairs were done to the structure, previously damaged by bombing, by the British army, although the repairs actually caused further damage to the original fabric of the building.[3] The MFAA Region 3 report for March 1944 refers to officers attending 'innumerable conferences' there in connection with the repairs.[4] After repair, the Palace was used as a NAAFI/EFI (Navy, Army and Air Force Institutes/ Expeditionary Forces Institutes) recreational centre for British personnel for the remainder of the war, since Naples and the surrounding area remained an important base area and leave destination. The various facilities of the recreational centre are set out in a plan (Figure 34—see also Figure 35) included in a brief pamphlet written by British monuments officer Captain Edward Croft-Murray (of the British Museum) that introduced military visitors to the building's history, and another short guidebook published in the following year has an afterword that reads[5]

> 'The NAAFI/EFI are proud to have been able to provide for the men of His Majesties' Forces in such a magnificent setting. They publish this booklet in order that those whom they serve may know a little of the history of their new Club.'

The MFAA *Final Report* seeks to present the damage to the palace optimistically:

> 'At least it can be said that the experience of the Royal Palace at Naples was never repeated in the course of the Italian campaign, and it should be stressed that the damage was to works of relatively secondary quality. The experience was worth the price.'[6]

Elsewhere in Campania, the Collier Commission's recommendations and *Administrative Instruction No. 10* also had no significant impact on the occupation of the Royal Palace at Caserta.[7] The political weight and military authority of AFHQ that occupied it was such that it could afford to ignore what were essentially its own orders. The occupation was complicated by the fact that the palace was already in use by the Italian authorities as a repository for over 500 paintings and 20,000 books evacuated from Naples. The requisition order provided for the entire palace to be taken over along with as much usable furniture as possible. While custodians were permitted to move the most valuable items into storage in the building, it seems that insufficient space was available.[8] The storage problem is reiterated in a March 1944 *Report on the Palace of Caserta* that also notes damage to the soft wood and fabric coverings of antique furniture requisitioned for use in officers' quarters and messes.[9] Croft-Murray admits that the best items had been stored and none of the damaged items were 'first-rate', but sets had been broken up and the furniture formed an integral part of the palace's interior décor. 'Wilful damage' had been done by souvenir hunters, some pictures had been stolen ('although it is impossible to say when or by whom') and there was some accidental damage to statues in the East Park. He concludes that much of the damage could have been avoided if AFHQ had notified the MFAA Sub-Commission earlier so safeguards to protect the palace could have been established from the beginning.

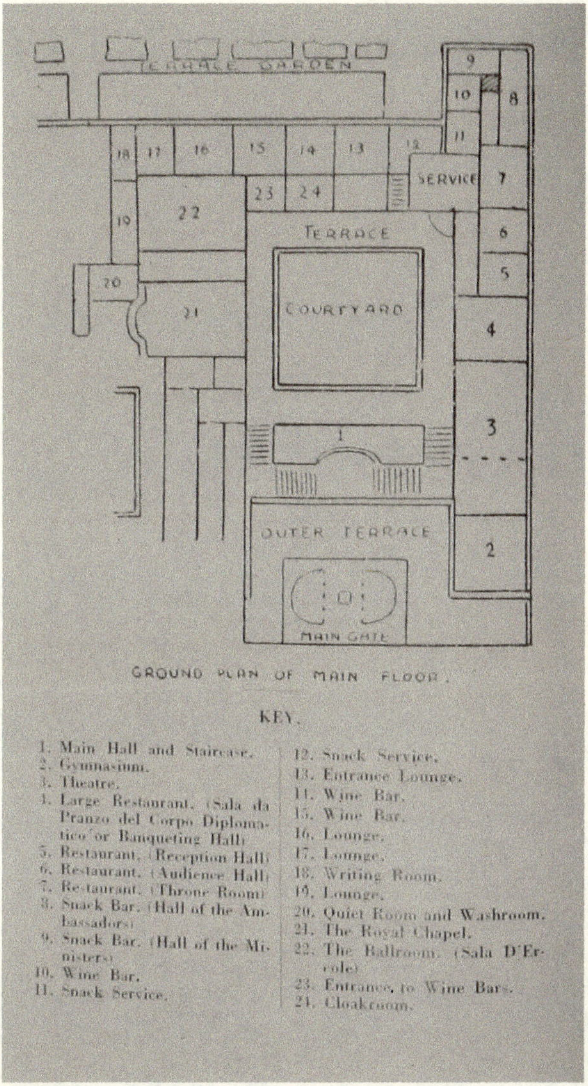

Figure 34: Plan showing the welfare facilities established for British troops in the Royal Palace of Naples, from NARA M1944, RG 239/0067, Edward Croft-Murray (Sub-Commission for Monuments, Fine Arts and Archives), *The Royal Palace of Naples: An Historical and Architectural Guide to the State Apartments* (1944).

Other problems relating to military occupation of historic buildings showed up at this time beyond Campania, in Apulia and Palermo. Unknown to Allied military authorities (including the MFAA Sub-Commission), the 13th-century fortress of Castel del Monte in Apulia, c. 50 km west of Bari, a two-star monument in the Harvard Lists, had been used by the Italian regional superintendencies as a refuge for evacuation of collections from

Figure 35: The 'Main Hall and Staircase' (labelled as '1' on the 1944 plan) of the Royal Palace of Naples (author's photograph).

urban museums, galleries, churches and libraries. The area came under British control in September 1943 and the castle was occupied by a Royal Air Force unit without consultation or control at about the same time as similarly uncontrolled requisition was taking place in Naples. Limited manpower meant that the building could not be visited by an MFAA officer or the refuge identified until late January 1944, when John Ward-Perkins undertook his inspection visits in south-eastern Italy. He reported that the RAF personnel had been 'quartered indiscriminately throughout', without regard for the building's contents, and that field ovens had been built in a courtyard against walls of rooms that housed the evacuated collections. Actual damage was 'limited to blackening and general squalor', but there had been a real risk of fire that might have devastated the material there. The British unit had moved on at the time of Ward-Perkins's visit, and he considered the American unit that had replaced it to be much less of a problem, as the Americans only used the castle roof and a staircase to access it. However, the ranking of Castel del Monte was raised to three stars in the 1944 *Lists of Protected Monuments* to reflect its contents as well as the building itself, with the hope that the building would not be re-occupied.[10]

Another such refuge, this time of materials evacuated from Naples, was located at the Loreto Abbey at Mercogliano (Prov. di Avellino). This was another structure of historic and cultural importance in itself, and like Castel del Monte, its function as a refuge initially was unknown to MFAA officers. However, when this became known, that knowledge enabled MFAA officers to successfully oppose threatened requisition by Canadian troops in late December 1944.[11] Experiences such as these relating to refuges for movable works of art (as well as the knowledge that Montecassino had served as such a refuge for material from the National Museum in Naples) undoubtedly led to the provision for discovery of 'repositories of stored materials' in *Administrative Instruction No. 10*. This provision was beneficial in securing their safety when such refuges containing paintings and sculpture from the churches and major galleries of Florence were encountered in the course of combat west of that city in July and August 1944.

Events in Palermo in February 1944 had already revealed some specific problems relating to the requisition and occupation of historic buildings even before *Administrative Instruction No. 10* was published, and also some of the more general risks of such occupation. While the importance of Palermo as an Allied military base had diminished by February 1944 with the development of Naples as the focus of Allied logistical and military government activity in Italy, nevertheless it continued to host large numbers of Allied military personnel. Even as the MFAA Sub-Commission's headquarters was in transit to Naples, US Naval Reserve Lieutenant Perry B. Cott (formerly of the Worcester [MA] Art Museum) was serving as Region I (Sicily) adviser on monuments and fine arts from his base in Palermo.[12] On 4 February 1944, Cott learned from the superintendent of galleries that the Royal Palace of Palermo had been requisitioned as a headquarters and training centre (including a gymnasium) for US military police, and that Italian staff had been ordered out of the building. Cott reported that when he went to the Palace to object to its requisition, he (among other things) 'suggested to Col. Hudson that "I did not approve of using a state apartment as a gymnasium"; there was no reply to my question'.[13] In this case, the deficiencies of the Zone Handbook Lists may, on the surface at least, have provided a loophole used to justify the requisition. For the very brief Zone Handbook Lists for Sicily (just thirteen sites in seven locations) did not include the entire Royal Palace, just the 12th-century Capella Palatina, with its spectacular mosaics and painted ceiling, located in the centre of the palace complex.[14] Thus, in a narrow technical sense, the requisitioning authority could argue that this did not contravene AFHQ, General Order Number 68 of 29 December 1943, whose basis was the Zone Handbook Lists. This discrepancy was corrected with the introduction in March 1944 of the much more comprehensive *Lists of Protected Monuments*, which included the entire Royal Palace, with the Capella Palatina included as a three-star structure within the zero-star complex as a whole.[15] However, by this time, the damage (literally) had been done. Less than three weeks after its initial requisition, fire broke out in a part of the palace occupied by US personnel. It is unclear whether the cause was electrical or a chimney fire, or even whether the Americans had actually caused it. The cost of repair was substantial, but the main concern was that it might potentially have spread to the decorated wooden ceiling of the Capella Palatina.[16] This demonstrated clearly one possible danger of partial occupation of an historic building or complex. The Italian superintendent, reporting the fire damage to Cott, highlighted other risks of partial occupation. He asks him to intercede with the commander of the military police headquarters to prevent 'other disasters', emphasising the need to keep the Capella Palatina separate and secure, and for the Americans not to force open doors or windows. If part of an historic building was occupied, it was difficult to secure any other part unless discipline was sufficiently tight to prevent occupying troops from exploring and entering sections of the building that were off-limits. The requisition was not lifted, although Cott made recommendations to reduce future risk, including a prohibition on the use of electric heaters in the complex, warnings about the use of fires and chimneys more generally, and the posting of 'off-limits' notices around the chapel.[17]

PREPARATIONS FOR THE OCCUPATION OF ROME

As noted, failure to protect historic buildings in Naples and reflection on its lessons ultimately proved beneficial for other Italian (and northern European) cities, including Rome. Preparations for the occupation of Rome were much more thorough than those for Naples, and time was available for plans (initially submitted at the end of December 1944) to be re-evaluated and improved in light of recommendations and improvements highlighted by the Collier Commission. For example, the practical details incorporated in *Administrative Instruction No. 10* were of immense value, including not only the improved dissemination of cultural intelligence in the *Lists of Protected Monuments* but also its production in a format suited to military needs, with grid references linking sites to military maps, concise entries and a basic indication of importance.

Changes in the organisation and deployment of MFAA personnel were also important. Thus, for example, the regional assignments of monuments officers were regarded in a more flexible manner that enabled surplus officers (whose regions were not yet under Allied occupation) to undertake planning tasks for their own region while gaining experience working in support of Gardner in Region III. Observations from Sicily and Naples about the need to incorporate MFAA issues into operational planning and the importance of forward deployment of specialist officers (to be present in that window of time when—as the Collier Commission put it—'everything is in a state of confusion' between combat and full control by reserve and administrative formations) meant that by the spring of 1944 specialist officers were assigned to operational headquarters (particularly 5th Army) and military government advanced parties. Thus the Region IV MFAA officer (Perry Cott, now transferred from Sicily) was assigned to go with the AMG 5th Army forward party to enter the city of Rome immediately on its liberation, while the MFAA officers assigned to the Army headquarters remained with them as they advanced beyond Rome. To some extent, separate provision in planning had always been made for the city of Rome and the rest of

Lazio, even though they were parts of the same region. However, late in the planning process Lazio was temporarily made a separate region under British Captain Basil Marriott (a peacetime architect), enabling Cott to focus on the city of Rome until the two areas were recombined in August 1944.[18]

Besides the distribution of *Lists of Protected Monuments* down to battalion level, specialist lists were drawn up and formatted that, for example, detailed monuments for units on their advance routes to Rome and (separately, for operational convenience) beyond Rome when they had passed through the city itself.[19]

There were, of course, lists of monuments for protection within the city of Rome itself. But, again, specialist lists were produced, including versions organised according to police precincts, with detailed map coordinates. These, along with detailed MFAA liaison with the chief of the Public Safety Division AMG 5th Army and the provost marshal of the 5th Army, were intended to facilitate rapid fixing of 'out-of-bounds' notices and posting of military guards on historic buildings and cultural institutions as appropriate. Besides the 'out-of-bounds' notices, inventory forms were printed to distribute to Italian authorities, and preparations were made to interview relevant government and museum officials. A pamphlet with information about the monuments and art of Rome was prepared for military personnel, and contacts were made with the Red Cross and Special Services (a US unit that organised rest facilities for troops) to plan tours of the city for troops once it was secure. The experience, planning and preparation paid off, as Cott entered the city on the evening of 4 June 1944, right at the start of its liberation, with the Advanced Regional AMG party that also included British Captain Humphrey Brooke, the regional archives specialist. As the MFAA *Final Report* justifiably claims, 'The occupation of Rome was in striking contrast to that of Naples'.[20]

CONCLUSION

In contrast to their failure to take precautions against damage caused by aerial bombardment, at the time of their invasion of mainland Italy, Allied armies had undertaken substantial preparation to protect cultural property in occupied territory. This was based on their practical experience in Tripolitania and Sicily, and the concerns and efforts of individual military personnel, civilian academics and museum staff (including the members of the American civilian commissions and committees) and some politicians.

These preparations included specialist officers as monuments and fine arts advisers and lists and maps to support them.

Nevertheless, these precautions were largely ineffective in the period from the Allied landings in Calabria and the Gulf of Salerno in September 1943, through the occupation of Naples in October, to spring 1944. The factors that brought about this failure were partly structural, organisational and logistical within the MFAA organisation. The place and relative importance of monuments and fine arts activities within general civil affairs duties had not been assessed and asserted accurately and effectively, so both civil affairs officers and monuments and fine arts specialists such as Gardner were overwhelmed and distracted by more immediately pressing needs in the confusion of the early days of the occupation of a large city like Naples. The importance for monuments protection of the window between combat itself and effective occupation and control by second-echelon formations became known in Sicily, but was not communicated early enough to help Naples. While documentary support (lists, maps) was theoretically available to officers and commanders who were not monuments and fine arts specialists, these were not distributed widely or effectively, and often were not produced in a format that was particularly easy to use by military personnel in the field.

However, the key issue in Naples was that existing preparations, instructions and international law relating to cultural property protection were not accorded sufficient respect or priority. Even leaving aside specialist personnel and the more specialised and detailed publications such as the AMGOT *Plan for Italy*, some provision was made for cultural property protection even in quite basic handbooks and documents such as the British *Manual of Military Law* and Zone Handbooks. Nevertheless, these were ignored because there was no perception among commanders and (for example) billeting officers that their higher command thought cultural property protection sufficiently important to prioritise it over other military activities that were assessed as more pressing. Hence Brigadier Bruxner-Randall could argue with Sir Leonard Woolley that occupation of the Museo Nazionale was a matter of military necessity because he had been given no reason to set the threshold of military necessity at any but the very lowest level. In reality, this was a matter of (in Eisenhower's words) military convenience. That was not necessarily a trivial issue. Finding another appropriate building for the medical stores depot may well have been a difficult matter with implications for other military activities. However, Bruxner-Randall had never been required to weigh that inconvenience against the importance of the museum and its contents in political and cultural terms.

If commanders perceived cultural property protection as unimportant (when they were aware of it as an issue at all), it is hardly surprising that some of their men engaged in casual and thoughtless looting and destruction because they had been neither educated nor instructed (in clear disciplinary terms) to do otherwise.

However, in this field, the Allied armed forces learned from their mistakes through mechanisms such as reports from monuments officers and from the Collier Commission of Enquiry and made changes that to a great extent prevented recurrence of the damage done in Naples. The contents of the letters, orders and administrative documents between December 1943 and May 1944 that advanced improvements in Allied cultural property protection practice and policy were not revolutionary. While they did introduce some relatively minor (but useful) changes, such as the substitution of the *Lists of Protected Monuments* for the Zone Handbook Lists, their key importance lay in the following dimensions:

Some, in particular Eisenhower's letter to commanders in December 1943 and Alexander's order in February 1944, served to emphasise in clear terms that the protection of historic buildings and their contents was important to the Allied high command. They emphasise the responsibility of commanders for such protection, a responsibility that was not new, but previously disregarded. They made it essentially impossible for commanders to argue that they were unaware of its importance.

Others, such as Allied Force Headquarters, *General Orders Number 68* (29 December 1943) and Headquarters Allied Armies Italy (Administrative Echelon) *Administrative Instruction No. 10: Preservation of Property of Historical or Educational Importance in Italy* (30 March 1944), besides reinforcing the message of responsibility and discipline, provide detailed advice and instructions on how commanders could discharge that responsibility. They reinforce the status and authority of monuments and fine arts officers. They also draw attention to documentary resources (lists in particular) available to commanders and provide for widespread and effective distribution of those resources. The procedures and practices set out in these documents were supported by other changes. These include improvements to the nature and format of lists available to military personnel (the compact printed booklets of *Lists of Protected Monuments* with military grid references and star-rankings) and organisational changes within the MFAA, with monuments officers incorporated in forward elements of military government structures and Army-level headquarters.

A final aspect of the Collier Commission's recommendations and the responses to them was educational. *Preservation of Works of Art in Italy*, produced in May 1943, is an example of a growing attempt to provide interested lower-ranking officers and ordinary soldiers with educational and cultural materials that encourage them to protect cultural property by engaging their interest in the subject rather than (or at least, in parallel with) emphasising its disciplinary aspects. The term 'propaganda' is often applied to such pamphlets and booklets in contemporary sources, in its original and literal sense of 'things to be propagated' rather than the political sense in which it is typically used now. *The Soldier's Guide to Sicily*, for example, produced before the invasion of the island, included very little cultural content, but later soldier's guides (which proliferated after the liberation of Rome), such as those to Rome and Florence, included a much higher proportion of such material. All of these lessons are as applicable to modern conflicts and stabilisation operations involving organised military forces as they were to the later stages of the Second World War in Italy. Preparation for cultural property protection based on obligations under international law, cultural intelligence (the lists and maps) and specialist cultural protection personnel are all vital, but its importance needs to be made clear to commanders and men alike.

Conclusions

On 24/25 August 1943 and between 13 and 26 September 1943, over 160 bombs struck the archaeological site of Pompeii. Those bombs were dropped by British, US and Canadian bombers.[1] The bombing of the archaeological site was accidental damage inflicted in the course of attacks against other targets nearby, primarily road and rail routes and bridges immediately to the west of the archaeological site. Most of this bombing was undertaken as an emergency response to a German counter-attack against the Allied beachhead on the Gulf of Salerno between 12 and 20 September. A successful counter-attack would have had a disastrous impact on Allied prosecution of the war against Nazi Germany. At such short notice, the application of airpower against transportation routes used to reinforce and supply that counter-attack was viewed (rightly) as one of the few means by which it might be defeated, in parallel with close air support of the battle itself. The German counter-attack was unsuccessful, and while it is impossible to quantify, it seems likely that this use of air power was an important factor in its defeat. There were no German troops in the ruins of Pompeii, and the Allied command never thought there were, despite the rumours that spread subsequently and have been so tenacious ever since. Even though the bombing was conducted in clear conditions with little opposition, 1943 bombing technology was such that it was impossible to attack targets so close to the archaeological site without some bombs hitting the archaeological site. The Allied military Monuments, Fine Arts and Archives organisation existed (but barely) at the time of the bombing of Pompeii, and there is no evidence that the presence of the heritage site was considered at all in the process of targeting nearby transportation systems. Even if it had been considered, the exigent military circumstances meant there were few practical alternatives open to Allied commanders that might have spared the site except prohibiting bombing anywhere in its vicinity—and 'in its vicinity' by 1943 standards probably meant several kilometres.

However, the bombing of ancient Pompeii played an important role in the development of Allied thought, policy and practice relating to cultural property protection. Alongside the destruction caused by bombing to the city of Naples and other Campanian towns such as Benevento, the bombing of Pompeii specifically was raised in discussions of bombing and damage to cultural heritage among civilian academics, museum professionals and politicians in the USA and in Britain, and also, it seems, among air force commanders such as Tedder. These discussions brought the problem of bomb damage to the fore of Allied cultural property protection and drove forward real changes in policy and tactics. While those changes had some successes, and the examples of Florence and Venice are highlighted in wartime reports, for the most part those successes were severely limited by contemporary bombing technology in conjunction with Allied political-military imperatives to bomb, even when it risked destruction and damage to heritage sites (and civilian lives).

Another driver of change in Allied wartime cultural property protection was the British military requisition and occupation of the Museo Nazionale in Naples from November 1943 to June 1944. Given the scale and importance of its collections from the site, this too had a close connection to ancient Pompeii. In conjunction with occupation of and damage to other historic buildings and cultural institutions in Naples, such as the Royal Palace and buildings of the University of Naples, the case of the National Museum motivated initial changes (December 1943) relating to the requisition and treatment of such buildings and other cultural property by Allied military personnel. The Collier Commission of Enquiry in turn led to further improvements in the spring of 1944. Those improvements, in response to experience and lessons learned, were successful in that they prevented a repeat of the problems seen during the occupation of Naples when Allied forces occupied Rome, Florence and other Italian cities.

These cultural property protection lessons relating to Pompeii have tended to be overlooked. Much of the post-war discussion of cultural property protection in wartime Italy has focused on the bombing of Montecassino. As already noted, this was not a typical example of war damage to cultural property, not even in wartime Italy, and much of the discussion relating to that site has taken the form of assigning blame, or of arguments made in hindsight about whether the Abbey itself was occupied by German troops and about the military value of the bombing. On the other hand, other issues raised by the bombing of Montecassino, such as the demilitarisation of 'immediate surroundings' of protected sites and definitions of cultural property (for example, the confusion between religious and historical significance in wartime definitions and debates) have not been explored so thoroughly.[2] In many ways, Pompeii and Naples provided (and continue to provide) a more fruitful and important focus of analysis and source of lessons learned for military cultural property protection.

Heritage sites and other forms of cultural property do not enjoy absolute immunity in conflict even under contemporary international law such as the 1954 Hague Convention, and it would be unreasonable to expect such immunity when civilian lives are not accorded it. Only ending wars will convey such complete protection of heritage sites and people. Otherwise their protection not only entails peacetime preparation but also potentially (politically, militarily, morally) complex decisions in wartime relating to military use and necessity, proportionality, distinction and humanity. Historic buildings and heritage sites do not enjoy total immunity from damage and destruction by other human factors—exposure by excavation and development, for example—so to expect more in wartime, when civilian and military lives enter into the calculation, seems unreasonable.[3]

The basic military cultural property protection lessons to be learned from the bombing of Pompeii (and of cultural sites in Naples, and Benevento) in 1943 are that protection requires CPP input into the planning of air operations, and the support of readily available and effectively presented cultural intelligence (typically in the form of inventories, databases, lists and maps) about cultural property in the area of operations. The urgency of the military context in which Pompeii was bombed shows that this requires peacetime preparation and planning—it needs to be embedded in military doctrine before the conflict, military personnel with CPP training need to be integrated into operational planning and targeting, and the intelligence data has to be available before the need for it emerges. In the case of Pompeii, taking the location of the heritage site into account when planning operations may not have prevented the bombing, but the discussion should at least have taken place, which, it seems, it did not.

The basic military cultural property protection lessons to be learned from the requisition and occupation of the National Museum and other cultural sites in Naples in 1943 are that while preparation (establishing policies, gathering cultural intelligence and so on) is important, practice must be evaluated and modified regularly in light of experience. The Allied responses to their CPP failures in Naples show that evaluation and change can make policy and practice more effective in the future. The failures in Naples also show that preparation in itself is not enough. Cultural property protection procedures and personnel need to be reinforced by clear statements and demonstrations of their importance throughout the chain of command, from the very top (Eisenhower), and by doctrine and education. At the same time, politicians and senior commanders must be willing to take responsibility for difficult decisions that might (on the one hand) have adverse impact on military operations or (on the other) lead to damage to cultural property when militarily necessary.

Another important general lesson to be learned from this wartime experience is that different types of conflict will place different demands on military cultural property protection. Western armed forces' recent cultural property protection experience has been mostly in counter-insurgency and post-conflict stabilisation missions. While we hope there will be no more large-scale, high-intensity conflicts comparable to the Second World War, that should not necessarily be taken for granted. The Second World War provides a valuable source of lessons that complement more recent experience.

The 1954 Hague Convention (Art. 3; Art. 4) assigns responsibility for protection of cultural property to the owning state as well as to potential enemies. That includes peacetime preparation for possible protection and evacuation of structures and movable material. The effective Italian in situ protection of objects in the National Museum in Naples (and other historic buildings and collections) with sandbags and wooden frameworks provides one lesson.[4] The more mixed success of Italian wartime evacuation policies provides another such lesson, since in some cases (Ancona, Tarquinia) evacuation undoubtedly saved or would have saved collections, whereas in other cases (Florence, for example, and the Naples collections sent to Montecassino) the secret dispersed refuges to which movable cultural property was evacuated actually placed their contents at more risk than if they had been left in situ.[5] The 1954 Hague Convention (Art. 4.1) also potentially requires the demilitarisation of the 'immediate surroundings' of a cultural site by the owning state, and the (unadopted) 1923 Hague Air Rules's definition of 'immediate surrounding' as a zone of 500 m from the site continues to be used by some states today.[6]

Some forms of damage are more preventable than others, and that may change over time. Deliberate, ideologically motivated damage to cultural property is extremely difficult to prevent. Allied CPP efforts to reduce damage to cultural sites by bombing were of limited success in the Second World War due to the inherent inaccuracy of bombing at that time, combined with political-military imperatives to continue bombing regardless of damage to cultural sites. Consequently, bombing was the cause of most damage to cultural property caused by the Allies in the Second World War, and even when measures were taken to reduce it, their success was limited. However, modern air-launched weapons, while not infallible, make modern bombing more accurate than that of the Second World War. Thus the measures designed to address this problem in that conflict (integration of CPP concerns in operational planning; availability and dissemination of cultural property intelligence in the form of lists, images and so on) can be employed more effectively in modern conflicts. On the other hand, as damage caused by bombing is reduced, other causes of damage become proportionately more important. Military use and occupation of historic sites and buildings continues to be a feature of modern conflicts, and Second World War lessons reflected in MFAA precepts relating to such activity (securing movable collections away from troops and civilians; controlling access within the building as well as external entrances; avoiding mixed occupation—military/civilian, different nationalities and different units) are still of great value.

The activities of US academics and museum professionals in 1943 provide a lesson in the potential for fruitful relationships between civilians and military CPP specialists, particularly in the provision of 'cultural intelligence' in the form of lists, maps and databases of cultural property to be protected. However, the deficiencies of some of the materials provided by the ACLS Committee and the Harvard Group (failure to integrate maps into military grids; small scale; excessive and sometimes irrelevant detail) emphasise the need for mutual military-academic understanding and discussion, preferably before a conflict occurs. However, such cooperation was less controversial in the Second World War when both countries were already at war, many academics were in uniform and there was broad backing for Allied war aims that (for the British, at least), were essentially national survival. In contrast, some contemporary academics' attitudes towards the armed forces are ambivalent or even hostile as the result of historical polarisation (for example, in the Vietnam War–era USA); contributing to the planning of potential conflict might be viewed as facilitating militarism and imperialism, and the moral issues at the heart of some contemporary conflicts are less clear-cut than those of the Second World War.

Likewise the wartime experiences of Allied monuments officers of effective cooperation with Italian civilian heritage authorities underline the importance of good relations between military CPP specialists and local stakeholders and communities, who typically are best placed to assign value to, and in many cases safeguard, their own cultural property. This undoubtedly influenced the emphasis in the 1954 Hague Convention on cooperation with, and rapid handover to, host nation authorities.[7]

Protection of heritage and protection of people are not mutually exclusive. While lives are paramount, heritage plays an important role in human, national and local identity, so important that in recent conflicts heritage professionals and ordinary citizens have risked and lost their lives protecting it. The protection of cultural property can be of great importance, both practical and symbolic, in holding together communities in times of conflict, and in reconstructing them when conflict has passed on.

Appendices

APPENDIX A

Bomb Damage to the Archaeological Site of Pompeii

Summaries from Contemporary Allied Documentation (see also Figures 1 and 2).

Works of Art in Italy: Losses and Survivals in the War. Part I—South of Bologna. **Compiled from War Office Reports by the British Committee on the Preservation and Restitution of Works of Art, Archives and Other Material in Enemy Hands (London: HMSO, 1945), pp. 49–50.**

'POMPEII (Napoli)

POMPEII was bombed severely and damage was done, especially in the area of the NUOVI SCAVI. In view of the conflicting accounts that have been published the detailed report of the Monuments and Fine Arts Sub-Commission can be quoted in full.

Regio I

Ins. VI. Casa del Criptoportico: Two roofs and four walls damaged; fresco of Mercury and Serpent unharmed.

Ins. VII. Casa Poquino [sic = Paquino] Proculo: Roof and upper parts of walls damaged.

Regio II

Ins. V. Palestra: Little damaged. Casa di Loreto [sic = Loreio] Tiburtino: Roof and rooms damaged; ceiling of oecus damaged.

Regio III

Ins. II. Casa di Trebio Valente: front wall and three frescoes of second style destroyed.

Ins. III. Shops and taverns completely destroyed. Scuola Juventutis: west wall damaged; one fresco of war trophies and frescoes on west wall gone.

Ins. IV. Casa di Iphigenia e Moralista: Peristyle and four rooms with frescoes of fourth style destroyed.

Regio V.

Ins. V. North of Villa delle Colonne e Musaico [sic]: Four rooms damaged; Tomb No. 34 destroyed.

Villa di Diomede: South West angle of garden damaged.

Regio VI

Ins. II. Casa di Sallustio: Tablinium, portico and several rooms destroyed, involving frescoes, notably "Actaeon and Diana".

Ins. VI. Casa dei Vettii; Damage very slight and all important frescoes intact.

Ins. XII. Casa del Fauno: Atrium and five (North East and North West) rooms destroyed with frescoes of first and fourth styles. This is the most unfortunate individual loss.

Regio VII

Temple of Apollo and Casa di Trittolemo: Dividing wall damaged, but damage to temple not serious. Atrium and six rooms of the Casa destroyed; also a shed containing the recently found archaic Greek terracotta revetments; these were broken, but are in process of restoration.

Ins. VIII. Casa del Marinaio: Destroyed; Roman pottery collection destroyed. Museum: South part completely destroyed.

Regio VIII

Foro Triangolario: Street and entrance hit, but damage insignificant.

Teatro grande: Three bombs hit the MEDIA CAVA, CRIPTA and SUMMA CAVA.

Tempio Dorico: Part of (rebuilt) podium destroyed: Palestra Sannitica: Portico and entrance partly destroyed.

Regio IX

Ins. XII. Edifizio del Cenacolo: Completely destroyed.

Insula occidentale

Casa del grande atrio: Four walls and one room with frescoes destroyed.

The Sub-director of the Monuments and Fine Arts Sub-Commission reports that the damage is far less than early accounts would suggest and that with the careful work of clearance and consolidation now in progress under the direction of Signorina Elia, it will leave little permanent trace on the excavation other than the disappearance of such ornamental detail as has been listed as destroyed.

The "Apollo" from the MUSEO NAZIONALE of NAPLES, stored at MONTECASSINO, was taken by the Germans to the Vatican.'

***Works of Art in Italy: Losses and Survivals in the War. Part II—North of Bologna* together with Regional Summaries and a Supplement to Part I. Compiled from War Office Reports by the British Committee on the Preservation and Restitution of Works of Art, Archives and Other Material in Enemy Hands (London: HMSO, 1946), p. 79.**

'At Pompeii, damage from the 156 bombs which fell within the excavated area was widespread. The bombs were, however, of a light calibre and the total of significant destruction is limited. The effect on the general appearance of the ruins, after clearance and consolidation, is almost negligible.'

'A number of museums and archaeological collections were damaged or suffered loss. The National Museum at Naples is untouched but the Antiquarium at Pompeii and the Museo Campano at Capua suffered direct hits.'

MFAA *Final Report: Campania* (25 November 1945), Appendix 1, 'Bomb Damage to Pompeii' (pp. 25–26):

'The following is a summary record of the more important damage to the excavated area of Pompeii. Numbers refer to the accompanying map [= Figure 2 in this book], upon which are shown the approximate locations of all bomb hits. Numbers in parentheses refer to a comprehensive list prepared by the Superintendency of Antiquities for Campania. It will be seen from the map that the greatest concentration of bombs fell near the Porta Marina, in the area of the oldest excavations, where less damageable detail had survived than elsewhere. The Forum itself and the adjacent public buildings suffered little permanent harm. The Via dell'Abbondanza sustained some detailed damage, but in no sense such as to mar the general effect after clearance and restoration.

1 (10) *Reg. I, Ins. VI: House of the Criptoportico.* Destruction of east wing of portico and south of atrium with four adjoining rooms. Painting of Mercury and Serpent unharmed.

2 (10) *Reg. I, Ins. VII: House of Paquius Proculus.* Roof and upper parts of walls damaged.

3 *Reg. IX, Ins. XII: Cenaculum* destroyed.

4 (13) *Reg. III, Ins. II: House of Trebius Valens.* Façade partially destroyed; second and third style paintings in cubicoli west and south of atrium and of adjacent triclinium also destroyed.

5 (14) *Reg. III, Ins. III: Shops* facing Via dell'Abbondanza destroyed.

6 (15) *Reg. III, Ins. III: "Schola Juventutis Pompeianae".* West wall destroyed together with fourth-style ornament, and trophy-painting of east wall.

7 (16 & 18) *Reg. III, Ins. IV: "House of the Moralist".* Surrounding wall of garden and of frescoed triclinium in the garden: stuccoes damaged. Also House of Iphigenia. West wing of peristyle destroyed with 3 rooms and fourth-style painted stuccoes of triclinium.

8 (11) *Reg. II, Ins. V: House of Loreius Tiburtinus.* Partial destruction of atrium and 3 rooms, one with fourth-style stuccoes; and the oecus with white-ground frescoes.

9 (23–26) *Reg. II: Palestra.* Very little significant damage. Two doors demolished.

10 (144–146) *Reg. VIII: Greater Theatre.* Three bomb hits, which demolished considerable tracts of Bourbon restoration.

11 (141, 147) *Reg. IX: Doric Temple.* A reconstructed portion of the podium and the well damaged.

12 (143) *Reg. VIII: Samnite Palestra.* Four columns of west side of portico damaged.

13 (142) *Reg. VIII: Triangular Forum.* Damage to propylaeon.

14 (97–102) *Reg. VIII: Temple of Apollo.* Three bombs, damaging portico and demolishing sheds containing important recently-excavated and restored terracottas. These have been mainly recovered in fragments capable once more of restoration. Damage to temple itself only to restored porticus.

House of Triptolemus adjacent, atrium and peristyle badly damaged.

15 (66–7) *Reg. VI, Ins. XIII: House of the Faun.* This important early house was badly damaged, 3 rooms north of atrium with first and fourth style painting and mosaics; and a considerable part of the tetrastyle atrium.

16 (77) *Reg. VI, Ins. XV: House of the Vettii.* Bomb on N.W. angle of peristyle did miraculously little damage. No significant damage to paintings, decent or indecent.

17 (50) *Reg. VI, Ins. II: House of Sallust.* Total destruction of small internal portico and four adjacent painted rooms, including the well-known "Actaeon and Diana".

18 (44, 46) *Via dei Sepolcri: Tomb No 34* and nearby portico damaged.

19 (47) *Via dei Sepolcri: Villa of Diomede.* Sustaining wall at south-west angle of peristyle collapsed.

20 (125, 126) *Reg. VII, Western Insula. House of the Large Atrium.* Part of atrium and rooms with fourth-style painting destroyed.

21 (156) *Antiquarium* beside the Porta Marina. Half demolished and serious losses to collections.'

APPENDIX B

Air Forces Organisation and Documentation

ALLIED AIR FORCES ORGANISATION DURING THE BOMBING NEAR POMPEII[1]

The air forces engaged in the bombing of Pompeii formed part of a command integrating US forces with those of the British Empire and Commonwealth. The highest level was Mediterranean Air Command, but operational command of activity related to the bombing of ancient Pompeii lay with Headquarters Northwest African Air Forces, which had both strategic and tactical components. The combat aircraft of each included bombers and fighters, although the distance from bases in North Africa and Sicily to Pompeii (until the establishment of airfields on mainland Italy, including, eventually, the Salerno area) meant that the latter played a very limited role in the bombing of the site.[2] A brief day-by-day contemporary account of operations from the perspective of Headquarters Northwest African Air Forces is provided by its *Operations and Intelligence Summary* (TNA AIR/51/253). This summary numbers the days of activity consecutively, each day being defined as the 24-hour period ending at 18:00 hrs on a particular date. Thus *Summary* 186 covers the 24 hours ending 18:00 25 August 1943, while *Summary* 205 covers the 24 hours ending 18:00 13 September 1943. Within these daily summaries, missions are also numbered, and sometimes further subdivided with letters. Weekly and monthly intelligence summaries produced at higher headquarters are also of great value in evaluating both targeting and contemporary damage assessment.[3]

Tactical Bomber Force[4]

The tactical components of Northwest African Air Forces engaged in the bombing of Pompeii formed part of the combined Tactical Bomber Force.

USAAF: 12th and 340th Bombardment Groups, equipped with B-25 Mitchell twin-engine medium bombers (also 47th Bombardment Group, which did not take part in these operations).

RAF: No. 326 (Light Bomber) Wing, equipped with Douglas Boston twin-engine light bombers. Composing 326 Wing were 18 and 114 Squadrons. The Tactical Bomber Force also included No. 3 (South African) Wing (equipped at this time with Boston and Baltimore light bombers), which played a limited role in these operations, and No. 232 (Light Bomber) Wing [RAF], which did not participate.

Northwest African Strategic Air Forces

The strategic bomber forces engaged in the 1943 bombing of Pompeii were components of the Northwest African Strategic Air Forces. They included both US and British-Canadian elements.

RAF/RCAF

No. 205 Group, subdivided into Nos. 231 (Bomber) Wing, 236 (Bomber) Wing, 330 (Bomber) Wing, and No. 331 Wing RCAF. These were in turn composed of squadrons (see below), two each for the RAF Wings and three for the Canadian. All were equipped with Vickers Wellington twin-engine medium bombers.

USAAF[5]

5th Wing USAAF, composed of 2nd, 97th and 301st Bombardment Groups equipped with B-17 four-engine heavy bombers (the 2nd BG did not take part in these operations).

42nd Wing USAAF, composed of 17th, 319th and 320th Bombardment Groups equipped with B-26 twin-engine medium bombers.

57th Wing USAAF, composed of 310th and 321st Bombardment Groups equipped with B-25 twin-engine medium bombers. Only the 310th operated in the vicinity of Pompeii.

RAF/RCAF DOCUMENTATION FOR THE BOMBING NEAR POMPEII

As noted above, the *Operations and Intelligence Summary* of HQ Northwest African Air Forces (TNA AIR/51/253) provides a comprehensive overview of each day's air operations at the highest level of command in the Mediterranean theatre.

Quite detailed documentation of the participation of the RAF and RCAF from Group down to Squadron level survives in the UK National Archives. Each Group, Wing and Squadron maintained its own *Operations Record*

Book (*ORB*) that included a record of each day's missions (and sometimes other activities) on a standard 'Summary of Events' form called a Form 540. At Squadron level, returning crews were debriefed by a squadron intelligence officer, who completed the Form 540, in some cases summarising the activities of the Squadron as a whole, in other cases listing each individual aircraft and crew and summarising (very briefly) each crew's report of what it had done. Thus it is possible to get a glimpse of what even individual crews thought they had bombed, and how successful they thought they had been.

Besides the *ORB*s, which for each formation are retained in separate files at the UK National Archives, there also survive at Wing level summaries of the orders sent down from Group, giving a prospective account of intended targets. In some cases, targets were changed in the course of a day, so multiple sets of orders cancel one another out, most notably and dramatically for the night of 13/14 September 1943. After the day's (or, typically, night's) operations, the Wings reported back to Group on standard *OPSUM* (Operations Summary) forms. Copies of the orders from Group and the *OPSUM*s are preserved at the National Archives in 'Appendix' files for each Wing. Thus, for example, No. 231 (Bomber) Wing's *Operations Record Book* is TNA AIR 26/283, while the corresponding appendix file is AIR 26/287. The numbers of the relevant documents are summarised below.

Northwest African Strategic Air Forces

HQ Northwest African Air Forces: *Operations and Intelligence Summary*: TNA AIR/51/253

RAF Group

No. 205 Group: *Operations Record Book*: TNA AIR 25/817

RAF/RCAF Wings

No. 231 (Bomber) Wing: *ORB*: AIR 26/283; Appendix AIR 26/287
No. 236 (Bomber) Wing: *ORB*: AIR 26/302; Appendix AIR 26/304
No. 330 (Bomber) Wing: *ORB*: AIR 26/437; Appendix AIR 26/438
No. 331 Wing RCAF: *ORB*: AIR 26/439

RAF/RCAF Squadrons

In No. 231 (Bomber) Wing
37 Squadron: *ORB* AIR 27/391
70 Squadron: *ORB* AIR 27/616

In No. 236 (Bomber) Wing
40 Squadron: *ORB* AIR 27/412
104 Squadron: *ORB* AIR 27/821
In No. 330 (Bomber) Wing
142 Squadron: *ORB* AIR 27/974
150 Squadron: *ORB* AIR 27/1011
In No. 331 Wing RCAF
420 Squadron RCAF: *ORB* AIR 27/1825
424 Squadron RCAF: *ORB* AIR 27/1834
425 Squadron RCAF: *ORB* AIR 27/1837

Northwest African Tactical Air Forces

HQ Northwest African Air Forces: *Operations and Intelligence Summary*: TNA AIR/51/253

Tactical Bomber Force

RAF/SAAF Wings
No. 3 (South African) Wing: *ORB* AIR 54/98 and 54/99
No. 232 (Light Bomber) Wing: (N/A)
No. 326 (Light Bomber) Wing: *ORB* AIR 26/434

RAF Squadrons in No. 326 (Light Bomber) Wing
18 Squadron: *ORB* AIR 27/244/31
114 Squadron: *ORB* AIR 27/882/77

SAAF Squadrons in No. 3 (South African Air Force) Wing
12 (SAAF) Squadron: *ORB* AIR 27/418/12; Appendix AIR 27/179
21 (SAAF) Squadron: *ORB* AIR 27/268; Appendix AIR 27/276
24 (SAAF) Squadron: *ORB* AIR 27/299; Appendix AIR 27/304

USAAF DOCUMENTATION FOR THE BOMBING NEAR POMPEII

The *Operations and Intelligence Summary* for Headquarters Northwest African Air Forces (TNA AIR/51/253) also includes summaries of operations conducted by USAAF formations.

The more detailed USAAF documentation consulted was produced at Group and Squadron level, and is more diverse than the RAF equivalent. It includes Group *Weekly Status and Operations Report* documents, compiled on standard forms (the War Department Army Air Forces Form no. 34) similar to the RAF Form 540s. These summarise the week's missions flown by the Group, with dates, timings, number and type of aircraft, bombing altitude, details of bombs dropped and some brief comments on the mission. They also include basic information on personnel, maintenance issues and consumption of fuel and ammunition. There are also more detailed Group and Squadron Mission or Sortie Reports, that provide a narrative (typically a single typescript page) of each individual mission, sometimes with additional pages documenting formations employed and crew composition. These were produced (and composed) by a Group Intelligence Officer. Unit War Diaries provide information too, although these tend to be variable in content and quality, quite often informal, and often reflect on personnel issues and day-to-day life in the unit rather than operational details. Most of the USAAF documents listed below are denoted by the IRIS catalogue numbers of the US Air Force Historical Research Agency, although others have been accessed on Wing and Group history sites where they have been transcribed from US National Archives records by enthusiasts and veterans.

TACTICAL BOMBER FORCE

12th Bombardment Group

12th Bombardment Group Sortie Reports (AFHRA IRIS 00077840)

340th Bombardment Group

340th Bombardment Group Daily Operational Journal (AFHRA IRIS 00083898)

340th Bomb Group Diary (AFHRA IRIS 00083912)

5TH WING

97th Bombardment Group

97th Bombardment Group Mission Reports (AFHRA IRIS 00081450)

97th Bombardment Group War Diary September 1943 (AFHRA IRIS 00081463)

301st Bombardment Group

Headquarters, 301st Bombardment Group (H), AAF, Office of the Intelligence Officer, *Narrative Mission Report*, 20 September 1943 (AFHRA IRIS 00081727)

57TH WING

310th Bombardment Group

310th Bombardment Group (M) AAF, *Headquarters and Group History*, September 1943 (AFHRA IRIS 00081977)

310th Bombardment Group *Mission Reports*, September 1943 at 57th Bomb Wing Association website: <http://57thbombwing.com/310thHistory/310_BG_1943-09.pdf> [accessed 4 August 2019].

HQ 310th Bombardment Group *Mission Summaries*, September 1943 at 57th Bomb Wing Association website: <http://57thbombwing.com/310thHistory/310_BG_1943-09.pdf> [accessed 4 August 2019].

42ND BOMBARDMENT WING

42nd Bombardment Wing: Air and Ground Cooperation—Salerno, Anzio, Cassino (AFHRA IRIS 00105103)

319th Bombardment Group

319th Bomb Group *War Diary*, September 1943 (AFHRA IRIS 00082333)

319th Bombardment Group *Outline History*, September 1943 (AFHRA IRIS 00082333)

319th Bombardment Group from *42nd Bombardment Wing Mission Summaries*, September 1943 (AFHRA IRIS 00105053)

320th Bombardment Group

320th Bombardment Group *Intelligence Narrative* No. 68, 29 August 1943 (AFHRA IRIS 00082367)

86th Fighter-Bomber Group

War Diaries of the 525th, 526th and 527th Fighter-Bomber Squadrons accessed at http://www.86fighterbombergroup.com/documents/

APPENDIX C

Applying 1944 US Eighth Air Force Accuracy Data to Pompeii

As noted above (Chapter 4), the 1947 United States Strategic Bombing Survey incorporated a detailed study of Eighth Air Force bombing missions in northern Europe between 1 September and 31 December 1944. This study provided accuracy data for B-17 and B-24 bombers bombing from a mean altitude of 21,000 ft in a range of visibility conditions, including 'Good to fair visibility—no cloud cover, no haze, and no smoke', which was taken to reflect, roughly at least, the daytime conditions over Pompeii in September 1943. Accuracy is expressed in terms of proportion of bombs judged (primarily from assessment of aerial photographs) to have hit within stated distances from their aiming point.[1]

Table 4: Percentage of bombs hitting within a specified distance of the aiming point

1000 ft (305 m)	½ mile (845 m)	1 mile (1609 m)	3 miles (4282 m)	5 miles (<8047 m)	More than 5 miles (>8047 m)
30%	64.9%	82.4%	91.5%	92.2%	7.8%

To apply this data to the bombing near Pompeii, the distance was measured between three known or possible aiming points (the intersection of the Naples-Pompeii autostrada, the Incrocio Paselli, and the Piazza Imbriani intersection east of Torre Annunziata), and both the closest (Porta Marina) and furthest (amphitheatre) points of the archaeological site.

The distance from each aiming point to the Porta Marina at Pompeii is recorded as Distance A. The distance from each aiming point to the east corner of the amphitheatre at Pompeii is recorded as Distance B.

Table 5: Distances between aiming points and closest and furthest points on the archaeological site of Pompeii

Aiming point	Distance A	Distance B
Junction of autostrada and SS18	941 ft/287 m	0.93 miles/1489 m
Incrocio Paselli	1828 ft/557 m	1.04 miles/1681 m
Torre Annunziata Piazza Imbriani	0.98 miles/1580 m	1.66 miles/2667 m

Additional points to reflect expected accuracy at those distances were interpolated between those provided in the US Strategic Bombing Survey, with the percentage of bombs that would be expected to fall within that distance from the AP calculated from the Strategic Bombing Survey data:

Table 6: Estimated percentage of bombs falling within specified radii measured from aiming point

Distance from AP	% bombs hitting within that distance
305 m (US SBS data provides no value for 287 m)	30%
500 m	45.08%
1000 m	68.05%
1500 m	78.20%
1700 m	82.71%
2700 m	86.11%

These percentage figures were then used to calculate the approximate percentage of bombs that would be expected to fall within each of a series of concentric rings centred on the aiming points to include the archaeological site.

Table 7: Data from Table 6 applied to radii from particular aiming points encompassing the archaeological site of Pompeii

	Approximate % bombs aimed at specified AP hitting within that ring
Between 305 m (1000 ft) and 1500 m (amphitheatre) from AP if AP is autostrada/SS18 junction	78.20–30 = 48.2%
Between 500 m (Porta Marina) and 1700 m (amphitheatre) from AP if AP is Incrocio Paselli	82.71–45.08 = 37.63%
Between 1500 m (Porta Marina) and 2700 m (amphitheatre) from AP if AP is Torre Annunziata Piazza Imbriani	86.11–78.21 = 7.9%

The total area of each ring was divided by the total area of the site of ancient Pompeii (c. 64 ha) and applied to the percentage figure above to give an estimate of the proportion of bombs dropped on a given aiming point that might have been expected to hit the site based on the 1944 Eighth Air Force data.

Table 8: Percentage of bombs dropped on particular aiming points estimated to fall on the archaeological site of Pompeii

	Area of ring	Area of ancient Pompeii (64 ha) expressed as % of area of ring	% of bombs expected to hit ancient Pompeii for that aiming point
Intersection of Naples-Pompeii autostrada and SS18, to between 305 m (1000 ft) and 1500 m (amphitheatre)	678 ha	9.44%	9.44 x 0.482 = 4.53%
Incrocio Paselli, to between 500 m (Porta Marina) and 1700 m (amphitheatre)	829 ha	7.72%	7.72 x 0.3763 = 2.91%
Torre Annunziata road junction, between 1500 m (Porta Marina) and 2700 m (amphitheatre)	1583 ha	4.04%	4.04 x 0.079 = 0.32%

We can apply these percentages to known numbers of bombs dropped by B-17 bombers on particular missions against targets near Pompeii. For example, on 14 September, the 97th Bombardment Group dropped 408 500 lb bombs on 'Pompei road junction'.

If their AP was the autostrada/SS18 junction, the bombs expected to fall within Pompeii archaeological site would be 408 x 4.53% = 18.

If their AP was the Incrocio Paselli, the bombs expected within Pompeii archaeological site would be 408 x 2.91% = 11.

At about the same time that day, the 99th Bombardment Group 'bombed Torre Annunziata junction'. Assuming their aiming point was the Piazza Imbriani again, and that the 99th dropped the same number of bombs as the 97th, then that mission might be expected to have hit the archaeological site of Pompeii with a single additional bomb (408 x 0.32% = 1.3).

APPENDIX D

RAF Medium Bombers' Use of Flares

The relevant *ORB*s do not provide much detail on the techniques and tactics used by RAF night bombers to illuminate targets near Pompeii, and so I tried to reconstruct them by using the relatively few timings (mostly of landings and take-offs) to assess whether illuminators invariably arrived before the bomb-carrying aircraft of their Squadron/Wing, whether some illuminators arrived at staggered times within their Wing's bombing slot to maintain illumination, and/or whether illuminators dropped their flares quickly and returned to their base or remained over the target for an extended period to maintain illumination.

NO. 231 WING

37 Sqn ORB

13 September (9 aircraft): Sgt. Noble (with 54 flares) took off at 1837 (second, 3 minutes after the first aircraft, 3 minutes before the next wave of 3). Three more took off after 1840 (the last at 1845). Noble was one of the last back, which might support the hypothesis that he arrived early and stayed over the target to maintain illumination. However, No. 231 Wing's other illuminator for its 2200–2220 bombing slot (Flt. Sgt. Lockhart, also of 37 Sqn., 54 flares) took off only 3 minutes after Noble and returned first in the squadron, 35 minutes before Noble, which runs contrary to that hypothesis.

15 September (16 aircraft): Sgt. Holland (54 flares) took off at 2000 (equal first in the squadron, 3 minutes before the next aircraft and 18 minutes before the last) and returned at 0250 equal ninth. The Wing's bombing slot was 2300 to 0001. The 231 Wing *ORB* indicates the Wing's other illuminator came from 70 Sqn.

70 Sqn. ORB

16 September: While the *ORB* is not entirely clear, Wellington 'G' (Sgt. Brasier) seems to have been the illuminator. It took off at 2015, 15 minutes after Sgt. Holland of 37 Sqn. The *ORB* reports 'Identified Torre Annunciata and whole area in light of flares of previous wave. Own flares dropped to

illuminate target roads. 1 x 4,000 lb'. Seven out of the 18 70 Sqn aircraft on the mission arrived after 'G' returned at 0300. [It is unclear whether the 1 x 4000 lb indicates that 'G' was carrying a 4000 lb in addition to its flares—a natural reading of the document, although no other aircraft carried flares alongside such a heavy bomb load].

The take-off and return times for 15/16 September support the idea that one illuminator (Sgt. Holland, 37 Sqn.) was scheduled to arrive early in the No. 231 Wing bombing slot, to be replaced by another (Sgt. Brasier, 70 Sqn.) to provide something approaching continuous illumination, a hypothesis reinforced by the statement that 'G' found the area 'in light of flares of previous wave', presumably those of Sgt. Holland of 37 Squadron, who had taken off 15 minutes before Sgt. Brasier.

NO. 331 WING RCAF

ORB *425 Sqn. RCAF*

13 September: The illuminator was 'A' (36 flares) which took off at 1809, first of 11 aircraft and 6 minutes before the next one (1815—the last took off at 1848). 'A' returned first. This fits with a scheme in which 'A' opened the illumination for No. 331 Wing (bombing between 2150 and 2200) and returned quickly.

15 September: 'L' is the only aircraft of the squadron reported as carrying flares, but only 18 of them, in a mixed load with 9 250 lb bombs. It took off at 2015, tenth out of 15 aircraft (and 30 minutes after the first), arriving back joint last. The timings suggest that this may have been intended to maintain illumination begun by an aircraft from another squadron in the Wing, the mixed load being analogous to that of the 'main force' of the Renault factory raid.[1]

Unfortunately the *ORB*s of the other squadrons (420, 424) in the Wing do not identify the illuminators or provide timings for this mission (or that of 13 September)

ORB *420 Sqn. RCAF*

24 August (Torre Annunziata): HE569 was the squadron's illuminator (carrying 36 flares), and took off first of 12 aircraft, but was forced to turn back for technical reasons.

29 August (Torre Annunziata): HZ414 dropped 88 illuminators [flares] over the target at 0058 from 8000 ft (2438 m). This is the only illuminating

aircraft for which the records actually give a time at which the flares were dropped. It was the first in the squadron to bomb, the next (HE973) being at 0101, the last (of 8) at 0109. The appendices to the No. 231 Wing *ORB* (AIR 26/287) give 'B', the notional bombing time for 331 and 231 Wings, as 0100 (with Nos. 236 and 330 Wings following at 0200), so HZ414 was opening the raid with its flares. Mk. V flares had a 2-minute internal delay, so flares dropped at 0058 from 8000 ft (1829 m) would have gone off at 0100 at 6000 ft, with HE973 then bombing at 0101. The other squadron *ORB*s of No. 331 Wing provide no useful information about illuminators for August beyond the fact that 424 Sqn. provided 1 illuminator (and 8 bomb-carrying aircraft) for the August 29 mission.

APPENDIX E

BBC Recording of Matthew Henry Halton at Pompeii, 29 September 1943

Transcription of archival sound recording held by the Imperial War Museum (London), IWM 1369, 1943-09-29, 'Canadian correspondent's [Matthew Henry Halton] commentary as British troops reach the Plain of Naples'.

'Naples lies before us, sparkling in the sun like a bowl of diamonds. The first phase of the Italian campaign is over. Yesterday and today, British soldiers of the Fifth Army broke through the two mountain passes connecting the Plain of Salerno with the Plain of Naples. The going was hard. We had to pay for every pillbox in the passes, and the German delaying forces fought with skill, and desperate courage. Nevertheless, they were beaten, and we are now debouched into the Plain of Italy, of Naples. I left the Eighth Army and its Canadians yesterday to visit the Fifth Army, and early today I was able to enter Pompeii—you can hear the enemy guns—with one of the first British units, a unit I had known in the far-off wasteland of Libya two years and a half ago. I speak now from Pompeii. I speak actually from the ruins of the Roman amphitheatre, nearly 2000 years old. I am standing on the high wall of this amphitheatre. It was used by the Germans as a gun position, with the result that we had to bomb it, and there is a gaping bomb crater right in the middle of the arena. Two thousand years ago these stones echoed to the cries and shouts of gladiators and tortured men, and now the wild sounds of exploding bombs and shells go echoing through them. It's quiet now, but perhaps our guns, or the enemy's, will start shooting again while I'm speaking. We stand on the wall of this amphitheatre, the spectacular scene before us is full of the memories of history and at the same moment, history is being made. As I speak these . . . [two loud bangs] . . . As I speak these words I . . . I can see the armoured cars of a celebrated British cavalry regiment probing down the lush lanes against the enemy rearguards three miles away on the side of Vesuvius. As I speak these words, British armoured cars are going through the ruined city of ancient Pompeii, 400 yards away. On the right is Vesuvius, the volcanic mountain, which spewed out its molten lava to bury Pompeii so long ago, and its white smoke plume drifts lazily into the sky. On the left, just below us, is the modern town of Pompei. Our first tanks are just coming down through the main square, clattering through at 30 miles an hour. As each tank turns the corner and roars into the square . . .—now those . . . those are our guns—and roars into the square, a torrent of hand-clapping and cheering runs down the street. And girls throw bouquets of lilies, and sweet-peas, and carnations. The shells from our guns a mile back are whistling over, from time to time, as you can hear. As I speak, enemy machine-gun nests in sight of this amphitheatre are holding up our advance for an hour or two. As I speak, a British armoured car is burning 200 yards away. Two German prisoners are standing sulkily beside a truck, and two of our soldiers are being buried in a garden. Two men who fought in many campaigns, from Alamein to Tunis, and now are stopped forever at the foot of Vesuvius, just after one of them had said "We are getting closer to home." Imagine for yourself the high ring of mountains behind us, the rich plain before us, the white ruins of Pompeii, Vesuvius on our right, and just below us, the Bay of Naples, and the battle, it seems, just ending.'

APPENDIX F

Cities Included in MAAF, *Ancient Monuments of Italy* (23 February 1944)

The names are in the anglicised forms given in the document.

Table 9: Cities included in MAAF, *Ancient Monuments of Italy*, Volume 1

Amelia	Florence (see Figure 28)	Modena
Ancona	Forli	Montefalco
Aosta	Frascati	Novara
Aquila (Abruzzi)	Gaeta	Orvieto
Aquileia	Genoa	Padua
Assisi	Grosseto	Parma
Bergamo	Lodi	Pavia
Bologna	Loreto	Pesaro
Cortona	Lucca	Piacenza
Cremona	Mantua	Pisa
Ferentino	Massa Maritima	Pistoia
Fidenza	Milan	Prato

Table 10: Cities included in MAAF, *Ancient Monuments of Italy*, Volume 2

Ravenna	Terracina	Tuscania
Reggio Emilia	Tivoli	Udine
Rimini	Todi	Urbino
Saronno	Tolentino	Venice (see Figure 29)
Spoleto	Treviso	Vercelli
Tarquinia	Trieste	Verona
Terni	Turin	Viterbo
		Volterra

The preface to the atlas names other cities with varying degrees of protection not included among the aerial photographs of the UK National Archive copy. These are Rome, Torcello (not included in the 'Venice' plate of the atlas), Arezzo, Ascoli Piceno, Borgo, Bracciano, Brescia, Como, Ferrara, Gubbio, Montepulciano, Perugia, San Gimignano, San Spolone [?], Siena, and Ragusa, Spalato and Zara on the Dalmatian coast.

Notes

INTRODUCTION

1. For the number of bomb hits, see Amedeo Maiuri, *Taccuino napoletano: Giugno 1940–luglio 1944* (Naples: Vajro Editore, 1956), p. 110 ('at least 160 bombs'). One hundred and sixty hits are recorded on a contemporary plan of bomb damage (Figure 1 in this book) produced at Pompeii by Italian staff and included in the report MFAA *Pompeii and Herculaneum*, p. 2, along with a lengthy and detailed report on the damage by the Italian staff. This plan was adapted by the Allied Monuments, Fine Arts and Archives Sub-Commission as 'Pompeii: Bomb-Damage 1943' for MFAA *Final Report: Campania*, p. 27—see Figure 2, and Appendix A. Laurentino García y García, *Danni di guerra a Pompei: Una dolorosa vicenda quasi dimenticata* (Rome: "L'Erma" di Bretschneider, 2006), pp. 24–25 n. 15 provides evidence and argument that the number of bombs was somewhat higher, which undoubtedly is true.

2. Maiuri, p. 110. García y García (p. 28) argues that Maiuri took a 'soft' line on the damage because of the delicacy of his political position vis-à-vis the Allies. It might also be argued that his perspective was a realistic one, given the circumstances under which the site was damaged and the general problems of its conservation. Mary Beard, *Pompeii: The Life of a Roman Town* (London: Profile Books, 2008), pp. 18–19 accurately characterises the wartime damage and post-war reconstruction of Pompeii as an episode in 'the slow death that the city has suffered since it began to be uncovered in the mid eighteenth century' rather than a unique cataclysm. For post-war restoration, see Renata Picone, 'Restauri di guerra a Pompei: Le Case del Fauno e di Epidio Rufo', in *Offese di guerra: Ricostruzione e restauro nel Mezzogiorno d'Italia*, ed. by Stella Casiello (Florence: Alinea Editrice, 2011), pp. 19–41.

3. *Works of Art in Italy: Losses and Survivals in the War*, Part II—*North of Bologna* together with Regional Summaries and a Supplement to Part I. Compiled from War Office Reports by the British Committee on the Preservation and Restitution of Works of Art, Archives and Other Material in Enemy Hands (London: HMSO, 1946), p. 79—see Appendix A. Also see [Sir Leonard Woolley], 'The War and Classical Remains in Italy. Supplied by the Archaeological Adviser, The War Office', *Antiquity* 72 (1944), 169–72 (p. 170).

4. García y García, pp. 18, 24–26. In wartime MFAA documentation Pompeii was ranked as a three-star site, the highest rating, comprising 'monuments of highest importance'. For the ranking of Pompeii, see, for example, United States Army Service Forces, *Civil Affairs Handbook. Italy. Section 17: Supplement on Cultural Institutions, Supplementary Atlas*, M353–17 (Washington, DC: US Government Printing Office, 4 January 1944), p. 28; definition of three-star monuments from United States Army Service Forces, *Civil Affairs Handbook. France. Section 17C: Cultural Institutions, Central and*

Southern France, M352–17C (Washington, DC: US Government Printing Office, 24 June 1944), p. xiv.

5. For example, Ingrid D. Rowland, 'The Wrong Way for Pompeii', *New York Review of Books*, 22 October 2013, <https://www.nybooks.com/daily/2013/10/22/pompeii-wrong-way/> [accessed 18 September 2018]: 'During World War II, the Allies dropped 156 bombs in the area around the site, in the misguided belief that German troops were hiding out among the ruins', repeated in the same author's book *From Pompeii: The Afterlife of a Roman Town* (Cambridge, MA: Harvard University Press, 2014), p. 251.

6. NARA M1944, RG 239/0067, MFAA Field Reports, Allied Force Headquarters, Office of the Commander-in-Chief [Gen. Dwight D. Eisenhower], *Historical Monuments*, 29 December 1943. 'Distinguishing military convenience from military necessity,' see Ronald T.P. Alcala, 'Babylon Revisited: Reestablishing a Corps of Specialists for the Protection of Cultural Property in Armed Conflict', *Harvard National Security Journal* 6 (2015), 206–54 (226).

7. Sir Kenneth Clark, director of the [British] National Gallery: 'even supposing it were possible for an archaeologist to accompany each invading force, I cannot help feeling that he would have great difficulty in restraining a commanding officer from shelling an important military objective simply because it contained some fine historical monuments'; Sir Eric Maclagan, director of the Victoria and Albert Museum: 'In violent fighting damage will happen anyway. . . . I do not think it would be the faintest use to have an official archaeologist at GHQ.' Both (writing in 1943) are quoted in Lynn H. Nicholas, *The Rape of Europa: The Fate of Europe's Treasures in the Third Reich and the Second World War* (New York: Vintage Books, 1995), p. 214. Both were correct, but took unrealistically extreme positions that failed to acknowledge the middle ground between 'no protection' and 'absolute immunity' on which wartime heritage protection works.

8. The key report is the typescript MFAA *Final Report: General*, and its specialised regional sections. See also Sir Leonard Woolley, *A Record of the Work Done by the Military Authorities for the Protection of the Treasures of Art & History in War Areas* (London: HMSO, 1947). For the Commission of Enquiry (the 'Collier Commission'), see pp. 176–80; 194–200. American monuments officer Mason Hammond made suggestions in a post-war letter to Huntington Cairns, secretary of the Roberts Commission, for peacetime training and education in cultural protection for US military personnel (NARA M1944, RG 239/0014, Correspondence, Hammond to Cairns, 8 April 1946). He advocated their familiarisation with its value 'so that there will not be the distrust and lack of cooperation which existed during this war', as well as provision of specialist monuments officers and inventories of cultural property.

9. Most conveniently accessed, with commentary including historical context, in Patrick J. O'Keefe and Lyndel V. Prott, *Cultural Heritage Conventions and Other Instruments: A Compendium with Commentaries* (Builth Wells, UK: Institute of Art and Law, 2011), pp. 16–42. For the development and contexts of the 1954 Hague Convention, see Roger O'Keefe, *The Protection of Cultural Property in Armed Conflict* (Cambridge: Cambridge University Press, 2006), pp. 92–195; Patrick J. Boylan, *Review of the Convention for the Protection of Cultural Property in the Event of Armed Conflict (The Hague Convention of 1954)* (London: City University, 1993).

10. At least, beyond their basic documentation in post-war official histories, especially those relating to military government of occupied territories. See Harry L. Coles and Albert K. Weinberg, *Civil Affairs: Soldiers Become Governors*. The United States Army

in World War II, Special Studies, 6 (Washington, DC: Department of the Army, 1964), pp. 860–76; F.S.V. Donnison, *Civil Affairs and Military Government: Central Organization and Planning*. History of the Second World War. United Kingdom Military Series (London: HMSO, 1966), pp. 211–36.

11. I am grateful to my UK Blue Shield colleague Paul Fox for making this point.

12. Although maps and inventories of cultural heritage were produced for some Asian countries (China, Japan, Korea, the Netherlands East Indies, Siam and Taiwan) during the Second World War, and US specialists were sent to Japan during its occupation. For the latter, see Carlotta Coccoli, 'Ricostruzione postbellica e patrimonio urbano in Giappone: Orientamenti di ricerca,' *Storia Urbana* 140–141 (2013), 5–16.

13. Memoirs: see, for example, Frederick Hartt, *Florentine Art under Fire* (Princeton: Princeton University Press, 1949); James J. Rorimer, *Survival: The Salvage and Protection of Art in War* (New York: Abelard Press, 1950).

14. Nicholas; Ilaria Dagnini Brey, *The Venus Fixers* (New York: Farrar, Straus and Giroux, 2009); Robert M. Edsell, *Monuments Men* (London: Preface Publishing, 2009).

15. *Guerra, monumenti, ricostruzione: Architetture e centri storici italiani nel secondo conflitto mondiale*, ed. by Lorenzo De Stefani (Venice: Marsilio Editori, 2011); Carlotta Coccoli, *Monumenti violati: Danni bellici e riparazioni in Italia nel 1943–1945. Il ruolo degli alleati* (Florence: Nardini Editore, 2017).

16. For a representative selection of studies, see *Kunsthistoriker im Krieg: deutscher militärischer Kunstschutz in Italien* 1943–1945, ed. by Christian Fuhrmeister and others (Cologne: Böhlau-Verlag, 2012).

17. Nicola Lambourne, *War Damage in Western Europe* (Edinburgh: Edinburgh University Press, 2001); Marta Nezzi, 'The Defence of Works of Art from Bombing in Italy during the Second World War', in *Bombing, States and Peoples in Western Europe 1940–1945*, ed. by Claudia Baldoli, Andrew Knapp and Richard Overy (London: Continuum, 2011), pp. 101–20; More generally on Italy, see Claudia Baldoli and Andrew Knapp, *Forgotten Blitzes: France and Italy under Allied Air Attack, 1940–1945* (London: Continuum, 2012). Richard Overy, *The Bombing War: Europe 1939–1945* (London: Allen Lane, 2013), pp. 472–73, 532–36, 544 provides some insights on the destruction of heritage in the context of a broader study of bombing in the Second World War.

18. See, for example, Alcala, p. 209.

19. To list just a few notable examples: Geoff Emberling, Katharyn Hanson and McGuire Gibson, *Catastrophe! The Looting and Destruction of Iraq's Past* (Chicago: Oriental Institute of the University of Chicago , 2008); Peter G. Stone, *Cultural Heritage, Ethics and the Military* (Woodbridge, UK: Boydell Press, 2011); *Destruction of Cultural Heritage in Iraq*, ed. by Peter G. Stone and Joanne Farchakh Bajjaly (Woodbridge, UK: Boydell Press, 2011); *Archaeology, Cultural Property, and the Military*, ed. by Laurie W. Rush (Woodbridge, UK: Boydell Press, 2012); *Cultural Heritage in the Crosshairs: Protecting Cultural Property During Conflict*, ed. by Joris Kila and James A. Zeidler (Leiden: Brill, 2013); Helen Walasek and others, *Bosnia and the Destruction of Cultural Heritage* (London: Routledge, 2016).

20. Laurie W. Rush, 'Cultural Property Protection as a Force Multiplier in Stability Operations: World War II Monuments Officers' Lessons Learned', *Military Review* 36 (March–April 2012), 36–43.

21. Alcala. The legal scholarship on the current international humanitarian legislation inevitably examines the historical contexts in which it developed—c.f. Roger O'Keefe,

Protection; Boylan, pp. 23–48; Jiří Toman, *The Protection of Cultural Property in the Event of Armed Conflict* (Aldershot, UK: UNESCO/Dartmouth Publishing, 1996).

22. All of these issues arise to some extent in the modern contexts addressed in the bibliography listed above. See also Roger O'Keefe and others, *Protection of Cultural Property: Military Manual* (Paris: UNESCO, 2016).

23. Baldoli and Knapp, pp. 40–41

24. Gabriella Gribaudi, *Guerra totale: Tra bombe alleate e violenze naziste. Napoli e il fronte meridionale 1940–1944* (Turin: Bollati Boringhieri 2005), especially pp. 89–173 (and pp. 386–406 on Benevento), provides a comprehensive and wide-ranging discussion of the impact of bombing on the civilian population of Campania; Simon Pocock, *Campania 1943: Enciclopedia della memoria*. Vol. II, *Provincia di Napoli*. Parte I, *Zona est* (Naples: Three Mice Books, 2009), provides vivid contemporary accounts of civilian experience of the bombing; Baldoli and Knapp address the issue of civilian casualties caused by Allied bombing of France and Italy as a central theme. On the casualty figures for Naples, see Gribaudi, pp. 161–62.

25. See Maiuri, pp. 164–65 on this issue. Maiuri records with appreciation MFAA Major Paul Gardner's decision to make Allied military personnel pay an entrance fee to visit the site when technically, like Italian troops in uniform, they were entitled to enter free of charge. He estimates that there were about half a million such visitors to the site in 1943–1945. The entrance fee for ordinary soldiers was 5 lire (10 lire for officers), totalling over 2.5 million lire. Besides the entrance fees, 700,000 lire of reconstruction funds were allocated for the ancient site of Pompeii in November 1943 for the period to June 1944 ([Gardner], *November Report*, p. 3). The *AMGOT Plan for Italy*, the military government planning handbook for the Allied invasion of Italy, sets a maximum rate of 50 lire a day for unskilled labourers employed by the Allies, so the entrance fees to Pompeii funded the equivalent of c. 50,000 man-days of employment for such labourers, and the reconstruction funds a further 14,000 man-days.

CHAPTER 1

1. I have used the term 'accidental' rather than 'collateral' for technical reasons. Written contemporary military definitions of collateral damage seem appropriate for what happened at Pompeii: 'Damage to personnel and property adjacent to, but not forming part of, an authorised target' (Annex 3B8 'Prevention of Collateral Damage', in [UK] Ministry of Defence, *Campaign Execution*. Joint Doctrine Publication 3–00 3rd edition, October 2009) <https://assets.publishing.service.gov.uk/government/> [accessed 3/8/18]. However, discussions with military personnel engaged in targeting suggest that 'collateral' is more typically used of damage and casualties caused when a weapon hits its intended target but its impact also causes damage beyond that intended target. In the case of Pompeii, bombs were aimed at particular targets but missed and hit the archaeological site instead, causing damage for which the term 'accidental' is perhaps more appropriate. Civilians sometimes regard 'collateral damage' as a cynical military euphemism for 'civilian casualties', which it is not.

2. García y García, pp. 31–34.

3. For the bombing on 24/25 September, see Maiuri, pp. 105–8.

4. For Operation Avalanche, the Salerno landings, see the British and US official

histories respectively by C.J.C. Molony, *The Campaign in Sicily 1943 and the Campaign in Italy, 3rd September 1943 to 31st March 1944*. The History of the Second World War: The Mediterranean and Middle East. Vol. V (London: HMSO, 1973), pp. 255–329; and Martin Blumenson, *Salerno to Cassino*. The United States Army in WWII: The Mediterranean (Washington, DC: Department of the Army, 1969), pp. 73–153. The Salerno force was the 5th U.S. Army commanded by the American Lieutenant-General Mark W. Clark, but including both the 6th U.S. Corps and the 10th (British) Corps. Avalanche was the primary Allied landing on mainland Italy, intended to secure the port of Naples as the basis for further operations. The British 8th Army, composed of British and Empire and Commonwealth forces, landed in, and advanced north from, Calabria and Apulia from 3 September 1943 as Operation Baytown, with the aim of drawing enemy troops away from the Salerno area, which was the main landing (Molony, *Campaign in Italy*, p. 223, quoting Montgomery).

5. Overy, pp. 510–46; Denis Richards, *The Fight at Odds*. Royal Air Force 1939–1945. Vol. 1 (London: HMSO, 1953), pp. 145–47: Genoa, Milan and Turin from June 1940; Naples first in October 1940, but especially from December 1942; Rome only from 19 July 1943. On the origins and history of Allied bombing of Italy more generally, see Baldoli and Knapp, esp. pp. 1–48. Pocock, pp. 213–14, notes bombs (probably intended for Naples) falling sporadically in areas around the modern town of Pompei in June and July 1943.

6. An introduction to Allied air forces organisation, organisational terminology and documentation is provided in Appendix B.

7. Appendix B: 'Air Forces Organisation and Documentation' examines these topics in more detail.

8. RAF Form 540s that make up the Operations Record Books at Group, Wing and Squadron level are classified 'Secret', and the USAAF Weekly Status and Operations Reports and Mission/Sortie Reports are classified 'U.S. Secret (= British Most Secret)'.

9. HQ Northwest African Air Forces, *Operations and Intelligence Summary 186 ending 18:00 25 August 1943* (TNA AIR/51/253) [hereafter *OIS* 186 (25/08/43)]. Contemporary analysis in Zuckerman, *Report*, pp. 101–4, characterises the mission of 24/25 August as the start of attacks against Torre Annunziata rail targets, a key point (in his view) for the movement of troops and supplies to the south of Italy by rail. The RAF official history, Denis Richards and Hilary St. George Saunders, *The Fight Avails: Royal Air Force 1939–1945*, Vol. II (London: HMSO, 1954), p. 327, presents this mission as part of the increasing weight of air attacks against railway marshalling yards in Italy in late August 1943, in preparation for the Salerno landings.

10. *ORB* No. 205 Group (24/08/43); appendices to *ORB* No. 236 Wing (24/08/43); App. B611 orders from the Group to its component Wings recording the aim 'To deny the enemy the use of the steelworks and marshalling yards, TORRE ANNUNZIATA' and the mission code-word 'SNUFF'.

11. *ORB* 104 Sqn. (24/08/43).

12. Aircraft were marked with individual letters for identification within the squadron. The phrase 'light to moderate heavy' is incomplete, and probably should read 'light to moderate heavy flak' [heavy calibre anti-aircraft fire] or 'light [flak] and moderate heavy [flak]', the latter according with the description in the 424 Sqn. RCAF *ORB* (24/08/43). Maiuri, p. 105, recounts seeing the light from the parachute flares while sheltering from the bombing.

13. *ORB* 424 Sqn. (24/08/43). The other relevant squadron *ORBs* are those of 425 Sqn. RCAF (11 aircraft), 420 Sqn. RCAF (12 aircraft) and 40 Sq. RAF (9 aircraft), all for 24/08/43.

14. *ORB* No. 205 Group (29/08/43), setting out the Torre Annunziata marshalling yards as the target for a mission on the night of 29/30 August, describes them as largely undamaged by the earlier mission.

15. D'Avino cited by García y García, pp. 31–32, supplemented by Maiuri, pp. 105–6. To put this in perspective, the damage to the site on this occasion, while serious where the bombs hit, seems to have been caused by no more than 4–6 bombs. Most of the Wellington bombers on this mission carried standard loads of 7 or 9 bombs (2 x 1000 lb + 5 x 500 lb; or 9 x 500 lb—*ORB* 420 Sqn. RCAF, 24/08/43), so the damage that night was the equivalent of just part of the bomb load of a single aircraft. Alone, 40 Sqn. RAF and 420 Sqn. RCAF (with 21 of the 48 aircraft bombing, the only ones recording the composition of their bomb loads) aimed a total of 147 high-explosive bombs (2 x 4000 lb, 8 x 1000 lb, 137 x 500 lb) and 35 small incendiaries at the intended targets. Thus of c. 300 bombs dropped in the mission as a whole, only c. 2% hit ancient Pompeii that night, which certainly argues against deliberate targeting of the ancient site.

16. Maiuri, pp. 107–8.

17. *OIS* 190 (29/08/43), Mission No. 632 b. The enemy fighters were identified as a mix of German Bf-109 and Fw-190 and Italian MC.202. In what the *OIS* describes as a 50-minute engagement, the bombers claimed 15 enemy fighters destroyed, 4 probable and 6 damaged (undoubtedly an exaggeration) for no loss, and the P-38s a single Bf-109 for one loss of their own.

18. *ORBs* of Nos. 205 Group, 236 Wing and 330 Wing (29/08/43).

19. Pocock, pp. 217–18

CHAPTER 2

The title of this section derives from *ORB* No. 205 Group (14/09/43) 'N.A.S.A.F [Northwest African Strategic Air Force] called for "everything we could put into the air"'.

1. Interdiction, 'air operations intended to isolate the battlefront by destroying, disrupting and delaying enemy forces, communications and supplies, often in areas far removed from the battle area' as defined by Ian Gooderson, *Air Power at the Battlefront: Allied Close Air Support in Europe* (London: Cass, 1998), p. 3. Strictly speaking, in the Second World War terms presented by Gooderson, operations around Pompeii overlapped the categories of interdiction and general air support, a distinction based on proximity to the land battlefront rather than on aims and activities. On definitions and characteristics of strategic bombing, in contrast, see Overy, pp. 9–14.

2. *OIS* 205 (13/09/43), Mission no. 107b; AFHRA IRIS 00081977, 310th Bombardment Group, *Headquarters and Group History* September 1943, Mission no.158; AFHRA IRIS 00082330, 319th Bombardment Group *Outline History*, September 1943, Mission no. 83.

3. Bombing by 319th BG took place between 1716 and 1803 hrs., from altitudes of 9300 to 12,000 ft (c. 2800–3700 m). The 310th BG (which bombed a few minutes earlier—the photos are timed at 1710 hrs—and from similar altitudes) dropped 854 bombs, while the 319th dropped 635 bombs.

4. 319th BG: AFHRA IRIS 00105053, *42nd Bombardment Wing Mission Summary*, 13

September 1943, 'Two strings [of bombs] crossed the road junction target running on into the town of POMPEII'.

5. NARA RG 18, Box 1187, USAAF 310th BG, 13/9/1943, image 005.

6. NARA RG 18, Box 1187, USAAF 310th BG, 13/9/1943, image 008.

7. García y García, p. 32. The mission timed at 1700 hrs was presumably that of the 310th BG and the one at 1730 hrs the 319th, if it was even possible for an observer on the ground to distinguish accurately between damage caused by the two attacks.

8. *OIS* 206 (14/09/43), Mission no. 116. For some reason, this fails to mention the participation of No. 330 Wing but *ORB*s at Wing and Squadron level confirm that the 91 aircraft included some from that formation.

9. Appendices to No. 330 Wing *ORB* (13/09/43), B655.

10. Appendices to No. 236 Wing *ORB* (13/09/43). Orders B652 and B653 have 'cancelled' pencilled across them. See Molony, *Campaign in Italy*, p. 314 n. 1 on the practical implications of changing plans at such short notice. The rapid changes in targeting attested here emphasise the urgency of the situation, and undoubtedly caused considerable stress for the planning staff and crews.

11. RAF bombers typically had fewer bomb hooks in their bomb bays than comparable American aircraft, and so were less capable of carrying small bombs in large quantities. This was largely irrelevant in the strategic role in which the Wellingtons were primarily employed, but sometimes a problem when operating closer to the battlefield, in close support or (as here) interdiction roles. See Gooderson, p. 128, and the near-contemporary *Effects of Close Air Support*, p. 9, noting that even RAF heavy bombers (such as Lancasters, bigger than the Wellington mediums) have only 14 bomb hooks while US heavy bombers have 40.

12. 90 x 250 lb and 45 x 500 lb specified in *ORB* 425 Sqn. (14/09/43). None of the other squadron *ORB*s specify bomb loads, but 4000 lb bombs are mentioned for 142 and 104 Sqns. There are also references to incendiary bombs used on the mission, typically smaller and carried in clusters.

13. The relevant ORBs are those of the constituent Wings and Squadrons of No. 205 Group (see Appendix B), all for 13/09/43.

14. According to their *ORB*, crews of 150 Squadron 'easily identified the target by light of flares and full moon'. See Chapter 4 and Appendix D.

15. *OIS* 206 (14/09/43), Mission nos. 121c (RAF Bostons), 121d (340th BG) and 121e (12th BG).

16. ORB No. 326 (Light Bomber) Wing (Night, 13–14/09/43). The reference is to Mercato San Severino on the railway between Sarno/Nocera and Avellino (see Zuckerman, *Report*, p. 139). The general area denoted lies north and east of Pompeii.

17. *ORB* 18 Sqn. (13/09/43). The grid reference, like others in these wartime documents, refers to the British grid system (also used by US forces), South Italy Zone, grid rN. I am very grateful to Oliver Madgwick of the UK Defence Geographic Centre for his initial help in developing my understanding of this system. <http://www.echodelta.net/mbs/eng-translation.php> provides conversion of wartime grids to latitude and longitude. The 18 Sqn. *ORB* shows that the Bostons looking for German road traffic found numerous targets. It refers to 'continuous streams of M.T. [motor transport]—over 100—seen moving NE from Nocera [Inferiore]-Castel San Giorgio (N5438—N5943)'. Many of these vehicles would have passed through Torre Annunziata and modern Pompei earlier on their journey.

18. Besides the highway intersection, the Circumvesuviana light railway runs roughly

north-south between the junction and the site, and its nearby bridge over the SS18 provided another possible target whose destruction would block road and rail traffic. The main Naples-Salerno railway line runs west-east c. 250 m south of this junction, with more bridges.

19. AFHRA IRIS 00077840, *12th Bombardment Group Sortie Reports*, 83rd and 434th Bombardment Squadrons, 13 September 1943. The documentation for the 340th BG, AFHRA IRIS 00083898, *340th Bombardment Group Daily Operational Journal Sortie Reports*, provides little detail beyond identifying the target ('Pompei rd jct'), number of aircraft (12), time (0112) and tonnage of bombs dropped (24). The only comments in the 'Remarks' column are 'Good. No flak'. US medium bombers typically were employed during the day in 'box' formations, but the reports of this mission specifically refer to individual bombing, and 12th BG had undertaken similar missions previously—see Chapter 4.

20. AFHRA IRIS, 00077840, *12th Bombardment Group Sortie Reports*, 83rd and 434th Bombardment Squadrons, 13 September 1943. These also give the grid reference for the target (N405385 = 40°44′54″ N, 14°28′48″ E), a little to the south of that given by the *ORB* of the RAF 18 Sqn. markers. However, the difference is minimal in 1943 bombing terms, and it clearly refers to the same intersection.

21. García y García, pp. 32–33; Maiuri, pp. 116–17 refers to the bombing of that night as having caused 'a hundred or more bombs to fall in the excavation zone' ('oltre un centinaio e piú di bombe cadute nella zona degli scavi'), an exaggeration even on the basis of Maiuri's own totals.

22. One instance of damage does not necessarily equate to a single bomb, but the magnitude of damage done in individual locations suggests this was rarely (if ever) the product of multiple bomb strikes in the same place.

23. Night of 14/15 September: *OIS* 207 (15/09/43) indicates that all major air activity on that night (both RAF and USAAF) was directed against targets in the Eboli-Battipaglia area, close to the Salerno battle area and some 45 km south of Pompeii. However, it is possible that one or more bombers dropped their bomb loads on Pompeii as the result of gross navigational errors. B-17s: These were used on the previous day at Torre del Greco, where the railway line from Naples to Salerno (via Pompei) passes between Vesuvius and the sea. See *OIS* 206 13/09/43 Mission no. 107a and AFHRA IRIS 00081463, *97th Bombardment Group War Diary September 1943*, p. 3 (14 September 1943).

24. Thomas F. Gulley, *The Hour Has Come: The 97th Bomb Group in World War II* (Dallas: Taylor Publishing Company, 1993), p. 125, specifically refers to bombs hitting the ancient site during the day on 14 September ('the bombs of the 414th Squadron overshot the target and fell into the ruins of the old city of Pompei'), apparently based on a contemporary source that is not cited.

25. *OIS* 206 (14/09/43) Mission nos. 117 c and d; AFHRA IRIS 00081463, *97th Bombardment Group War Diary*, p. 3 (14 September 1943); AFHRA IRIS 00081450, *97th Bombardment Group Mission Reports* (14 September 1943).

26. NWAAF *Air Intelligence Weekly Summary* No. 44, p. 28, captioned 'Pompeii Catches Hell Again'. The only alternative date for the image is 13 September, perhaps depicting the daytime bombing by USAAF medium bombers, but as noted above, despite their target being described as 'ROAD JUNCTION AT POMPEII' in *OIS* 205,

more detailed accounts indicate the aiming points on 13 were actually closer to Torre Annunziata. The Incrocio Paselli is not under attack in this photograph.

27. Damage at the Incrocio Paselli (described on 15 September): Maiuri, p. 118.

28. *OIS* 206 (14/09/43), Mission no. 117 c.

29. Zuckerman, *Report*, p. 103.

30. Bombers: *OIS* 207 (15/09/43), Mission no. 124 b. Zuckerman, *Report*, p. 102, refers specifically to B-25s (and A-36 dive-bombers) operating in the Torre Annunziata area on 15 September.

31. Photo: Pocock, p. 224; the bomb plot is NARA RG 18, Box 1190, USAAF 310th BG, 15/9/1943, image 008.

32. Fighter-bombers and dive-bombers: *OIS* 207 (15/09/43), Mission nos. 131 a. (A-36s of 27th Fighter-Bomber Group 'bombing targets of opportunity' at Torre Annunziata and elsewhere); 131 d. ('20 P-40s attacked Eboli and Torre Annunziata dropping 12 x 250 lb bombs. Dock and railroad hit at Torre Annunziata'). During the early stages of the battle at Salerno, fighter and fighter-bomber missions were flown either from Royal Navy aircraft carriers off-shore, or at long range (over 150 miles—240 km) from bases in Sicily, limiting their ability to strike as far north as Pompeii–Torre Annunziata. Some Allied fighter aircraft were based on airfields within the beachhead by 13 September, and others used those airfields for refuelling and emergency landings. However, the 27th FBG, equipped with the A-36, an early Allison-engine dive-bomber version of the P-51 Mustang, did not transfer from S. Antonio in Sicily to Sele in the Salerno beachhead until 16 September. See Molony, *Campaign in Italy*, pp. 268–73, 299, 302, 311, 323; *RAF Narrative*, Vol. 1, p. 162 n. 1; Blumenson, pp. 147–48.

33. Maiuri, pp. 118–19.

34. Given that the *Diario delle incursioni* records its fifth incursion as the night of 14/15 September ('14–15 settembre: notturna'), presumably the sixth incursion ('16 settembre: notturna') was actually the night of 15/16 September even though the air forces' documentation records this attack as ending at 23:57 on 15 September. There was no significant air activity in this area on the night of 16/17 September, as the RAF night bombers were attacking more distant targets, at Cisterna and Littoria. The mission of 15/16 September is documented in *OIS* 208 (16/09/43) Mission No. 134a, and the *ORBs* (and their appendices) of No. 205 Group and its constituent Wings and Squadrons.

35. Appendix C16 to the *ORB* of No. 231 Wing (15/09/43).

36. *ORB* No. 205 Group (15/09/43).

37. *ORB* 70 Sqn. (15/09/43)

38. Pocock, pp. 225–26; Angelo Pesce, *Scafati e l'agro: Cinquant' anni fa la Guerra* (Scafati: Comune di Scafati, 1993), pp. 16–21, provides an overview of the bombing of modern Pompei and nearby communities including the attack of 15 September, and its impact on the civilian population. Four-thousand-pound bombs were also dropped on Torre Annunziata—for example, the two squadrons (37 and 70) of No. 231 Wing dropped a total of 5 4000 lb bombs (4 on Torre Annunziata, 1 on Pompei) and 483 250 lb GP bombs. See OPSUM (*Operations Summary*) for 15/16 September 1943 in the appendix volume to the *ORB* of No. 231 Wing.

39. García y García, p. 33.

40. Ibid. If the 'sixth incursion' ('*16 settembre: notturna*') was actually the night of 15/16 September, as suggested above, then it is likely that the seventh ('*18 settembre: not-*

turna') was the night of 17/18 September. This interpretation of the dates corresponds best with the missions attested in the military documents, which give bombing times in the early hours of the morning of 18 September.

41. *OIS* 210 (18/09/43), Mission no. 176 (night of 17/18 September).

42. AFHRA IRIS 00077840, *12th Bombardment Group Sortie Reports*, 434th Bombardment Squadron, 18 September 1943 on Pompei; AFHRA IRIS, 00083898, *340th Bombardment Group Daily Operational Journal* provides little information beyond the target ('Pompei RR jct'), number of aircraft (10), time (0430) and tonnage of bombs dropped (20). The only comment in the 'Remarks' column is 'Good'. AFHRA IRIS 00077840, *12th Bombardment Group Sortie Reports*, 81st, 82nd and 83rd Bombardment Squadrons, 18 September 1943 on Torre Annunziata, with eight, ten and six aircraft respectively.

43. Clearly the modern town was being used as a general identification feature to aid crews in locating their aiming point, and was not a target in its own right, although undoubtedly bombs drifted off target and hit the modern town (as well as the archaeological site). The *ORB* for 18 Sqn. RAF, which marked the Pompeii target for the 12th BG, gives the grid reference N403386 (40°44′55″ N, 14°28′39″ E), on the SS18 c. 200 m west of the 12th BG grid reference. This may be a transcription error in the *ORB* (the 18 Sqn. *ORB* for 13/14 September gives N405386), but even so, the discrepancy made very little practical difference in terms of hitting the target.

44. García y García, p. 33.

45. García y García, p. 31.

46. *OIS* 212 (20/09/43) Mission nos.188 c and d.

47. AFHRA IRIS 00081727, 301st BG (H), *Narrative Mission Report*, 20 September 1943.

48. The grid references provided (N385409 = 40°46′09″ N, 14°27′23″ E; N378407 = 40°46′03″ N, 14°26′53″ E; N385405 = 40°45′56″ N, 14°27′23″ E) for the road junction and highway bridge claimed destroyed are 0.5–1 km north of Torre Annunziata, towards Boscoreale and Boscotrecase, and 1.5–2 km north-west of ancient Pompeii. Either these are incorrect, or they attest to bombing that was very scattered, deliberately or otherwise.

49. I am very grateful to Simon Pocock for drawing my attention to this photograph (from NARA) and for providing me with an initial copy of it. He reproduces it himself in Pocock, p. 227.

50. For the damage to the House of the Faun, see García y García, pp. 82–85 and Appendix A (pp. 222, 225) above.

51. *ORB* No. 326 (Lt. Bomber) Wing (21–22/09/43). *OIS* 214 (22/09/43) Mission 211b (re. night of 21/22 September) specifically reports that these road intruder operations included bombing of marshalling yards at Torre Annunziata by aircraft of No. 326 Wing.

52. *ORB* No. 3 (SAAF) Wing, App. 45, Mission no. 106 with *ORB* 12 (SAAF) Squadron, App. DD (one Boston dropped four 250 lb bombs 'on edge of and in town' of Torre Annunziata and another dropped '2 NE and 2 in town').

53. USAAF *Combat Chronology*, 23 September. Sarno, 12 km north-east of Pompei, had been bombed by 24 B-25s of the US 12th and 340th BGs during the day on 23 September—*OIS* 215 (23/9/43), Mission no. 221c. Also see Molony, *Campaign in Italy*, pp. 339–40.

54. USAAF *Combat Chronology*, 25 September (Sarno, Nocera) and 26 September

(Sarno); Molony, *Campaign in Italy*, p. 342 (both). *OIS* 217 (25/9/43), Mission no. 24, further daytime bombing of Sarno by US B-25s. See also Pesce, pp. 25–26, citing the contemporary diary of Franco d'Alessandro, on low-level incursions by Allied aircraft attacking German motor transport. *War Room Monthly Summary*, September 1943, p. 5, shows just 34 bomber sorties flown by Allied air forces on 27 September compared to 343 on 20 September, the reduction largely due to deteriorating weather.

55. See Pesce, pp. 129–32 with photographs on pp. 145–49; Pocock, pp. 234–38. *OIS* 220 (28/09/43) reports the defeat of the German counter-attack 'at N-4438 (near Pompeii)'—in fact at the bridge over the River Sarno between Pompei and Scafati—on the evening of 28 September.

CHAPTER 3

1. The only exception to this was the mission of the night of 24/25 August, undertaken before the Salerno landings. As already noted, this was a more properly strategic mission, directed against the steelworks and railway marshalling yards at Torre Annunziata.

2. While "autostrada" is normally translated as 'highway' or 'motorway' in English, these terms give a misleading impression of the rather basic character of this road in 1943. Nevertheless, its direct nature made it an important link between Naples and the south at the time. An extension of this autostrada (the modern A3) to Salerno was opened in 1961, bypassing the modern town of Pompei. Subsequently it was extended from Salerno to Reggio Calabria. Much of the description here is written in the past tense, reflecting the situation in 1943, but in fact, besides the autostrada extension beyond Pompei, the key components of transport infrastructure remain largely the same today.

3. Zuckerman, *Report*, pp. 94, 101–4.

4. For example, appendices to *ORB* of No. 330 Wing (15/09/43), orders from No. 205 Group, specify one of the aims of the night's mission as 'to block the roads in these towns [Torre Annunziata and Pompei] by dropping "BLOCKBUSTERS" on them.' Blockbusters were 4000 lb (1814 kg) bombs. Zuckerman, *Report*, pp. 53–56, reflects on the effectiveness of bombing to produce road blocks for the purposes of interdiction, and specifically recommends (p. 55) 4000 lb bombs for greater demolition effect.

5. García y García, p. 26: 'Possiamo comunque ragionevolmente ipotizzare che il vero bersaglio fosse la statale e la ferrovia.' ('We can perhaps reasonably hypothesise that the main road and the railway were the true target').

6. *RAF Narrative*, Vol. 1, pp. 144–68, covers the air operations at Salerno from 8–16 September.

7. Molony, *Campaign in Italy*, p. 299.

8. Molony, *Campaign in Italy*, pp. 290–91, 293–95. For a contemporary intelligence summary of the counter-attack, see TNA WO 204/96, Allied Force Headquarters, Office of the Assistant Chief of Staff G-2, *Weekly Intelligence Report* No. 56, to 1200B 18 September 1943.

9. Molony, *Campaign in Italy*, p. 310.

10. Molony, *Campaign in Italy*, pp. 309–12, 316. Blumensen, *Salerno to Cassino*, pp. 115–18, 125. Blumensen identifies the artillery battalions (presumably correctly) as the

158th and 189th and notes that they expended 3650 rounds in about four hours on the evening of 13 September.

11. Molony, *Campaign in Italy*, pp. 313–23. Blumensen, *Salerno to Cassino*, p. 136—'The battle seemed won' by the time of Eisenhower's visit to the beachhead in the afternoon of 17 September.

12. Molony, *Campaign in Italy*, pp. 324–44; Pesce, pp. 124–30, provides a detailed and vivid account of the advance through, and combat in, Scafati, Pompei and Torre Annunziata. TNA WO 204/967, Allied Force Headquarters Office of the Assistant Chief of Staff G-2, *Weekly Intelligence Report* No. 58, to 1200A 2 October 1943, pp. 1, 7.

13. García y García, p. 21.

14. *319th Bomb Group War Diary*, 14 September 1943.

15. *340th Bomb Group Diary*.

16. Molony, *Campaign in Italy*, pp. 238–52. It was untrue that the 8th Army was advancing to 'rescue' 5th Army, although this impression was given in some British public sources (see Blumenson, p. 138–43) and reflected in some of the air force documentation. Elements of 5th Army and 8th Army linked up at Auletta, on 20 September, well after the German counter-attack had already been defeated by 5th Army (Blumensen, p. 138).

17. Orders from No. 205 Group to No. 231 Wing, in No 231 Wing *ORB* (14/09/43 and 15/09/43), Appendices C15 and C16.

18. As an example at Wing level, *ORB* No. 330 Wing (15–16/09/43): 'The target was the road communications between TORRE ANNUNZIATA and POMPEI. The fighting at SALERNO was proving particularly heavy and it was essential to hamper and delay the enemy while the 8th ARMY was on its way to the battle area from the south.'

19. *ORB* 104 Sqn. (14/09/43 and 15/09/43).

20. Molony, *Campaign in Italy*, pp. 293–95. The intelligence report included in *OIS* 204 (12/09/43) notes, 'it is thought that reinforcements have arrived in the area between Naples and the Northern end of the beach-head. Considerable M/T [motor transport] traffic was again observed to be moving in the direction of the beach-head from the South, from the Foggia area, and from the area N. of Naples . . . heavy M/T movement reported headed S towards Naples and a 50-car train headed S. towards the Formia area.'

21. Appendices to the *ORB* of No. 236 Wing (13/9/43), discussed p. 26; *ORB* 142 Squadron (13–14/09/43).

22. No. 231 Wing *ORB* (13–14/09/43) 'With enemy armoured vehicles located North of the Salerno Bridgehead as their main objective. . . .'; and 15/16 September 'still striking at the enemy's communications and armoured vehicles South of Naples . . .'.

23. 310th BG *Mission Report* for 13 September (57th Bomb Wing Association website: <http://57thbombwing.com/310thHistory/310_BG_1943-09.pdf> [accessed 4 August 2019]) records '15–20 M/T 4–5 miles E of target heading W. Many trucks on road just S of target, heading unknown. Some M/T activity reported at target. 40–50 railroad cars on siding just SW of road junction on edge of town of Torre Annunziata', and the same unit's *Mission Summary* 174, for 15 September, refers to '30–40 M/T [motor transport] heading E on road near Pompeii'.

24. *ORB* 70 Sqn. (13–14/9/43).

25. *RAF Narrative*, Vol. 1, p. 152, characterises the main object of the night bombing of Pompeii as 'the prevention of enemy reinforcements from reaching the battle zone'.

26. Molony, *Campaign in Italy*, p. 305

27. Molony, *Campaign in Italy*, p. 326 (also see pp. 306, 314–15).

28. TNA AIR 23/1509, *NAAF Notes on Air Operations: July–October 1943*.

29. *OIS* 207 (15/09/43), Mission no. 123 (Battipaglia-Eboli roads); *ORB* No. 205 Group (14/09/43); *ORB* No. 330 Wing, App. B657 (14–15/09/43) specifies 121 sorties (32 for No. 231 Wing, 23 for No. 236 Wing, 23 for No. 330 Wing and 43 for No. 331 Wing); also Molony, *Campaign in Italy*, p. 315. 14 September was the peak of air activity in the Mediterranean that month. *War Room Monthly Summary* for September 1943 gives a total of 2278 sorties flown that day, 890 of them by bombers.

30. *OIS* 208 (16/09/43) Mission no. 134 (Torre Annunziata and Pompeii roads) gives 123 sorties; *ORB* No. 330 Wing, App. B659 (15–16/09/43) gives a total of 127 sorties (32 for No. 231 Wing, 28 for No. 236 Wing, 24 for No. 330 Wing and 43 for No. 331 Wing); also Molony, *Campaign in Italy*, p. 318.

31. *ORB* 424 Sqn. RCAF (15–16/09/43).

32. Molony, *Campaign in Italy*, p. 307; *RAF Narrative*, Vol. 1, p. 159. *ORB* 424 Sqn. RCAF (13/09/43) expresses the squadron's dismay at the decision to retain No. 331 Wing in North Africa, describing it as 'quite a shock'.

33. Appendix C15 to *ORB* No. 231 Wing (14/09/43).

34. Molony, *Campaign in Italy*, pp. 314–15. See also *OIS* 206 (14/09/43) and *OIS* 207 (15/09/43).

35. Blumenson, *Salerno to Cassino*, p. 148.

36. García y García, p. 21.

37. Molony, *Campaign in Italy*, p. 315. This was certainly the worst-hit area, especially Eboli, which was targeted with a staggering total of 894.6 tons (909 tonnes) of bombs in the week of 11–17 September. However, in the same week, the Pompeii targets received 390.9 tons (397 tonnes) and Torre Annunziata 398.4 tons (405 tonnes: NWAAF *Air Intelligence Weekly Summary* No. 44, p. 28).

38. Zuckerman, *Report*, pp. 93, 94b on Benevento as a transportation target. It was struck by 208.5 tons (212 tonnes) of bombs (bridge) and 117 tons (119 tonnes—marshalling yards) between 11 and 17 September: NWAAF *Air Intelligence Weekly Summary* No. 44, p. 28. The cathedral of Benevento was almost completely destroyed and 'the lower town between the DUOMO and the PONTE VANVITELLI has been obliterated [and is] a mass of ruins'—*Works of Art in Italy: Losses and Survivals in the War*. Part I—*South of Bologna*. Compiled from War Office Reports by the British Committee on the Preservation and Restitution of Works of Art, Archives and Other Material in Enemy Hands (London: HMSO, 1945), p. 7; and Part II, pp. 78, 137. See Francesco Delizia, 'Benevento: ricerca archeologica e ricostruzione della città,' in *Guerra, monumenti, ricostruzione*, pp. 410–15 (and on the wider impact of the bombing on the city, Gribaudi, pp. 386–406). See Coccoli, *Monumenti violati*, pp. 38–103 for a wider discussion of bomb damage in Campania, including Benevento and Naples, and subsequent reconstruction.

39. *War Room Monthly Summary* for September 1943, p. 7: 'The air offensive was switched from communications to airfields on 17th.' TNA AIR 23/1509, *NAAF Notes on Air Operations: July–October 1943*: 'The immediate threat to the bridgehead was now reduced and our air effort was directed to the outer ring of communications once more.' The *OIS*s for subsequent days show that while much effort continued to be expended on transportation targets in Campania, more distant strategic targets, such as airfields at Ciampino, Cerveteri and Viterbo and marshalling yards at Pisa, again were targeted in great strength by both US and British air forces.

CHAPTER 4

1. For definitions of interdiction and strategic bombing, see above (Chapter 2, n.1). In contrast, at Montecassino in February 1944, air power (including medium and heavy bombers) was used in a close-support role, supporting troops in direct contact with the enemy on the ground (Molony, *Campaign in Italy*, p. 713). Such concentrated use of bombers (especially heavy bombers) for close support was unusual, but repeated on a number of occasions in Normandy in 1944 (see Gooderson, pp. 125–64).

2. 104 Sqn. *ORB* (24/08/43).

3. 104 Sqn. *ORB* (24/08/43); 40 Sqn. *ORB* (24–25/08/43), aircraft 'B' recorded 'explosion seen in air over target which looked like aircraft' and 'Q' 'A/C seen to crash just NW of target at 2217 hrs approx.' Pocock (p. 217) notes that the bodies of two crew members were recovered by the Italian navy and buried on Capri.

4. 424 Squadron *ORB* (24/08/43).

5. *OIS* 190 (29/08/43), Mission No. 632b and *OIS* 191 (30/09/43), Mission No. 636a cover the daytime and night missions respectively. The former was conducted by 51 B-26 medium bombers of the 17th and 320th Bombardment Groups (USAAF), escorted by 40 P-38 fighters of the 1st Fighter Group (USAAF). The latter comprised 78 Wellington bombers of Nos. 231, 236 and 330 Wings RAF and No. 331 Wing RCAF. The RAF/RCAF night bombing is also documented in *ORB*s, including those of No. 205 Group and Nos. 236 and 330 Wing.

6. As examples, *ORB* 150 Sqn. (13/08/43): 'located target by flares and moonlight'; *ORB* 142 Sqn. (13/08/43) 'A full moon but very little activity was seen' (suggesting either the absence of visible movement on the ground, or, perhaps, the absence of opposition—it is unclear which is meant). The downside of moonlight was that it facilitated enemy interception.

7. For example, *ORB* 104 Sqn. (13/08/43): 'the attack by our aircraft was carried out in good weather'.

8. AFHRA IRIS 00105053, 42nd *Bombardment Wing Mission Summary* (13 September 1943), p. 3: 'CAVU [Ceiling and visibility unlimited] with moderate haze' for Torre Annunziata–Pompeii; AFHRA IRIS 00081450, *97th Bombardment Group (Heavy) Mission Report* (14/09/43): '[Weather] over target: good and good visibility'; AFHRA IRIS 00081727, *301st Bombardment Group (Heavy) Narrative Mission Report*: 'Weather 2 to 3/10th [i.e., 20–30% cloudy] en route with slight haze at the target'. 310th BG records indicate 'CAVU with haze' for both Torre Annunziata day missions on 13 and 15 September.

9. *ORB* No. 330 Wing (13–14/09/43): 'Full moon. . . . Slight ground haze did not prevent successful identification of the target'; *ORB* 424 Sqn. (15/09/43): 'visibility was good but somewhat hazy'; *ORB* 114 Sqn. (21/09/43, night): 'Slight haze was found over the target but not sufficient to interfere with operations'.

10. 104 Sqn. *ORB* (15/09/43): 'Bombing considered good, but many bomb bursts were obscured by clouds of dust and smoke.'; 424 Sqn. *ORB* (15/09/43): 'Much smoke and dust over TORRE ANNUNZIATA caused by fires and exploding bombs'.

11. No. 231 Wing *ORB* (13/09/43): 'no opposition from the target, but 3–4 heavy guns from the coastal area'; 424 Sqn. *ORB* (13/09/43): 'no flak or S/L [searchlights] from the target, but S/L were operating and some inaccurate flak was shot up from Naples' [both 13 September].

12. *ORB* 40 Sqn. (13/09/43): 'opposition encountered was negligible.'

13. *ORB* 114 Sqn. (13/09/43): 'The only opposition was one searchlight which held an aircraft for just under five seconds'; *ORB* 424 Sqn. (13/09/43): 'One unidentified aircraft was seen at 21:50 hrs flying at 8000 ft.' *ORB* 104 Sqn. (13/09/43): 'Opposition encountered was nil to slight, although several reports of night fighters were made, no attempts at interception were made'; *OIS* 206, Mission No. 116 (14/09/43) reports that one aircraft was intercepted by a night fighter presumed to be a Junkers JU-88, which broke off its attack after an exchange of fire.

14. For example, *OIS* 207 (15/09/43), Mission no. 134; *ORB* 40 Sqn. (15/09/43); *ORB* 420 Sqn. (15/09/43); *ORB* 424 Sqn. (15/09/43). Pesce (p. 20) writes of German anti-aircraft batteries dispersed to the north and south of the Santuario church in Pompei firing furiously that night, but this is not reflected in the accounts written by their RAF and RCAF targets. Paradoxically, he also records (p. 19) that the *lack* of anti-aircraft defences around Pompei was one of the factors cited in a petition from the civic authorities to the German commander that very same day, asking him to move troops and artillery away from the undefended town.

15. For example, *OIS* 207, 'Day 14th September Additional', Mission no. 131 includes a range of fighter and fighter-bomber activities specifically in the Torre Annunziata area, involving A-36s of 27th FB Group (131a), P-38s (131c) and P-40s (131g). By then several squadrons of RAF and USAAF fighters had been flown in to landing fields at Tusciano and Paestum within the beachhead (Molony, *Campaign in Italy*, pp. 298–99, 311, 323; *RAF Narrative*, Vol. 1, p. 162 n. 1). Before then, fighter cover in the Salerno area had depended on Royal Navy aircraft carriers, and RAF and USAAF fighters operating from bases in southern Italy and Sicily over 150 miles (240km) away (Molony, *Campaign in Italy*, pp. 228, 263; *RAF Narrative*, Vol. 1, pp. 18, 43).

16. For this reason, the absence from the Mediterranean of radio bombing aids such as Gee and H2S, already in use by the Allies in northern Europe, was not a factor in the damage done to ancient Pompeii. These were essentially navigational aids that helped crews locate their targets, especially in poor weather, and locating the targets was not a particular problem in the bombing around Pompeii. The issue was actually hitting targets that were visible without causing accidental damage beyond those targets. At any rate, these radio aids largely were not available in Italy until very late 1943 and 1944, when they were of value in the poor weather conditions encountered there later (*RAF Narrative*, Vol. 1, p. 198; Alun Granfield, *Bombers Over Sand and Snow: 205 Group RAF in World War II* (Barnsley, UK: Pen and Sword Aviation, 2011), pp. 247–48, 252, 256).

17. García y García, p. 26: 'bombardamenti anche diurni'.

18. Sir Charles Webster and Noble Frankland, *Annexes and Appendices*. The Strategic Air Offensive Against Germany 1939–1945, Vol.4 (London: HMSO, 1961), pp. 37–38. In addition, a proportion of bombs might be subject to 'gross errors of various kinds' that went well beyond the normal factors, such as mechanical failures of bomb release equipment: *Effects of Close Air Support*, p. 42.

19. For this claim, attributed to Norden's salesman-publicist partner Ted Barth, see Stephen L. MacFarland, *America's Pursuit of Precision Bombing, 1910–1945* (Washington, DC: Smithsonian Institution, 1995), p. 100, and Stewart Halsey Ross, *Strategic Bombing by the United States in World War II* (Jefferson, NC: McFarland & Co., 2003), p. 128. The famous claim that Norden sights could drop a bomb 'into a pickle-barrel' also seems to have originated with Barth. Both MacFarland and Ross provide valuable discussion of

the hyperbole relating to the Norden sights and its roots in the pre-war US ideology of precision bombing. Albert L. Pardini, *The Legendary Norden Bombsight* (Atglen, PA: Schiffer Books, 1999) is technically informative but uncritical. Tami Davis Biddle, 'British and American Approaches to Strategic Bombing: Their Origins and Implementation in the World War II Combined Bomber Offensive', *Journal of Strategic Studies* 18 (1995), 91–144 (pp. 110–14); and W. Hays Parks, '"Precision" and "Area" Bombing: Who Did Which, and When?' *Journal of Strategic Studies* 18 (1995), 145–74 both assess the influence of the Norden sight on US bombing strategy and ideology, and its reality relative to RAF 'area' bombing. See also Baldoli and Knapp, esp. pp. 7, 18, 34.

20. The United States Strategic Bombing Survey, *Bombing Accuracy, USAAF Heavy and Medium Bombers in the ETO*. Military Analysis Division (January 1947), Exhibit (= Table) 'R' and p. 12 (mean bombing altitude).

21. The Eighth Air Force was more likely to meet opposition of various kinds that would reduce accuracy and its larger formations are likely to have reduced mean accuracy (see US Strategic Bombing Survey, *Bombing Accuracy*, p. 12). On the other hand, the Eighth Air Force data was generated more than a year after the bombing of Pompeii, so presumably crews were more experienced and bombing techniques had improved. The bombing near Pompeii on 20 September was conducted from an altitude similar to the mean altitude for the Eighth Air Force data, while that of 13 September was lower (15,800 ft compared to 21,000 ft = 4816 to 6400 m).

22. *Effects of Close Air Support*, p. 9, para. 20: 'Their [bombing] pattern is usually elongated in the direction of flight' here refers specifically to British and US medium bombers, but the principle is more generally applicable.

23. The best evidence for navigation comes from the RAF documents discussed on p. 62, but the same was true for the USAAF. For example, the 301st Bombardment Group *Mission Reports* of 20 September indicate a heading of 45° (SW to NE) when bombing Torre Annunziata and 90° (W to E) against Sarno. *320th Bombardment Group Mission 068, Intelligence Narrative* No. 68, Day Operation, 29 August, indicates a bomb run heading of 80° for a mission by B-26 medium bombers against Torre Annunziata marshalling yards. See also Figure 6 (50°).

24. *OIS* 206 (14/09/43) Mission no. 117 b.

25. *OIS* 206 (14/09/43) Mission no. 117 c.

26. This exact correspondence is coincidental, as the calculation was done to provide a baseline figure rather than an exact number. In fact, as noted above, the *Diario delle incurzioni* actually attributes that damage to the night of 14/15 September, when there was no recorded significant Allied air activity in the area. D'Avino may have mistakenly attributed the day's damage to the following night. The additional bombs that one might expect due to the elongated distribution predicted above may have been offset by the lack of opposition around Pompeii when compared to the northern European targets attacked by the Eighth Air Force, as well as the lower bombing altitude employed (15,800 ft compared to a mean altitude of 21,000 ft for the Eighth Air Force data) and the smaller number of aircraft used against the same target.

27. US Strategic Bombing Survey, *Bombing Accuracy*, p. 12; *Effects of Close Air Support*, pp. 7–11—noting that, weight for weight, medium bombers were at least two and a half times as effective as heavies, and plane for plane (despite heavies carrying greater bomb loads), about the same. For area targets, medium bombers are characterised as

less satisfactory, because precise accuracy was less important and the greater load carried by the heavies was more important against such targets.

28. AFHRA IRIS 00081977, *310th Bombardment Group (M) AAF Headquarters and Group History September 1943*, Mission 158 provides the number of bombs dropped, and AFHRA IRIS 00082330, *Outline History 319th Bomb Gp. September 1943*, Mission 83.

29. AFHRA IRIS 00081977, *310th Bombardment Group (M) AAF Headquarters and Group History September 1943*, Mission 161.

30. These tactics are extensively documented and described in contemporary accounts and by aircrew who used them. See, for example, *Fighter/Bomber Tactics*, pp. 20–21. While these are British documents, the tactics employed are explicitly described as applying to both British and American formations. Also see Dale J. Satterthwaite, *Truth Flies with Fiction: Flying B-25 Bombers into Battle during 1944* (Bloomington IN: Archway Publishing, 2014), pp. 44, 55–a contemporary diary by a B-25 pilot of the 340th BG; Steve Pace, *B-25 Mitchell Units of the MTO* (Oxford, UK: Osprey Publishing, 2002), pp. 22–25 (quoting Capt. Henry L. Colman of the 434th BS, 12th BG).

31. *Fighter/Bomber Tactics*, p. 25; *320th Bombardment Group Mission 068, Intelligence Narrative* No. 68, Day Operation, 29 August, describing an attack on Torre Annunziata marshalling yards, illustrates the formation employed by its 24 B-26 bombers, with four boxes of 6 aircraft. Each box is arranged in two 'arrowheads' of 3 aircraft, one behind the other, and the Group as a whole is arranged with the boxes disposed in a diamond formation, one leading, followed by two side by side, and the fourth trailing. In contrast, AFHRA IRIS 00105103, *42nd Bombardment Wing: Air and Ground Cooperation—Salerno, Anzio, Cassino*, p. 11, describes in detail a 'trail' formation of boxes used in a mission against the Battipaglia-Eboli road on 15 September 1943, with the initially echeloned formation changing to 'a long, narrow line of 6 ship elements in trail' between Capri and the Initial Point. 'Each element [=box] leader is on the bombsight solving for range and deflection, in other words, six individual bomb runs are being made.'

32. Satterthwaite, p. 55 (writing of 31 January 1944, when 340th BG was engaged primarily in daytime missions rather than the night missions it flew against targets near Pompeii): 'When the sight got lined up with the target, the bombardier pushed the button on the pendant which caused the bombs to drop. The bombardiers in the trailing airplanes would drop their bombs on cue from the front ship. There was of course a human factor, and the bombs were scattered quite a bit. The outfit had a reputation for plowing up graveyards all over southern Italy.'

33. Satterthwaite, pp. 55, 69, 77. The Mark IX was also used by British Wellington bombers bombing targets near Pompeii. *RAF Narrative*, Vol. 1, p. 243, refers to Marauders (B-26) having Norden sights by early 1944, while Mitchells (B-25) used the 'less precise Mk. IXE'. While this is an RAF document, it clearly refers to the USAAF, as the RAF had no Mitchells in the Mediterranean.

34. Pace, p. 26 (quoting Capt. Henry L. Colman of the 434th BS, 12th BG). While the intention was to equip all B-25s and B-26s with the Norden M-9, production delays meant that heavy bomber units and related training units were given priority. Even when a surplus over heavy bomber requirements became available, at first a maximum of 25% of light and medium bombers were fitted with the M-9 as they were manufactured, and priority in supplying overseas medium bombers went to the 341st Bombard-

ment Group in India. Sufficient production to begin installing the M-9 in all light and medium bombers was only achieved at the end of 1943—see Pardini, pp. 117, 145–53 (including p. 147 on the Estoppey D-8).

35. AFHRA IRIS 00105103, *42nd Bombardment Wing: Air and Ground Cooperation—Salerno, Anzio, Cassino*, p. 11, describes how the 'trail' formation of boxes used against the Battipaglia-Eboli road on 15 September 1943 produced a spread of bombs along the road in clusters 'evenly spaced in overall distance of a mile and a half.'

36. *Effects of Close Air Support*, pp. 10–11, estimates the chances of hitting a bridge target 200 x 30 ft (61 x 9 m) with a single bomb in 1944 were 1:200 for the Mediterranean Allied Tactical Air Force and 1:800 for the (British) Desert Air Force, so 60% and 20% respectively for every 200 bombs dropped, and 99.3% and 70% respectively for every 1000 bombs dropped. Besides the general issues of accuracy highlighted here, there were also what are described as 'gross errors' caused by major technical and/or navigational issues. For example, the AFHRA IRIS 00105053, *42nd Bombardment Wing Mission Summary* for 13 September 1943, p. 3, records, in the context of a mission by the 319th BG targeting the Torre Annunziata road junction '47 [100 lb] bombs salvoed after target—faulty bomb mechanism.' There is no evidence these hit ancient Pompeii, but given that the bombs of other aircraft on this mission spread along the road from Torre Annunziata to Pompeii, it is quite possible. At any rate, it gives a general indication of the kinds of problems that might occur.

37. Sir Charles Webster and Noble Frankland, *Preparation*. The Strategic Air Offensive Against Germany 1939–1945, Vol. 1 (London: HMSO, 1961), p. 211, quotes a Bomber Command report from spring 1940 suggesting that only 50% of average bomber crews 'might be expected to find and bomb the right target in good visibility,' but then only if it were near a substantial navigational marker like the coast or a major river.

38. *ORB* No. 231 Wing, Appendix C14 (15–16/09/43). The routing is over Cap Bon in Tunisia, towards the island of Ponza off the coast of Lazio, then turning south-east towards Ischia, then across the Bay of Naples skirting south of the city itself (avoiding its anti-aircraft guns) to cross the coast south of Vesuvius. The orders also specify 'Aircraft are NOT (R[epeat]) NOT to fly EAST of a line running from CAP BON to PONZA.' This is a rather indirect route, but presumably was specified for deconfliction purposes to avoid the Allied air defences of Sicily and shipping in the Bay of Salerno. See also *ORB* No. 231 Wing (13–14/09/43). *ORB* 70 Sqn. (13–14/09/43) provides examples of individual aircraft ('M,' 'O') reporting sightings of all these landmarks (Ponza, Ischia, Capri, Torre Annunziata).

39. *ORB* No. 231 Wing Appendices (13–14/09/43 and 15–16/09/43).

40. The numbers of aircraft for each wing come from the appendices to the Wing *ORB*s recording the orders for those nights' missions sent down from No. 205 Group. For comparative bombing concentration figures, see Webster and Frankland, Vol. 1, pp. 388–89 on the attack on the Renault factory at Billancourt near Paris, 6 February 1942, with an average concentration of 121 aircraft per hour (including a ten-minute period with 59 aircraft, for an hourly average of 354). This was considered high for its time, compared to the heaviest previous concentration of 80 aircraft per hour. However, the 127 Wellington bombers used in that two-hour period against targets near Pompeii on 15 September represented almost all the RAF strategic bombers available in the Mediterranean theatre. The only other activity by Wellingtons recorded that night is 'nickel-

ing' (leaflet dropping) around Benevento and Foggia by two aircraft of No. 330 Wing (*OIS* 208, Mission 134b).

41. Actual bombing times: *ORB* 420 Sqn. RCAF (24–25/08/43); 'B Hour' at 22:00: *ORB* No. 236 Wing Appendix B16 (24/08/43).

42. *ORB* 425 Sqn. RCAF provides particularly good evidence on this point for the nights of 13/14 and 15/16 September. These conditions of visibility contrasted significantly with those encountered by Allied bombers over Germany for much of the war, where weather often made it difficult to navigate to, locate and identify targets.

43. *ORB* 420 Sqn. RCAF (24-25/08/43); *ORB* 424 Sqn. RCAF (15–16/09/43).

44. *ORB* 70 Sqn. (15–16/09/43).

45. Pesce, p. 20, diary of Franco d'Alessandro, describing the bombing of the night of 15 September: 'i razzi sospesi in aria in grande quantità e quasi continuamente diffondevano all'intorno quella caratteristica luce giallastra' ('the many flares that hung in the sky and spread, almost continuously, and everywhere, their distinctive yellowish light'); Maiuri, p. 105 on 24/25 August: 'luce folgorante dei bengala lanciati con i paracadute, una luce spietata, planetaria da lento bolide in fiamme' ('the dazzling light of flares dropped on parachutes, a merciless, cosmic light given off by their slow-burning fires'); and p. 110 on the bombing in September: '. . . di notte, con gran lusso di razzi e di bengala folgoranti e fumiganti che dovevano scrutare ogni angolo riposte e che, dall'alto del vecchio casale dell'Aquila, davano a volte l'impressione terrificante dell'incendio delle rovine' ('. . . and at night, with an extravagant display of illuminating candles and dazzling, smoking, flares that shone into every nook and cranny and which, from our viewpoint on the old Casale dell'Aquila, sometimes gave the terrifying impression that the ruins themselves were ablaze').

46. For RAF use of illuminating flares in northern Europe, see Webster and Frankland, Vol. 1, pp. 209, 229, 386–88. For the Mediterranean, Granfield, p. 37, on the RAF bombing of Tobruk, 20/21 January 1941. Figure 15 shows a Wellington IC bomber T2508, 'LF-O' of 37 Squadron in Egypt in 1941. The Latin motto painted on it, *Defaecamus luces purpuras* ('We shit purple lights'), alludes to its flare-dropping role. For No. 8 Group as the Pathfinder Force and the evolution of its techniques, Webster and Frankland, Vol. 1, pp. 418–36.

47. Appendices to the *ORB* of No. 231 Wing, orders from No. 205 Group to No. 231 Wing (13/09/43) 'Method and times of illumination as decided by officers i/c [in charge of] operations' and (15/09/43) 'Illumination as required by Wings'.

48. Detailed information is not provided consistently. No. 231 Wing *ORB* (15–16/09/43) for 15/16 September 1943 records one illuminator each from 37 Squadron (out of 18 aircraft total) and 70 Squadron (16 aircraft), but for 13/14 September just two illuminators from 37 Squadron (out of 9 aircraft) and none from 70 Squadron (7 aircraft). *ORB* 40 Sqn. (for 13/09/43) reports one illuminator from 11 aircraft. *ORB* 425 Sqn. RCAF (for 13/09/43) records 1 aircraft (of 11) with flares; for 15/09/43, 1 aircraft (of 15) with a mixed load of HE bombs and flares; *ORB* 420 Sqn. RCAF (for 24/08/43) records one illuminator (from 12 aircraft) and (for 29/08/43) one illuminator from 8 aircraft for another mission against Torre Annunziata. As for the crews to whom the task of illumination was allocated, *ORB* 37 Sqn. for September 1943 records 24 illumination sorties that month shared unevenly among 15 different crews. While Sgt. Noble's crew, who illuminated for targets east of Pompeii on 13 September, served as illuminator on

three other occasions that month, the other crew illuminating for the squadron that night (commanded by F. Sgt. Lockwood) only did so that one time during the month, and Sgt. Holland's crew, illuminating targets west of Pompeii on 15 September likewise only illuminated once.

49. See Appendix D. *ORB* 424 Sqn. RCAF (24/08/43): 'Most captains reported flares dropped on time and on the right spot' reinforces the idea of a timed scheme.

50. 104 Sqn. *ORB* 13/9/43 for 13 September states 'Flares were dropped at intervals', although it is unclear whether this means individual aircraft dropped flares at intervals or whether it refers to intervals between aircraft dropping loads of flares. Illuminating aircraft might remain over the target for extended periods dropping flares at intervals to keep the illumination going—see Webster and Frankland, Vol. 1, pp. 386–88, for such techniques in northern Europe before the development of more elaborate pathfinder tactics. However, there is no specific reference to this practice in the contemporary documentation relating to Pompeii.

51. For RAF wartime flares, see *RAF Narrative*, Vol. 5, pp. 229–30; *British Explosive Ordnance* (Washington, DC: US Department of the Navy, Ordnance Systems Command, 1946), pp. 143–57, especially pp. 147–53 on the various types of 4.5 in. flares; and pp. 179–81 on cluster projectiles 270 lb No. 1 (7 x 4.5" flares) and No. 2 (4 x 4.4" flares). The 4.5 in. reconnaissance flare (individually and in clusters) was standard for finding and marking targets until the development of more sophisticated marking methods. See also John A. MacBean and Arthur S. Hogben, *Bombs Gone: The Development and Use of British Air-Dropped Weapons from 1912 to the Present Day* (Wellingborough, UK: Patrick Stephens Ltd., 1990), p. 109.

52. For example, *ORB* 70 Sqn. (15/09/43) aircraft 'P': 'Target well illuminated on arrival and this was continued while aircraft was in area. Roads stood out clearly and junction target identified'. The sorts of problems that might be encountered with use of flares included the dazzling of bomb-aimers, especially in hazy conditions, and 'the wide scatter and the drift of the flares made it difficult to choose the centre point at which to aim.'—see *RAF Narrative*, vol. 5, p. 229.

53. 70 Sqn. *ORB* (13/09/43).

54. 40 Sqn. *ORB* (13/09/43).

55. *OIS* 206, Mission No. 116 (13–14/09/43); *OIS* 208, Mission No. 134 (15–16/09/43).

56. Webster and Frankland, Vol. 1, pp. 387–89.

57. Webster and Frankland, Vol. 1, p. 388: of the 38 flash photographs taken by 14 bombers in the attack that showed enough detail to be plotted, 35 (including at least one from each aircraft) were taken within a mile of the centre of the factory. 'This was a good sign.' There is, unfortunately, very little comparative data for RAF night bombing accuracy applicable to the Pompeii targets (at night, in clear Mediterranean conditions including moonlight, minimal opposition, using early- to mid-war technology). Most of it relates to the difficulties of finding even urban area targets in northern European weather conditions, rather than the accuracy of bombs dropped on a clearly visible target. For the same reason, the absence of some of the radio aids that came in to RAF use in northern Europe in 1942, such as Gee and H2S, is not relevant to this account as they helped aircraft find their target rather than place bombs on it. At any rate, these radio aids were not available in Italy until February and March 1944 (Granfield, pp. 247–48).

58. Granfield, p. 242: introduction of the improved Mk XIV stabilised bombsight in No. 205 Group in February 1944.

59. *Fighter-Bomber Tactics, December 1943–1944*, p. 29.

60. British Bombing Survey Unit, *The Strategic Air War Against Germany: Report of the British Bombing Survey Unit* (London, Cass, 1998, a reprint of TNA AIR 10/3866, 1949), Figure 8. One square mile equates to a circle of 993 yards (908 m) radius. As already noted, the west and east limits of the archaeological site of Pompeii lie between 287 and 1489 m respectively from the autostrada/SS18 aiming point (557–1681 m from the Incrocio Paselli, 1580–2667 m from Torre Annunziata Piazza Imbriani). These *British Bombing Survey* figures are for targets in Germany, where, even in the summer, average visibility would be poorer, but they give an indication of the magnitude of the accuracy issues.

61. *ORB* 18 Sqn.; *ORB* 114 Sqn.; *ORB* No. 326 Wing. For technical details of these TIs and incendiary bombs, *RAF Narrative*, Vol. 5, pp. 229–30; *British Explosive Ordnance*, pp. 127–39, 68–71, 71–75; and MacBean and Hogben, pp. 109–12 on TIs. The 250 lb TI was standard at this time. Incendiaries as target markers, typically in conjunction with sky markers, had been used elsewhere by the RAF, and their use was a normal pathfinder practice in northern Europe—*RAF Narrative*, Vol. 5, p. 229, on the use of TIs and incendiaries together; Webster and Frankland, Vol. 1, p. 386, on the evolution of the 'Shaker' technique in 1942). Incendiaries were not used much in the missions near Pompeii, and are only attested for the Torre Annunziata bombing of 24 August (40 Sqn. RAF and 420 Sqn. RCAF employed—besides high-explosive bombs, 35 small incendiaries) and for the 13 September bombing of routes east of Pompeii (104 Sqn., 'bombs and incendiaries were dropped'). Obviously incendiaries were less effective than high explosive bombs against roads, railways, and concrete bridges.

62. *British Explosive Ordnance*, p. 127.

63. Pace, p. 21–22, quoting Capt. Henry L. Colman of the 434th Bombardment Squadron.

64. *Fighter/Bomber Tactics*, pp. 26–28, discusses such activities, referring to 'about 9 or 10 trips on this type of work' and mentioning, besides Sciacca, attacks on Battipaglia and Altamura (in Apulia). The *Operations and Intelligence Summaries* record other instances, including *OIS* 200 (8/09/43), Missions No. 68 a and b, night of 7/8 September against Metaponto marshalling yards, with four Bostons of No. 326 Wing dropping 510 x 4 [lb] I.B. from 1500–5000 ft (457–1524 m) followed by 15 B-25 of 12th BG bombing from 8000–10,000ft (2438–3048 m) on 'flares and incendiaries dropped by the Bostons'; *OIS* 204, Missions 101 a–c night of 12/13 September against Auletta road junction and Corleto (town) (three Bostons of No. 326 Wing for each target and B-25s of 12th BG and 340th BG).

65. See, for example, AFHRA IRIS 00077840 *12th Bombardment Group Sortie Reports*, 434th Bombardment Squadron, 18 September 1943, 'individual bombing of Pompei'.

66. AFHRA IRIS 00077840, *12th Bombardment Group Sortie Reports*, 83rd Bombardment Squadron, 18 September 1943 for Torre Annunziata. The 114 Sqn. *ORB* reports 'All the 4 lb incendiaries overshot in the south westerly direction but the 30 lb incendiaries of 2 a/c [aircraft] fell on the crossroads specified as the actual aiming point'. 18 Sqn. *ORB* (13/09/43) on the bombing of the 'Pompei road junction' '6 x 250 TI and 540 4 lb incendiaries dropped accurately clearly illuminating target'.

67. Satterthwaite, pp. 55, 69, 77; Pace, p. 26 (quoting Capt. Henry L. Colman of the 434th BS, 12th BG). Regarding the accuracy of the B-25s, the 18 Sqn. *ORB* (19/09/43, 'Pompei Road Junction') reports 'close pattern [of own incendiaries] across target. Clear

illumination was provided for the bombers whose bursts were seen among the incendiaries'. 114 Sqn. *ORB* (13/09/43), however, notes for a similar mission (against San Severino) 'subsequent high explosive bombing by B25s was of a higher standard than on previous occasions', suggesting the technique was not invariably accurate.

CHAPTER 5

1. For a discussion of proportionality, see pp. 86–88.

2. *ORB* 40 Sqn. (15/09/43).

3. This partial break in the overpass over SS18 is also shown from ground level in another archive photograph, IWM NA7459, 29 September 1943, discussed on pp. 76–78, and reproduced here as Figure 20.

4. *OIS* 205 covers the 24-hour period ending 18:00 on 13 September 1943. Attacks began in the Pompeii area between 17:00 and 18:00 on that date, so too late for the damage inflicted that day to be included in that *OIS*.

5. Zuckerman, *Report*, pp. 101–2. See also *OIS* 191 (30/08/43), p. 8 re. Mission no. 636a against Torre Annunziata on 29/30 August, 'much rolling stock is destroyed, and the line to Salerno is temporarily blocked, while the line to Naples has been hit'.

6. Zuckerman, *Report*, p. 102.

7. Maiuri, p. 118: 'passiamo per mucchi di calcinacci, carogne di cavalli, porte sfondate: penso con rimorso al nostro bravo vetturino del giorno innanzi, sperando che l'abbia fatta franca. Il corso di Torre Annunziata, tra valanghe di pietrame e groviglio di fili elettrici, irriconoscibile; era stato colpito poche ore dopo il nostro passagio. L'ultima casa, quella del mio povera amico Luigi Jacono, infermo e paralizzato, e fortunamente intatta; fuori dell'abitato, a quel dolce sole di settembre, si pedala più franchi e sereni.'

8. Freeman, quoted in Pesce, p. 130.

9. Pesce, p. 160. The delay caused by German rear guards is also mentioned in the vivid BBC radio report recorded by Matthew Henry Halton in the Pompeii amphitheatre just as the town was being liberated on 29 September 1943 (IWM 1369, 1943-09-29, transcribed in full in Appendix E): 'As I speak, enemy machine-gun nests in sight of this amphitheatre are holding up our advance for an hour or two'.

10. IWM NA7459, 29 September 1943 (depicting the bridge at 40°44'52.70" N, 14°28'47.61" E). This is reproduced by Pesce (p. 148, but without full reference) and García y García, (p. 25, credited, in turn, to Pesce).

11. Zuckerman, *Report*, p. ii, Conclusion 1.

12. *ORB* 40 Sqn. (15/09/43).

13. Allied Force Headquarters, Office of the Assistant Chief of Staff G-2, *Weekly Intelligence Report* No. 56, p. 2, echoed by the post-war *RAF Narrative*, Vol. 1, pp. 152, 154.

14. Molony, *Campaign in Italy*, p. 315.

15. Zuckerman, *Report*, p. ii, Conclusion 1.

16. Zuckerman, *Report*, pp. 94, 101–4; *Report on Operation Strangle;* and *RAF Narrative*, Vol. 1, pp. 306–21. There is also some useful and relevant general reflection on the success of aerial interdiction derived largely from subsequent experience in Normandy in *Effects of Close Air Support*. On Zuckerman and Strangle, see Overy, pp. 536–37.

17. Also in Zuckerman's published account, Solly Zuckerman, *From Apes to Warlords: An Autobiography, 1904–46* (London: Collins, 1988), pp. 209–11, where (quoting his

own earlier words) he reiterates his conclusion that enemy movement had not been prevented, but that nevertheless, 'the offensive against rail targets in Sicily and Southern Italy had been an "outstanding success". The two factors which contributed most to the outcome of the offensive, I went on to say, "were the destruction and damaging of rolling stock and repair facilities". Largely because of this, "the Sicilian and Southern Italian rail systems had become practically paralysed by the end of July 1943—as the result of attacks on only six railway centres, Naples, Foggia, San Giovanni, Reggio, Messina, Palermo". . . . [T]he most economic way to disrupt communications was not to cut lines but to attack "large railway centres which contain important rail facilities and large concentrations of locomotives and rolling stock"'. On planning for Normandy, see Zuckerman, *Apes to Warlords*, pp. 217–45. Also see Baldoli and Knapp, pp. 27–29.

18. On railway lines, see Zuckerman, *Report*, p. 41, noting that cuts and craters were easy to repair and had little effect. *Report on Operation Strangle*, p. 5, argues that large numbers of rail cuts could overwhelm the repair organisation, and that railway lines tended to be thinly defended if at all, so were 'inexpensive' targets. Bridges: Zuckerman, *Report*, p. v.—'Railway and road bridges are uneconomical and difficult targets, and in general do not appear to be worth attacking except where special considerations demand it in the tactical area'. In general, Zuckerman (*Report*, pp. 57–60) is very sceptical about targeting bridges, noting that they were difficult to hit and claiming that there was little effect even when they were hit. The later analysis of *Strangle* was more positive about this, noting that 'Bridges are one of the most difficult types of bombing targets. In normal circumstances however, if successfully attacked, they form a positive block which may take a day to several weeks to repair'. The report includes them among the vulnerable points of the Italian rail system and advocates them as primary targets for medium bombers. (*Report on Operation Strangle*, p. 4). The change in emphasis may be explained by the increasing accuracy of such attacks between autumn 1943 and spring 1944 improving from an average of 196 tons of bombs dropped per bridge destroyed between 22 October 1943 and 22 January 1944, to less than 62 tons in May 1944. This was partly due to improvement after the poor winter weather (not a factor in the September bombing near Pompeii), but also to better equipment and tactics, including the equipping of South African Air Force B-26 Marauder bombers with Norden bomb sights—see *Bombing Accuracy of Marauder Squadrons*. See also the accuracy data in *Effects of Close Air Support*, pp. 10–11.

19. Zuckerman, *Report*, Preface. p. v, points 20 and 21 and pp. 55–56; *Effects of Close Air Support*, pp. 3, 26, which states: 'The following bomb densities are required for adequate interdiction' of road traffic—5 bombs per acre (0.405 ha) in heavily built up areas, 20 bombs per acre in suburban areas and 10 bombs per acre in close country where traffic is unable to move off-road to by-pass the block. This approach is 'uneconomical' in open country. *Report on Operation Strangle*, p. 5, makes attacks on road targets a second priority after railways, given the extent of the Italian road network, but argues that road targets become relatively more important as the rail system is degraded, and advocates in particular the use of medium bombers against major road bridges.

20. Zuckerman argued for prioritising destruction of locomotives, rolling stock and their associated repair facilities at a few key rail centres on the basis of his analysis of the air campaign in southern Italy, including the attacks against Torre Annunziata (*Report*, p. v). However, even he acknowledged that 'it may be a vital necessity in certain situations to attempt to disrupt enemy movement suddenly by means of air attacks', citing (p.

29) attacks against the Eboli-Battipaglia area as a successful example. Zuckerman's arguments did not shape Allied air interdiction strategy, however. While *Strangle* focused on the rail system, it targeted a wider range of rail targets than those advocated by Zuckerman, including bridges, marshalling yards and the railway lines themselves (*Report on Operation Strangle*, pp. 4–5). The authors of that *Report* argue (p. 3) that the large quantity of rolling stock available to the Germans and their extensive repair facilities meant that to focus exclusively on such targets was ineffective.

21. As, essentially, does García y García, pp. 18, 25–26.

22. See Chapter 10. These rules of engagement are set out in the preface (pp. 1–2) to the atlas of aerial photographs of cities annotated with cultural sites MAAF, *Ancient Monuments of Italy*, produced by Headquarters Mediterranean Allied Air Forces, 23 February 1944, and under the signature of Brigadier-General Lauris Norstad, USA, director of operations of MAAF. These protocols are repeated as Appendix C-5 (pp. 47–48) to the post-war MFAA, *Final Report: General*.

23. *RAF Narrative*, Vol. 1, Appendix 2: 27th and 86th Fighter-Bomber Groups, each composed of four squadrons with a nominal strength of 13 aircraft, for a total of 104. At the time of the 5th Army landings at Salerno, they were based at Barcellona Pozzo di Gotto and nearby S. Antonio on the north-east coast of Sicily, but moved into airfields in the Salerno beachhead in the course of the battle, as discussed below, n. 25.

24. *Fighter/Bomber Tactics*, pp. 1–7, includes some discussion of A-36 bombing tactics.

25. As shown by *War Room Monthly Summary* for September 1943, p. 6 (237 A-36 beachhead air cover sorties on 14 September alone, compared to 321 by P-38s, 123 by RAF Spitfires and 59 by US Spitfires), and the *War Diaries* of the A-36 Fighter-Bomber Squadrons (525th, 526th and 527th) of 27th Fighter-Bomber Group. The A-36 had a notional combat radius of c. 550 miles (885 km). It was c. 300 km from Barcellona Pozzo di Gotto to Pompei and c. 250 km to the closest point on the Gulf of Salerno coast. Even with additional fuel tanks, the A-36 could patrol over the beachhead area for only about an hour (see 526th FBS *War Diary*, 9 September 1943). The *War Diaries* show that the 27th FB Group was established on the airstrip at Sele, near the archaeological site of Paestum, only on 16–17 September. Some of the unit's aircraft had begun to use the landing strip as an advanced base (often in emergencies) a few days before that, although German counter-attack led to delays, with transport aircraft conveying unit personnel from Sicily being turned back on occasion due to danger from ground combat—see 527th FBS *War Diary* (14/09/43). The first A-36 missions flown in the Pompeii area, armed reconnaissance around Torre Annunziata, were conducted on 15 September (525th FBS *War Diary*—also see *OIS* 207 [15/09/43], Mission No. 131a—A-36s of 27th FB Group 'bombing targets of opportunity' at Torre Annunziata and elsewhere). Such missions were at the limits of the A-36s' endurance from Sicily, particularly when carrying bombs, and it is likely that they were actually flown from Sele, or by aircraft from Sicily that refuelled at Sele.

26. Zuckerman (*Report*, p. 58) states 'It is fairly clear that the U.S. 500 lb [General Purpose] G.P. bomb, which was most frequently used, was practically never sufficiently powerful to achieve the desired object, even when a direct hit was scored on a bridge. . . . In general, it seems that only direct hits by 50% C.W. 1000 lb or probably 2000 lb bombs are likely to be effective against brick, reinforced-concrete or masonry bridges.' The general assumption in wartime documentation relating to air attacks on bridges in Italy

is that a direct hit by a 1000 lb bomb might be required, and consequently by August 1944, at least, British medium bombers attacking bridge targets were loaded with 1000 lb bombs rather than larger numbers of 500 or 250 lb bombs. See *Bombing Accuracy of Marauder Squadrons*, pp. 1–2 (the assumption that a direct hit from a 1000 lb bomb would be required), and p. 3 (normal bomb load used against bridge targets by DAF [Desert Air Force] medium bombers 4 x 1000 lb; also *Report on Operation Strangle*, p. 13, advocating 1000 lb G.P. or Semi-Armour-Piercing bombs.

27. *MFAA Final Report: General*, pp. 25–26.

28. Given that individuals such as monuments officer Ernest De Wald and Mortimer Wheeler (with his MFAA connections) believed ancient Pompeii was bombed due to an (incorrect) judgement that there were German troops in the site (see Chapter 6), it seems likely that this belief was widespread within the organisation as a whole.

29. Hague Convention (IV) 1907, *Regulations*, Article 27, set out in International Committee of the Red Cross, *International Humanitarian Law*: <https://ihl-databases.icrc.org/customary-ihl/eng/docs/v2_rul_rule38> [accessed 30 May 2017]. Aerial bombing is not specified as a type of 'bombardment' in Article 27, since it was in its infancy in 1907, but bombardment here can be taken to include aerial bombing on the basis of Regulations, Article 25, which refers to (my italics) 'attack or bombardment, *by whatever means*, of towns . . .', etc. See Roger O'Keefe, *Protection*, pp. 23, 26.

30. [British] War Office, *Manual of Military Law* (London: HMSO, 1929, reprinted 1939), Chapter XIV [as Amendments No. 12 of 1936], 'The Laws and Usages of War on Land', p. 3 (Hague) and p. 33, art. 133. The *Manual of Military Law* used in the Second World War was essentially the 1929 edition. However, even at the time of its publication in 1929, it was noted (p. iii, 'Note by Editor to Seventh Edition') that Chapter XIV was not entirely up to date. This chapter was updated in its entirety with *Amendments* (No. 12) in 1936. The 1939 reprint of the *Manual* (p. iii, 'Note to 1939 Reprint') omitted all of the 1929 version of Chapter XIV except for its appendices, and refers to the 1936 *Amendments* No. 12 for its substantive contents; United States War Department, *Basic Field Manual FM 27-10: Rules of Land Warfare* (Washington, DC: US Government Printing Office, 1940), p. 14, no. 58 (quoting Hague [IV] 1907 directly).

31. *Manual of Military Law (Amendments No. 12)*, p. 33, art. 136.

32. Roger O'Keefe, *Protection*, p. 24; *Manual of Military Law* (*Amendments* No. 12), p. 33, note 1 on art. 133. Another anachronism also cited in the *Manual* is Article 27's requirement that such buildings be marked with 'distinctive and visible signs which must be notified to the enemy beforehand', something that would be difficult to achieve with any clarity given the altitudes from which bombing was conducted by 1943 (*Manual of Military Law* [*Amendments* No. 12], p. 33, arts. 134–35, with n. 2–4).

33. MAAF, *Ancient Monuments of Italy*, p. 2, No. 3 (i).

34. Roger O'Keefe, *Protection*, p. 25; Alcala, p. 215. See also W. Hays Parks, 'Air War and the Law of War', *Air Force Law Review* 32 (1990), 1–225 (p. 31). *Regulations*, Article 23 (g) of Hague Convention (IV) 1907 <https://ihl-databases.icrc.org/customary-ihl/eng/docs/v2_rul_rule50> [accessed 3 August 2019] also forbade destruction and seizure of enemy property unless 'imperatively demanded by the necessities of war' (repeated in the *Manual of Military Law* (*Amendments* No. 12), p. 75, art. 406), but in the context of the German counter-attack against Salerno, the Allies could have made a strong argument that such necessity existed.

35. Text available at https://ihl-databases.icrc.org/applic/ihl/ihl.nsf/

INTRO/275?OpenDocument [accessed 3 August 2019]. On the Hague Air Rules and their status during the Second World War, see Overy, pp. 29–30, 32, 237–38; Parks, 'Air War and the Law of War', pp. 25–36; the discussion that follows is based on the approaches taken by Roger O'Keefe, *Protection*, pp. 44–51, and Alcala, pp. 215–17.

36. Roger O'Keefe, *Protection*, pp. 46–47; Alcala, pp. 215–17.

37. While the bombing near Pompeii was not in direct support ('close air support') of land forces in the target area, it was interdiction (or 'general air support' in Second World War terms—see Gooderson, p. 3) inextricably tied up with the land operations nearby in the Gulf of Salerno, so application of Article 24 (4) would seem appropriate. Parks, 'Air War and the Law of War', p. 32, argues that when the Hague Air Rules were drafted 'immediate neighbourhood . . . of land forces' 'certainly was perceived' as meaning within artillery range of ground combat (which Pompeii was not). However, it is difficult to envisage how such a definition could have been maintained in 1943. Article 24 (3) seems to be intended to apply to essentially strategic bombing, and so would be relevant to the attack that damaged Pompeii in August, before the Salerno landings. In that case, the argument would focus on whether or not the bombing could be considered 'indiscriminate'. Article 24 (3) and the discriminate/indiscriminate distinction is relevant to much of the damage done to cultural property by strategic bombing in the Second World War.

38. Protocol Additional to the Geneva Conventions of 12 August 1949, and relating to the Protection of Victims of International Armed Conflicts (Protocol I), 8 June 1977 <https://ihl-databases.icrc.org/ihl/INTRO/470> [accessed 3 August 2018]; Roger O'Keefe and others, *Military Manual*, §§10 (p. 3) on Additional Protocol I and §§113 (p. 34) on proportionality and cultural property.

39. As set out in [UK] Ministry of Defence, *Campaign Execution*. Joint Doctrine Publication 3-00 (third edition, October 2009) <https://assets.publishing.service.gov.uk/government/> [accessed 3/8/18], Annex 3B—'Joint Action Targeting Process'. 'Principles of Lawful Targeting' is Annex 3B5. See also Roger O'Keefe and others, *Military Manual*, §§84–110 (pp. 26–33) on targeting and §§112–21 (pp. 34–36) on incidental/collateral damage under contemporary international humanitarian law.

40. [UK] Ministry of Defence, *Campaign Execution*, Annex 3B8 'Prevention of Collateral Damage'. Roger O'Keefe and others, *Military Manual*, §§116–21 (pp. 35–36) on weapons selection and collateral damage estimation.

41. I am grateful to Paul Fox for highlighting these factors.

42. Regarding planning, note the changes to No. 205 Group's intended operations on 13 September, discussed on pp. 25–26. See Parks, 'Air War and the Law of War', p. 33 on the failure of the Hague Air Rules to accommodate the dynamic nature of targeting even from a 1920s perspective.

43. Under the terms of modern international law incorporating the concept of proportionality, the discussion should also take into consideration the 'cultural value of the object, building or site likely to be harmed' (Roger O'Keefe and others, *Military Manual*, §§114 = p. 34). Clearly Pompeii was a site of high cultural value, as reflected in the three-star—highest—ranking assigned to it in wartime Monuments, Fine Arts and Archives Sub-Commission documentation. It might have qualified for some form of special or enhanced protection, requiring that a decision to bomb nearby be made at a high level of command. However, collateral damage estimation that the anticipated damage to the site would not result in its total destruction would also factor into that judgement.

44. 1954 Hague Convention for the Protection of Cultural Property in the Event of Armed Conflict, Art. 4 on 'immediate surroundings'; Arts. 8–11 and *Regulations* 11–16, Special Protection; Second Protocol (1999), Arts. 10–14, Enhanced Protection. See O'Keefe and Prott, pp. 21, 48–49.

45. *Hague Draft Rules of Aerial Warfare*, Article 26 (7), text from <https://ihl-databases.icrc.org/applic/ihl/ihl.nsf/INTRO/275?OpenDocument> [accessed 3/8/18]: 'A State which accepts the provisions of this Article should abstain from making use of the historic monuments and the zone surrounding them for military purposes or for the benefit of its military organization in any manner whatsoever.' Presumably 'a State which accepts the provisions of this Article' should be taken to refer to any state (including, potentially, Germany) rather than just the state in which the historic monument was situated (Italy). Germany was not invited to the 1922 Washington Conference that established the committee that drafted the Hague Air Rules (Parks, 'Air War and the Law of War', p. 27) and so may not have observed them even if they had been generally accepted.

46. 1954 Hague Convention, *Regulations*, Art. 8.3 in O'Keefe and Prott, p. 21. In fact, this very issue had to be addressed in the granting of Special Protection as a 'centre containing monuments' to the Vatican City under Hague 1954, requiring agreement of the Italian authorities to move or de-militarise elements of their military and transportation infrastructure (including a segment of the Via Aurelia) running close to the boundaries of Vatican City. See Boylan, pp. 55–56 incl. n. 13; UNESCO, *International Register of Cultural Property under Special Protection* (2015), p. 11, <http://www.unesco.org/new/fileadmin/MULTIMEDIA/HQ/CLT/pdf/Register2015EN.pdf> [accessed 3 August 2018]. Roger O'Keefe and others, *Military Manual*, §§130–132 (pp. 39–40), argue that current international humanitarian law forbids military use of the 'immediate surroundings' of cultural property, citing the relationship between the abbey of Montecassino and the German Gustav Line in 1944 as an example.

47. It could also be argued that military necessity was a less clear-cut factor (in legal terms, at any rate) in the case of the bombing that damaged Pompeii in August, before the Salerno landings. Like strategic bombing more generally, the attacks in August were not so constrained or motivated by immediate and urgent circumstances on the ground as the September attacks, and so the August attacks might (theoretically, had the Rules been binding) be challenged under Hague Air Rules Article 24 (3), requiring a case to be made that the August bombing was not 'indiscriminate'.

48. On the relationship between the Monuments, Fine Arts and Archives organisation and the Allied Air Forces in September 1943, and after the improvements of early 1944, see Chapters 9 and 10.

CHAPTER 6

Much of the material in this chapter also appears in Nigel Pollard, '"Bombing Pompeii!!! Why Not the Pyramids?" Myths and Memories of the Allied Bombing of Pompeii, August–September 1943', in *Critical Perspectives on Cultural Memory and Heritage: Construction, Transformation and Destruction*, ed. by Veysel Apaydin (London: UCL Press, 2020), pp. 239–51.

1. *12th Bombardment Group Sortie Reports*, 83rd Bombardment Squadron, 17 September 1943.

2. *ORB* 70 Sqn. (15/09/43).

3. Maiuri, p. 107. I have not found any other evidence for this broadcast besides Maiuri's account, but there is no particular reason to disbelieve the substance of his recollection. The broadcast is not one of those catalogued in Maura Piccialuti Caprioli's *Radio Londra 1940–1945: Inventario delle trasmissioni per l'Italia* (Rome: Ministero per I Beni Culturali ed Ambientali, 1976), but her evidence is clearly fragmentary. As Maiuri notes, the Radio Londra broadcast included an undertaking that no further damage would be done to Pompeii, which, of course, subsequently proved untrue.

4. Maiuri, pp. 107–8, states that a 'little group' (rather than a headquarters) of Germans was in the hotel. See also Pesce, p. 20 (citing the contemporary diary of Franco d'Alessandro). Maiuri (p. 109) discusses German military dispositions around (but not in) the site, as does d'Alessandro's diary (in Pesce, pp. 19–20).

5. *Giornale d'Italia*, 27 August 1943, p. 1; *Giornale d'Italia*, 29–30 August 1943, p. 3; *Kölnische Zeitung*, 28 August 1943, p. 2. See García y García, p. 21. All three include similar information, referring to damage to the Arch of Drusus in the Forum, the House of Romulus and Remus, and the Antiquarium, as does the coverage of Pompeii in 'Leonardo's "Last Supper" Intact Amid Raid Debris,' *New York Times*, 27 August 1943, p. 4 [dateline London, 26 August], which cites 'Rome radio' as its source. Also see a (subsequent) letter from E.H. Keeling M.P. to Secretary of State for Air Sir Archibald Sinclair (in TNA T 209/1, Keeling to Sinclair, 10 December 1943 [pp. 23–24]), which notes that 'The Germans did not fail to publish photographs of the damage, for anti-British propaganda.'

6. 'Naples Railways Again Bombed', the *Times* [London], 26 August 1943, p. 3.

7. See, for example, *Collier Evidence*, p. 3; Col. Edgar Erskine Hume [US], Allied Regional Civil Affairs Officer in Campania in October 1943, stated 'I have been told by many people in Naples that damage caused by Allied troops in the Palace [the Royal Palace of Naples] was the subject of much adverse comment among people from all classes of society and that sometimes there was the statement that "even the Germans did not do that"'.

8. Asa Briggs, *The War of Words. The History of Broadcasting in the United Kingdom*, Vol. III (Oxford: Oxford University Press, 1970), pp. 435–41.

9. See, for example, 'Pompeii Bombed', the *Times* [London], 15 September 1943, p. 4; the *Times* [London] 17 September 1943, p. 3; 'Pompeii's Fiery Gamut Rounded Out By Bombers', *Chicago Daily Tribune*, 15 September 1943, p. 4; 'Tanks Lash Allies', *New York Times*, 15 September 1943, p. 1.

10. The immediate context of Maiuri's entry for 4 September 1943 is the initial (but secondary) British landing in Calabria on 3 September 1943. However, his reflections here anticipate the main Allied landing in the Gulf of Salerno on 9 September and events beyond that. This emphasises that, despite its appearance, *Taccuino napoletano* is not a straightforward version of Maiuri's contemporary diary.

11. Maiuri, pp. 209–10 (my translation).

12. Maiuri, pp. 119–20 (my translation).

13. Relman Morin, 'Most Naples Art Treasures Survive Fight', *Washington Post*, 7 October 1943 [dateline Naples, 2 October], p. 15.

14. My transcription of 'Canadian correspondent's commentary as British troops reach the Plain of Naples', Imperial War Museum catalogue 1369, 1943-09-29. The complete transcription is given here as Appendix E.

15. For example, Relman Morin, 'New Disaster Visits Ancient City of Pompeii,' *Washington Post*, 2 October 1943 [dateline 29 September], p. 9.

16. Morin, 'Most Naples Art Treasures Survive.'

17. John O'Reilly, 'Pompeii Hails Clark's Troops,' *New York Herald Tribune*, 2 October 1943 [dateline 29 September], p. 1, which contains more details of the damage (including that to the Antiquarium) than the other reports, states 'During bombings to drive the Germans from positions around the ruins a number of old structures were reduced to rubble.'

18. Maiuri, p. 109, in the entry attributed to 4 September 1943, discussed p. 95 and n. 10 above, anticipating German resistance to the Salerno landings.

19. Quoted in Pesce, pp. 19–20. D'Alessandro also refers to anti-aircraft batteries located north and south of the Santuario (the 19th-century cathedral of Pompei) 'firing furiously' against RAF bombers that very same night, which seems to contradict the notion that there were no anti-aircraft defences.

20. UK National Collection of Aerial Photography, ACIU NA 0685 4006 reproduced here as Figure 5 (low resolution) and 16–19 (details).

21. Herbert L. Matthews, 'Naples Goes Mad with Joy as Grim Allied Push Ends,' *New York Times*, 2 October 1943 (dateline Naples, 1 October 1943), pp. 1, 3.

22. NARA M1944, RG 239/0015, Correspondence, Col. Henry C. Newton, *Report on Conversation with Herbert Matthews*, 24 April 1944, p. 2.

23. On Wheeler and British military cultural property protection, see Chapters 7 and 9; on Wheeler as showman, Gabriel Moshenka and Tim Shadla-Hall, 'Mortimer Wheeler's Theatre of the Past,' *Public Archaeology* 10 (2011), 46–55. Wheeler's biographer Jacquetta Hawkes refers to his 'habit of self-dramatization' and reports the view of Arnold (later Lord) Goodman, a member of his unit, that 'his commanding officer . . . was playing a dramatic role—the role of a conventional soldier, which inevitably in his hands became larger than life.' Jacquetta Hawkes, *Adventurer in Archaeology: The Biography of Sir Mortimer Wheeler* (London: St. Martin's Press, 1982), pp. 7–8.

24. Mortimer Wheeler, *Still Digging. Interleaves from an Antiquary's Notebook* (London: Michael Joseph, 1955), pp. 1–2. The date for the anecdote is provided by a contemporary letter—see Hawkes, p. 224. L.C. Carr, *Tessa Verney Wheeler: Women and Archaeology Before World War Two* (Oxford: Oxford University Press, 2012) accurately describes Wheeler's *Still Digging* as 'a racy and charmingly caustic autobiography.'

25. Wheeler's observation is correct for the standard contemporary GSGS 4228 1:25,000 Allied military maps of the area. See sheets 185-III NW *Boscotrecase* and 185-III SW *Castellamare di Stabia* (July–August 1943).

26. Wheeler, *Preservation*, p. 1.

27. TNA T 209/1, Keeling to Secretary of State for Air Sir Archibald Sinclair 10 December 1943 [pp. 23–24] refers to Wheeler's 'striking evidence of damage to Pompeii which could have been avoided if the R.A.F. had expert knowledge at their disposal'; also in TNA T 209/1 Keeling to Attlee [Deputy Prime Minister], 19 December 1943 [p. 22].

28. See Morin, 'Most Naples Art Treasures Survive,' reporting Maiuri: 'The newest excavations are irreparably injured. . . . The Strada dell'Abbondanza is ruined beyond restoration.' Also 'Naples Preserved Most of Its Art,' *New York Times*, 7 October 1943, p. 5: 'Professor Maiuri said that the Via dell'Abbondanza in Pompeii's new excavations had been severely damaged'; and *Works of Art in Italy:* Part I, p. 49, reproduced in Appendix A below. In contrast, inspection of the site in April 1944 (see p. 102), identified (in

MFAA *Pompeii and Herculaneum*, p. 46) the Porta Marina/Antiquarium as the area of heaviest damage.

29. Spike Milligan, *Mussolini: My Part in His Downfall* (London: Penguin Books, 1980), p. 51.

30. 'Damage at Pompeii,' the *Times* [London] 9 November 1943, p. 3. As noted on pp. 94–95, no Allied newspaper accounts contemporary with air missions that damaged the site suggest ancient Pompeii was occupied by Germans or targeted deliberately. They reflect official communiqués describing the targets as nearby transportation routes.

31. MFAA *Pompeii and Herculaneum*, p. 1.

32. MFAA *Final Report: General*, p. 26. It actually refers to 'the earlier raid on Pompeii'. It is unclear whether this is a reference solely to the bombing on 24 August 1943, or whether 'earlier' here is to be taken as relative to the later bombing of Treviso, Verona, Vicenza and Ravenna mentioned previously in the same passage. Regardless, it emphasises that monuments officers had no special insight into the planning of such operations unless personally involved.

33. The Allies and Axis/German media competed to depict one another as careless or downright rapacious of cultural property after the Allied invasion of Sicily in July 1943—see Nicholas, p. 231.

34. Pre-war debates about bombing led to exaggerated perceptions of its accuracy and effectiveness among both military and civilians—see Overy, pp. 19–55, and here, pp. 57–59; 141–46. Naivety regarding the realities of bombing in 1943 is emphasised by Maiuri's claim in a newspaper interview that he had tried to signal Allied bombers away from the site (in Morin, 'Most Naples Art Treasures Survive Fight', p. 15) and García y García's (p. 26) modern incomprehension that bombers might hit the site in error even in daytime, in clear view.

35. See García y García, p. 24 n. 14, for the contemporary story that the 19th-century Santuario della Madonna of modern Pompei (listed as a zero-star heritage site in wartime MFAA lists) was the real target of the bombing because of the concentration of people sheltering there, but the commander of the Allied bombers had 'sacrificed' the archaeological site to 'save' the Santuario by bombing the Roman town instead of the modern church.

36. The only possible evidence I have seen for the propagation of this story from the centre is 'When Allies Struck at Foggia and Pompeii,' *New York Times*, 5 October 1943, p. 3. A photograph of damage to the ancient Case dei cenacoli colonnati (via dell'Abbondanza, *Reg.* IX, *Ins.* xii—see García y García, p. 157) is captioned 'In Pompeii this Nazi gun position was bombed into a mass of ruins'. The photograph shows no indication of German use, and the location would be a poor one for artillery. The picture is credited as 'British Official', although it is unclear whether the caption was also provided by British official sources. If so, then it was deliberate disinformation. Not all Allied military visitors accepted deliberate bombing of German forces as the cause of the damage, and aircrew, perhaps aware of the limitations of their own weapons systems, may have been less susceptible to it than others. Satterthwaite (p. 40), a B-25 pilot who visited Pompeii in 1944, writes of the area where the brothel is located: 'One of our stray bombs made a direct hit on that section of the ruins. The irony of this is not lost on us.'

CHAPTER 7

1. For Hammond's arrival and subsequent activities, see MFAA *Final Report: General*, pp. 2–3; [Maxse], *Report for August*; [Hammond—Maxse], *Memorandum*, p. 1.

2. NARA M1944, RG 236/0062, MFAA Field Reports, AMGOT Adv. HQ Syracuse [Capt. Mason Hammond], *Condition of Monuments in the Syracuse Area*, 2 August 1943.

3. [Maxse], *Report for August*; NARA M1944, RG 239/0067, MFAA Field Reports, AMGOT HQ [Capts. M. Hammond and F.H.J. Maxse], *Progress Report for the Month of September of the Office of Fine Arts and Monuments*, 7 October 1943; Palermo: [Maxse], *Report for August*; [Hammond—Maxse], *Memorandum*, p. 2; TNA FO 371/37330/24, HQ AMG [Capts. Mason Hammond and F.H.J. Maxse], *Report of the Advisers on Fine Arts and Monuments in AMGOT for October 1943*, 1 November 1943. See Coccoli, *Monumenti violati*, pp. 39, 55–74.

4. Woolley, (*Record*, p. 20). Modern definitions of the roles of military cultural property protection specialists, established with knowledge of the Second World War experience, are quite wide-ranging. The 1954 Hague Convention (Art. 7.1) merely states that such personnel are 'to secure respect for cultural property in the event of armed conflict and to co-operate with the civilian authorities responsible for safeguarding it', but given the broad definition of 'safeguarding' and harm (Arts. 3 and 4), it is clear that a range of pro-active activities are implied. Certainly guarding sites under occupation is envisaged, but also participation in planning, targeting and collateral damage estimation for air and ground operations—see Alcala, pp. 247–53, esp. 251–53; Roger O'Keefe and others, *Military Manual*, §§66–70 (pp. 20–22).

5. On the origins and development of Allied military cultural property protection activities in the Second World War, see MFAA *Final Report: General*, pp. 1–17; Woolley, *Record*, pp. 5–25; Coles and Weinberg, pp. 860–76, which compiles extracts from key contemporary documents; Donnison, pp. 211–36; Nicholas, pp. 209–44; Edsell; Dagnini Brey; and now, in particular, Coccoli, *Monumenti violati*, pp. 29–53.

6. See Chapter 5. Besides the prohibition of bombardment of historic buildings set out in *Manual of Military Law* (*Amendments* No. 12), p. 33, art. 133 based on Hague Convention (IV) 1907, *Regulations*, Article 27, there are sections pertaining to the treatment of historic buildings and cultural institutions such as museums in occupied enemy territory. These include *Manual of Military Law* (*Amendments* No. 12), p. 79, art. 429, that forbids requisition of such buildings for accommodation of troops unless 'it is a military necessity' and also 'any seizure, destruction or wilful damage to the property of such [cultural, religious or humanitarian] institutions, or to historic monuments, or works of science or art'; and p. 80, art. 431 requiring respect for and forbidding appropriation of 'pictures, collections of works of art, and archives.' This derives primarily from the authority of Hague Convention (IV) 1907, Article 56 'The property of municipalities, that of institutions dedicated to religion, charity and education, the arts and sciences, even when State property, shall be treated as private property. All seizure of, destruction or wilful damage done to institutions of this character, historic monuments, works of art and science, is forbidden, and should be made the subject of legal proceedings.'

7. *Che cosa hanno fatto gli Inglesi in Cirenaica* (Rome: Ministero della Cultura Populare, 1941). The second edition (which I used) is dated July 1941.

8. *Che cosa hanno fatto gli Inglesi*, unnumbered photographs between pp. 40 and 41. Some graffiti give the names and units of individual soldiers and a date, and these and a large drawing of a kangaroo leave little doubt that they were done by British/Australian soldiers (but see below for their context). Such graffiti were a typical but relatively harmless form of vandalism (they were mostly done in pencil) to cultural sites through the later course of the war, recorded at Pompeii and elsewhere.

9. 'Cyrenaica and Tripolitania (Ancient Monuments),' House of Commons, *House of Commons Debate* (5 August 1943, vol. 391, col. 2485): 'The museum at Cyrene was practically cleared of all exhibits when the Axis forces first retreated from Cyrenaica in January, 1941, but a few large pieces remain. On this occasion the museum was securely closed as soon as possible after the building came into our hands. After our withdrawal from Cyrenaica on this occasion, the Italians prepared a propaganda pamphlet in which they purported to enumerate the acts of vandalism perpetrated by our troops during our three months' occupation of the territory. Among other things they alleged that the Australian troops did very considerable damage to the exhibits in the Cyrene museum and they published a photograph showing a large quantity of broken vessels and damaged statues said to have been taken in the Cyrene museum. Investigations made during this last [1942] occupation of Cyrenaica proved conclusively that this photograph was not taken in the Cyrene museum at all. It was in fact a photograph of a small shed adjacent to the museum in which the Italian archaeologists had collected a large number of broken vessels and damaged statues and were in the process of piecing them together. The photograph published by the Italians was therefore grossly misleading and in no way supported the charges made against our troops'. Woolley, *Record*, p. 11: 'When Cyrene was finally re-taken, we were able to establish the fact that all this evidence has been deliberately falsified by the Italians. The broken statues had been broken, not recently by our troops, but in antiquity; they were photographed not in the Museum galleries but in the workshops where the "formatori" had been building them up from fragments collected in the course of the excavations. The statues that had stood upon the empty pedestals had been carried off by the Italians themselves and were in Tripolitania. The rooms on whose walls Australian soldiers had inscribed their names were not the art galleries, but empty rooms, whose walls already bore Italian graffiti of a precisely similar sort. The damage done by our troops was in fact negligible.' This was based on conclusions by Professor Alan Rowe, who had excavated at Cyrene before the war and visited from Alexandria during the second British occupation of Cyrenaica (Woolley, *Record*, p. 14).

10. TNA T 209/19, Ward Perkins, *Report on Conservation of Antiquities in Cyrenaica* [after 20th July 1943], p. 3 (with Appendix B): 'The damage done to the museum at Cyrene has received a great deal of publicity. In particular, on the withdrawal of the Italians during the first occupation the local population looted and overturned the collections and the records housed in the stores and they were followed by British and Australian troops, who recorded their presence in the usual manner on the walls. The resulting mess was duly photographed and illustrated in the propaganda publication *Cosa hanno fatto gli inglesi nella Cirenaica*. These facts are admitted by Dr. PESCE, former Inspector of Antiquities for Cyrenaica. It does appear however to be established, despite any special pleading to the contrary, that Imperial troops did do a lot of thoughtless damage. Statues were overturned and chipped and in some cases fired on, and quantities of minor antiquities were looted.' Ward-Perkins also notes (p. 8) that while many of the

archaeological records from Cyrenaica had been moved to safety in Tripolitania by the Italians, all the records, plans and photographs from Pesce's most recent excavations at Cyrene and Tolmeta were lost during the occupation.

11. Woolley, *Record*, pp. 5, 11. See Christopher Edens, 'Woolley, Sir (Charles) Leonard (1880–1960), archaeologist', *Oxford Dictionary of National Biography*. September 23, 2004. Oxford: Oxford University Press <http://www.oxforddnb.com/view/10.1093/ref:odnb/9780198614128.001.0001/odnb-9780198614128-e-37021> [accessed 7 September 2018]. There is a brief overview of these developments in Nicholas, pp. 215–17, 236–37.

12. 'Cyrenaica and Tripolitania (Ancient Monuments)': 'When the British Forces advanced into Libya in the autumn of 1942 immediate steps were taken for the preservation of any archaeological monuments which might come into our possession during the course of the occupation.'

13. Woolley, *Record*, pp. 11–12. See Coccoli, *Monumenti violati*, pp. 40–41.

14. On Wheeler see Jane McIntosh, 'Wheeler, Sir (Robert Eric) Mortimer (1890–1976), archaeologist and broadcaster.' *Oxford Dictionary of National Biography* (Oxford: Oxford University Press, October 4, 2012) <http://www.oxforddnb.com/view/10.1093/ref:odnb/9780198614128.001.0001/odnb-9780198614128-e-31825> [accessed 7 September 2018]; Wheeler, *Still Digging*; Hawkes; Carr. Vivid glimpses of Wheeler's personality are provided by Carr, pp. 17, 76, 189: 'a man of overwhelming personality. . . . he did nor censor himself'; and Hawkes, p. 7: 'martinet'; pp. 3–5: 'daemonic . . . concentrated'; p. 216: 'exactly the kind of undertaking . . .'.

15. Wheeler, *Antiquaries Paper*, pp. 7, 6a, 12; Wheeler, *Preservation*, pp. 1–2. This is echoed in Wheeler's 1955 autobiography, *Still Digging*, pp. 153–54: 'the Secretary of State had unhappily been misinformed. . . . .at the time of our advance into Cyrenaica and Tripolitania in 1942–43 no steps of any kind had been taken by our military authorities to safeguard museums, records, works of art, "monuments", whether during the active process of occupation or during the subsequent military administration.' Hawkes (p. 219) describes this as 'one of his few published attacks on the Establishment'.

16. Wheeler's accounts are preserved in his own *Antiquaries Paper*, pp. 4–7; and *Preservation*, pp. 1–2 (in which with unusual modesty he refers to himself merely as 'a combatant officer who happened to be on the spot'); and *Still Digging*, pp. 152–60. Also see Woolley, *Record*, pp. 12–17 (a predictably more prosaic account than Wheeler's).

17. See Roger Ling, 'Perkins, John Bryan Ward– (1912–1981), archaeologist', *Oxford Dictionary of National Biography* (Oxford: Oxford University Press, September 23, 2004), <http://www.oxforddnb.com/view/10.1093/ref:odnb/9780198614128.001.0001/odnb-9780198614128-e-31802> [Accessed 7 September. 2018]. Ward-Perkins's name is given in both hyphenated and unhyphenated forms (and at least once as 'J.B.W. Perkins') in contemporary documents, but he himself used the hyphenated form consistently after the Second World War. For this reason I do so too, except when quoting documents that do otherwise. I am grateful to his son Bryan Ward-Perkins for clarification.

18. Wheeler, *Still Digging*, p. 153.

19. Wheeler, *Still Digging*, p. 155. TNA FO 371/37330/1, Major J.B. Ward Perkins, R.A., *Damage to Antiquities in Tripolitania* [before 7 August 1943] [pp. 5–28], p. 1, mentions the second break-in and that no active measures were taken by the Divisional authorities to prevent a recurrence after the first.

20. Wheeler, *Still Digging*, pp. 155–56.

21. Wheeler, *Still Digging*, pp. 157–59. Secretary of State Henderson's August 1943 statement in Parliament summarises these activities but gives the impression they were the result of British preparations rather than the improvisation described by Wheeler: 'In the case of Tripolitania, similar steps were taken as in Cyrenaica to retain in the employ of the military administration the Guardians, both Arab and Italian, who were responsible under the Italian administration for safeguarding the sites. In addition the skilled Italian archaeologists who remained in the country have been kept on the payroll of the British military administration. The large and important museum at Sabratha is completely intact and is being very carefully guarded. Steps have also been taken to safeguard the ruins at this site. The advice of several experienced archaeologists has been obtained and an archaeologist has been seconded to the British military administration at Tripolitania in order further to advise the Deputy Chief Civil Affairs Officer on the measures which should be taken to safeguard all the ruins in the territories.'

22. Wheeler, *Still Digging*, pp. 157, 159–60; *Summary of Paper on Archaeology in the War Zone*, p. 6a (Mareth Line); Woolley, *Record*, p. 15 (four months, August, invalided to Cairo).

23. A number of Ward-Perkins's reports are preserved in the UK National Archives. In TNA T 209/19: Major J.B. Ward Perkins, R.A., *Memorandum on the Antiquities of Tripolitania and Cyrenaica and on the Future of Archaeological Research in these Two Countries* (1943), (pp. 5–6); idem, *Cyrenaica: The Future of Archaeological Research*; idem, *Report on Conservation of Antiquities in Cyrenaica*, (1943), (pp. 7–15); idem, *The Future of Archaeological Research in Tripolitania*, (1943), (pp. 33–45). In TNA FO 371/37330/1, idem, *Damage to Antiquities in Tripolitania* (before 7 August 1943), (pp. 5–28); idem, *Report on Conservation of Antiquities in Tripolitania* (before 7 August 1943), (pp. 10–24). Arab houses and mosques in Tripoli: *Damage to Antiquities in Tripolitania*, Appendix A. Woolley, *Record*, p. 13, mentions reports submitted (separately) by Wheeler and Ward-Perkins in January and February 1943, but those of Ward-Perkins I have seen clearly date to July and August 1943 or a little later. *Memorandum on the Antiquities of Tripolitania and Cyrenaica* (p. 2) indicates it was written at the London Museum, presumably in a period of home leave after he had been invalided to Cairo.

24. Arch of Septimius Severus: *Damage to Antiquities in Tripolitania*, p. 2. Damage caused by traffic of troops at Lepcis Magna (especially men of the 7th Armoured Division on their way to shows in the Roman theatre, with agreed safeguards 'very grudgingly and incompletely observed') and at Sabratha: *Damage to Antiquities in Tripolitania*, pp. 1–4. Damage 'considerable and cumulatively serious', *Report on Conservation of Antiquities in Tripolitania*, p. 7.

25. Wheeler, *Antiquaries Paper*, p. 6: 'Let me interpolate that since then the appointment [held by Ward-Perkins] has been allowed to lapse for I learn that at the present moment Major Ward Perkins is elsewhere and there is no one in charge of the antiquities of Cyrenaica and Tripolitania beyond a partial and inadequate vigilation of Cyrenaica from Alexandria. In other words, the moment outside pressure was relaxed, the structure fell to the ground.' Woolley, *Record*, pp. 15–17.

26. Woolley, *Record*, p. 8: 'He had to be of an age which justified his exemption from combatant duties and, for the most part men already serving in the forces had to be found.'

27. Attempts by British civilian academics and other figures prominent in civilian life

to exercise influence over wartime cultural property protection were kept at arm's length in part by the restriction of the remit of the Macmillan Committee (see pp. 122; 147–48) to post-war restitution issues. To some degree this was necessary, because given direct British experience of the war (and bombing in particular), the perception that civilian 'connoisseurs' might determine strategy to protect enemy monuments was unacceptable to many. In the face of these limitations, the British approach to wartime cultural property protection is sometimes characterised as 'military' in comparison to the 'civilian' approach of the US, where the civilian committees were also important (Woolley, *Record*, p. 6: 'the necessary work in the field was essentially a military responsibility and could only be performed by military personnel under the exclusive control of the Commander-in-Chief concerned'). In fact, while the US civilian committees were of tremendous importance in *supporting* (rather than directing or managing) US military cultural property protection, the Roberts Commission sometimes over-estimated its own importance vis-à-vis the War Department and was more or less tactfully rebuked for it on occasion by the War Department—see, for example, Nicholas, pp. 275–81, on the case of Colonel Henry C. Newton.

28. 1954 Hague Convention, Article 7.2, 'to plan or establish in peace-time, within their armed forces, services or specialist personnel whose purpose will be to secure respect for cultural property and to co-operate with the civilian authorities responsible for safeguarding it.'

29. Wheeler, *Still Digging*, pp. 165–89. In relation to the severity of the German counter-attacks against the Salerno beachhead in the Allied bombing of Pompeii (Chapter 3, above), note Wheeler's account (pp. 171–72) of assembling an emergency scratch force of gunners armed as infantry to counter a breakthrough on 15 September. See also Hawkes, pp. 219–32.

30. Quoted at length in Wheeler, *Still Digging*, pp. 160–62. Presumably Wheeler means Alfred Clapham, who was president in June 1943, unless his published account reflects later confusion and the actual recipient of the letter was Cyril Fox, a close friend of Wheeler and his successor as keeper of the National Museum of Wales, elected president of the society shortly afterwards, in March 1944. Wheeler himself was director, an elected member of the society's council ranking below its president.

31. Wheeler, *Antiquaries Paper*, p. 9.

32. Keeling and others had already raised the question of protection of monuments in Italy in Parliament: 'Ancient Monuments and Art Treasures, Italy (Protection),' House of Commons, *House of Commons Debate* (12 October 1943, vol. 392, cols. 692–94). Surviving correspondence includes: TNA FO 371/37330/20, Wheeler to Dixon, 9 December 1943 [p. 3]; in TNA T 209/1: Keeling to Sinclair, 10 December 1943 [pp. 23–24]; Keeling to Mann, 12 December 1943 [p. 17] (mentioning that Forsdyke had a copy of Wheeler's report); Mann to Keeling, 13 December 1943 [p. 16]; Keeling to Attlee, 19 December 1943 [p. 22] (including mention of the 6 December All-Party Amenities Group meeting); TNA T 209/19, Wheeler to Mann, 10 January 1944 [p. 4] (from the London Museum, enclosing copies of Ward-Perkins's reports from North Africa, Wheeler's own *Preservation* report and his *Antiquaries* paper).

33. The visitors' book pages for that meeting of the Society of Antiquaries show that Wheeler's paper was attended by a range of his existing friends and contacts related to the issues under discussion (J.G. Mann, Cyril Fox), influential museum directors and curators such as Sir Frederic Kenyon and T.D. Kendrick of the British Museum and Sir

Eric Maclagan of the Victoria and Albert Museum, Conservative member of Parliament Hugh Molson, men who were already involved in monuments-protection activities in the services or would take on such roles later (Woolley, Geoffrey Webb, Christopher Norris) and important Roman archaeologists such as Jocelyn Toynbee, K. St. Joseph and Ian Richmond. John Ward-Perkins's father, Bryan (whose grandson Bryan deciphered his signature for me), also attended. I am grateful to Magda Kowalczuk of the Society of Antiquaries library for providing copies of the relevant pages.

34. Wheeler, *Still Digging*, pp. 160–61; *Preservation*; *Antiquaries Paper*, pp. 11–12.

35. Wheeler, *Preservation*, p. 1.

36. Wheeler, *Antiquaries Paper*, p. 3 (four stages); p. 10 (strategic bombing). The reference to Padua was unfortunately prescient given the destruction by Allied bombing of the Mantegna frescoes in the Ovetari Chapel of the Eremitani Church there less than two months later.

37. Much of the relevant correspondence is preserved in the file TNA T 209/1. TNA T 209/1, David Lindsay [Earl of Crawford, formerly a member of the House of Commons] to Keeling, 23 September 1943 (pp. 43–46), refers to the possibility of avoiding unnecessary damage by bombing 'alternative targets—e.g. different parts of a railway line, or alternative marshalling yards. . . . One target may be adjacent to some famous building: another (perhaps equally good) at a safe distance'. TNA T 209/1, J.G. Mann, *Notes of Address, House of Commons*, 26 October 1943 (pp. 26–28), a hand-written document, repeats this idea ('Railway lines and communications can be bombed at alternative spots with equal effect') as well as suggesting that preventing damage from attack (especially from 'bombardment through ignorance') should be prioritised over subsequent salvage of the damaged structures.

38. Woolley, *Record*, p. 21, suggests twelve regional officers and two more at headquarters, had a strictly regional deployment been followed through to the end of the war in Italy.

39. Wheeler, *Antiquaries Paper*, p. 12 (and pp. 7–8 on Italian authorities and their precautions). See Carlotta Coccoli, 'I "fortilizi inespugnabili della civiltà italiana": la protezione antiaerea del patrimonio monumentale italiano durante la Seconda Guerra Mondiale.' In *Pensare la prevenzione: Manufatti, usi, ambienti*. Atti del XXVI Convegno di Studi Scienze e Beni Culturale, Bressanone, 13–16 luglio 2010 (Venice: Editore Arcadia Ricerche, 2010), pp. 409–18.

40. Woolley as archaeological adviser and 'two or three other officers of lesser rank sent out' in Wheeler, *Preservation*, pp. 11–15 (quotation from p. 14).

41. Wheeler, *Still Digging*, pp. 161–65; Wheeler, *Antiquaries Paper*, p. 7 (on Sicily): 'Discovery that no action was being taken on the British side but that two American officers were being appointed by Allied Force Headquarters at Algiers to deal with this problem'. Hawkes, pp. 218–19.

42. *AMGOT Plan for Italy*, p. 9 (= §68) and *General Administrative Instruction* No. 8, 'Monuments and Fine Arts' (on an unnumbered page). While the copy in the UK National Archives was used for the subsequent invasion of mainland Italy (hence nominally *Plan for Italy*), a contemporary minute attached to that copy (11 September 1943) notes that it was taken in its entirety from the 'Sicily edition' except for some marked changes, additions and omissions made between the two invasions. The only such modifications relating to monuments and fine arts are a change in title from 'Antiquities and Monuments' or just 'Monuments', to 'Fine Arts and Monuments'.

43. *AIM Planning Instruction No. 12, Civil Relations.* 141F/3073/A, 14 June 1943, appended as Annexure 14 of *Collier Evidence.* Here Sicily itself is identified only by its code name 'HORRIFIED' in an attempt to maintain secrecy regarding the destination of the invasion force, although the range of monuments identified—Greek, Saracen, Norman, Angevin—make this clear to any reader with a basic knowledge of Mediterranean history. The NARA copy of this document is appended to the report of the December 1943–January 1944 Collier Commission in Naples as evidence that instructions had been given to protect monuments (*Collier Evidence,* Annexure 14—see Part Three).

44. TNA WO 220/277, War Office Directorate of Civil Affairs, *Sicily Zone Handbook,* Part I: *People and Administration,* June 1943, p. 43. Zone handbooks with similar lists were also produced for regions of Italy before the invasion of the mainland, including TNA WO 220/321, *Zone Handbook No. 6 Campania,* Part I: *People and Administration,* August 1943, p. 51, and TNA WO 220/330, *Zone Handbook No. 8 Lazio,* Part I: *People and Administration,* August 1943, pp. 65–66. These remained in use until March 1944, when they were superceded by the *Lists of Protected Monuments* (see Part Three).

45. [Mediterranean Expeditionary Force Headquarters], *Soldier's Guide to Sicily* (MEF 2754/2/6–43, June 1943), pp. 8–10. Intended distribution: *Collier Report,* p. 13. However, it included no specific instructions on how to treat historic buildings.

46. See [Hammond—Maxse], *Memorandum,* p. 1. At this time Hammond also produced a booklet *Brief Notes for CAOs* [Civil Affairs Officers] *on the Care and Preservation of Monuments.*

47. See *Works of Art in Italy:* Part I, pp. 11–12 (Catania), p. 28 (Messina: 'The town was a constant target for our bombers and suffered heavily') and pp. 39–40 (Palermo). Part II, pp. 72–75 ('Palermo suffered the most grievously and more than sixty churches were destroyed or damaged . . . most of the casualties were among the Baroque churches'). Nicholas, pp. 224–25; Zaira Barone, 'Danni bellici. Tutela dei monumenti, restauri e ricostruzioni in Sicilia: I casi di Randazzo e Taormina', in *Guerra, monumenti, ricostruzione,* pp. 445–56; Dagnini Brey, pp. 62–64

48. TNA T 209/2 is the committee's minute book, and its membership and terms of service are provided as an enclosure with letters from retired Archbishop of Canterbury Cosmo Lang and Churchill's private secretary Anthony Bevir inviting Mann to join the committee (TNA T 209/1: Lang to Mann, 15 April 1944 [p. 10]; Bevir to Mann, 7 May 1944 [p. 11]; membership and terms of service [p. 12]).

CHAPTER 8

1. Overviews of the creation of the US civilian commissions are provided by Coccoli, *Monumenti violati,* pp. 33–38, and Nicholas, pp. 209–22. It is worth noting again the substantially greater level of mobilisation and militarisation of wartime British society that meant that the British equivalents of many of the US civilian members of the Roberts Commission, Harvard Group and ACLS Committee had already been in the armed forces for several years by 1943. While, as noted, Sir Leonard Woolley was 63, Mortimer Wheeler 53 and most British monuments officers well into their thirties (Ward-Perkins was young at 32), Dinsmoor was 57, Constable 56, Finley 53, Macleish 51, Taylor 40, Cairns 38, Walker 37 and Sumner Crosby 34. Undoubtedly this affected their outlook, particularly on the balance between military and civilian roles.

2. NARA M1944 RG 239/0010, Correspondence, Finley to Stone, 30 November 1942; NARA M1944 RG 239/0010, Correspondence, Stone to Roosevelt, 8 December 1942; NARA M1944 RG 239/0010, Correspondence, Roosevelt to Stone, 28 December 1942; NARA M1944 RG 239/0010 Correspondence, Roosevelt to Stone, 24 April 1943 (including quotation).

3. NARA M1944 RG 239/0010, Correspondence, Hull to Roosevelt, 21 June 1943; on solicitation of members, see NARA M1944 RG 239/0010, Correspondence, Hull to Finley, 16 July 1943, formally requesting Finley serve as vice-chairman. Later (October 1943) letters from Cairns inviting W.G. Constable, Rufus Morey and Sumner Crosby to join the Commission are also preserved (NARA M1944, RG 239/0010, Correspondence, Cairns to Constable; Cairns to Morey; Cairns to Crosby [all 8 October 1943]).

4. NARA M1944, RG 239/0010, Correspondence, American Commission for the Protection and Salvage of Artistic and Historic Monuments in Europe [Press Release], 25 August 1943, p. 1. By that time Supreme Court Justice Owen J. Roberts had agreed to chair the commission, as Harlan Stone, the original choice, was unable to do so due to pressure of work on the Supreme Court (NARA M1944, RG 239/0013, Correpondence, Stone to Finley, 22 July 1943). The other members announced at that time were Finley (vice-chair), Huntington Cairns (also of the National Gallery, secretary/treasurer), Lehman, Archibald MacLeish (librarian of Congress), Dinsmoor, Taylor, and Paul J. Sachs (Harvard, Fogg Art Museum). The membership was later increased (see above, n. 3) to include W.G. Constable (Boston Museum of Fine Art), Rufus Morey (Princeton) and Sumner Crosby (Metropolitan Museum of Art in New York).

5. NARA M1944 RG 239/0010, Correspondence, Hull to Roosevelt, 21 June 1943; NARA M1944 RG 239/0010, Correspondence, Finley to Stone, 30 November 1942. The other wartime function mentioned is compilation of lists of cultural property appropriated by Axis forces and authorities and then, in the post-war period, there is engagement with the process of restitution of such cultural property.

6. See Chapter 9. At this time the US Army Air Forces (as their title suggests, and unlike the RAF) were a semi-autonomous component of the US Army rather than an entirely autonomous force (which they did not become—as the US Air Force—until 1947). The force was known as the Army Air Corps until 1942, the title of which survived in certain contexts. Thus, for example, most officers such as Mason Hammond technically continued to hold Army Air Corps commissions.

7. Creation of the Harvard Group: Nicholas, pp. 209–10; for the establishment and membership of the subcommittee, NARA M1944, RG 239/0016, Correspondence, William L.M. Burke, *Official Report* [1945], pp. 2–3.

8. NARA M1944, RG 239/0016, Correspondence, William L.M. Burke, *Official Report* [1945], p. 3. Concerns expressed within the ACLS Committee over duplicating Harvard Group activities with questionnaires of their own indicate that this was one of their methods.

9. NARA M1944, RG 239/0098, American Defense–Harvard Group, Committee on the Protection of Monuments, *List of Monuments in Italy: Region of Campania* (June 1943). This is a subsection of *List of Monuments South Italy. Regions: Abruzzi e Molise; Apulia; Basilicata; Calabria; Campania* that in turn is part of *List of Monuments in Italy*. In its general introduction this indicates it was accepted by the [US] War Department in June 1943. Coccoli, *Monumenti violati*, pp. 34–38, provides an overview of the American-produced documentation.

10. The general introduction to *List of Monuments in Italy* provides the following definition of the star rankings: 'No attempt has been made to list every monument that should be preserved. Only important monuments are listed. Those of greater importance are marked with one star (*). Those of greater significance have two stars (**). Those of extreme importance have three stars (***)'.

11. The authors are listed in the general introduction to *List of Monuments in Italy*. Besides Levi, Blake, Bloch and Lehmann were Smith College art historians Ruth Wedgewood Kennedy, her husband Clarence Kennedy, and Rensselaer W. Lee; medieval Latin scholars E.A. Lowe and Leonardo Olschki; Boston Museum of Fine Arts curator Georg Swarzenski; and D. Randall MacIver, a former Egyptologist who had later lived in Italy.

12. The other three-star entries for Campania are the National Museum in Naples (then housing the city's primary art collection as well as its archaeological collections), the Bibliotheca Nazionale in Naples, ancient Herculaneum, the Arch of Trajan at Benevento, the Greco-Roman site of Paestum and the Certosa di San Lorenzo at Padula.

13. NARA M1944, RG 239/0098, American Defense–Harvard Group, Committee on the Protection of Monuments, *Short List of Monuments: Italy* (June 1943), condenses the contents of the Campania long list into just over two typescript pages with 38 monuments, essentially the two- and three-star ones from the long list. For the Zone Handbook Lists (53 monuments on two pages for Campania) see Chapters 7, 11 and 12; Army Service Forces, *Civil Affairs Handbook. Italy. Section 17: Supplementary Atlas*, p. 28.

14. The early history of the ACLS Committee is documented in a series of reports and minutes from 1943: NARA M1944, RG 239/0010, Correspondence, Committee of the ACLS on the Protection of Cultural Treasure in War Areas, *Minutes of the First Full Meeting*, 25 June 1943; NARA M1944, RG 239/0010, Correspondence, Committee of the ACLS on the Protection of Cultural Treasure in War Areas [Dinsmoor], *Summary for the Month of July 1943*, 3 August 1943; NARA M1944, RG 239/0057, Committee of the ACLS on the Protection of Cultural Treasure in War Areas, *Report of the Committee on Collection of Maps, Lists and Descriptions of Art Objects, and Other Information*, 3 November 1943; NARA M1944, RG 239/0095, Reports of the ACLS Committee, *Report on the Activities of the Committee of the ACLS on the Protection of Cultural Treasure in War Areas*, 31 December 1943.

15. Among the latter, Dinsmoor's wife, Zillah Pierce Dinsmoor, and Marguerite (Lévy) Focillon, the widow of French art historian Henri Focillon, are at least mentioned.

16. Touring Club Italiano, *Guida d'Italia: Italia meridionale. Secondo volume: Napoli e dintorni* (Milan: Touring Club Italiano, 1927), between pp. 384–85.

17. NARA M1944, RG 239/0156, Maps Showing Areas to be Spared Destruction/Europe: Hungary-Italy, *Naples Suburban-East*, p. 209. This was subsequently reproduced in a printed civil affairs handbook: Army Service Forces, *Civil Affairs Handbook. Italy. Section 17: Supplementary Atlas*. The level of detail provided by the Frick maps varies considerably, according to the detail shown on the base map copied. While ancient Pompeii and its surroundings are depicted on a tiny scale within a huge tract of suburban Naples and rural Campania, the ancient site of Paestum (as 'Paestum/Pesto') gets its own map that shows individual ancient buildings.

18. The European countries were Albania, Austria, Belgium, Bulgaria, Czechoslovakia, Denmark, France, Greece, Holland, Hungary, Italy, Rumania and Yugoslavia.

19. However, as discussed in Chapter 9, similar moral and philosophical consider-

ations were prominent in British civilian circles comparable to those of the American academics considered here. The range of motivating factors is just as relevant today as it was then. See, for example, Roger O'Keefe and others, *Military Manual*, §§3–6 (pp. 1–2), characterising the rationales for military cultural property protection as essentially three: (1) 'Abstract', that is, moral, philosophical, and intellectual. '[C]ultural property forms a vital part of the cultural identity of individuals, communities, peoples and all humanity'. (2) 'Strategic'. Failure to protect cultural property 'endangers mission success' by provoking hostility from the local population. It is useful for enemy propaganda, and it may diminish support at home and among allies. It can produce income for enemies from looting and illicit trade. It can embitter a conflict, making peace and reconciliation more difficult; by contrast, protecting cultural property 'can win hearts and minds'. (3) 'Legal'.

20. NARA M1944, RG 239/0010, Correspondence, [Charles Rufus Morey], Appendix E of Committee of the ACLS on the Protection of Cultural Treasures in War Areas, *Minutes of the First Full Meeting*, June 25 1943 (Morey's authorship is noted on p. 5); NARA M1944, RG 239/0095, Reports of the ACLS Committee, Committee of the ACLS on the Protection of European Cultural Material [cover letter to questionnaire, c. June 1943], p. 1. The counter-propaganda value of the Roberts Commission was recognised and highlighted frequently by the Office of War Information (OWI)—for example, an autumn 1943 OWI memo emphasises that a key objective in publicising the Roberts Commission was 'to counteract . . . the recent, frequent Nazi line that Americans are "barbarians" trying to "tear down Europe's culture"' (NARA M1944, RG 239/0016, Correspondence, Eugene Rosenfeld [OWI] to A.H. Feller [OWI], *Commission for Protection and Salvage of Artistic and Historic Monuments in Europe*, October 1943).

21. NARA M1944, RG 239/0015, Correspondence [Charles Rufus Morey], *Outline of a Lecture on the Protection of Cultural Treasures* [c. October 1943].

22. See Eugen Weber, 'Western Civilization', in *Imagined Histories: American Historians Interpret the Past*, ed. by Anthony Molho and Gordon S. Wood (Princeton: Princeton University Press, 1998), pp. 206–21; Gilbert Allardyce, 'The Rise and Fall of the Western Civilization Course', *American Historical Review* 87 (1982), 695–725. 'A characteristically American invention'—Allardyce, p. 699.

23. J.C. Stobart, *The Grandeur that was Rome*: *A Survey of Roman Culture and Civilisation* (London: Sidgwick and Jackson, 1912). Stobart's preface explicitly refers to his book's 'point of view [as] that of humanity and the progress of civilisation . . . [t]he value of Rome's contribution to the lasting welfare of mankind'; the book makes extensive use of illustrations of art and archaeology (including Pompeii) and draws heavily on (then) recent discoveries at Pompeii. My own (forthcoming) study of wartime accounts of visits to Pompeii and Rome by British military personnel on leave suggests that they were largely technically skilled lower-middle-class and working-class men. They were in great part self-educated (by reading books such as Stobart's) rather than graduates with advanced training in Classics.

24. This concept still provides a central rationale for the contemporary UNESCO World Heritage List and the 1954 Hague Convention (Art. 1) that in defining cultural property refers to 'property of great importance to the cultural heritage of *every* people' (my italics). Taken in conjunction with that Convention's Preamble ('damage to cultural property belonging to any people whatsoever means damage to the cultural heritage of all mankind, since each people makes its contribution to the culture of the world'), this

argues for universality. See Roger O'Keefe, *Protection*, pp. 103–4, 212, for interpretation of (and problems with) this aspect of the 1954 Hague Convention. Roger O'Keefe and others, *Military Manual*, §§4 (p. 1), provides a more diverse modern definition that retains a notion of universality as one potential factor: 'cultural property forms a vital part of the cultural identity of individuals, communities, peoples *and all humanity*' (my italics).

25. Poland: [Morey], *Outline of a Lecture*, pp. 1–2; 'would not seem important to a foreigner': [Morey], *Outline of a Lecture*, p. 6. For more local definitions of cultural property alongside 'universal' ones, see (again) O'Keefe and others, *Military Manual*, §§ 4 (p. 1)—'cultural property forms a vital part of the cultural identity of *individuals, communities, peoples* and all humanity' [my italics]); §§45 (p. 13)—'Whether a specific object, structure or site is of such importance [i.e. to merit protection] is first and foremost a question for the state on whose territory it is situated. If this state, in good faith, considers given movable or immovable property to be of great importance to its cultural heritage, the property is "cultural property"'.

26. NARA M1944, RG 239/0095, Reports of the ACLS Committee, American Defense–Harvard Group, *The Safeguarding and Care of Works of Art and of Monuments of Cultural Importance in Occupied Countries* [1943], p. 1. This equates (in part) to Roger O'Keefe and others, *Military Manual*, §§5 (pp. 1–2) 'strategic' (failure to protect cultural property 'endangers mission success' by provoking hostility from the local population . . . by embittering a conflict making peace and reconciliation more difficult; protection of cultural property 'can win hearts and minds'). See Rush, 'Cultural Property Protection as a Force Multiplier' as a discussion of this 'pragmatic'/'strategic' rationale.

27. NARA M1944, RG 239/0095, Reports of the ACLS Committee, American Defense–Harvard Group, *The Safeguarding and Care of Works of Art*, p. 2; [Morey], *Outline of a Lecture*, p. 6. Inventories of cultural heritage to be protected, produced for military use by the Harvard Group and the ACLS Committee and subsequently used for US Army Civil Affairs handbooks, include the names and addresses of local civilian heritage officials (including, for example, Amedeo Maiuri, in both the Harvard Lists and British Zone Handbooks for Campania). The importance of effective cooperation between monuments officers and such officials is repeatedly stressed in MFAA reports from Italy, from Hammond in Sicily onwards. In 1943–45, cooperation with local heritage authorities in occupied areas was legally an aspect of Hague Convention 1907 (IV), *Regulations*, Article 43, that required the occupier to respect and uphold existing local law whenever possible. The 1954 Hague Convention (Articles 5 and 7—see Roger O'Keefe and others, *Military Manual*, §§70 = p. 22; §§195–200 = pp. 58–60) also emphasises the importance of military cooperation with the responsible national civilian authorities in occupied territory and more generally (§§82 = p. 26) 'local communities including their religious and other leaders'.

28. [Morey], *Outline of a Lecture*, pp. 4–5. This organizing principle (division into churches, houses, monuments and cultural institutions) is not used in early versions of lists prepared for military use, but it is employed in the later printed versions used in US Civil Affairs handbooks. See, for example, United States Army Service Forces, *Civil Affairs Handbook. Italy. Section 17A: Cultural Institutions, Central Italy*, M353–17A (Washington, DC: US Government Printing Office, 6 July 1944).

29. [Morey], *Outline of a Lecture*, p. 6; NARA M1944, RG 239/0095, Reports of the ACLS Committee, Committee of the ACLS on the Protection of European Cultural

Material, *Questionnaire No. 1: Italian & Balkan Peninsulas & Their Approaches* [c. June 1943], p. 2.

30. While a similarly conservative definition of cultural property is given in the 1954 Hague Convention (Art. 1, 'monuments . . . ; archaeological sites; groups of buildings . . . of historical or artistic interest; works of art; manuscripts, books and other objects of artistic, historical or archaeological interest; . . . scientific collections and important collections of books and archives' as well as buildings such as museums, libraries and refuges intended to house the above), legal commentary and current practice typically employ a broader definition (including e.g. 'indigenous cultural objects or sites')—see Roger O'Keefe and others, *Military Manual*, §§82, p. 25. Protection in conflict of natural heritage and intangible cultural heritage (included respectively in the UNESCO *Convention Concerning the Protection of the World Cultural and Natural Heritage 1972*—the '1972 World Heritage Convention'—and *Convention for the Safeguarding of the Intangible Cultural Heritage* 2003—see O'Keefe and Prott, pp. 77–91, 148–61) are current concerns that were not addressed in Second World War cultural property protection. In fact, it was sometimes felt that even a fairly narrow and tangible definition of cultural heritage was too diffuse. A memo from John Walker to David Finley (both of the [US] National Gallery, and both members of the Roberts Commission) rejected a proposal from the Film Library at the New York Museum of Modern Art to class cinema film and film archives in Germany as protected cultural property, because that might distract monuments officers from 'the main objective, i.e. to look after the great and irreplaceable works of art.' (NARA M1944, RG 239/0015, Correspondence, Walker to Finley, 20 July 1944 and Barry to Macleish, 8 July 1944).

31. [Morey], *Outline of a Lecture*, p. 18.

32. NARA M1944, RG 239/0067, AMG Region 1, Sicily, Advisers for Monuments, Fine Arts and Archives [Capt. F.H.J. Maxse; Lt. P. Cott], *Monthly Report for November of the Advisers for Monuments, Fine Arts and Archives*, 1 December 1943, p. 4.

33. NARA M1944, RG 239/0015, Correspondence, Col. Henry C. Newton (War Department), to Cairns (Roberts Commission), 10 April 1944 (Newton's emphasis). Beyond the desire to protect cultural heritage for secular reasons, this may have reflected some concerns relating to the exacerbation of denominational differences among Christians in the US.

34. NARA M1944 RG 239/0010, Correspondence, Hull to Roosevelt, 21 June 1943.

35. Nicholas, pp. 221–27; [Hammond—Maxse], *Memorandum*, pp. 1–2.

36. NARA M1944 RG 239/0014, Correspondence, Hammond to Finley [September-October 1943], datable from context, since he mentions the arrival of Maxse (6 September 1943) but not that of Perry Cott on 29 October.

CHAPTER 9

1. MFAA *Final Report: General*, p. 25: 95% of the damage to major monuments by Allies caused by air bombardment.

2. MFAA *Final Report: General*, p. 26.

3. NARA M1944 RG 239/0010, Correspondence, Hull to Roosevelt, 21 June 1943; NARA M1944 RG 239/0010, Finley to Stone, 30 November 1942.

4. Roberts Commission, *Special Meeting*, p. 5: Archibald Macleish asked whether

the maps were not only going to Civil Affairs 'but actually to the Bombing Command and . . . with some support and backing. . . . I believe we still do not know that they go to the Bombing Command with anything more than a suggestion that they be looked at . . .'; NARA M1944, RG 239/0015, Correspondence, McCloy (War Department) to Finley (Roberts Commission) 9 October 1943: 'I am advised by the US Army Air Force that your assumption that the maps are used in the planning of aerial operations is correct'. McCloy also claimed in a later letter to the Roberts Commission (NARA M1944, RG 239/0015, Correspondence, McCloy to Finley, 23 October 1943) that 'arrangements now exist whereby these [monuments] officers are made available to the bomber command.' Even if such arrangements existed in theory (and there is no other evidence for them), certainly no monuments officers were engaged with air forces planning in any practical way at this time.

5. Herbert L. Matthews, 'Raid Is Explained', *New York Times*, 20 July 1943, pp. 1, 4. See also 'Planner Explains First Rome Raid. Vatican and Famous Churches Guarded Against Accident.' *New York Times*, 25 August 1943, p. 3; Coccoli, *Monumenti violati*, pp. 143–44; Overy, pp. 522–25; Nicholas, p. 235.

6. *Works of Art in Italy*: Part I, pp. 58–61. San Lorenzo is of 4th century AD origin, substantially reconstructed in the 13th century. A single bomb hit the nave of the church, destroying its roof and the western façade and causing substantial damage to the interior, including destruction of the fine 12th-century pulpit. On the other hand, the 6th-century eastern core of the church was largely unscathed.

7. Herbert L. Matthews, 'Italian Art Under Shellfire', *Harper's Magazine*, 1 May 1945, 559–68 (p. 561).

8. NARA M1944, RG 239/0015, Correspondence, Col. Henry C. Newton, *Report on Conversation with Herbert Matthews*, 24 April 1944.

9. NARA M1944, RG 239/0015, Correspondence, American Commission for the Protection and Salvage of Artistic and Historic Monuments in Europe, *American Scholars Work to Save Europe's Cultural Heritage* [c. 27 October 1943], p. 3. Date from attached cover letter.

10. 'AMG "Medics" Provide First Aid to Italy's Many Artistic War Casualties', *Stars and Stripes—Italy*, 16 December 1943, pp. 1–2 (typescript copy in NARA M1944, RG 237, 0067).

11. Roberts Commission, *Special Meeting*, p. 5; ibid. p. 14 for Hilldring's views expressed directly: 'I wouldn't be in as good a position today as I am if we had the same thing in our force as the RAF. They wonder how, with the RAF's program of variable [sic = area?] bombing, we are going to weave this thought of the [Roberts] commission in with it, where does it fit?' Finley on Naples, and Dinsmoor on Pompeii, ibid., pp. 6, 12.

12. Biddle; Parks, '"Precision" and "Area" Bombing'; Baldoli and Knapp, pp. 7, 34. It is notable that civilian inhabitants of Naples who lived through it typically perceived American bombing as *less* precise than British—see Gribaudi, pp. 91–93.

13. See Woolley, *Record*, pp. 28 (quoting US MFAA officer Col. Henry C. Newton): 'hopelessly insufficient in number and not suitable for the purposes required, though "excellent as a basis for further exploration of the problem"'. The underlying accuracy problem was noted by the director of the Bombing Survey Unit, Solly Zuckerman, *Apes to Warlords*, p. 211 (discussed pp. 149–50): 'I found that a street map, copied from Baedeker and marked to show important buildings that were to be avoided, was now to be included in the briefing kit for each Italian town that was likely to be a target. I fear,

however, that I did not have enough faith in the bombing accuracy of the aircrews to believe that this could be of real value.'

14. 'Ancient Monuments and Art Treasures, Italy (Protection)', 12 October 1943.

15. TNA T 209/1, Keeling to Sinclair, 10 December 1943 [pp. 23–24]: 'I enclose copy of letter addressed to Attlee. Attached to it is a note by Wheeler. It contains striking evidence of damage to Pompeii which could have been avoided if the R.A.F. had had expert knowledge at their disposal. The Germans did not fail to publish photographs of the damage, for anti-British propaganda.'

16. FO 371/37330/3, Molson to Anthony Eden [Foreign Secretary], 21 September 1943 [pp. 3–4], quoting the Bishop of Chichester (George Bell, a central figure in the opposition to British area bombing) over the possible appointment of 'some connoisseur' and suggesting (in a handwritten postscript) Blount [sic] for the job. Molson also claimed, unfairly, that Woolley needed a counterpart because 'his interest in buildings does not, so far as I know, extend much beyond 500 BC'; TNA T 209/1 Lindsay to Keeling, 23 September 1943 [pp. 43–46] also recommends Blunt. However, nothing came of this, partly because the general idea was dismissed as admirable but impractical (TNA FO 371/37330/3, G.E. Millard [Foreign Office] to R.H. Melville [Air Ministry], 10 October 1943 [pp. 7–8]) and partly because Blunt, publically exposed as a Soviet spy in 1979, was otherwise occupied working for MI5 at the time.

17. TNA T 209/1, Keeling to Mann, 13 October 1943 [p. 33]; a draft of a memo prepared for submission to the War Cabinet by Forsdyke, Mann and others (TNA T 209/1, *The Protection of Cultural Monuments and Works of Art*, November 1943 [pp. 72–73, but various other drafts are included]) reports that 'a very brief list' of places in Italy had already been submitted to Bomber Command in North Africa.

18. Webster and Frankland, Vol. 1, pp. 299–336; the 'Butt Report' of August 1941, assessing the accuracy of RAF strategic bombing at that time, is included as Appendix 13 of Webster and Frankland Vol. 4, pp. 205–13; Overy, pp. 263–79, 288–99.

19. TNA T 209/1, 'Maclagan's Suggestions' [November 1943?] [p. 83], typed notes with handwritten title.

20. TNA T 209/1, Mann to Lindsay, 27 September 1943 [pp. 50–51]. But see Overy, pp. 180–81 on evidence of ambivalence in British public attitudes towards bombing others.

21. Baldoli and Knapp, p. 33, on the origins of this distinction in British policy in 1942. The fact that strategic bombing was largely conducted against enemy home territory (especially Germany and Austria) and close air support and interdiction against enemy-occupied territory (Italy after the armistice of September 1943, and France and the Low Countries throughout the war) underpinned this dichotomy.

22. TNA T 209/6, Sinclair to Macmillan Committee, 28 July 1944 [pp. 9–11].

23. The rationales for MAAF engagement with the protection of cultural heritage are set out in UKNA AIR/51/184/21, 16 February 1944, memo to Tedder's successor as MAAF commander, US Lieutenant-General Ira Eaker, by his deputy, RAF Air Marshal John Slessor: 'Apart from the [inherent] merits of the case—which I think are very strong—I think it is most important from the point of view of repercussions in the House of Commons and Congress, and on public opinion towards the Air Forces in Britain and America to ensure that our orders on the subject are clear and reasonable.'

24. TNA T 209/1, Keeling to Mann, 13 October 1943 [p. 33]: 'were you able to see a copy of the list sent out to Tedder, and are you satisfied with it?'

25. TNA T 209/1, Keeling to Sinclair, 10 December 1943 [pp. 23–24].

26. TNA FO 371/37330/24, HQ AMG [Capts. Mason Hammond and F.H.J. Maxse], *Report of the Advisers on Fine Arts and Monuments in AMGOT for October 1943*, 1 November 1943, p. 7; NARA M1944, RG 239/0067, MFAA Field Reports, HQ AMG Monuments, Fine Arts and Archives Sub-Commission [Maj. P.K. Baillie Reynolds], *First Monthly Report, for November 1943*, 4 December 1943, p. 3; NARA M1944, RG 239/0067, MFAA Field Reports, HQ ACC, Sub-Commission for Monuments, Fine Arts and Archives [Maj. P.K. Baillie Reynolds], *Third Monthly Report, for January 1944* [nd, c. February 1944], p. 2.

27. Zuckerman, *Apes to Warlords*, p. 211, suggests he took the issue to Tedder, who responded positively, although other evidence (below) suggests Tedder himself already had an interest in the issue that he was actively pursuing by the start of October. MFAA *Final Report: General*, p. 7 states 'there is no evidence that the information [Zuckerman] requested and received ever reached competent headquarters', implying that the activities of Zuckerman and Tedder/Norris (see below) were entirely separate.

28. Philip Ziegler, 'Zuckerman, Solly, Baron Zuckerman (1904–1993), scientist and public servant.' *Oxford Dictionary of National Biography* (Oxford: Oxford University Press, 10 January 2013)
<https://www.oxforddnb.com/view/10.1093/ref:odnb/9780198614128.001.0001/odnb-9780198614128-e-53466> [accessed 15 April 2019].

29. NARA M1944, RG 239/0067, MFAA Field Reports, HQ AMG Monuments, Fine Arts and Archives Sub-Commission [Maj. P.K. Baillie Reynolds], *First Monthly Report, for November 1943*, 4 December 1943, p. 3. Zuckerman's account (*Apes to Warlords*, p. 211) differs from the contemporary report in detail but not in substance, and confirms that he was familiar with the ACLS maps ('a street map, copied from Baedeker and marked to show important buildings that were to be avoided') while doubting their practical value.

30. See Coccoli, *Monumenti violati*, pp. 75–85.

31. Shinnie went on to become an important figure in British research in the archaeology of Africa after the war.

32. NARA M1944, RG 237/0067, MFAA Field Reports [Major J.B.W. Perkins (sic)], *Prevention of Unnecessary Bombing of Works of Art: Air Force Measures*, WP/0322, 3 February 1944. The original report had been compiled by Fl.-Lt. Christopher Norris, a pre-war art historian serving in the RAF. In addition to historic buildings and the permanent locations of major art collections, Norris had included a list of nine known or suspected temporary refuges for movable works of art (including Montecassino, to where materials evacuated from Naples had been sent in the first instance), most of which were initially unknown to the MFAA and not included on other lists. This had caused a number of problems, not least those at Castel del Monte near Bari, identified by Ward-Perkins on the same trip. See Nigel Pollard, 'Refuges for Movable Cultural Property in Wartime: Lessons for Contemporary Practice from Wartime Italy,' *International Journal of Heritage Studies* (2019). http://dx.doi.org/10.1080/13527258.2019.1678052.

CHAPTER 10

1. MFAA *Final Report: General*, p. 7.

2. MAAF *Ancient Monuments of Italy*. This is substantially fewer than the 'about a

hundred' mentioned in Ward-Perkins's report, and the preface to the atlas includes the names of several cities not included among the aerial photographs in the UK National Archives copy. The loose-leaf nature of the atlas raises the possibility that the UK National Archives copy is incomplete. However, the preface (p. 2) states that photographs of some towns were not available at the time of its compilation, but would be added later. Rome itself is a particularly curious omission, although given the number of cultural sites there, it may have been treated separately. No such exceptional circumstances would seem to explain Siena, also missing.

3. United States Army Service Forces, *Civil Affairs Handbook. Italy. Section 17B: Cultural Institutions, Central Italy*, M353-17B (Washington, DC: US Government Printing Office, July 1944), pp. 124–27; the ACLS Frick Map includes a similar number of sites to the *Civil Affairs Handbook*.

4. See Woolley, *Record*, pp. 28–29 (quoting US MFAA officer Col. Henry C. Newton): 'much superior to the maps. . . . since each photograph clearly indicates terrain features and other essential information. The picture itself clearly represents the area as the pilot and the bombardier actually observe it. The [Civil Affairs] Handbooks will be of great assistance but cannot be compared with an aerial photograph . . .'

5. Hague Convention (IV) 1907, *Regulations*, Article 27.

6. MFAA *Final Report: General*, p. 7. NARA M1944, RG 239/0067, MFAA Field Reports, ACC Sub-Commission for Monuments, Fine Arts and Archives [Maj. Ernest T. De Wald], *Fifth Monthly Report, for March 1944*, 9 April 1944 does not specifically mention such a meeting, although it does have a section (on p. 3) entitled 'Air Force Measures' on MAAF's production and dissemination of *Ancient Monuments of Italy* and its preface. This report also includes as an attachment *Function of Monuments, Fine Arts and Archives Sub-Commission*, 23 March 1944, that lists among its major functions to 'maintain liaison with ground *and air-forces* [my italics] in order to furnish them with information concerning historic monuments within their respective theatre of operations.' On the assignments to Army headquarters, MFAA *Final Report: General*, p. 8.

7. The signal (essentially setting out the rules of engagement contained in MAAF, *Ancient Monuments of Italy*) went out under the signature of Tedder's successor, US Lieutenant-General Ira Eaker. It was drafted by his deputy, RAF Air Marshal John Slessor, with Norstad's input, as shown in TNA AIR 51/184/21, memo from Slessor to Eaker, 16 February 1944. In it, Slessor states 'there must be no "passing the buck" to lower formations and we must accept our full responsibility.'

8. MFAA *Final Report: General*, p. 26, repeated in Woolley, *Record*, p. 29.

9. C.J.C. Molony, *Victory in the Mediterranean*. Part I, *1st April to 4th June 1944*. The History of the Second World War: The Mediterranean and Middle East. Vol. VI. (London: HMSO, 1984), pp. 33–44, 157–61.

10. TNA CAB 79/71/11, War Cabinet Chiefs of Staff Committee *Minutes*, 1 March 1944, p. 1 [p. 2].

11. TNA CAB 79/71/12, War Cabinet Chiefs of Staff Committee *Minutes*, 2 March 1944, p. 3 [p. 4].

12. The USAAF *Combat Chronology* for 1944 records relevant missions on 11 March (medium bombers, Florence marshalling yards); 23 March (B-26s, Florence Campo di Marte); 11 April (B-26s, Siena marshalling yards); 22 April (US P-47 fighter-bombers, Siena marshalling yards); 1 May (mediums, Florence Campo di Marte and Florence [sic]); 2 May (mediums, Florence/Campo di Marte and WNW of Florence); 23 May

(mediums, marshalling yards on the Florence-Empoli line); 26 May (mediums, rail targets in the Florence area).

13. Baldoli and Knapp, p. 40.

14. W. Jackson, *Victory in the Mediterranean.* Part III, *November 1944–May 1945.* The History of the Second World War: The Mediterranean and Middle East. Vol. VI. (London: HMSO, 1988), pp. 304–5; *RAF Narrative*, Vol. 2, pp. 192–96.

15. As Overy (p. 533) observes, Venice had already been bombed, in breach of the MAAF rules of engagement, on 20 April 1944 by USAAF bombers that treated it as a target of opportunity when their primary target (Trieste) could not be located.

16. *RAF Narrative*, vol. 2, pp. 278–80. The crews reported that their bombing had been accurate, and the realisation that Vatican territory had been struck in error only came when Vatican officials lodged a complaint. The British Chiefs of Staff excused the bombing by analogy with MAAF's statement on the status of churches in the city of Rome.

17. *Works of Art in Italy*, Part II, pp. 39–40. See Coccoli, *Monumenti violati*, pp. 348–50.

18. Three-stars: Army Service Forces, *Civil Affairs Handbook. Italy. Section 17B*, p. 111.

19. Matthews, 'Italian Art Under Shellfire', p. 3, on this attack states 'the compounded errors of human beings and complicated mechanisms will inevitably spill stray bombs hundreds of yards from the briefed aiming point', noting that the Eremitani church was only 800 yards (731 metres) from the railroad station that was the briefed aiming point, so it was impossible to guarantee that all the bombs would fall in the intended target pattern.

20. MFAA *Final Report: General*, p. 26; *Works of Art in Italy*, Part II, pp. 55–56 (Treviso); 60–66 (Verona); 66–69 (Vicenza). See Coccoli, *Monumenti violati*, pp. 350–52 on Treviso and pp. 353–54 on Verona; Baldoli and Knapp, p. 184 on Treviso.

21. *Works of Art in Italy*, Part II, p. 131.

22. Overy, pp. 572–82; Baldoli and Knapp, pp. 30–32; Nicholas, pp. 282–85; Lambourne, pp. 67–73. On tactical bombing in Normandy, see Gooderson.

23. Jerrold F. Elkin, 'Application of the Open City Concept to Rome 1942–1944', *Air Force Law Review* 22 (1980), pp. 188–200, provides a thorough review. See also H. Wayne Elliott, 'Open Cities and (Un)defended Places', *The Army Lawyer* (April 1995), 39–50 (especially pp. 45–46); Nicholas, p. 235.

24. Nicholas, pp. 243, 257–59. Ultimately the Germans chose not to defend either Rome or Florence, and the Allies did not attack the latter directly, choosing to encircle and isolate the city from the west. Nevertheless, massive damage was inflicted by German demolition of the Arno bridges, in part perhaps motivated by the speed with which Allied forces had advanced through and beyond Rome earlier that summer.

25. NARA M1944, RG 239/0015, Correspondence, Finley to McCloy, 2 October 1943. Roger O'Keefe, *Protection*, pp. 41–42, shows that the concept of historic towns as 'sanctuaries of art' had its roots in proposals by the Nederlandsche Oudheidkundige Bond in 1918–19.

26. Roberts Commission, *Special Meeting*, pp. 8 (Finley), 10–11 (Hilldring, Bundy), 14 (Bundy).

27. NARA M1944 RG 239/0015, Correspondence, McCloy to Finley, 23 October 1943.

28. NARA M1944, RG 239/0010, Correspondence, Finley [Memo], 27 October 1943.

29. A contemporary Allied report lists eight official deposits for Rome and Lazio (Cantalupo Sabina, Capraola, Casamari, Civitacastellana, Gennazzano, Montecassino, Tarquinia and Tivoli) and notes that the contents of most were returned to Rome and/or the Vatican by June 1944 (MFAA *Final Report: Lazio*, pp. 28–30). On the reconcentration of collections in Rome and the Vatican, see Nicholas, pp. 241–43; on the role of the Vatican, see Micol Forti, '"I trasporti possono iniziati da oggi, 15 novembre 1943": Il ruolo del Vaticano nella salvaguardia del patrimonio artistico italiano,' in *Musei e monumenti in guerra 1939–1945: Londra, Parigi, Roma e Berlino*, ed. by Teresa Calvano and Micol Forti (Città del Vaticano: Edizioni Musei Vaticani, 2014), pp. 149–65. On the issue of refuges for portable works of art in wartime Italy, see Pollard, 'Refuges.'

30. MFAA *Final Report: Lazio*, pp. 24, 30.

31. Nicholas, p. 251; Dagnini Brey, pp. 31–35; Pollard, 'Refuges'; TNA T 209/30/3, Headquarters Allied Commission APO 394, Subcommission for Monuments, Fine Arts and Archives. *Report on the German Kunstschutz (MFA&A Branch) in Italy Between 1943 and 1945*. 20914/MFAA. 30 June 1945, pp. 2–4. On the wider issue of protection and damage in Florence and Siena at this time, see Coccoli, *Monumenti violati*, pp. 177–99.

32. MFAA officer Frederick Hartt stated in a contemporary report, 'according to all advices available in Rome the works of art had all been moved back into Florence subsequent on the German declaration that Florence was an open city. The presence of the great works of Art [sic] from Florence museums and churches still in highly exposed positions came therefore as a considerable surprise': TNA T 209/17/2, 2nd Lt. Frederick Hartt, USAAF, Allied Military Government, Office of the Monuments and Fine Arts Officer [sic], Region VIII, *Report on Deposits of Works of Art*, RVIII/31/MFAA/10.1, 22 August 1944, p. 1 [p. 7]; see MFAA *Final Report, General*, p. 13.

33. NARA M1944, RG 239/0015, Correspondence, Rt. Rev. Michael J. Ready (NCWC) to Cairns, 4 May 1944, with attached memorandum.

34. Elliott (p. 46) argues that 'open city' declarations in the Second World War (citing the example of Manila in 1941–1942 as well as Rome) typically were attempts to use the cultural status of a city as leverage to protect it regardless of the presence of lawful military objectives.

35. NARA M1944, RG 239/0015, Correspondence, McCloy to Finley, 7 May 1944, in response to Finley's letter of 19 April.

36. The Vaucher Commission was more properly the Commission for Protection and Restitution of Cultural Material established by the Conference of Allied Ministers of Education on 19 April 1944. It was essentially a vehicle for representatives of allied nations under German occupation, on which Britain and the US had observer status. For the wording of the resolution, see TNA T 209/5/2 [p. 32] and NARA M1944, RG 239/0010, *Resolution Adopted by the Vaucher Committee*, 10 July 1944.

37. See NARA M1944, RG 239/0010, Correspondence, William Bell Dinsmoor, *Destruction of Cultural Monuments in France by "Carpet Bombing"* [July 1944]. This also includes the resolution by the Vaucher Committee (10 July 1944), the supporting resolution by the Roberts Commission (27 July 1944) and a cover letter from Chief Justice Roberts as chair of the commission to Henry L. Stimson, the secretary of war (18 August 1944). On the British side: TNA T 209/2, Committee for the Restitution of Works of Art in Enemy Hands, *Minutes*, 2 August 1944, p. 2 [p. 20] for sympathy but refusal; TNA

T 209/5/2, Mann [as secretary of Macmillan Committee] to Vaucher Commission, 8 August 1944 [pp. 28–29] on interference with military matters; TNA T 209/5/2, C.P. Harvey [for Vaucher Commission] to Macmillan Committee, 13 July 1944 [pp. 30–31, with the terms of the resolution appended on p. 32]; TNA T 209/5/2, Maclagan to Mann, 20 June 1944 [pp. 53–56].

38. NARA M1944, RG 239/0098, American Defense–Harvard Group, Committee on the Protection of Monuments, *List of Monuments: Central Italy. Lazio* (June 1943), p. 33 (the abbey and its library are each assigned two stars); United States Army Service Forces, *Civil Affairs Handbook. Italy. Section 17A: Cultural Institutions, Central Italy*, M353–17A (Washington, DC: US Government Printing Office, 6 July 1944). p. 17 (two stars); *Lists of Protected Monuments: Lazio* p. 17 (three stars). The last two of these were actually published after the bombing of the Abbey, but prepared beforehand.

39. The decision-making process and the destruction of the Abbey are discussed thoroughly and effectively by David Hopgood and David Richardson, *Monte Cassino: The Story of the Most Controversial Battle of World War II* (Cambridge MA: Da Capo Press, 2002).

CHAPTER 11

1. Peter G. Stone, 'The Challenge of Protecting Heritage in Times of Armed Conflict', *Museum International* 67 (2016), 40–54, identifies seven.

2. These were the deliberate burning of the Biblioteca della Società Reale in Naples by German troops on 12 September 1943; and again by German troops, of the Neapolitan State Archive and collections from the Museo Civico Filangieri that had been evacuated to the Villa Montesano at San Paolo Belsito near Nola, on 30 September 1943, apparently in revenge for the killing of a comrade nearby. See *Works of Art in Italy*, Part I, p. 37; Part II, pp. 80–84; MFAA *Final Report General*, p. 27; Riccardo Filangieri, 'Report on the Destruction by the Germans, September 30, 1943, of the Depository of Priceless Historical Records of the Naples State Archives', *The American Archivist* 7.4 (1944), pp. 252–55; MFAA *Final Report Campania*, p. 19. Besides being advertised prominently in contemporary British and US newspaper reports (pp. 175–76), these examples of deliberate destruction were used to characterise German attitudes in a booklet later published for circulation to Allied troops, NARA M1944, RG 239/0063, MFAA Field Reports, Allied Force HQ, *Preservation of Works of Art in Italy*, 8 May 1944, p. 2. The other prominent example of deliberate damage was the destruction of the Roman ships recovered from Lake Nemi in the Alban Hills, burned in their lakeside museum by German soldiers (MFAA *Final Report General*, pp. 12, 27; *Works of Art in Italy*: Part I, p. 38).

3. Colonel Geoffrey Webb, (British) director of monuments and fine arts at SHAEF (so for the Allied invasion of northwestern Europe), singled out the importance of the Naples experience and the subsequent Commission of Enquiry in establishing effective policies and emphasising command responsibilities in protecting cultural sites in occupied areas (TNA T 209/2, Committee for the Restitution of Works of Art in Enemy Hands, *Minutes*, 13 June 1944, p. 4 [p. 14]).

4. See Emberling, Hanson and Gibson; and *The Destruction of Cultural Heritage in Iraq*, that address a number of important issues and instances. On failure to provide adequate security for mosques (including the Al-Askari mosque in Samarra) as a fac-

tor in sectarian violence, see Benjamin Isakhan, 'Creating the Iraq Cultural Property Destruction Database: Calculating a Heritage Destruction Index', *International Journal of Heritage Studies* 21 (2015), 1–21. http://dx.doi.org/ 10.1080/13527258.2013.868818

5. As argued by Rush, 'Cultural Property Protection as a Force Multiplier in Stability Operations'.

6. [British] War Office, *Manual of Military Law*, Chapter XIV, para. 429; United States War Department, *Rules of Land Warfare*, pp. 81–82, para. 318.

7. NARA M1944, RG 239/0062, MFAA Field Reports, AMG HQ [Capt. M. Hammond], *Position of Advisers on Fine Arts & Monuments in AMG*, 24 October 1943. The key points of this memo are re-iterated and developed further in another memo by Hammond addressed to what he describes as the 'Advisory Committee on the Preservation of Monuments and Works of Art in London and Washington': NARA M1944, RG 239/0062, MFAA Field Reports, AMG HQ [Capt. M. Hammond] *Conservation of Monuments and Works of Art*, 1 November 1943.

8. The 2003 Coalition invasion of Iraq, as cited above, provides a vivid example of the continuing crucial importance for cultural property protection of this transitional period between combat operations and stabilisation/occupation.

9. Molony, *Campaign in Italy*, pp. 324–44.

10. Photograph captioned 'A company of men has set up its office between the columns (Doric) of an ancient Greek temple of Neptune, built about 700 B.C.', 22 September 1943, online version, <https://catalog.archives.gov/OpaAPI/media/531170/content/arcmedia/media/images/43/1/43-0050a.gif> [accessed 16 July 2019]. The attribution to Neptune/Poseidon is a conventional one, and probably the temple was dedicated to the goddess Hera. News of this reached the Roberts Commission, and David Finley remarked 'I understand there is an office, for example, in the Temple of Paestum. That is probably something the high command could avoid if there was someone to call the fact to his attention that it is a Greek temple of importance' (Roberts Commission, *Special Meeting*, p. 7).

11. Herbert L. Matthews, 'Croce Fears Loss of Art Treasures', *New York Times*, 28 September 1943, p. 4.

12. 'Refugees Tell How Nazis Lay Naples Waste', *New York Herald Tribune*, 30 September 1943, pp. 1–2 (Palazzo Reale and opera house); Seymour Korman, 'Allies Drive for Rome as Naples Falls', *Chicago Daily Tribune*, 2 October 1943, p. 4 (quotation).

13. Herbert L. Matthews, 'Primitive Man in Naples', *New York Times*, 13 October 1943, p. 22: 'As a group the Nazis are primitives and as individuals they are spiritually stunted adolescents. What they can't understand they have a lust to destroy, whether it is the creative and self-respecting human being or the things such a human being creates'; see also Morin, 'Most Naples Art Treasures Survive Fight', p. 15; 'Naples Preserved Most of Its Art'.

14. *Collier Report*, pp. 4–6. In addition to the Royal Palace itself, offices in the adjacent Bibliotheca Nazionale were ransacked and there was damage and looting at the nearby Castel Nuovo, including the desecration of 15th-century tombs and decapitation of the mummies they contained.

15. *Collier Evidence*, p. 3

16. *Collier Report*, pp. 6 (82nd Airborne Division); 7–8 (general); *Collier Evidence*, p. 2 (Gardner).

17. *Collier Evidence*, pp. 44–46 (Huggan), pp. 46–47 (Bruxner-Randall), pp. 49–51

(McCall). Relations and coordination between AMG and the British (57th Area) and US (Peninsular Base Section) static base formations that did much of the requisitioning in Naples were generally poor, and similar problems of military occupation extended to civilian hospitals: C.R.S. Harris, *Allied Military Administration of Italy 1943–1945*. History of the Second World War United Kingdom Military Series (London: HMSO, 1957), p. 92.

18. For an overview of conditions in Naples and the military government issues they raised, see Harris, *Allied Military Administration of Italy*, pp. 84–92. Norman Lewis, *Naples '44* (London: Collins 1978), provides a vivid (and justly famous) personal account of the account of life in Naples under Allied occupation.

19. [Gardner], *Division of Fine Arts*, p. 1.

20. Wheeler, *Preservation*, p. 2.

21. [Gardner], *Division of Fine Arts*, p. 4; NARA M1944, RG 239/0067, HQ Region 3 AMG [Maj. Paul Gardner], *December Report of the Division of Fine Arts*, 10 January 1944, p. 3.

22. [Gardner], *Division of Fine Arts*, p. 3.

23. Letter from Lush (at AMG Headquarters 15th Army Group) to [British] Major-General Sir Brian Robertson, deputy chief administrative officer, AFHQ Advance Administrative Echelon, 12 December 1943, included as *Collier Evidence*, Annexure 3. Robertson, the senior Allied logistical officer in Italy, responded to Lush unsympathetically, arguing that criticisms of the behaviour of Allied troops were unjustified and (for example) noting that while military occupation of public areas in Naples was 'unsightly', 'squares and parks in England and S Africa are being similarly disfigured' [Robertson was South African].

24. *Collier Report*, p. 15

25. See Harris, pp. 95–98, on this separation as a wider issue.

26. NARA M1944, RG 239/0067, MFAA Field Reports, HQ ACC Sub-Commission for Monuments, Fine Arts and Archives [Maj. P.K. Baillie Reynolds], *Fourth Monthly Report, for February 1944*, 10 March 1944, p. 1. See Coccoli, *Monumenti violati*, pp. 70–71, on this problem.

27. These issues are all set out in NARA M1944, RG 239/0067, MFAA Field Reports, HQ AMG Monuments, Fine Arts and Archives Sub-Commission [Major P.K. Baillie Reynolds], *Second Monthly Report, for December 1943*, 4 January 1943 (quotation from p. 2).

28. Wheeler, *Antiquaries Paper*, p. 11; Woolley's recommendations are set out in his memo submitted to the chief civil affairs officer, 'The Commandeering of the Naples Museum for Military Purposes', 7 December 1943, *Collier Evidence*, Annexure 1.

CHAPTER 12

1. NARA M1944, RG 239/0098, American Defense–Harvard Group, Committee on the Protection of Monuments, *List of Monuments in Italy: Region of Campania* (June 1943), p. 4.

2. The pre-war Touring Club Italiano guides provide a detailed account of the museum's contents and layout at that time (Touring Club Italiano, *Napoli e dintorni*, pp. 187–265).

3. Maiuri, pp. 90–92, 112–15. On the evacuation of movable cultural property from Naples and other centres in Campania, see Pollard, 'Refuges'; Benedetta Gentile and Francesco Bianchini. *I misteri dell'Abbazia: Le verità sul tesoro di Montecassino* (Florence: Casa Editrice Le Lettere 2015), pp. 32–35, 147–54; Stella Casiello, 'Prevenzione, ricostruzione e restauri a Napoli e in Campania: Criteri, metodi, esperienze,' in *Musei e monumenti in guerra 1939–1945: Londra, Parigi, Roma e Berlino*, ed. by Teresa Calvano and Micol Forti (Vatican City: Edizioni Musei Vaticani, 2014), pp. 250–62; Dagnini-Brey, pp. 21–22; MFAA *Final Report, Campania*, p. 18. Copies of the wartime inventory of the archaeological collections sent from Naples to Montecassino, and of all the materials eventually received in Rome (see below), are preserved in the War Damage Collection of the British School at Rome (Box E, MFAA Inv. Nos. 70 and 71).

4. Maiuri, pp. 112–15; seated Mercury from Stabiae; dancing faun; Apollo from Pompeii; Pompeian ephebe; small 'dancer'; Mercury at rest; sleeping satyr; drunken Silenus; small ephebe from Pompeii; five 'dancers'; two 'wrestlers' and the bronze head conventionally identified as that of Aulus Gabinius, are the individually crated works listed, with others (two deer, a range of philosopher and ruler busts) crated in groups (MFAA Inv. No. 71, BSR War Damage Documents Box E). For the Villa of the Papyri sculpture, see Carol C. Mattusch, *The Villa dei Papiri at Herculaneum: Life and Afterlife of a Sculpture Collection* (Los Angeles: J. Paul Getty Museum, 2005), pp. 189–94 ('wrestlers' as "Boy Athletes"); 195–15 ('dancers' as *peplophoroi*); 216–22 (seated Hermes/Mercury); 230–33 ('Aulus Gabinius' as 'Herm-head'); 321–26 (drunken Silenus/satyr).

5. Maiuri, pp. 92, 145–47; MFAA *Final Report: Campania*, pp. 18–19. The material evacuated to Montecassino was moved from there by elements of the German Hermann Goering Division in October 1943, long before the Allied bombing of the Abbey. After a period at the Division's Headquarters near Spoleto, much of it was forwarded to Rome and the Vatican for safe-keeping. However, a portion (including paintings and Herculaneum bronze sculptures) was instead sent to Germany, supposedly as a gift for Goering himself. Ultimately it was recovered from the great repository of looted cultural property at Alt-Aussee in Austria and returned to Naples (see Pollard, Refuges; Gentile and Bianchini).

6. Maiuri, pp. 124–25. The Royal Society library had been burned by the Germans on 12 September, the day on which the garrison commander declared martial law throughout the city.

7. Morin, 'Most Naples Art Treasures Survive'; 'Naples Art Treasures Found Mainly Unscathed,' *New York Herald Tribune*, 7 October 1943, p. 3.

8. 'Unique Collection of Art Treasures Taken Away by Germans in Italy,' *New York Times*, 10 November 1943, pp. 25–26. According to Maiuri (pp. 145–47) this had become public knowledge on 7 November.

9. *Paris-Soir* cited in the index files of the Roberts Commission: NARA M1944, RG 239/0121 [Roberts Commission], *Geographical Working Files: Italy, Naples*, 6 October 1943; Maiuri, pp. 133, 136.

10. [Gardner], *Division of Fine Arts*, p. 1. The 75% estimate is given by Gardner in his subsequent monthly report (1 December 1943).

11. [Gardner], *November Report*, p. 3; Maiuri, pp. 136–38. Maiuri's account (published in 1956) sets everything a few days later, noting that he himself initially was at Pompei, but all of Gardner's reports and the Collier Commission report specify 17 November. For an overview, see Coccoli, *Monumenti violati*, pp. 103–5.

12. NARA M1944 RG 239/0067 HQ 5th Army AMG Region 3 [Major Paul Gardner], memo to Col. Edgar Erskine Hume, 18 November 1943 (attached to [Gardner], *Division of Fine Arts*); *Collier Evidence*, p. 7 on inflammable materials and oxygen.

13. It is important to note that this characterisation of the planned requisition as 'military convenience' rather than 'military necessity' is not my own anachronistic, retrospective, civilian perspective, but a view held by numerous contemporary military officers, including not only the members of the Collier Commission (pp. 194–97) but also individuals who had commanded men in battle in the First and/or Second World War (including Mortimer Wheeler and Paul Gardner) and who consequently might be presumed to be sympathetic to the needs of British and American wounded. Even if a historic building had to be occupied for these purposes, it could be argued that the Museo Nazionale was of such exceptional importance (one of only two 'three-star' monuments in Naples in the 'Harvard Lists') that it could and should have been spared regardless.

14. Woolley, 'Commandeering of the Naples Museum', *Collier Evidence*, Annexure 1; also see Maiuri, pp. 130–31, 138–39 on the various meetings and preparatory work.

15. [Gardner], *December Report*, p. 2; Maiuri, pp. 133, 140.

16. [Gardner], *December Report*, p. 2.

17. NARA M1944, RG 239/0067, MFAA Field Reports, HQ AMG Monuments, Fine Arts and Archives Sub-Commission [Major P.K. Baillie Reynolds], *Second Monthly Report, for December 1943*, 4 January 1943, p. 2.

18. Woolley certainly claimed credit early on for many of the improvements in organisation and practice detailed below, and perhaps justifiably so. A US report on the potential establishment of a British equivalent to the Roberts Commission (NARA M1944, RG 239/0010, Correspondence, *Artistic and Historic Monuments* [c. February 1944?]) summarises a memo (5 February 1944) by Woolley. On his inspection visit to Italy, Woolley states, he found the organisation 'admirable in theory [but] not adapted to conditions in the field', with officers who were not deployed where they were most needed and who 'lacked the authority necessary for the performance of their duties'; accordingly, Woolley claims, he 'remodelled' it, with some officers 'attached to the fighting commands.' 'As a result of Sir LW's recs., Gen. Eisenhower issued general orders . . .' A letter (NARA M1944, RG 239/0018, Correspondence, Woolley to Dinsmoor, 2 March 1944, outlining the history of monuments protection and the development of Woolley's own role in it includes the claim that on his visit to Sicily and Italy he 'advised certain modifications which on the whole have been approved and put into force'; that the application of the Civil Affairs regional system for allocating personnel had proved problematic for Fine Arts, so it was 'my conclusion' that officers should be pooled; that monuments officers should be of higher rank 'so as to give them the necessary authority'; and 'I urged' separation of Education and Fine Arts.

19. NARA M1944, RG 239/0067, MFAA Field Reports, HQ Region 3 AMG [Maj. Paul Gardner], *Monuments of Fine Arts and Cultural Institutions Occupied by Allied Troops*, 20 December 1944.

20. Preserved as Annexure 16 of *Collier Evidence*. Peninsula and Peninsular (noun and adjective, referring to Italy) are both employed inconsistently in its title.

21. NARA M1944, RG 239/0067, MFAA Field Reports, Allied Force Headquarters, Office of the Commander-in-Chief [Gen. Dwight D. Eisenhower], *Historical Monuments*, 29 December 1943.

22. Preserved as Annexure 18 of *Collier Evidence*.

23. NARA M1944, RG 239/0067, MFAA Field Reports, HQ Region 3 AMG [Major Paul Gardner] [untitled] memo to Public Relations Office, 25 February 1944, p. 5, 'this General Order, however, has had no effect on the occupations of historical monuments in this region even though listed in the Zone Handbook.'

24. NARA M1944, RG 239/0067, MFAA Field Reports, HQ ACC, Sub-Commission for Monuments, Fine Arts and Archives [Maj. P.K. Baillie Reynolds], *Third Monthly Report, for January 1944*. [nd, c. February 1944], p. 2: 'It is perhaps unfortunate that the "Zone Handbook" lists, which are by no means exhaustive, should have been given such high authority.'

25. NARA M1944, RG 239/0018, Correspondence, Woolley to Dinsmoor, 2 March 1944: 'Of course [the Zone Handbook lists] do not compare with the lists supplied by Harvard and Washington; but the C-in-C could not possibly have extended his veto for army use to all the monuments given in these exhaustive lists and it was the brevity of the Zone Handbook lists that recommended them.' Woolley in TNA T 209/2, Committee for the Restitution of Works of Art in Enemy Hands, *Minutes*, 25 May 1944, p. 1 [p. 9]: 'but the difficulty was to get [the lists] through in sufficient numbers to the subordinate officers in the field. The lists in the F.O. Zone Handbooks being shorter had been found more useful than the lists prepared at Harvard.' Dinsmoor in the minutes of the previous meeting of the Macmillan Committee, 16 May 1944, pp. 2–3 [pp. 6–7]: 'There had been difficulties in ensuring the distribution [of the US-produced documentation] to subordinate officers in the field, and danger of supplying them with too much detail'.

26. *Collier Report*, pp. 4–8.

27. *Collier Report*, p. 3.

28. *Collier Evidence*, p. 6.

29. *Collier Report*, p. 3.

30. NARA M1944, RG 239/0063, MFAA Field Reports, HQ Region 3 ACC [Maj. Paul Gardner], *June 1944 Report of the Division of Fine Arts, Region 3, ACC*, I July 1944, p. 3.

31. *Collier Report*, p. 18.

32. *Collier Report*, p. 21.

33. *Collier Report*, pp. 19–20.

34. *Collier Report*, p. 17.

35. *Collier Report*, pp. 19–20.

36. Rush, 'Cultural Property Protection as a Force Multiplier'.

37. *Collier Report*, pp. 12, 21.

38. Headquarters ACMF, *Property of Historical and Educational Importance in Italy—Preservation of*. 17 February 1944. See Coccoli, *Monumenti violati*, p. 107.

39. NARA M1944, RG 239/0067, MFAA Field Reports, Headquarters Allied Armies Italy (Administrative Echelon), *Administrative Instruction No. 10: Preservation of Property of Historical or Educational Importance in Italy*, 30 March 1944 (typescript). A typed or printed version is included in each part of the *Lists of Protected Monuments*.

40. *Lists of Protected Monuments: Campania*. This is a typescript, as is *Lists of Protected Monuments: Sicily*. *Lists of Protected Monuments: Lazio* and subsequent volumes were produced as printed booklets.

41. The recommendations of the *Collier Report* (p. 19) particularly single out the star-ranking system as 'the essential feature of such lists', perhaps explaining why it was adopted for the *Lists of Protected Monuments*.

42. The grid references provided are single points rather than (e.g.) polygons, some-

times with quite imprecise results. Thus, for example, the *Lists of Protected Monuments: Campania* grid reference for Pompeii is N4139, a point adjacent to the House of Caecilius Iucundus (V.1.26) that in itself gives little indication of the extent of the site around it. This is still a recurring issue in incorporating cultural data into 'no-strike' lists for military use.

43. NARA M1944, RG 239/0063, MFAA Field Reports, Allied Force HQ, *Preservation of Works of Art in Italy*, 8 May 1944, p. 2. The NARA copy is one forwarded from Maj. Gen. Hilldring to the Roberts Commission, with a cover letter dated 16 May 1944. See Coccoli, *Monumenti violati*, p. 108.

44. NARA M1944, RG 239/0067, MFAA Field Reports, HQ ACC, Sub-Commission for Monuments, Fine Arts, and Archives [Maj. J B. Ward Perkins], *Attached Documents Relative to Preservation of Monuments and Fine Arts in Italy*, 1 June 1944.

CHAPTER 13

1. MFAA Final Report: General , p. 4

2. MFAA *Final Report: General*, p. 7. Its evacuation by the British is described as 'under way' by early April (NARA M1944, RG 239/0067, MFAA Field Reports, ACC Sub-Commission for Monuments, Fine Arts and Archives [Maj. Ernest T. De Wald], *Fifth Monthly Report, for March 1944*, 9 April 1944, p. 3), presumably in response to the recent publication of *Administrative Instruction No. 10*, but clearly that was an optimistic report.

3. MFAA *Final Report: Campania*, p. 9: 'Its eventual repair and occupation as a soldier's club by NAAFI/EFI [see pp. 201–3], despite a few acts of high-handed "restoration" by the troops involved, unquestionably save[d] the badly damaged fabric from further disintegration'; p. 16 'Sadly shaken by some 23 direct bomb hits then despoiled by civilians and troops prior to and during occupation of city. Considerable repair work done by Genio Civile and Army Engineers, not always under proper supervision.' Woolley, *Record*, p. 28 'needless destruction of several damaged but reparable features.'

4. NARA M1944, RG 239/0067, MFAA Field Reports, HQ Region 3 ACC [Maj. Paul Gardner], *March Report of Division of Fine Arts*, 1 April 1944, p. 3.

5. NARA M1944, RG 239/0067, MFAA Field Reports, Edward Croft-Murray (Sub-Commission for Monuments, Fine Arts and Archives), *The Royal Palace of Naples: An Historical and Architectural Guide to the State Apartments* (1944); Felice De Filippis, *The Royal Palace of Naples* (1945). The facilities included a theatre and cinema, a restaurant, tea rooms, bars, lounges, valeting facilities, a welfare office and a shop.

6. MFAA *Final Report: General*, p. 6.

7. Despite the palace being a three-star monument in the *Lists of Protected Monuments: Campania* that formed the basis of the *Instruction* (upgraded from two stars on the Harvard Lists, perhaps due to the presence of the evacuated collections). It is now on the UNESCO World Heritage List.

8. NARA M1944, RG 239/0067, MFAA Field Reports, HQ Region 3 AMG [Maj. Paul Gardner], *Requisition of Entire Palazzo Reale at Caserta*, 13 December 1943. Gardner's comment 'If military necessity requires' requisition of furnishings suggests a weary familiarity with 'military necessity' advanced as a pretext for misappropriation of all kinds.

9. NARA M1944 RG 239/0067, MFAA Field Reports, HQ ACC Sub-Commission for Monuments, Fine Arts and Archives [Capt. E. Croft-Murray], *Report on the Palace of Caserta*, 23 March 1944.

10. This discussion of the Castel del Monte and Mercogliano refuges was previously published in Pollard, 'Refuges'. NARA M1944, RG 239/0067, MFAA Field Reports, Major J.B.W. Perkins [sic], *Art Collections Stored at CASTEL DEL MONTE (Prov. BARI)*, WP/0321, 6 February 1944; NARA M1944 RG 239/0067, MFAA Field Reports, AMG HQ Monuments, Fine Arts and Archives [Maj. J.B. Ward Perkins], *Monuments, Fine Arts and Archives in APULIA*, 29 January 1944, pp. 1–2; *Works of Art in Italy:* Part II, p. 77. MFAA *Final Report: Apulia, Calabria, Lucania*, p. 13. The fortress of Castel del Monte is on the current UNESCO World Heritage List <https://whc.unesco.org/en/list/398> [accessed 09/07/19].

11. [Gardner], *December Report*, p. 3. See Pollard, 'Refuges'.

12. Cott was in Sicily from 29 October 1943 and he and Fred Maxse remained there until March 1944, when the Sicily office was closed and responsibility returned to Italian civilian authorities (MFAA *Final Report: Sicily*, p. 3).

13. NARA M1944, RG 239/0067, MFAA Field Reports, HQ ACC Sub-Commission for Monuments, Fine Arts and Archives [Maj. P.K. Baillie Reynolds], *Fourth Monthly Report, for February 1944*, 10 March 1944, p. 3; NARA M1944 RG 239/0067, MFAA Field Reports, AMG Sicily Region HQ Adviser on Monuments, Fine Arts and Archives [Lt. P. Cott], *Requisition of Palazzo Reale, Palermo*, 6 February 1944 (quotation on p. 1).

14. 'Appendix I: Works of Art' in TNA WO 220/277, War Office Directorate of Civil Affairs, *Sicily, Zone Handbook:* Part I, p. 43.

15. *Lists of Protected Monuments: Sicily*, p. 2. The palace, including the chapel, is now on the UNESCO World Heritage List as part of 'Arab-Norman Palermo and the Cathedral Churches of Cefalú and Monreale' <https://whc.unesco.org/en/list/1487> [accessed 09/07/19].

16. MFAA *Final Report: Sicily*, p. 16. '[Overall] No damage done except from fire during occupancy by troops. Repairs 422,700 lire. Capella Palatina endangered but saved without harm.'

17. NARA M1944, RG 239/0067, MFAA Field Reports, R. Soprintendenza ai Monumenti della Sicilia to Lt. Perry Cott, 23 February 1944 (translation) appended to letter ACC Sicily Regional HQ Advisers on Monuments, Fine Arts and Archives [Lt. Perry Cott], *Fire at Palazzo Reale, Palermo*, 24 February 1944 (that includes Cott's recommendations).

18. The planning and preparation is summarised in NARA M1944, RG 239/0067, MFAA Field Reports, HQ Region 4 AMG [Maj. Ernest T. De Wald], *Report of Division MFAA Region IV to Date*, 1 March 1944 and MFAA *Final Report: General*, pp. 10–11.

19. NARA M1944, RG 239/0067, MFAA Field Reports, AMG Region 4, Division of Monuments and Fine Arts, *Protected Monuments in AMG Region 4 Between the Front Lines and Rome* [c. January 1944]; NARA M1944, RG 239/0067, MFAA Field Reports, AMG Region 4, Division of Monuments and Fine Arts, *Protected Monuments in AMG Region 4 Above and Beyond Rome* [c. January 1944].

20. Nicholas, p. 249; MFAA *Final Report: General*, pp. 10–11. The latter (p. 11) refers to 'some uneasy moments' in Rome including plans to requisition the 'Farnesina Palace' [sic—presumably the Villa Farnesina] as a billet for Canadian nurses and the Palazzo Venezia as a Red Cross Enlisted Men's Club, but both were 'successfully fought and . . . with good will and patience all around.'

CONCLUSIONS

1. Not 'bombed 156 times by the RAF in August 1943' as stated by Hugh Eakin, 'Cultural Casualties of War,' *Wall Street Journal*, 17 May 2013.

2. Religious significance clearly should be a crucial factor in defining cultural property for protection, perhaps more important than general historical significance (see Isakhan), and one which is largely taken for granted today. However, wartime thinking on this (and the balance between the historical and religious significance of Montecassino Abbey) was quite confused, as shown in Chapter 8.

3. My only significant criticism of García y García is that he seems to suggest Pompeii *did* deserve some such complete immunity (pp. 18, 25–26) and his outrage at the damage to the site (inflicted under exigent circumstances at a critical time of the war) seems disproportionate relative to the damage done by its mere exposure to the elements over the centuries, and the consequent conservation problems. Beard's (pp. 18–19) characterisation of wartime damage as an episode in 'the slow death that the city has suffered since it began to be uncovered in the mid-eighteenth century' seems more proportionate.

4. See Coccoli, *Monumenti violati*, p. 92; 'I "fortilizi inespugnabili"'; Casiello, 'Prevenzione, ricostruzione e restauri a Napoli'; Nezzi; and *Works of Art in Italy*, Part I, pp. 33–37, on the successes of in situ protection in Naples including the Museo Nazionale, Monteoliveto church (Sant'Anna dei Lombardi), S. Domenico Maggiore and S. Giovanni a Carbonara; and the notable failure at Santa Chiara, where the protective wooden scaffolding added fuel to the fire that severely damaged the church. The Italian wartime publication *La protezione del patrimonio artistico nazionale dalle offese della guerra aerea* (Florence: Le Monnier, 1942) provides more information on protective measures in general, including vivid photographs.

5. This experience and its implications for modern evacuation policies are discussed in detail in Pollard, 'Refuges.'

6. For example, Switzerland. See Rule no. 6 of *Switzerland's Regulation on Ten Basic Rules for the Protection of Cultural Property* (2013) cited at <https://ihl-databases.icrc.org/customary-ihl/eng/docs/v2_cou_ch_rule38> [accessed 15 November 2019].

7. See, for example, 1954 Hague Convention Art. 5.2 on military occupation, emphasising the need for 'close cooperation with [national] authorities.'

APPENDIX B

1. This overview derives from 'Appendix 1: Air Organisation and Chain of Command of Forces Engaged in the Invasion of Italy as at 3rd Sept. 1943', in *RAF Narrative*, Vol. 1; and Appendix XII of the published RAF official history (Richards and Saunders), 'Order of Battle, Mediterranean Air Command, 10th July, 1943', along with information from the material documenting the bombing itself.

2. In addition to the strategic and tactical components, Northwest African Air Forces also included coastal, reconnaissance, troop-carrier and training elements. Besides the Tactical Bomber Force, the fighter and fighter-bomber components of Northwest African Tactical Air Force included the British Desert Air Force assigned to support the British 8th Army in southern Italy, and the US 12th Air Support Command operating in support of 5th Army in the Salerno area. Support by the Tactical Bomber Force was divided between the two armies.

3. NWAAF, *Air Intelligence Weekly Summary* No. 44; *War Room Monthly Summary*, September 1943.

4. An RAF medium bomber squadron had an initial establishment (paper strength) of 20 aircraft, a light bomber squadron of 16 or 24. A USAAF Bombardment Group was composed of Bombardment Squadrons, somewhat smaller than RAF squadrons, with 12 aircraft in a heavy bombardment squadron, 13 in a medium squadron. The Group was a more important level of organisation in the USAAF than the Squadron, and this is reflected in the contemporary documentation. USAAF Groups (typically of three or four squadrons) were roughly equivalent to RAF Wings (typically two or three squadrons), and a USAAF Wing was roughly equivalent in size to an RAF Group.

5. The highest US national command structures in the Mediterranean were Twelfth Air Force, which contributed bombers to the Northwest African Strategic Air Force and provided a major component (12th Air Support Command) to Northwest African Tactical Air Force. However, Twelfth Air Force did not exercise operational control of these elements; Ninth Air Force, which had bombers in the Mediterranean theatre of operations at this time, was not engaged in operations near Pompeii.

APPENDIX C

1. United States Strategic Bombing Survey, *Bombing Accuracy*, Exhibit (= Table) 'R' and p. 12 (for mean bombing altitude).

APPENDIX D

1. Webster and Frankland, Vol. 1, pp. 387–89.

Bibliography

Alcala, Ronald T.P., 'Babylon Revisited: Reestablishing a Corps of Specialists for the Protection of Cultural Property in Armed Conflict', *Harvard National Security Journal* 6 (2015), 206–54.

Allardyce, Gilbert, 'The Rise and Fall of the Western Civilization Course,' *American Historical Review* 87 (1982), 695–725.

Archaeology, Cultural Property, and the Military, ed. by Laurie W. Rush (Woodbridge, UK: Boydell Press, 2012).

Baldoli, Claudia, and Andrew Knapp, *Forgotten Blitzes: France and Italy under Allied Air Attack, 1940–1945* (London: Continuum, 2012).

Barone, Zaira, 'Danni bellici. Tutela dei monumenti, restauri e ricostruzioni in Sicilia: I casi di Randazzo e Taormina', in *Guerra, monumenti, ricostruzione*, pp. 445–56.

Beard, Mary, *Pompeii: The Life of a Roman Town* (London: Profile Books, 2008).

Biddle, Tami Davis, 'British and American Approaches to Strategic Bombing: Their Origins and Implementation in the World War II Combined Bomber Offensive', *Journal of Strategic Studies* 18 (1995), 91–144.

Blumenson, Martin, *Salerno to Cassino*. The United States Army in WWII: The Mediterranean (Washington, DC: The Department of the Army, 1969).

Boylan, Patrick J., *Review of the Convention for the Protection of Cultural Property in the Event of Armed Conflict (The Hague Convention of 1954)* (London: City University, 1993).

Briggs, Asa, *The War of Words. The History of Broadcasting in the United Kingdom*, Vol. III (Oxford: Oxford University Press, 1970).

British Bombing Survey Unit, *The Strategic Air War Against Germany: Report of the British Bombing Survey Unit* (London: Cass, 1998, a reprint of TNA AIR 10/3866 of 1949).

British Explosive Ordnance (Washington, DC: US Department of the Navy, Ordnance Systems Command, 1946).

Carr, L.C., *Tessa Verney Wheeler: Women and Archaeology Before World War Two* (Oxford: Oxford University Press, 2012).

Casiello, Stella, 'Prevenzione, ricostruzione e restauri a Napoli e in Campania: Criteri, metodi, esperienze', in *Musei e monumenti in guerra 1939–1945: Londra, Parigi, Roma e Berlino*, ed. by Teresa Calvano and Micol Forti (Vatican City: Edizioni Musei Vaticani, 2014), pp. 250–62.

Che cosa hanno fatto gli Inglesi in Cirenaica (Rome: Ministero della Cultura Populare, 1941).

Coccoli, Carlotta, 'I "fortilizi inespugnabili della civiltà italiana": la protezione antiaerea del patrimonio monumentale italiano durante la Seconda Guerra Mondiale', in *Pensare la prevenzione: Manufatti, usi, ambienti*. Atti del XXVI Convegno di Studi Scienze e Beni Culturale, Bressanone, 13–16 luglio 2010 (Venice, Editore Arcadia Ricerche, 2010), pp. 409–18.

Coccoli, Carlotta, 'Ricostruzione postbellica e patrimonio urbano in Giappone: Orientamenti di ricerca,' *Storia Urbana* 140–41 (2013), 5–16.

Coccoli, Carlotta, *Monumenti violati: Danni bellici e riparazioni in Italia nel 1943–1945. Il ruolo degli alleati* (Florence: Nardini Editore, 2017).

Coles, Harry L., and Albert K. Weinberg, *Civil Affairs: Soldiers Become Governors*. The United States Army in World War II, Special Studies, 6 (Washington, DC: The Department of the Army, 1964).

Cultural Heritage in the Crosshairs: Protecting Cultural Property during Conflict, ed. by Joris Kila and James A. Zeidler (Leiden: Brill, 2013).

Dagnini Brey, Ilaria, *The Venus Fixers* (New York: Farrar, Straus and Giroux, 2009).

Delizia, Francesco, 'Benevento: ricerca archeologica e ricostruzione della città' in *Guerra, monumenti, ricostruzione*, ed. by Lorenzo De Stefani (Venice: Marsilio Editori, 2011), pp. 410–15.

Destruction of Cultural Heritage in Iraq, ed. by Peter G. Stone and Joanne Farchakh Bajjaly (Woodbridge, UK: Boydell Press, 2011).

Donnison, F.S.V., *Civil Affairs and Military Government: Central Organization and Planning*. History of the Second World War. United Kingdom Military Series (London: HMSO, 1966).

Edens, Christopher, 'Woolley, Sir (Charles) Leonard (1880–1960), archaeologist,' *Oxford Dictionary of National Biography* (Oxford: Oxford University Press, September 23, 2004) <http://www.oxforddnb.com/view/10.1093/ref:odnb/9780198614128.001.0001/odnb-9780198614128-e-37021> [accessed 7 September 2018].

Edsell, Robert M., *Monuments Men* (London: Preface Publishing, 2009).

Elkin, Jerrold F., 'Application of the Open City Concept to Rome 1942–1944,' *Air Force Law Review* 22 (1980), 188–200.

Elliott, H. Wayne, 'Open Cities and (Un)defended Places,' *The Army Lawyer* (April 1995), 39–50.

Emberling, Geoff, Katharyn Hanson, and McGuire Gibson, *Catastrophe! The Looting and Destruction of Iraq's Past* (Chicago: Oriental Institute of the University of Chicago, 2008).

Filangieri, Riccardo, 'Report on the Destruction by the Germans, September 30, 1943, of the Depository of Priceless Historical Records of the Naples State Archives,' *The American Archivist* 7.4 (1944), 252–55.

Forti, Micol, '"I trasporti possono iniziati da oggi, 15 novembre 1943": Il ruolo del Vaticano nella salvaguardia del patrimonio artistico italiano,' in *Musei e monumenti in guerra 1939–1945: Londra, Parigi, Roma e Berlino*, ed. by Teresa Calvano and Micol Forti (Vatican City: Edizioni Musei Vaticani, 2014), pp. 149–65.

García y García, Laurentino, *Danni di guerra a Pompei: Una dolorosa vicenda quasi dimenticata* (Rome: "L'Erma" di Bretschneider, 2006).

Gentile, Benedetta, and Francesco Bianchini, *I misteri dell'Abbazia: Le verità sul tesoro di Montecassino* (Florence: Casa Editrice Le Lettere 2015).

Gooderson, Ian, *Air Power at the Battlefront: Allied Close Air Support in Europe* (London: Cass, 1998).

Granfield, Alun, *Bombers over Sand and Snow: 205 Group RAF in World War II* (Barnsley, UK: Pen and Sword Aviation, 2011).

Gribaudi, Gabriella, *Guerra totale: Tra bombe alleate e violenze naziste. Napoli e il fronte meridionale 1940–1944* (Turin: Bollati Boringhieri 2005).

Guerra, monumenti, ricostruzione: Architetture e centri storici italiani nel secondo conflitto mondiale, ed. by Lorenzo De Stefani (Venice: Marsilio Editori, 2011).

Gulley, Thomas F., *The Hour Has Come: The 97th Bomb Group in World War II* (Dallas: Taylor Publishing Company, 1993).

Harris, C.R.S., *Allied Military Administration of Italy 1943–1945*. History of the Second World War. United Kingdom Military Series (London: HMSO, 1957).

Hartt, Frederick, *Florentine Art under Fire* (Princeton: Princeton University Press, 1949).

Hawkes, Jacquetta, *Adventurer in Archaeology: The Biography of Sir Mortimer Wheeler* (London: St. Martin's Press, 1982).

Hopgood, David, and David Richardson, *Monte Cassino: The Story of the Most Controversial Battle of World War II* (Cambridge MA: Da Capo Press, 2002).

House of Commons, 'Cyrenaica and Tripolitania (Ancient Monuments),' *House of Commons Debate* (5 August 1943, vol. 391, col. 2485).

House of Commons, 'Ancient Monuments and Art Treasures, Italy (Protection),' *House of Commons Debate* (12 October 1943, vol. 392, cols. 692–94).

Isakhan, Benjamin, 'Creating the Iraq Cultural Property Destruction Database: Calculating a Heritage Destruction Index', *International Journal of Heritage Studies* 21 (2015), 1–21. http://dx.doi.org/ 10.1080/13527258.2013.868818

Jackson, W., *Victory in the Mediterranean*. Part III, *November 1944–May 1945*. The History of the Second World War: The Mediterranean and Middle East. Vol. VI (London: HMSO, 1988).

Kunsthistoriker im Krieg: deutscher militärischer Kunstschutz in Italien 1943–1945, ed. by Christian Fuhrmeister, Johannes Griebel, Stephan Klingen, and Ralf Peters (Cologne: Böhlau-Verlag, 2012).

La protezione del patrimonio artistico nazionale dalle offese della guerra aerea (Florence: Le Monnier, 1942).

Lambourne, Nicola, *War Damage in Western Europe* (Edinburgh: Edinburgh University Press, 2001).

Lewis, Norman, *Naples '44* (London: Collins, 1978).

MacBean, John A., and Arthur S. Hogben, *Bombs Gone: The Development and Use of British Air-Dropped Weapons from 1912 to the Present Day* (Wellingborough, UK: Patrick Stephens Ltd., 1990).

MacFarland, Stephen L., *America's Pursuit of Precision Bombing, 1910–1945* (Washington, DC: Smithsonian Institution, 1995).

Maiuri, Amedeo, *Taccuino napoletano: Giugno 1940-luglio 1944* (Naples: Vajro Editore, 1956).

McIntosh, Jane, 'Wheeler, Sir (Robert Eric) Mortimer (1890–1976), archaeologist and broadcaster'. *Oxford Dictionary of National Biography* (Oxford: Oxford University Press, October 4, 2012) <http://www.oxforddnb.com/view/10.1093/ref:odnb/9780198614128.001.0001/odnb-9780198614128-e-31825> [accessed 7 September 2018].

Mattusch, Carol C., *The Villa dei Papiri at Herculaneum: Life and Afterlife of a Sculpture Collection* (Los Angeles: J. Paul Getty Museum, 2005).

Milligan, Spike, *Mussolini: My Part in His Downfall* (London: Penguin Books, 1980).

[UK] Ministry of Defence, *Campaign Execution*. Joint Doctrine Publication 3-00 (third edition, October 2009) <https://assets.publishing.service.gov.uk/government/> [accessed 3/8/18].

Molony, C.J.C., *The Campaign in Sicily 1943 and the Campaign in Italy, 3rd September 1943 to 31st March 1944*. The History of the Second World War: The Mediterranean and Middle East, Vol. V (London: HMSO, 1973).

Molony, C.J.C., *Victory in the Mediterranean. Part I, 1st April to 4th June 1944*. The History of the Second World War: The Mediterranean and Middle East. Vol. VI (London: HMSO, 1984).

Moshenka, Gabriel, and Tim Shadla-Hall, 'Mortimer Wheeler's Theatre of the Past,' *Public Archaeology* 10 (2011), 46–55.

Nezzi, Marta, 'The Defence of Works of Art from Bombing in Italy during the Second World War', in *Bombing, States and Peoples in Western Europe 1940–1945*, ed. by Claudia Baldoli, Andrew Knapp, and Richard Overy (London: Continuum, 2011), pp. 101–20.

Nicholas, Lynn H., *The Rape of Europa: The Fate of Europe's Treasures in the Third Reich and the Second World War* (New York: Vintage Books, 1995).

O'Keefe, Patrick J., and Lyndel V. Prott, *Cultural Heritage Conventions and Other Instruments: A Compendium with Commentaries* (Builth Wells, UK: Institute of Art and Law, 2011).

O'Keefe, Roger, *The Protection of Cultural Property in Armed Conflict* (Cambridge: Cambridge University Press, 2006).

O'Keefe, Roger, Camille Péron, Tofig Musayev, and Gianluca Ferrari, *Protection of Cultural Property: Military Manual* (Paris: UNESCO, 2016).

Overy, Richard, *The Bombing War: Europe 1939–1945* (London: Allen Lane, 2013).

Pace, Steve, *B-25 Mitchell Units of the MTO* (Oxford: Osprey Publishing, 2002).

Pardini, Albert L., *The Legendary Norden Bombsight* (Atglen, PA: Schiffer Books, 1999).

Parks, W. Hays, 'Air War and the Law of War', *Air Force Law Review* 32 (1990), 1–225.

Parks, W. Hays, '"Precision" and "Area" Bombing: Who Did Which, and When?' *Journal of Strategic Studies* 18 (1995), 145–74.

Pesce, Angelo, *Scafati e l'agro: Cinquant' anni fa la Guerra* (Scafati: Comune di Scafati, 1993).

Piccialuti Caprioli, Maura. *Radio Londra 1940–1945: Inventario delle trasmissioni per l'Italia* (Rome: Ministero per I Beni Culturali ed Ambientali, 1976).

Picone, Renata, 'Restauri di guerra a Pompei: Le Case del Fauno e di Epidio Rufo', *Offese di guerra: Ricostruzione e restauro nel Mezzogiorno d'Italia*, ed. by Stella Casiello (Florence: Alinea Editrice, 2011), pp. 19–41.

Pocock, Simon, *Campania 1943: Enciclopedia della memoria*, Vol. II, *Provincia di Napoli. Parte I, Zona est* (Naples: Three Mice Books, 2009).

Pollard, Nigel, 'Refuges for Movable Cultural Property in Wartime: Lessons for Contemporary Practice from Wartime Italy,' *International Journal of Heritage Studies* 26 (2020), 667–83. http://dx.doi.org/10.1080/13527258.2019.1678052.

Pollard, Nigel, '"Bombing Pompeii!!! Why Not the Pyramids?" Myths and Memories of the Allied Bombing of Pompeii, August–September 1943', in *Critical Perspectives on Cultural Memory and Heritage: Construction, Transformation and Destruction*, ed. by Veysel Apaydin (London: UCL Press, 2020), pp. 239–51.

Richards, Denis, *The Fight at Odds*. Royal Air Force 1939–1945, Vol. 1 (London: HMSO, 1953).

Richards, Denis, and Hilary St. George Saunders, *The Fight Avails*. Royal Air Force 1939–1945: Vol. II (London: HMSO, 1954).

Rorimer, James J., *Survival: The Salvage and Protection of Art in War* (New York: Abelard Press, 1950).

Ross, Stewart Halsey, *Strategic Bombing by the United States in World War II* (London: McFarland & Co., 2003).

Rowland, Ingrid D., 'The Wrong Way for Pompeii', *New York Review of Books*, 22 October 2013 <https://www.nybooks.com/daily/2013/10/22/pompeii-wrong-way/> [accessed 18 September 2018].

Rowland, Ingrid D., *From Pompeii: The Afterlife of a Roman Town* (Cambridge: Harvard University Press, 2014).

Rush, Laurie W., 'Cultural Property Protection as a Force Multiplier in Stability Operations: World War II Monuments Officers' Lessons Learned', *Military Review* 36 (March–April 2012), 36–43.

Satterthwaite, Dale J., *Truth Flies with Fiction: Flying B-25 Bombers into Battle during 1944* (Bloomington, IN: Archway Publishing, 2014).

Shepherd, Elizabeth J., 'Le foto aeree della II Guerra Mondiale conservate in aerofototeca nazionale e il loro potenziale informative per la sicurezza nazionale', *Bollettino di archeologia on line*, 6 (2015), 111–30 <http://bollettinodiarcheologiaonline.beniculturali.it/wp-content/uploads/2018/12/VI-2015-1-4.-E.-J.-Shepherd-.pdf> [accessed 08/087/19].

Stobart, J.C., *The Grandeur that Was Rome: A Survey of Roman Culture and Civilisation* (London: Sidgwick and Jackson, 1912).

Stone, Peter G., *Cultural Heritage, Ethics and the Military* (Woodbridge, UK: Boydell Press, 2011).

Stone, Peter G., 'The Challenge of Protecting Heritage in Times of Armed Conflict', *Museum International* 67 (2016), 40–54.

Toman, Jiří, *The Protection of Cultural Property in the Event of Armed Conflict* (Aldershot, UK: UNESCO/Dartmouth Publishing, 1996).

Touring Club Italiano, *Guida d'Italia: Italia meridionale*, Vol. 2, *Napoli e dintorni* (Milan: Touring Club Italiano, 1927).

United States Army Service Forces, *Civil Affairs Handbook: Italy*, Section 17: *Supplement on Cultural Institutions, Supplementary Atlas*, M353–17 (Washington, DC: US Government Printing Office, 4 January 1944).

United States Army Service Forces, *Civil Affairs Handbook: France*, Section 17C: *Cultural Institutions, Central and Southern France*, M352–17C (Washington, DC: US Government Printing Office, 24 June 1944).

United States Army Service Forces, *Civil Affairs Handbook: Italy*, Section 17A: *Cultural Institutions, Central Italy*, M353–17A (Washington, DC: US Government Printing Office, 6 July 1944).

United States Army Service Forces, *Civil Affairs Handbook: Italy*, Section 17B: *Cultural Institutions, Central Italy*, M353–17B (Washington, DC: US Government Printing Office, July 1944).

United States Strategic Bombing Survey, *Bombing Accuracy, USAAF Heavy and Medium Bombers in the ETO* (Washington, DC: Military Analysis Division, January 1947).

United States War Department, *Basic Field Manual FM 27-10: Rules of Land Warfare* (Washington, DC: US Government Printing Office, 1940).

Walasek, Helen with contributions by Richard Carlton, Amra Hadžimuhamedović,

Valery Perry, and Tina Wik, *Bosnia and the Destruction of Cultural Heritage* (London: Routledge, 2016).

[British] War Office, *Manual of Military Law* (London: HMSO, 1929, reprinted 1939).

Weber, Eugen, 'Western Civilization', in *Imagined Histories: American Historians Interpret the Past*, ed. by Anthony Molho and Gordon S. Wood (Princeton: Princeton University Press 1998), pp. 206–21.

Webster, Sir Charles, and Noble Frankland, *Preparation*. The Strategic Air Offensive against Germany 1939–1945, Vol. 1 (London: HMSO, 1961).

Webster, Sir Charles, and Noble Frankland, *Annexes and Appendices*. The Strategic Air Offensive against Germany 1939–1945, Vol. 4 (London: HMSO, 1961).

Wheeler, Mortimer, *Still Digging. Interleaves from an Antiquary's Notebook* (London: Michael Joseph, 1955).

[Woolley, Sir Leonard], 'The War and Classical Remains in Italy. Supplied by the Archaeological Adviser, The War Office', *Antiquity* 72 (1944), 169–72.

Woolley, Sir Leonard, *A Record of the Work Done by the Military Authorities for the Protection of the Treasures of Art & History in War Areas* (London: HMSO, 1947).

Works of Art in Italy: Losses and Survivals in the War. Part I, *South of Bologna*. Compiled from War Office Reports by the British Committee on the Preservation and Restitution of Works of Art, Archives and Other Material in Enemy Hands (London: HMSO, 1945).

Works of Art in Italy: Losses and Survivals in the War. Part II, *North of Bologna*, together with Regional Summaries and a Supplement to Part I. Compiled from War Office Reports by the British Committee on the Preservation and Restitution of Works of Art, Archives and Other Material in Enemy Hands (London: HMSO, 1946).

Zuckerman, Solly, *From Apes to Warlords: An Autobiography, 1904–46* (London: Collins, 1988).

Index

Note: Page numbers in bold indicate illustrations.